Network-Centric
WARFARE

How Navies Learned to Fight Smarter
through Three World Wars

Network-Centric
WARFARE

How Navies Learned to Fight Smarter through Three World Wars

NORMAN FRIEDMAN

NAVAL INSTITUTE PRESS
Annapolis, Maryland

Naval Institute Press
291 Wood Road
Annapolis, MD 21402

Library of Congress Cataloging-in-Publication Data
Friedman, Norman, 1946-
    Network-centric warfare : how navies learned to fight smarter through three world
wars / Norman Friedman.
        p. cm.
    Includes bibliographical references and index.
    ISBN 978-1-59114-286-7 (alk. paper)
  1. Naval art and science—History—20th century. 2. Communications, Military—
History—20th century. 3. Command and control systems—History—20th century.
4. Military surveillance—History—20th century. 5. Naval history, Modern—20th
century. 6. United States—History, Naval—20th century. 7. World War, 1914-1918--
Naval operations. 8. World War, 1939-1945—Naval operations. 9. Cold War. I. Title.
    V53.F745 2009
    359.4'2—dc22

2008054722

Printed in the United States of America on acid-free paper

14 13 12 11 10 09   9 8 7 6 5 4 3 2
First printing

Contents

Preface

This book reflects personal experience. Early in my career, in the course of a study conducted for the U.S. Defense Advanced Research Projects Agency (DARPA), I realized that the Soviet combination of long missile range and horizon-range sensors implied that the Soviet fleet was designed on information- or picture-centric lines. After giving several lectures on U.S. versus Soviet style in fleet tactics, I was invited to participate in a Naval War College study on how U.S. over-the-horizon antiship missiles might be targeted. My coauthor, Captain Hal Cauthen, USN, later said that he had often been told that our paper, "Information Support for Over-the-Horizon Targeting" (NWC/ARP[CS]-129E), which was submitted in November 1976 and declassified on 31 December 2006, had proved very influential. The paper proposed the picture-centric approach the U.S. Navy took. The project alerted me to the subtleties of modern picture-centric naval warfare, which at that time meant using the U.S. Ocean Surveillance Information System (OSIS) as a tactical tool, the development of the Naval Tactical Data System (NTDS) and its successors, and efforts to merge over-the-horizon and horizon-limited information to give commanders what they needed.

Many years later, it seemed that new network-centric concepts such as the Joint Chiefs' Vision 2010 and the U.S. Army's new command system were really elaborations of what I had seen at the War College in 1975–76. For several years the Naval Training Command sponsored my lectures on network-centric warfare at facilities such as the Naval Sea Systems Command (NAVSEA) Headquarters in Washington, China Lake, Point Mugu, Port Hueneme, Patuxent River, and Lakehurst. I am grateful to my audiences for sharpening my own perceptions and for enriching my understanding with accounts of their own. I have also benefitted from audience reactions to my lectures on network-centric naval warfare (and network-centric warfare in general) before official and unofficial audiences in the United States and abroad, particularly in Britain and in Australia.

In 2002 Andy Marshall, director of net assessment for the Office of the Secretary of Defense, sponsored my study of naval command and control as a model that might make the ideas of network-centric warfare much more vivid. The current book is partly based on the net assessment study (which was not releasable to the public), but it adds considerable further information. It is, moreover, limited to unclassified and declassified sources. For more details of command and control systems, the reader is referred to the various editions of my *Naval Institute Guide to World Naval Weapon Systems* and my *Seapower and Space* (2000).

I am grateful to all who helped in the original study, particularly the librarians of the Center for Naval Analyses (led by Greg Kaminski); the historians at the U.S. Navy Operational Archives at the Washington Navy Yard; Dr. David Stevens and the historians of the Royal Australian Naval Historical Branch; Captain Christopher Page, RN, and his staff of the Royal Navy Historical Branch; the staffs of the U.S. and British national archives; the staff of the Grumman Historical Center; and the staff of the French defense archives (naval section). For the present book, I added research at the U.S. National Archives, at the NAVAIR historical archive at the Washington Navy Yard, and at the archives of the U.S. Naval War College. Special thanks go to Dr. Evelyn Cherpak of the Naval War College, to Ken Johnson of the National Archives, to Greg Kaminski of the Center for Naval Analyses (CNA), to Curtis Utz of the NAVAIR archive, and to Josef Straczek, formerly of the Royal Australian Naval Historical Branch. I benefited heavily from discussions with Dr. Nicholas Lambert, who has been particularly interested in British ocean surveillance before World War I. Christopher C. Wright, editor of *Warship International*, provided some valuable documentation. Charles Haberlein of the Naval Historical Center helped with photographs and insights. Curtis Utz was also very helpful with both documents and photographs. I also appreciate the assistance of the U.S. Naval Institute photo archive staff. Versions or parts of this book were read by Christopher Carlson, David C. Isby, and Dr. Nicholas Lambert. They made many valuable comments, but the opinions and errors in this book are my own.

Except as noted, all photographs are U.S. Navy official.

Above all I am grateful to my wife, Rhea, for her support and encouragement, for her toleration of piles of paper and unreadable reference books, and also for her editorial advice.

Introduction

T his book is an alternative to what often seem excessively abstract and arcane theories of network-centric warfare. When the late Adm. Arthur K. Cebrowski coined that phrase something more than a decade ago, he thought he had invented a totally new way of war that would cure the problems he had experienced in air-strike warfare. Admiral Cebrowski took particular umbrage at suggestions that his child was actually "NTDS (the Naval Tactical Data System) on steroids." This book argues that was exactly the case. NTDS exemplified naval command and control practices invented more than a century ago. The idea is that information gathering and handling can reduce the numbers of men and platforms and weapons. Information is not in itself a weapon. It is an enabler that makes weapons more effective—if it is properly used.

How much information is needed determines how difficult it is to implement this sort of warfare. The main factors are the area involved, the size of the forces, the variety of the objects in the operational area (because the ones that matter must be distinguished from the others), and the pace of operations. Network-centric warfare is really *picture-centric* warfare, a kind of warfare based on using a more-or-less real-time picture of what is happening. How real time it must be depends on the pace and scale of operations. What suffices for a global naval situation, using ships moving great distances at 20 knots, is hardly good enough over shorter distances with airplanes moving at 600 knots. How complete the picture need be depends on how it is to be used. How well must nontargets be distinguished in the overall picture? This kind of warfare came to navies first because they dealt with wide areas in which relatively small forces were dispersed. It is only now coming to armies that deal with large numbers packed into limited areas.

The basic measure of success is whether the picture is saturated, whether it can handle enough objects to offer a usable picture of reality. No matter how the picture is created, entering data on each object takes time. Objects are entered one at a time, whether by human plotters or by computers. Inevitably, objects move before their positions can be entered, so the picture is always slightly inaccurate. The more the objects, or the faster they move, the less delay is acceptable. As picture-keeping requirements exploded after World War II, both on tactical and the wide-area scales, computers had to be adopted and then improved to keep pace.

Once a picture exists, it can be shared, at least potentially, among users. They can also contribute to a common picture, and they can use this shared awareness of a situation to work together. Advocates of network-centric warfare tend to emphasize the sharing and cooperation, but these actions are pointless without the picture created in the first place. This book shows how different navies learned to create and exploit tactical and wide-area pictures, beginning before World War I. These navies' experiences illuminate what network-centric warfare can do, what it needs to make it work, and what it cannot do. Current applications, for example, to land warfare, are far more demanding than the naval ones described here, but many of the lessons carry over. Unfortunately, it is a lot easier to evaluate the network surrounding the picture than to understand whether the picture is adequate. When money became tighter, the projects to create a family of common operating pictures (COPs) were largely sidetracked, but work on communications continued apace. Yet, the picture is much more important than the network. Admiral Cebrowski argued that, given a common picture, unit commanders could self-synchronize—could do what was needed with minimal instruction. The picture, however, was not enough; the unit commanders had to understand their higher commander's intent. He had to make sure they did not interfere, or waste common resources.[1]

The picture makes for a distinctive style of warfare, with its own characteristic tactics. It is not just a less-expensive means of conducting the sort of operations that might have been common in a prenetted era. An excellent tactical picture should give us the ability to choose targets more intelligently and to operate much faster, because we have a far better idea of what we are doing. It encourages us to use precision rather than area-bombardment weapons. We trade numbers of weapons and ships and airplanes and troops and vehicles for much better information about what is happening. We may be able to build much lighter and more mobile forces, better adapted to a world in which crises arise suddenly in widely separated places. That the United States has been fighting a war in Iraq since 2003 should not blind us to the likelihood that we may face other aspects of the same war in places like the Philippines and even in South America, probably well before all troops can leave Iraq and Afghanistan. Buying the right systems may give us enormous advantages *if we understand how to fight the new way.* If we buy the new systems but not the tactical style that goes with them, we will lose capability, even against those who have not invested in similar equipment.

Another phrase for the new kind of war is *precision warfare*. The tactical picture is to be so precise that it can be used to direct weapons to specific places. Hence, many weapons are now guided, not by seekers, but by navigational systems, usually the Global Position System (GPS). In effect, their seekers are the dispersed surveillance sensors and the associated means of data fusion.

How can the new style of war be visualized?

As a first example, think of a television crime drama set in Los Angeles. It begins with a night view of a suburban house. Suddenly a police helicopter appears, its spotlight shining down on the house. Its loudspeaker blares, "We know you are in there; come out and surrender." This is a picture-centric operation. The helicopter is dispatched on the basis of a tactical picture maintained at police headquarters. The sensors feeding into the picture are the burglar alarms in individual houses. Headquarters takes into account its knowledge of overall criminal activity in deciding where to send its limited force of helicopters. The tactical picture-helicopter combination is a way of dealing with the problem of space, a vast urban area in which houses like the one the helicopter visits are dispersed.

The alternative is many men on the beat. It was abandoned as unaffordable. The new system requires much greater capital investment per officer. Each alarm offers only a fleeting opportunity to capture a criminal, so reaction speed (using the helicopter) is very important. The new system depends critically on its surveillance system. It is vulnerable, for example, to false alarms.

How can the systems be compared? A police force is intended to make citizens feel safer. The policeman on his beat was a visible deterrent. He caught relatively few criminals, but he did make citizens feel safer by deterring casual street crime. The effect of deterrence (crimes not committed) is difficult or impossible to measure. The helicopter is more likely to catch criminals—but ordinary citizens may not realize that they are safer. Casual street crime may be unaffected. To make analysis more complicated, it is now argued that the same criminals commit casual crimes and burglaries, so that arresting them for the former may dramatically reduce the latter. The police problem is not too different from the classic trade protection problem of convoy versus hunting (the latter is actually surveillance driven).

A second, more fanciful example is a classic Western movie in which a lone sheriff awaits the arrival of a gang of gunslingers. He plans to make his stand crouching behind the bar of a saloon. In modern terms, the bar is his horizon. His only over-the-horizon sensor is his ear. He hopes that the creaking of a floorboard will indicate his enemy's arrival. To fire his gun, he has to pop his fire control sensors—his eyes—into the sight of the enemy. That gives the enemy tactical warning. The gun-slingers can outshoot the sheriff, so he is doomed.

In this fanciful version of the story, the town's general store has a time machine for sale. If the sheriff comes to our time, can he solve his problem? He can wire the ceiling of the bar with the little television cameras often advertised to monitor children, malevolent dogs, and nannies. Imagine that none of them covers a very wide angle, so the sheriff cannot act on the basis of any one camera. He needs a way of fusing all the pictures together. Moreover, he needs more than the set of pictures at any one time. He needs tracks—courses and speeds for each object the cameras detect. Tracks tell him where those objects (people, perhaps also animals like cats and dogs) are going. They give him some idea of which ones matter and which ones don't. Whatever mechanism the sheriff buys has to track multiple objects simultaneously because the sheriff cannot know how many gunmen he faces, or indeed whether those in the saloon will be limited to gunmen. In modern terms, he needs a *track-while-scan* system. It has to process the output of each camera to decide that it is seeing a real object (a potential target), it has to associate detections a few moments apart to form tracks, and it has to project each track ahead and compare that projection with further data to see whether the object has changed course and speed.

The output of the system is a diagram (a tactical picture) of movement on the floor of the saloon beyond the bar. If the picture is good enough, the sheriff's six-gun no longer seems to be the right weapon. Why bother to pop up, reacquire the target, and shoot? Why not buy a bullet that can simply be told to go to the spot the system expects the target to occupy a few moments hence? Such a weapon could be fired from behind the bar, or indeed from a convenient bank vault. The sensors, the computer, the software (to make sense of the sensor data), the real-time tactical picture, *and the geographically guided weapon* add up to a kind of network-centric warfare. Note that unless the sensors and the weapons are properly aligned, the weapons will miss.

Every attack the sheriff makes is a surprise attack. The enemy is always under surveillance good enough for targeting. He never knows what to expect. At the least, he always feels the strain of knowing that he may suddenly become victim rather than attacker. Also, because the weapon no longer depends on a line-of-sight sensor (the sheriff's eyes), it need not be fired from very close to its target. It can be an *over-the-horizon weapon*. One shooter can attack multiple widely separated targets—in this case, an entire gang of gunmen. Information on any one target is fleeting. The gunmen may flee the saloon. The ideal weapon ought to reach them before they can get behind cover.

The picture can be distributed to other users, who can support the sheriff. The gunslingers may not know which of several potential shooters will attack, making them even more uncomfortable. How can commander's (sheriff's) intent be disseminated? To what extent does the picture promote independent but cooperative action? To what extent does it empower a centralizing commander who cannot delegate authority?

The rub is that the system must somehow identify the objects it tracks. It is one thing if the movie is *High Noon* and the streets are deserted as the citizens wait at home to see whether the sheriff survives the gunfight. What if some of those on the street are deputies supporting the sheriff? If the mayor's wife or daughter enters the saloon? What if the gunfighters are in disguise? The sensors can see that *someone* is moving, and where, but can they identify that someone? Whoever builds the system becomes interested in adding further sensors specifically to aid in identification, such as floorboard sensors to estimate the weight of whoever or whatever triggers the main system.

What if the sensors cannot be sure of detecting targets? If the system misses some of the gunslingers altogether? How well should the sheriff be protected while firing his long-range weapons?

Imagine that the sheriff faces successive groups of gunslingers. Perhaps the first is easily cut down, but others may come to understand what the sheriff is doing. They may have their own general store. Perhaps they can place their own sensors in town, to form their own tactical picture. They will probably conclude that the best counter to a kind of warfare relying so heavily on information (in the form of a tactical picture) is to destroy information—deception rather than the physical destruction of numerous redundant sensors. What seemed at the outset a quick means of dispatching gunslingers becomes a subtle cat-and-mouse game.

Both examples are forms of strike warfare. So is most naval warfare. It is impossible to occupy the sea, so much of the point of naval warfare is to destroy enemy shipping and aircraft. Many other operations—such as delivery of supplies on a just-in-time basis—can be likened to strike warfare. However, ground warfare is different. Troops occupying ground, even temporarily, have important effects on an enemy. They can certainly benefit from a picture of what is happening beyond their horizon, but they have to do more than simply destroy enemies.

Ultimately, war is about violent persuasion. How does a precise tactical picture contribute? One current theory is effects-based operations (EBO). The picture makes it possible for us to obtain the desired effects on the mind(s) of the enemy without causing trouble by hitting what we should not, for both moral and political reasons. Unfortunately, foreign cultures are difficult to understand. We may be unable to understand the effects of our attacks. Our forbearance may or may not do any good. EBO was tried in Serbia. We concentrated on the assets of those supporting Serbian dictator Slobodan Milosevic. We hoped that by sparing the civilian population, we would not drive it into his hands (as is common in air campaigns). Did that work? Skeptics can find many reasons for the Serbian withdrawal.

The alternative idea, elaborated by the late Col. John Boyd, USAF, is that accelerating the pace of operations may in itself so dishearten an enemy as to cause his collapse. Boyd thought in terms of what he called the observation/orientation/decision/action (OODA) loop or cycle of military operations: Observation is succeeded by orientation (understanding what has been seen), by decision, and then by action, after which the actor returns to observing. If one side's OODA loop runs much faster than the other's, the slower opponent is always several steps behind, and the gap accelerates. Boyd attributed the 1940 collapse of France to an OODA-loop disaster. The Taliban defeat in Afghanistan may have been a similar case in point.

The examples in this book come from a simpler world in which destroying point targets—generally ships—was the point, so that issues like EBO versus OODA did not arise. Navies developed picture-centric warfare on two levels. The wide-area level is ocean surveillance. Ocean surveillance data is now probably the key to the kind of international naval cooperation the U.S. Navy espouses in the strategy it announced in 2007. Thus, the U.S. Navy is trying to develop a cooperative common operating picture of world sea movements. The U.S. Coast Guard's Project Deepwater is built around a detailed picture of the offshore situation, and a major current U.S. national goal is to develop Maritime Domain Awareness. A major NATO contribution to the ongoing war is to develop an accurate current picture of sea movements in the Mediterranean, which may become the basis for emergency action. One lesson of that effort was that netting sensors provided far more and better information than simple patrols. The more local version of the operational picture is the tactical situational awareness a Combat Direction Center develops. Clearly we think that picture-centric warfare offers enormous advantages, particularly against more tradition-minded enemies. Will other countries adopt the sort of warfare we are developing? How compelling are its advantages? How can we tell whether a prospective enemy has netted his forces? How can we compare or evaluate different netted systems?

The "kill chain" often used to describe attacks is a kind of OODA loop with more steps: the target is detected, classified, and localized and the decision is made to attack, a fire control solution is found, the attack is launched, and then its results are assessed. In theory, picture-centric warfare compresses the chain because the picture shows both the target and an approximate track. It collapses to choosing a target already seen, making its track precise enough for attack, attacking, and assessing the results. The kill chain emphasizes the need to understand a tactical situation and to observe the results of action. Another alternative is to split operations into situational awareness (what is there, who is there, and localization), target engagement (a combat-direction system function involving tracking and therefore prediction), and battle damage assessment. Situational awareness information need increases with sensor and weapon ranges and with the rise of remote sensors, which extend the space involved. Another stress is the need for better target identification to satisfy more exacting rules of engagement. More target engagement information is needed to handle faster targets, using more effective electronic countermeasures (ECM), which must be engaged at a greater rate (because of their numbers and the range at which they must be engaged). Assessment becomes more difficult as stand-off range increases, as precision munitions are used (because their effects are more localized, hence more difficult to observe in a gross way), and in the face of better countermeasures, which may mask effectiveness. This split makes clearer the ways in which a system can be overloaded or saturated. It may not be able to list enough objects, it may not be able to classify or localize (including track) enough objects, and it may be unable to deal with countermeasures, many of which add false targets.[2] The examples in this book illustrate these kinds of limitation and measures taken to overcome them.

PART 1 The Radio Era

Radio made network-centric warfare possible by providing distant command centers with nearly real-time information and by making remote command and control possible. Thus, the advent of radio, at the beginning of the twentieth century, is the beginning of this story.

CHAPTER 1

Ocean Surveillance: World War I

The British Royal Navy's ocean surveillance system, developed before World War I and used successfully during that war, was the first application of network-centric warfare. It is difficult for us to appreciate how revolutionary the British method was, partly because the U.S. Navy (and, for that matter, the Imperial Japanese Navy) learned from the Royal Navy during World War I and then adopted the same methods. That the British ideas really were unique becomes obvious in retrospect only when British and German World War I performance is compared.

Fisher in the Mediterranean

Admiral Sir John Fisher invented network- (actually picture-) centric warfare. It seems to have been the core of his naval revolution.[1] As Mediterranean Fleet commander in 1899–1902, Fisher faced a classic British naval problem.[2] His fleet was more powerful than any of his three widely separated potential enemies: the French at Toulon in the Mediterranean and at Brest in the Atlantic, and the Russians in the Black Sea. At least in theory, if all three combined, they were superior to his fleet. Fisher could not split his fleet to blockade the French in Toulon while watching the Turkish Straits for the Russians. If he could meet each fleet before it joined the others, he could defeat it. In 1903 a Royal Naval War College game demonstrated how such a strategy would succeed.[3] Fisher needed a way of predicting his enemies' movements (to intercept them at sea).

Fisher's solution was a new kind of naval intelligence service, the "all-seeing eye" of his fleet. Past Mediterranean commanders had financed agents and had received reports from merchant ships touching at the Mediterranean Fleet base of Malta, but Fisher seems to have been the first to understand that communications intelligence could provide ocean surveillance: a picture of where enemy forces were *and where they were going*. In a pre-radio age, the commander of each enemy fleet received his sailing orders by telegraph. Even postsailing changes (delivered by fast ship) would originate with telegrams to ports. For Fisher the key was that the British owned most of the world's cables, and that many of them came ashore (for their signals to be boosted) at Malta. For example, to avoid interception by the Germans, the French communicated with their Russian allies via the Mediterranean—and Malta. Similarly, the cable between France and North African ports passed through Malta. Fisher made private arrangements to receive copies of the telegrams, and he created a code-breaking cell to process them.[4] He boasted that he often read important telegrams before their intended recipients did. Fisher set up a large plotting table at Admiralty House in Malta, in effect a war room showing where enemy ships and fleets were, based on all available intelligence. In 1902 the British director of naval intelligence said that he could locate any named French ship within a quarter-hour.[5] He meant that he could find the relevant file that quickly, and that his files showed whether the ship was in a particular port or at sea in a particular ocean, not where it was within, say, a fifty-mile radius. Only Fisher's all-seeing eye could hope to do that.

Given the intelligence picture, the fleet had to be fast enough to intercept one enemy fleet after another. Fisher therefore successfully pressed his fleet's engineers to increase sustained speed. (At this time fleets cruised at low speed to avoid destructive vibration.)[6] This need for strategic speed explains why Fisher was so interested in the steam turbine, which solved the problem. Fisher also became interested in the sort of increased firepower that would enable his fleet to deal quickly with one enemy before breaking off to deal with the others. He could not afford serious damage during the initial fights. In particular, he had to protect his ships against underwater hits. Hence, his early interest in improving gunnery to the point where it would outrange the torpedoes enemy capital ships and cruisers might deploy. These considerations led him to order the chief constructor at his Malta fleet base, William H. Gard, to sketch fast all-big-gun battleships and cruisers, which in turn became HMS *Dreadnought* and HMS *Invincible*.

Overall, Fisher thought he had solved the central British naval problem—too few resources to cover too much space or too many enemies—with intelligence-driven ocean surveillance and a fast centrally commanded force. His success appealed to an Admiralty facing bankruptcy in 1903–4. "Radical Jack" was made First Sea Lord, equivalent to a U.S. chief of naval operations (CNO), in 1904. He brought his Mediterranean ideas and a sense that the Royal Navy was vital to protect Britain against starvation by attacks on her maritime trade. That contrasted with a conventional view that the navy's role was mainly to deal with enemy fleets.

Cruisers were the immediate problem. They were used to watch enemy ports, as fleet scouts, and to protect trade. For example, the Royal Navy estimated that a fleet needed three cruisers for every two battleships. Such numbers were affordable as long as cruisers were cheap—which meant as long as a ship could be either fast and small or large and slow. In the 1890s, however, machinery became much more efficient; large, fast cruisers were built. With the advent of lightweight armor, these ships could stand up to fire. Now it took a large, expensive armored cruiser to deal with another such ship. In 1898 the First Lord of the Admiralty (equivalent to the U.S. secretary of the Navy) told the cabinet that the French saw cruisers rather than battleships as the most effective threat against Britain.[7] The French understood that their naval threats might bankrupt the British, a practice they called *guerre industrielle*. British policy required a battle fleet that matched those of the next two powers, at that time France and Russia, but the British also needed numerous cruisers for trade protection. Since the new cruisers were about as expensive as battleships, in effect, the Royal Navy was building two battle fleets at once, a pace it could not sustain.

Fisher was most interested in building the sort of intelligence net he had had in the Mediterranean and a war room at the Admiralty (set up in 1905 to display the current situation).[8] The code-breaking cell in Malta moved to the Admiralty. In August 1904, just before assuming office as First Sea Lord, Fisher wrote that the old system of station fleets had to be discarded because "telegraphy has been enormously developed, hence transmission of orders, and mutual conference of thought enormously bettered . . . united squadrons under one Master Mind [i.e., the Admiralty] are infinitely stronger than a number of isolated squadrons. . . . [Any] enemy will be the objective of the 'Mind' in command, and that enemy will be hunted and destroyed." In August 1907: "Neither Nelson nor St. Vincent . . . could possibly possess the knowledge of the Admiralty octopus, with its antennae and its tentacles feeling everywhere and concentrating the knowledge in its brain." And, in September 1908: "no-one has any notion what an immense accession of strength the British Navy has obtained by the marvelous development of wireless telegraphy. It is par excellence the weapon of the strongest navy."[9]

A 1908 paper attacks "naval critics [who argue that] in war time the whole of the naval forces in home waters ought to be placed under the direct control of . . . the Commander-in-Chief afloat [who] should not be interfered with." The Admiralty, rather than the commander at sea, could exploit political and military intelligence information normally concentrated in London. Similarly, information obtained by outlying stations and vessels (both official and commercial) was normally collected by shore stations and then transmitted to the Admiralty, rather than to a fleet at sea. Because they reported by radio, even the fleet's scouts in effect reported both to the fleet commander and to the Admiralty. The Admiralty would guide the fleet to the point of contact. Then the local commander would take over, exploiting his far better knowledge of local conditions. Even then "the Admiralty may, through various sources, obtain information that some act of the enemy is likely to wreck the whole or some portion of the [Admiral's] plans, hence [it must know] exactly at any moment . . . the disposition of the forces and their movements in the immediate future."

That the core of Fisher's "system" was to transfer authority from officers at sea to the Admiralty (hence to the First Sea Lord) explains why he was so controversial, and so hated. The division between strategy and tactics was weakening because radio so greatly expanded the tactical area. As for speed, "no vessel can be considered to be within the tactical area if she is so far off that she cannot reach the scene of action in time to take part in the battle."[10] In this light Fisher's dramatic new warships were the consequences of his new approach to naval warfare, not his main accomplishments.

If potential enemies understood how heavily Fisher depended on intelligence, they might cut it off. Thus the War Room and the Naval Intelligence Division did not figure in Fisher's public or even semipublic papers. However, it is difficult to miss the meaning of the master mind and its information. Admiral Fisher often claimed that he was creating a "New Testament" navy. Did he mean new-generation ships like HMS *Dreadnought*? Or did he mean a new way of operating the Royal Navy? Fisher was famously familiar with the Bible and often used biblical references. A key New Testament phrase is "faith, not works," which might translate to "communications/intelligence, not numbers."

Fisher gave his War Room its first test in 1905, ordering it to track the Russian squadrons sent from the Baltic to Port Arthur. Its first triumph was to prove that one was going via Singapore rather than, as had been expected, Batavia. It also correctly estimated the position of the Japanese fleet, which differed from what had been telegraphed. In a 1908 exercise, the War Room ran an hourly (i.e., nearly real-time) plot of warships in the North Sea.

Radio (wireless, in British parlance) made it possible for the Admiralty to use the War Room picture to command its forces in more-or-less real time. Among Fisher's first investments as First Sea Lord was a navy-owned shore wireless network, whose main stations (Cleesthorpe and Horsea in England, and Malta and Gibraltar in the Mediterranean) could transmit to ships 500 miles at sea.[11] All were connected to the Admiralty by cable. Wireless was so important that, despite this investment, Fisher bought new stations in 1908. Cleesthorpe and Horsea were upgraded to a range of over 1,000 miles. A powerful station was installed at the Admiralty. New transmitters were ordered for British warships. Given shorter-range stations abroad, the Admiralty enjoyed global command and control. It could send messages to stations in colonies throughout the world via British-owned cables (which amounted to most of the world's cables). They could be repeated by wireless. No other country in the world enjoyed similar capability.

Contemporary observers thought German and American radio technology more advanced. Both relied on tactical radio in 1914, whereas the British continued to emphasize visual signals (flags and lights). This apparent British backwardness was probably associated with awareness of how radio intercepts could be used for ocean surveillance. There were also technical problems. Sets could not be tuned precisely, so radio operators found it difficult to distinguish signals in heavy traffic. Also, 1911 Home Fleet tests showed that a coded hundred-word message took ten minutes to transmit (only five if not coded), but thirty-five to code and twenty-five to decode. By 1914 the Royal Navy wanted a coding machine, but tests that year apparently did not produce a satisfactory one.

Flotilla Defense

Fisher came to see the War Room and vectoring as a way of dealing with the evolving British strategic problem, which after 1905 was less a war against France and Russia but more one against Germany. In contrast to the open ocean, North Sea distances were so short that destroyers and submarines could cross it. Their torpedoes could sink the largest battleship. Perhaps conventional fleets should be reserved for oceanic warfare. Perhaps the Royal Navy should dominate the North Sea with flotillas of destroyers and submarines. The War Room could vector them out to meet the Germans.[12] Fisher seems to have conceived such flotilla operations in embryonic form as Mediterranean commander; he wrote that the Mediterranean Fleet (but not the Channel Fleet) needed cooperation with destroyers. Fleet commander A. K. Wilson forced a retreat, but the idea was revived as soon as he retired in March 1907. The flotillas had to be fast enough to exploit perishable information. A new communications center was set up specifically for flotilla control at Sheerness, at the mouth of the Thames.

Flotilla defense was widely understood within the Royal Navy. When he proposed concentrating all the modern British battleships off Portugal for a 1910 exercise, First Lord of the Admiralty Reginald McKenna wrote the prime minister that the country would be safe because "our destroyers and submarine flotillas, which are the true defense against invasion, will be stationed on the East Coast."[13] This particular exercise tested the War Room. Fisher's successor, First Sea Lord Admiral A. K. Wilson, used it to control a division of battleships operating off Vigo. He had to mobilize enough staff to run the room around the clock, as it would be used in wartime.

How good this defense was depended on what it was supposed to do. Fisher's "all-seeing eye" might miss a few ships steaming out into the North Sea, but not the lengthy preparation for invasion. Scouts in the North Sea would not miss massive invasion convoys. Destroyers and submarines could be vectored to destroy them. Nothing the German battle fleet could do on a smaller scale would have much wartime effect because British destroyers and submarines would preclude any close blockade by the Germans of the British coast.[14] Unfortunely, the British 1913 maneuvers showed that German invasion convoys *could* evade the scouts. Fisher's picture-centric concept became workable only because of the success of radio intelligence.

Trade Protection

Fisher eliminated the traditional dispersed British squadrons. Was he calling back the legions to deal with the German threat in home waters? Understanding the squadrons' role suggests otherwise. They had been established largely to deal with the threat to British commerce, surface raiders. With the advent of armored cruisers, no one could maintain enough sufficiently powerful ships. Fisher's War Room offered an alternative: vectoring. Fisher's battle cruisers were exactly what this strategy required. Fisher transformed the recently formed Admiralty trade section into the sort of shipping surveillance center he needed.[15] Shipping surveillance translated into raider surveillance. Given records of which ships did *not* arrive as expected, it was possible to estimate where ships fell victim to raiders. Moreover, any merchant ship with a radio (many had them by 1914) would probably send a message, probably giving her location, before being silenced. Estimated raider positions at particular dates could be strung together to guess a raider's course and speed, and so to predict its future position. In the winter of 1911–12, British naval intelligence began work on a means of evasively routing fast merchant ships, given knowledge of raider tracks. The spread of British ocean surveillance (intelligence gathering) to East Asia and to South America proves that the Royal Navy retained its global focus.[16]

As in the Mediterranean or the North Sea, to be vectored efficiently a raider-killer had to be fast. She also had to be able to receive radio messages at the longest possible ranges at sea, to take advantage of new information discovered by the War Room. Fisher's favorite capital ship, the battle cruiser, met both requirements. The first battle cruisers traded armor and some firepower for much higher speed, about twenty-seven knots. They were described as superior replacements for the armored cruisers whose construction was bankrupting the Royal Navy: one *Invincible* could defeat any two conventional armored cruisers. That made no great sense if the ships were to be used in traditional roles; buying enough battle cruisers to populate focal areas and to work with the fleet would only bring quicker bankruptcy. After three British battle cruisers were blown up at Jutland, historians tended to dismiss them as a blunder. Ocean surveillance and picture-centric operations make the battle cruiser an entirely rational response to the problems the Royal Navy faced.

One indication of the new way of operating is a scheme the Admiralty promoted in 1909 for Dominion navies (and a projected Indian navy) in the Pacific.[17] Each was encouraged to buy a "fleet unit" consisting of a battle cruiser and fast scout cruisers. Individual fleet units would hunt down raiders. In the event that a fleet was needed outside European waters, it could be formed out of the Dominion units. When hunting, the ships would form a scouting line (line abreast). Ocean surveillance would give only an approximate raider location, but the extended line would make up for that imprecision. Only Australia built the requested fleet unit, and it never functioned as envisaged. (The battle cruiser was transferred to the Grand Fleet early in World War I.) The Empire Fleet concept was revived after World War I. This time the units were heavy cruisers. The scouting line function was taken over by cruiser-borne scouting aircraft.

Much as in the Los Angeles television crime drama example given in the introduction, the new technique was a way of destroying raiders, rather than of protecting merchant ships directly. Its rationale was that, over the first months of a war, all the raiders would be destroyed. Much the same was said of the U.S. picture-driven antisubmarine warfare (ASW) strategy of the 1960s, based on a different sensor (SOSUS, Sound Surveillance System). In 1960 the U.S. Navy estimated that over the first three months of a war, Soviet submarines would sink a hundred merchant ships each month—but by the end of the three months, the Soviet submarine force would be gone.

Ocean surveillance could also support British trade warfare, including a blockade of Germany. Geography placed Great Britain at the mouth of the North Sea, through which shipping to Germany flowed. By 1914 the British lacked sufficient cruisers to block the entrance to that sea, but they could vector cruisers to intercept particular ships—if their routes were known. That is how the World War I blockade of Germany was conducted.

Radio as Ocean Surveillance Sensor

Radio generally transmitted its signals in all directions, not only to the intended recipient, hence it was an obvious source of intelligence. Ships, both merchant and naval, use unique call signs (as addresses for radio messages). Because a ship still must identify herself to her listeners, call sign tracking and traffic analysis can continue even if enemy codes cannot be read.[18] Moreover, until well after World War II, most radio messages were sent by hand. Each of the few radiomen aboard a ship had a characteristic "fist," which a skilled intercept operator could distinguish. Range could be estimated, albeit crudely, by signal strength. In 1904 it was discovered that the direction to the transmitter could be measured (radio DF, or direction finding). A DF net can make it easier to identify particular ships (whose locations may be known from other information) with intercepted call signs. That information, in turn, can provide code-breaking clues.

It is not clear to what extent the pre-1914 Admiralty relied on code breaking and radio direction finding. British records suggesting that radio direction finding was introduced in 1914 may be unreliable. Instructions for the 1909 maneuver cautioned that officers should refrain from the popular pastime of code breaking to predict enemy movements. One purpose of the exercise was to find out what could be done without that source of information since "in actual war the difficulties to be solved would be much enhanced by the lack of acquaintance with the enemy's methods."[19]

Radio does have a major drawback as a surveillance technique. It requires the enemy's cooperation. If the enemy used his radio indiscriminately, he could be tracked. If he realized how much he was giving away, he might accept the disadvantages of radio silence. It appears that before 1914 many naval officers were aware of the danger that their codes might be broken, but few seem to have realized that simply transmitting radio signals would allow their ships to be tracked. Not too long after World War I British naval code breaking, but not naval DF, was revealed.[20] Code breaking may have acted as a kind of cover for the ocean surveillance DF net. A future enemy would surely change codes but might not realize the danger inherent in any emission.

Testing the Surveillance System: Exercises

The ashore headquarters of two of the three fleets involved (Red and Blue) had operational control for the British summer 1909 maneuvers. Each fleet had a string of war signal stations. Each fleet's ashore headquarters (a naval center) communicated with each fleet via designated radio (W/T) sending and receiving ships acting as the Admiralty radio station. (The Red fleet used Cleethorpes for transmission.) After Fisher left the Admiralty early in 1910, much of his thinking survived. Close blockade was essentially abandoned (except for a brief revival in 1912, in the guise of attack at source). The 1912 War Orders envisaged a scouting line of destroyers and light cruisers well offshore, reporting to the Admiralty by radio. Given an indication of a German breakout or a raid, the Admiralty could vector the battle fleet cruising further north, out of reach of German coastal craft.[21]

By this time many in Britain feared seaborne invasion. In both the 1912 and 1913 fleet exercises, the Germans managed to land troops, although there were claims that gamesmanship had made the exercises inconclusive.[22] Both exercises tested detailed fleet control by the Admiralty.[23] Commanding the fleet in both the 1912 and 1913 maneuvers, Admiral Sir George Callaghan reported that Blue (the British) could neither prevent raids nor quite bring the Red fleet to action. Surveillance seems to have been stymied by good British radio discipline on both sides. Callaghan concluded that radio surveillance could not detect raids in time to intercept them. The problems of the 1912 and 1913 exercises convinced Callaghan that he had best cruise the North Sea with his battle fleet in random sweeps to deter an enemy who could never be sure he was *not* nearby. He could hardly be sure that the War Room would detect an enemy sortie in time to vector him into position to meet it. At the outset of war the following year, the Royal Navy threw a scouting line of light cruisers across the North Sea, but the Grand Fleet executed Callaghan's sweeps.

As in 1909, in 1913 each side had a shore headquarters. The 1913 exercise revealed a major problem. Local commanders imagined that the War Room in the Admiralty had a clearer picture of the situation than they had. They surrendered initiative: surely they should await War Room orders. This problem was repeated throughout World War I. One striking form was an inability of light forces, such as destroyers and cruisers, to report frequently enough. Apparently junior commanders did not realize that the picture in the War Room consisted at least partly of what they reported. Much the same applied to the fleet plot Admiral Sir John Jellicoe introduced.

The Red fleet used the naval center at Sheerness, which would have controlled North Sea flotillas in wartime, as its headquarters "for the distribution of intelligence on the Red side." The 1913 exercises seem to have shown that it could not handle its communications load. Captain George Ballard, recalled from retirement to solve the coastal patrol problem, wanted to decentralize, creating six local command centers, each with its own war room. How these war rooms would have coordinated with that in the Admiralty was never clear.

Red orders for 1913 stated that "it is to be taken as an axiom that the fewest possible signals should be made by WT [radio]. . . . WT signals are constantly of help to an opponent. . . . On the other hand, instances have occurred of important information not being sent." The British solution was broadcast. Instead of signaling back and forth, ships copied signals included in fleet broadcasts, the messages being transmitted under coded or otherwise concealed headings. Broadcasting drastically reduced the value of traffic analysis, making it much more difficult to deduce the structure of the force at sea. It also became more difficult to deduce operations by noting which transmitters spoke to which other transmitters at any given time. The U.S. Navy adopted a similar broadcast system in the 1920s (initially called the "no receipt" system because no ship acknowledged receiving a message). Without receipts, a ship might never know that the intended recipient had missed a message. The U.S. solution was to number all messages; each ship guarded (received) all Fleet Broadcast messages. The U.S. Navy called this the Fox broadcast, after the old phonetic letter for *F*.

Fleet Surveillance in World War I

World War I began with a War Room failure in the Mediterranean: the escape of the German battle cruiser *Goeben* and the accompanying light cruiser *Breslau*.[24] The Admiralty had two forces in the Mediterranean, a pair of battle cruisers (which could have handled *Goeben*) and a cruiser squadron commanded by Rear Admiral Ernest Troubridge. The situation was complicated by the lag between the outbreak of war and the British declaration of war. The Admiralty felt that it had to deal with the greatest threat, which was that *Goeben* would upset French mobilization by attacking the stream of transports carrying French troops from North Africa. Intelligence was frustrated because the German commander made his own decisions at sea, rather than responding to instructions from Berlin. He did not radio ahead to make arrangements for his reception in Turkey, so code breaking would have added little.

Troubridge's cruisers became a backup, assigned by the Admiralty to what it considered a less-likely interception position. Once Troubridge encountered the German ships, he shadowed them. In effect he was a tattletale, and the War Room could have tried to vector other ships on the basis of his information. He seems to have passed too little information for that to happen, and the battle cruisers were too far away to reach *Goeben* if the latter ran at full speed. No one, including Troubridge, seems to have realized that he might have damaged the German ship badly enough to slow her so that the two British battle cruisers could catch up. He later explained his failure to attack on the ground that his force would have been destroyed. Reaching Turkey, *Goeben* later attacked Russia to force that country into the war on Germany's side, with enormous consequences. Court-martialed, Troubridge argued that his instructions had been poorly drafted and imprecise. The body of signals he cited during the court-martial show how little the Admiralty knew of the situation, or of the real threat the German force presented.

Then the situation improved. The great surprise of World War I was poor German radio discipline. Probably, as in Fisher's day in the Mediterranean, the British had expected to rely on their shore intelligence network to report the sortie they expected soon after war broke out. No spy network was likely to survive very long after that. The prewar structure adapted to intelligence-based ocean surveillance was well suited to exploit German talkativeness and the German code books it received soon after the outbreak of war. The dramatic story of how the Russians found a book clutched in the arms of a drowned German sailor may have been intended to conceal earlier code-breaking activity. The Royal Navy acted after the war as though its wartime picture-keeping system had all been extemporized by gifted amateurs. The volume of messages was so large that civilians had to be recruited to handle them. However, some of those involved were probably prewar Navy professionals.

The code breakers were insulated from the all-source plots, prohibited from creating their own plot based on decoded messages. There may have been fear that the information in the plot could contaminate their conclusions. Code breaking produced numerous false alarms because it was based on deduction from indirect evidence. The Germans never, for example, broadcast a signal ordering their fleet to sea. Rather, the code breakers used indicators such as orders to U-boats not to attack in particular areas, or to minesweepers to open a particular channel. Insulation denied the radio direction finders the insights into German operating practices gained by code breaking. Some of the compartmentalization seems to have been broken in 1917.

The Admiralty set up two separate receiver nets. The "B" service operated radio direction finders; the "Y" service intercepted messages for decoding. The two were separate for technical reasons. A DF station of this era swung a coil or equivalent directional antenna across the radio signal, seeking either a maximum or a null (which was easier to detect). Thus the direction finder received only a fraction of the signal because for much of the signal's duration it was not listening. It is not clear to what extent the "B" service existed before 1914.

At the outset, with the surveillance system undeveloped, the British followed the prewar policy of patrolling. It proved dangerous because no British patrol could pen U-boats in their German bases. U-boats and fast surface ships could lay mines in patrol areas and they could torpedo ships in British waters. The most dramatic case in point, and probably the reason fleet patrols were largely abandoned in favor of surveillance-directed sorties, was the mining and loss of the modern battleship HMS *Audacious* in October 1914. In British eyes this single event critically reduced the essential margin of superiority the British fleet enjoyed.

In December 1914 the surveillance system showed what it could do. The German battle cruisers sortied to raid the British coast. Ocean surveillance detected them in time for interception. Then came an unpleasant surprise: the battle squadron commander, Admiral Warrender, steered for the current position of the Germans rather than for a calculated interception point. No one had ever explained how he should use track data. He never contacted the enemy. Commanders of lighter craft that did make contact failed to report it—they failed to provide the information essential to developing that contact into something useful. Prewar exercises had never impressed on these officers that they were, in effect, the sensors of the system once contact was made.

In May 1916 the British Grand Fleet intercepted the German High Seas Fleet on the far side of the North Sea. That the battle happened at all demonstrates the success of British ocean surveillance. That the Germans called it Skaggerak—after the Danish strait near the battle area—shows how little they understood what had happened. They assumed that the British were steering for the Skaggerak because they planned ultimately to penetrate the Baltic and attack the German coast there. Their own fleet was headed for the British coast. They assumed that, after earlier raids, the British would be patrolling their coast, and that the German fleet could thus cut off and destroy some limited British force. To the Germans, Jutland was a kind of gigantic traffic accident, in which the British just happened to be athwart the route of the German fleet. The German official history made it clear that the appearance of the British fleet was a terrifying surprise. Other German documents show sensitivity to a possible British attack on the Baltic coast, hence the German interpretation of the British operation.[25]

British performance was not perfect. The accepted account of the intelligence or ocean surveillance background to Jutland is that the initial warning of the German sortie came from code breaking. Jellicoe sortied but seems to have assumed that it was probably a false alarm. He thought that, having foregone the advantages of the long nights of the winter of 1915–16, the Germans most likely had decided never to come out. By the spring of 1916 he was claiming victory without battle. On the night of the sortie, the duty officer in the Admiralty, Rear Admiral Sir Thomas Jackson, the director of operations, reportedly asked the code breakers not "where is the German fleet?" but "where is the call sign of the German flagship?" Presumably, he did not realize that the Germans habitually changed call signs when they went to sea (the code breakers did know). Jackson reportedly signaled Jellicoe that radio DF indicated the Germans had not yet sailed. (Their flagship's call sign was still in harbor.) However, this account is unlikely because in 1916 the code breakers and the DF plotters were in separate intelligence compartments. Probably DF stations had not yet detected any German activity outside harbor. Jackson may not have been sure that code breaking gave unambiguous evidence. The Jackson story served a political purpose within the Admiralty: the code breakers wanted to gain importance in comparison with the DF plotters. Jackson may have been a scapegoat for an embarrassing Royal Navy performance.

After the battle, the Germans signaled their planned course home because preparations had to be made to meet damaged ships and to clear paths through minefields. It differed radically from the one Jellicoe assumed. The Admiralty code breakers provided Jellicoe with what he needed to intercept the High Seas Fleet at dawn. Following his instinct rather than the intelligence he received, Jellicoe lost his chance to reengage the Germans. The Jackson episode was used to explain why: Jellicoe's faith in the arcane ocean surveillance system had already been broken. Skeptics point out that Jellicoe was prone to nervous exhaustion. He may never have seen the postbattle signal.

The Admiralty failed to use its War Room picture to vector the other strike force it controlled, the Harwich Force of destroyers and cruisers—the World War I descendant of the destroyer hunting groups envisaged years earlier for flotilla defense. The problem was incomplete information. The Admiralty signaled Jellicoe what it knew, but he did not signal back what he planned to do. Sending out the Harwich Force was risky. Navigation was poor. It and the Grand Fleet might well have met—and fought—at night. Perhaps, had Jellicoe more fully understood the War Room concept, he would have kept the Admiralty more fully informed, and it could have wielded its other force.

Code breaking worked: with only one exception, every German fleet sortie from December 1914 onward was known in advance, and interception was attempted.[26] However, the British never completely trusted intelligence-based ocean surveillance. They also wanted positive surveillance by scouts. Since surface ships were too vulnerable, they relied on submarines. By 1916 British submarine radios had sufficient range for them to perform effectively as scouts. Their surveillance role was considered so important that standing orders prohibited patrolling submarines from attacking ships they saw until after they had radioed sighting reports.[27] By the end of the war, the Germans' experience with their own (ineffective) radio intelligence organization was causing them to tighten radio discipline, so that the last fleet sortie (April 1918) was spotted only by a British submarine (*J 1*). Ironically, it was not reported because the submarine commanding officer (CO) thought he was seeing only a routine minelaying support mission, and the War Room became aware of the sortie only when the battle cruiser *Moltke* lost a propeller and had to arrange help.

Protecting Trade in World War I

When hunting German raiders in 1914, the British lacked the numbers to form the envisaged scouting lines. Hunts therefore took somewhat longer than might have been expected. Seeking the cruiser *Emden*, pursuers often missed by about fifty miles—the error a scouting line would have overcome. The most powerful German force, Rear Admiral Maximilian Graf von Spee's cruiser squadron, was destroyed in the single application of the battle cruisers' original concept. The two victorious British battle cruisers were vectored to the South Atlantic on the basis of reports not only of Spee's victory but also of estimates of his probable future course.

U-boat positions were plotted, in the same manner as the positions of surface raiders. Unfortunately, even a surfaced U-boat could generally see an approaching surface ship before being seen, so it could dive before being spotted by a surface ship vectored to its vicinity. Once submerged, U-boats could not easily be reacquired for attack, although by 1917 hydrophones made it possible to detect and track them at short range. Only British submarines could catch surfaced U-boats; they accounted for a substantial fraction of U-boat kills. Unfortunately, they were not fast enough to exploit radio intelligence, nor numerous enough to blanket routes to U-boat operating areas. They patrolled some focal areas. U-boats were mobile mainly on the surface, so the presence of submarines (and aircraft) dramatically reduced their mobility, hence their productivity

Given limited U-boat mobility, a fast liner could be vectored out of its way on the basis of the U-boat picture. The late Patrick Beesley once pointed out that evasive routing saved most fast British liners during the initial (1915) U-boat offensive. The War Room was already keeping track of their courses. They could receive evasion commands because, unlike many merchant ships, they had radios. In Beesley's view, *Lusitania* was sunk because of poor staff work, which caused her not to be rerouted in time. Her master disobeyed an Admiralty instruction to zigzag because a U-boat was nearby. (Her captain wanted to reach port on time.) Accounts of the *Lusitania* sinking treat the zigzag order casually. The Admiralty could never have afforded to explain to merchant commanders just how good its information was, hence how precisely its orders were to be heeded.

Attempts in 1916–17 to prearrange secret evasive routes in the Mediterranean failed miserably. There were so many merchant ships at sea, spread out so widely, that U-boats were likely to find them. Evasion required something more like real-time control of merchant ships. That was impractical given the vast number of ships at sea at any one time.

Convoy was not revived at the outset because it seemed that too many escorts would be required.[28] This was the same argument that had killed the convoy strategy about half a century earlier—it took something powerful and expensive to deal with a raider, and that something was in short supply. In 1915–16 it seems to have been assumed that the minimum convoy escort would be numerous destroyers. But destroyers were also badly needed by the Grand Fleet, which was the shield against a possible German naval attack on the British Isles, and for narrow-seas operations further south, against potential German surface raiders operating from the Belgian coast. Many British destroyers had limited endurance and also little seagoing capability. There was also a real fear that concentrating merchant ships would merely improve the chances of a U-boat firing from long range into a convoy, a technique called a "browning shot."[29] This seems to have been a carryover from analyses of torpedo use during a fleet engagement. In fact, U-boat skippers preferred to fire at particular ships from relatively short ranges. It was argued that adoping a convoy strategy would be equivalent to a considerable net loss of shipping. Ships already loaded had to wait for others to form convoys, and merchant ships would steam slowly in company (nor was it clear to naval officers that merchant masters could even steam in formation, never having practiced that prewar). The War Room's success in locating U-boats must have encouraged officers in the Admiralty to think that just a bit more work on passive submarine detection would make this sort of dislocation unnecessary.

When the United States entered the war in April 1917 with over sixty large destroyers, British perceptions suddenly changed. To everyone's surprise, it did not take many, or even one, destroyer to deal with a U-boat. Moreover, escorts were needed only within a few hundred miles of the British coast. U-boats could not find targets in the open ocean. Armed trawlers and the oldest British coastal destroyers would do. They generally did not have to face down serious surface opposition thanks to the Grand Fleet, guided by the War Room.

Convoys had unsuspected virtues. Concentrating merchant ships into groups emptied the sea. U-boats often simply could not find their targets. They were forced into focal areas that could be patrolled. A U-boat that found a convoy could not attack so many ships in the available time. Intelligence could now be used for evasion because every convoy had at least one radio-equipped warship in company, and because the numbers were now manageable by the War Room.

In the 1920s successive British governments tried but failed to abolish submarines by treaty. When that failure was accepted in 1930, the Royal Navy rethought what would be needed in a future ASW war. New plans were laid to build escorts, but there was no hope of building enough. The Royal Navy therefore showed continuing intense interest in intelligence-based interception. With the advent of asdic (sonar), it seemed that fast surface ships really could search the area of uncertainty around an interception position. Tactics were devised for cases in which a submarine was located within an area, and early in World War II destroyers were assigned alternative armaments as units of ASW striking groups. These efforts failed because it turned out that prewar and wartime asdic had far too slow a search rate.

U.S. Naval Surveillance during World War I

During World War I, both because they were integrating U.S. ships into the Grand Fleet and probably because they hoped to make the U.S. Navy a postwar security partner, the British revealed to American officers their ability to track the German High Seas Fleet.[30] This openness may also have seemed necessary to convince the Americans, who were quite free with their radios, to adopt British-style strict radio discipline and sophisticated coding. Americans were receptive, partly because the prewar U.S. fleet seems to have been unique in developing radio as a tactical sensor. In a 1913 exercise, Fleet Radio Officer Lt. C. S. Hooper successfully estimated the range to an opposing fleet by monitoring the strength of signals he received from it. The Navy then sought radio direction finders for capital ships and cruisers. They could track an enemy fleet, and they were also useful for navigation, using coastal radio stations. After some false starts, a successful shipboard direction finder was deployed in the fleet in 1916. As cover for the tactical role, the direction finders were called radio compasses. The British did not follow suit when they learned of this practice during World War I, perhaps because American battleship officers showed no interest. (There had been little attempt to explain why it was worthwhile.)

However, when they deployed to Europe during World War I, numerous junior officers manning destroyers and other antisubmarine craft found their direction finders extremely useful. They ran down U-boats, having intercepted and DFed their transmissions. U.S. ships could also steer convoys clear of U-boats on this basis. The same officers found their direction finders useful for navigation, for example, in fog. Overall, the U.S. approach to radio direction finding might be characterized as platform- rather than network-centric.

Lessons?

Radio ocean surveillance required an unwittingly cooperative target. Secrecy became absolutely essential. [Few of those using the fruits of surveillance could be allowed to understand how the system worked, hence decide how far to trust the information they received from a distant authority.] They were, however, often putting their lives on the line. To what extent could they trust data collected and interpreted remotely? How could (or should) they be convinced to trust systems whose workings or character or limitations were necessarily being withheld from them in the interest of security? *This problem is still with us.* It is inherent in any netted form of wide-area operation. One example is the skepticism of many U.S. officers in the 1980s who were expected to fire Tomahawk missiles on the basis of ocean surveillance data.

Another Point of View: The German Navy in Narrow Seas

The Imperial German Navy seems to have developed a very different kind of picture-centric warfare. From the 1890s on, the Germans saw the British as their future naval enemies.[31] As long as the Germans had the weaker fleet, they sought an equalizer. Like the British navy's Sir John Fisher, Admiral Alfred von Tirpitz, architect of the German navy, was a mine and torpedo specialist. He naturally thought in terms of combining guns and underwater weapons. To do that he had to keep his surface fleet away from his torpedo craft. Initially, the only way to do that seemed to be to keep them well apart. At first it seemed to Tirpitz that the British would feel compelled to attack the German Baltic coast. A British fleet trying to force the straits could be damaged by mines and by torpedo boats, particularly if the Germans gained control of the Danish coast through invasion. The small German battle fleet, operating in the North Sea, would suffice to deal with whatever survived. This particular idea died when the German General Staff refused to dilute its planned attack on France sufficiently to provide the forces for Denmark; the German army saw no point in naval warfare.

Tirpitz shifted his focus to the North Sea, although the idea of using coastal weapons (mines and torpedo boats) as equalizers must have remained attractive. German strategic exercises showed that minefields could damage an approaching British fleet. After considerable debate, the November 1912 German tactical orders envisaged combat in the Heligoland Bight, that is, just off the German coast and the naval base of Wilhelmshaven. The fleet would take the strategic defensive, but it would seek to damage the British by frequent energetic sorties. Now the Germans imagined fighting a battle in the presence of exactly those coastal weapons (now including coastal guns) that had to be kept well away from the fleet a few years before. When war broke out in 1914, the German fleet retreated to base, under the cover of minefields and fully manned coastal guns. Their leadership disregarded intelligence that showed the British would stay well offshore in the event of war.[32]

Thus, the Germans saw coast defense as a trap for which their fleet was the bait. Americans and Britons emphasized the ability to protect particular places inland.

When they seized the Flanders coast early in World War I, the Germans moved their combined-arms coastal operation there. Their techniques apparently became the basis for Soviet naval command and control.[33] In Marinekorps Flandern, the Germans used coast defenses as the basis for submarine and destroyer offensive operations they called "kleinkrieg," or small-scale warfare, to distinguish it from major fleet actions.[34] They threatened the dense cross-Channel traffic supporting the northern part of the Allied army in France. From the outset the Germans saw Flanders as an all-arms operation based on a central command ashore. Their first step on seizing the Flanders coast was to set up a radio station. The reconnaissance arm consisted of the surface force and, to some extent, German seaplanes based in Flanders. Scouting required a geographical reference; by 1918 German seaplanes had possibly the world's first radio aid to air navigation. Defensive measures included motor torpedo boats and also remote-controlled (wire-guided) explosive boats, the latter to destroy the monitors with which the British shelled the coast. Control required centralized surveillance, both by coastal positions and by aircraft. The Flanders operation was successful enough for the British to consider landing substantial forces on the coast to end it. A postwar British attempt to understand Marinekorps Flandern was frustrated because the Germans destroyed their command and control equipment, publications, and bunkers before abandoning the Flanders coast.[35]

The Mediterranean Sea Powers

France and Italy were also interested in a narrow sea: the Mediterranean. As British allies during World War I, both were probably initiated into the ideas of plotting and central control using intelligence-based ocean surveillance. During World War II, the French Admiralty seems to have acted as an operational headquarters on roughly the lines adopted by the British Admiralty. In 1939–40 the French Navy formed anti-raider hunting groups that would not have been effective without vectoring.[36]

The rationale of the post–World War I *contre-torpilleur* (in effect, destroyer killers) was that Italian naval strategy would be to maintain sea communications in the Eastern Basin of the Mediterranean while attacking French maritime communications in the Western Basin.[37] They would rely on light forces built around their three new light cruisers ("Esploratori"), their heavy destroyers (*Leone* class), and their best destroyers for frequent thirty-six to forty-eight-hour raids. This would be a larger-scale version of the attacks on shipping in the Downs by the German force based in Flanders. As during World War I, fights between light forces would be decided much more by gunnery than by torpedoes. Without a large cruiser force, the French considered the best counter to be super destroyers, which they called *contre-torpilleurs*. Once the prototype had run very successful trials, they decided to build up a force of thirty such ships. Unlike the large destroyers of, say, the Royal Navy, they were not destroyer leaders. Instead, they were intended to operate independently in groups of three. Since the raids would likely be conducted in good weather (so that the Italian strike force could run out and back at maximum speed), the *contre-torpilleurs* were conceived for maximum speed under the same conditions. The conventional French destroyers would work with their battle fleet.

The Italians clearly intended to intercept convoys or important merchant ships. Strike groups had to be vectored into position because extensive searches would make them vulnerable. The Italian naval headquarters (Supermarina) was a tracking center equivalent to the British Admiralty; during World War II it vectored Italian units to attack specific convoys.[38]

CHAPTER 2

Ocean Surveillance after 1918

United States

After 1919 the U.S. Navy saw the Japanese as its most likely future enemy. It hoped to emulate British World War I success in tracking the Japanese battle fleet. Code breaking was its main source of information. The U.S. Navy initially stole Japanese codes, and then it created a successful code-breaking organization.[1] By the mid-1930s, U.S. code breakers thought they had complete insight into Japanese naval operating practices, gained by listening in on the regularly scheduled Japanese Grand Maneuvers. Sometimes decoded signals also provided technical information, the most celebrated case being the information that the rebuilt battleship *Nagato* was much faster than the U.S. Navy had imagined. The decision to limit the new *South Dakota* class to twenty-four knots was reversed. This window closed after 1936: maneuvers were canceled as a result of the demands of the war in China. Tactical or technical developments, which became important after 1936, were probably missed because of effective Japanese security.[2] Examples probably include the new night torpedo tactics employing the Type 93 "Long Lance" oxygen torpedo. The degree to which earlier Japanese thinking was penetrated seems to have made U.S. naval intelligence officers overconfident of their understanding of the Imperial Japanese Navy on the eve of war.

Unfortunately, the Japanese chose to change their naval high command code system in 1940, leaving only traffic analysis—which the Japanese understood and tried to subvert. Ironically, Americans were reading a system the Japanese regarded as far more secure: the diplomatic code the U.S. government called Purple. The decoded messages discussed in the context of Pearl Harbor are all diplomatic. The highest-level of them offered no clue whatever to detailed intentions, merely information that war would soon break out. Messages that, in retrospect, might have provided clues—for example, demanding detailed information about ship locations in Pearl Harbor—were in low-level codes and were therefore left for later treatment

The usual supplement was radio direction finding (DF), but during the 1920s the Japanese relied on medium frequency (MF) radio, which could be intercepted only by three Asiatic Fleet stations (Beijing, Guam, and Olongapo). None had a DF set, and they were not linked, so it was impossible to take cross-bearings. The situation suddenly improved as the Japanese, like the U.S. Navy, adopted high frequency (HF) radio, which had intercontinental range. Unlike MF signals, HF signals can travel in various ways, the most important being ground (surface) wave and sky wave (reflection off the ionosphere). It is relatively easy to DF the surface wave, but the sky wave is far more difficult.

Experience of the Japanese 1930 maneuvers convinced the U.S. communications intelligence that it badly needed HF/DF to track the Japanese fleet.[3] Initially, U.S. experts doubted that it could be done. However, messages intercepted during the 1933 Japanese exercise showed that they had a viable HF/DF system. The U.S. Naval Research Laboratory was ordered to produce an equivalent. In 1939 the U.S. Navy's Mid-Pacific Strategic HF/DF Net became operational.[4] It was first tested, with limited success, in Fleet Problem Nineteen (1938).[5] Not until 1939 did U.S. DF stations in the Pacific approach the Japanese in number and quality of equipment, and they were not considered comparable until 1940. Even then, notes on the 1940 Fleet Problem (exercise) suggest that much remained to be done in terms of tracking, net control, bearing reports, and search for transmissions "before any of the nets would be able to obtain a fix, even on a loquacious station."[6] However, according to a 1943 internal analysis "at the present time we have outstripped the Japanese, as well as other nations, in the quality of D/F apparatus as well as in skill of 'tracking.'"[7] Presumably because they were using radio intelligence themselves, the Japanese were well aware of their vulnerabilities. Through the 1930s they tried to reduce them.[8]

All radio intelligence was handled by a unit nominally part of the naval communications system, Op-20G, hence separate from the Office of Naval Intelligence (ONI). (The two would be merged postwar.)[9] Probably the split was intended to conceal communications-intercept work.

There was an additional complication. In 1940 the U.S. fleet moved to Pearl Harbor to deter further Japanese expansion in East Asia. Protection depended on ocean surveillance. Because the fleet's move to Pearl Harbor was expected to be temporary, key facilities—such as its fleet tracking center—did not move with it. Fleet commander Adm. James O. Richardson protested that its new base was far more dangerous and that, moreover, it lacked necessary infrastructure—such as its intelligence center.

When he became Pacific Fleet commander in 1941, Adm. Husband E. Kimmel had a fleet intelligence officer with his own organization, cognizant of what American code breakers knew. Kimmel's intelligence officer collated the products of Op-20G and ONI plus the fleet's own long-range scouting aircraft. In effect Kimmel had a small all-source center in his fleet. He moved ashore because, he said, his staff was too large to go to sea aboard his flagship. That gave his intelligence officer continuous access to current intelligence. There was nothing like enough bandwidth to pipe that information to a flagship at sea. By this time the U.S. Navy was beginning to form task forces out of its centralized fleets. Their commanders had their own intelligence staffs, collecting and evaluating local information. Kimmel was therefore sliding into the position the First Sea Lord occupied in Britain, with access to wide-area surveillance information, on the basis of which he could deploy task forces. However, the U.S. Navy also still envisaged operations by an integrated Pacific Fleet.

In June 1941 Kimmel ordered the creation of the Combat Intelligence Center at Pearl Harbor. It seems to have been responsible for attacks on Japanese fleet codes and also for maintaining a plot of Japanese warships and merchant ships. It was denied information on the Japanese diplomatic codes, probably because secure communications capacity between the U.S. mainland and Hawaii was limited. Famously, when the Japanese message amounting to a war warning was discussed in the White House, the decision was not to phone Pearl Harbor—because the phone was a radio and could easily be intercepted (ultimately the message was cabled—and it was received far too late). OpNav in Washington was not an operational headquarters, hence had never had much of an intelligence center. It did have a chief of naval operation's flag plot, which in December 1941 showed the American estimate of where Japanese forces were—as a gauge of whether they were about to attack.[10]

The Japanese could not conceal the rising tension that suggested they were going to war because the U.S. government was reading their diplomatic traffic. On 27 November 1941 the U.S. government sent a war warning message to Pacific commands, ordering them to take actions envisaged under the current war plan (WPL 46). They included setting up air patrols. The war warning pointed to a potential attack against the Philippines, but it had wider implications. Presumably the assumption that the Japanese would attack the Philippines but not Hawaii was based largely on observed Japanese naval capabilities and current activity—on the fruits of ocean surveillance. The exercises the U.S. Navy had monitored suggested that Japanese carriers did not have the range to attack it and the Japanese were not known to fuel ships at sea.[11] The Japanese solved that problem (by learning to fuel at sea) well after U.S. access to their fleet exercises ended. Those at Pearl Harbor knew that attacks on that base had ceased to be a fixture of U.S. fleet exercises in the late 1930s. The reason, which may have been forgotten, was that the fleet received patrol aircraft (Catalinas), which so outranged carrier bombers that they could detect enemy carriers before they struck. Effective surveillance required numbers. By 1941 long-range patrol bombers were so urgently needed in the Atlantic that there were not enough left at Pearl Harbor.

The Japanese disabled the HF transmitters on board the task force headed for Pearl Harbor. Silence in itself might have alerted the U.S. Navy. Other forms of surveillance, such as submarine patrols, might have picked up the Pearl Harbor task force. The Japanese therefore moved fleet radio operators to ports in the Mandated islands to create deception traffic.[12] The U.S. surveillance system was to be left with the impression that it knew the locations of at least some of the carriers. The apparent location in the Mandates made sense if the carriers' role was to interdict any American naval thrust toward the Philippines, where the Americans assumed the Japanese would strike.

U.S. radio ocean surveillance was the victim of its own success. Without it, the U.S. Navy would have maintained submarines (of which it had enough in 1941) off Japanese bases to observe sorties by Japanese warships. They would probably have reported at least the departure of the Pearl Harbor task force, with its tankers. That might have caused the Pacific Fleet to mount surveillance flights.

Once World War II broke out, the Pacific Fleet (Pacific Ocean Areas) took control of operations in the Central Pacific. Forces in a separate Southwest Pacific theater were controlled from Australia by Gen. Douglas MacArthur. The naval component of MacArthur's command descended from the earlier Asiatic Fleet that fled the Philippines. Each shore headquarters controlled a forward-based numbered fleet (Third or Fifth for Central Pacific, depending on the fleet commander, Seventh for Southwest Pacific). Under the numbered fleet commander came task forces. In the October 1944 invasion of the Philippines, elements of Third and Seventh fleets came together. Pacific Fleet provided the fast carrier force (Third Fleet), which provided distant cover against Japanese fleet intervention and which could also deal with shore-based Japanese aircraft. MacArthur's Seventh Fleet, which could advise but not command Third Fleet, provided the landing force and shore bombardment ships. There was no unity of command. Intelligence and patrol resources still reported back to two separate headquarters. Some information was circulated between the two, but often with considerable time lags.

Southwest Pacific acquired a March 1944 Japanese fleet operational plan soon after it was produced. What was processed in Australia could not easily be transmitted to Hawaii, and thence to Third Fleet commander Adm. William F. Halsey Jr. Third Fleet obtained its copy that October, shortly before the invasion. The document emphasized using surface striking forces to destroy invasion shipping.[13] Some Third Fleet intelligence officers interpreted this to mean that the Japanese meant to use their carriers to draw off the Third Fleet, letting the surface forces in. The late arrival of the key document gave them much too little time to influence thinking higher up in Third Fleet. No one realized the magnitude of the U.S. success achieved a few months earlier at the Battle of the Philippine Sea (the "Marianas Turkey Shoot"). The Japanese carrier-based naval air arm, but not the carriers, was destroyed. Unaware that the Japanese lacked replacement pilots, many in the U.S. Navy criticized Adm. Raymond Spruance, the commander in the Philippine Sea, for letting the Japanese carriers escape. Given the enormous effectiveness of carriers throughout the Pacific War, their destruction naturally became Admiral Halsey's key objective, reinforced by his orders from Central Pacific commander Adm. Chester W. Nimitz. Halsey's staff rejected the decoy idea altogether (it may not have been presented to Halsey himself).

The Japanese had three separate main fleet formations, southern, central, and northern (decoy carriers). Halsey's aircraft attacked the central force, sinking one of its three battleships. His pilots reported that it had turned back. Surveillance by Seventh Fleet land-based patrol aircraft might have shown otherwise, but Halsey was unaware of any such reports. When the decoy northern force approached, he turned to attack it, unaware that it was toothless. He left the central route into Leyte Gulf uncovered. The central attack force turned back and very nearly disrupted the landings. Reports that it had turned back were apparently disregarded, or were kept from Admiral Halsey.[14] A desperate defense by the light Seventh Fleet force covering the landing stopped it, in the Battle off Samar. As that happened, Admiral Nimitz asked Halsey why he had not detached his own battleships to guard against the central force attack.[15] Halsey turned back and missed the opportunity to sink the whole northern (decoy) force but was also too late to intervene off Samar. It has been suggested that the fault was really that of Seventh Fleet commander Adm. Thomas C. Kinkaid, who was responsible for defending the landing area and who never asked Halsey whether he planned to keep battleships in the strait; apparently he simply assumed that Halsey would detach his battleships. Such assumptions are also failures of netting information, or of maintaining proper situational awareness.

Fortunately, this was nearly the last gasp of the Japanese fleet, certainly the last time there was enough of it to cause serious coordination problems. When the Japanese launched a surface attack at the Okinawa landing in April 1945, the fast carriers defended the operation by attacking and sinking the approaching Japanese ships. Whatever coordination problem had existed in the Philippines had been solved.

United Kingdom

World War I experience apparently showed the British that stovepiped use of sensors (such as separation between code breaking and direction finding) had seriously limited the effectiveness of ocean surveillance. In 1937 they therefore created an all-source Operational Intelligence Centre (OIC) in the Admiralty. Out-station OICs were created to serve naval forces in East Asia, the expected future theater of naval war, and then to serve the Mediterranean Fleet.[16]

HF Interception

By 1930 the Royal Navy, like others, was adopting HF radio for long-range communication.[17] All radio transmitters create both a ground wave, which follows the earth's surface, and a sky wave. At some frequencies, the sky wave bounces off a conducting layer in the atmosphere and hence comes back to earth at long range. This phenomenon gives HF its global range. The Royal Navy immediately began experimenting with HF/DF. A 1930 Confidential Admiralty Fleet Order describes early experiments: "There appears to be a general idea that these HF waves are immune from D/F. This is, however, not the case. A modern shore station can take bearings up to 25 MHz, but the results are not reliable unless it is possible to take the mean of a number of bearings." This is why the Germans imagined, incorrectly, that it would be impossible to exploit short signals. "In effect this means that a ship transmitting continuously on HF will probably disclose her position to enemy D/F stations; an occasional short transmission will, however, not necessarily do so. In a ship the problem of taking HF bearings is more difficult, but even in this case a modern D/F set will give some indication of the direction of a transmitter if the frequency is not greater than about 12 MHz. Special apparatus of this nature has been fitted in HMS *Queen Elizabeth* for trial." According to a later account (1932), accurate bearings could be taken where either the ground wave was uninfluenced by the sky wave (i.e., at relatively short ranges) or at longer ranges at which the sky wave was reflected to the earth, beyond the range of the ground wave. By 1932 the Royal Navy had an experimental Adcock sky wave HF/DF for shore use. (Ship installation was more difficult.) An Admiralty HF/DF station was set up in the United Kingdom for use in fleet exercises. At this time the verdict was that a fleet using HF would be vulnerable to DF, but not so much as a fleet using the earlier low frequency (LF) sets. After 1932, the annual confidential discussion of radio direction finding still mentioned that shore stations would be effective at HF, but omitted mention of the British station. That suggests that construction of a fleet tracking DF net began at about that time. The 1934 summary states that the direction to a 30 MHz signal may be determined to within ten degrees accuracy (the upper limit of long-range DF was given as 40 MHz).

Many Royal Navy ships were fitted for low frequency DF (up to 375 Hz). From the navy's point of view, as other navies increasingly shifted from low and medium frequencies to HF, DF would be less and less useful tactically, unless a shipboard HF/DF device could be perfected. This was modified in a September 1934 Admiralty confidential fleet order (CAFO). The maximum for reliable DF in any direction from a ship was 300 to 600 Hz, but if antennas were mounted higher than all others in a ship, it might be possible to get reliable results at 12 MHz. Useful bearings, particularly around certain angles from the ship's head, had been obtained in fleet exercises at up to 8.7 MHz. It was, moreover, "dangerous to assume that enemy vessels cannot take bearings on the auxiliary waves (2 and 2.3 MHz). As the frequency increases, the risk of disclosing the position of the transmitting ship tends, however, to decrease. It is unlikely that ships will at present succeed in taking a DF bearing on frequencies higher than 5 MHz." The first British shipboard HF/DF sets were probably fitted late in 1935.[18] In 1937 the upper limit for shipboard DF was given as 20 MHz, and for shore based, 40 MHz.[19]

The British learned to tell whether one signal came from the same radio as another. They mechanized the previous practice of recognizing a radio operator's "fist" under the cover name TINA (a contraction of Sepentina).[20] It could be used by an operator who lacked the aural memory to associate a "fist" with a particular operator. In addition, identifications could be stored and compared. However, ships could evade identification by "fist" by replacing their operators. In radio fingerprinting (RFP) the characteristic waveform emitted by the radio was captured by a high-speed oscilloscope, the trace of which was photographed. Records of measurable parameters made it possible to recognize a particular transmitter (associated, reasonably, with a particular ship). A DF net could locate an emitter twice. If fingerprints showed that it was the same ship, then the two locations could be associated into a track—which is what ocean surveillance systems need. The fingerprinting idea was important in many later ocean surveillance systems, such as post–World War II Western acoustic nets using acoustic signatures (in effect, fingerprints) and in surface ocean surveillance using, among other things, radar fingerprinting.

Fingerprinting made it possible to track an emitter that had not previously been heard. The *Bismarck* chase is the classic case in point. Admiral Gunther Luetjens in effect provided the British with his radio fingerprints when he sent a lengthy account of the action in which HMS *Hood* was sunk.[21] He considered that safe because he was still being shadowed by two British cruisers. Then he broke free; he knew he was clear when he could no longer detect the cruisers' radar pulses. He now sent a *thirty-minute* signal to Berlin. Radio fingerprinting showed that the long signal came from the ship that had sent shorter ones while she was being shadowed. Unfortunately for the British, the stations that picked up the long signal were all located in the UK. The battleship was at about the same latitude, so there were no cross-bearings. Interpretation was difficult. Was the ship, which the British thought (correctly) had been damaged, trying to get home to Germany through the Greenland Strait, or was she heading for a shipyard in France? Ultimately, the British solved their problem. Their crude DF data cued an airplane (a U.S.-supplied Catalina), which found the *Bismarck*. That must have particularly galled Germans in Berlin who repeatedly told Luetjens to limit himself to three-character messages, which they thought were too short to be DFed.

Aircraft

Aircraft dramatically changed ocean surveillance. At sea, they extended a cruiser's area of vision, so that the scouting lines envisaged by the British before World War I were no longer essential. That is why British cruisers all carried scout seaplanes, which their designers made considerable sacrifices to accommodate. On a more strategic scale, aircraft made possible a version of the sort of observational blockade the Royal Navy abandoned in 1912. They could periodically overfly an enemy base to determine whether the enemy's warships had sortied. Early in World War II, the Royal Navy bought a U.S. land-based reconnaissance bomber, which they called the Maryland, specifically to reconnoiter German naval bases. Aerial photos helped cue the *Bismarck* chase by spotting the presence and then the absence of *Bismarck* and her companion cruiser *Prinz Eugen* (other intelligence added to the picture). Geography made it easier for the Admiralty to guess where the ships were headed: the most likely outlet to the Atlantic was the Denmark Strait, between Greenland and Iceland. Using a chart, the Admiralty could estimate when the German battleship would reach the straits, and it assigned cruisers to watch that passage. Radar made it possible for two cruisers to cover the broad width of the Denmark Strait, and thus to cue the interception force, HMS *Hood* and HMS *Prince of Wales*. Later, when *Bismarck* broke free, DF cued not further British ships but rather a long-range airplane (a U.S.-supplied Catalina) capable of searching a wide enough area to have a good chance of finding her. This was a network-centric operation. The fruits of the flying boat's search went, not to the flagship of the force pursuing *Bismarck*, but rather to the Admiralty, which was assembling a picture of the situation.

Aerial photographs offered evidence of the state of preparation for a sortie, such as how deeply she was apparently loaded. This sort of information could be melded with other kinds of intelligence and with radio DF. Hence, the famous story of the aftermath of a successful Italian manned torpedo ("chariot") attack on two British battleships in Alexandria harbor. Because it bottomed them rather than capsizing them, and because the harbor was shallow, their decks remained above water. The British continued to conduct normal business on the ships' decks. Relying on aerial photographs, the Italians concluded mistakenly that their attack had failed and that the ships were still operational. That helped dissuade them from what might have been devastating action by their own fleet.

The Japanese appreciated the potential of reconnoitering their enemy's base from the air, so they developed the Mitsubishi G3M ("Nell") and G4M ("Betty") ultralong-range land-based reconnaissance bombers. The concept was so foreign to U.S. and British practice that both navies grossly underestimated the range of these aircraft. They sank HMS *Prince of Wales* and HMS *Repulse* when the British thought them beyond the range of Japanese land-based aircraft. These aircraft never carried out the intended mission of overflying Pearl Harbor.

Command Relationships

During World War II, the British had no way of merging Admiralty and local (at-sea) plots. There was never remotely enough bandwidth, particularly secure bandwidth, to do so. The story of Convoy PQ-17 illustrates the issue. Like its predecessors, this June 1942 convoy to Russia faced multiple German threats: strike aircraft, U-boats, and a potential surface attack by the battleship *Tirpitz* lying in a Norwegian fjord. The convoy escorts, which could deal with air and submarine attacks, could not handle the battleship. If it appeared, the convoy would disperse to cut losses—in which case much of it might well be destroyed by the aircraft and the U-boats. However, the Germans had only the one battleship. Operating in distant support, the British Home Fleet could pounce if the German battleship came out. The *Tirpitz* problem would be solved permanently at a reasonable price.

The main source of information about the battleship was broken German radio traffic: not a command to the ship (which would have come by teletype, via the buoy to which she was moored), but indications such as orders to minesweepers to clear particular obstacles down the fjord, or to U-boats not to attack a large ship in a particular area. This information went to the Admiralty, rather than to the convoy escort flagship. Conversely, the escort commander was much more aware of local conditions, such as weather that might make the battleship particularly vulnerable to attack by Home Fleet aircraft.

When the Admiralty received what seemed to be definite indications that the battleship would come out, First Sea Lord Admiral Sir Dudley Pound suggested that the convoy scatter. Its commander objected; given the weather, hence the likelihood that British carriers could strike, surely the *Tirpitz* would not come out. After considerable soul searching, Admiral Pound ordered the convoy to scatter. *Tirpitz* went back up her fjord (not to be sunk until 1944), and the convoy was massacred.

Admiral Pound was quite ill (he would die within six months), and possibly his judgment was poor. However, the destruction of the convoy was really the result of the inherent split in authority between the Admiralty and the convoy, based on the way in which British ocean surveillance developed. The issue was the usual one in a netted system: Who has the best information—if there is such a thing as best.

Halsey suggested various reasons for not detaching his fast battleships to cover Leyte Gulf. When he read the Japanese defensive plan, he was impressed not by the idea of using surface forces to break up an invasion, but by the idea that their land-based aircraft could shuttle-bomb a U.S. fleet; he saw his battleships as essential cover for his carriers—which were powerful but vulnerable (the lesson of the Turkey Shoot had not been assimilated). Similarly, Halsey argued that his carriers were still vulnerable to night surface attack. Overall, he saw his fast battleships as so integral to his force that he could hardly imagine detaching them.

There is interesting command-and-control evidence: Halsey chose the fast battleship *New Jersey* (rather than a cruiser, as Admiral Raymond Spruance used) as his flagship. Detaching the battleships to guard Leyte Gulf would have meant losing touch with the core of the Third Fleet, its fast carriers. Moving from one flagship to another would not have been a trivial matter, as Japanese Vice Admiral Takeo Kurita certainly discovered in the same battle. There was no way to move the crucial wide-area plots providing situational awareness, or the mass of other information or, for that matter, the staff which used that information.

CHAPTER 3

Net versus Net:
The Battle of the Atlantic

World War II submarine warfare depended heavily on ocean surveillance. Based on his World War I experience of convoy warfare, Captain (later Grossadmiral) Karl Doenitz developed wolf pack tactics in the 1930s. They were intended to solve the convoy problem: to find convoys despite the vastness of the ocean and then to destroy the numerous targets they presented. As it had been in the World War I Royal Navy, surveillance was mainly intelligence driven, by code breaking.[1] Occasionally, such information was supplemented by air reconnaissance. The shore data fusion center predicted convoy tracks. It also kept track of U-boat position and status. Given the inaccuracy inherent in this kind of surveillance, it took a scouting line (wolf pack) of U-boats to find a convoy. Once a convoy had been found, the scouting line massed to attack.[2] Given a fixed total of U-boats, Doenitz chose to assign a large number to each wolf pack and so to engage fewer convoys, rather than engage more convoys with fewer U-boats each. His theory seems to have been that more U-boats per convoy would sink a larger fraction of each convoy. He may also have thought that longer or denser patrol lines were needed to make up for the vagaries of intelligence-based ocean surveillance.[3]

Until 1944 and the advent of the snorkel, U-boats could make reasonable speeds and cover significant distances only on the surface. Aircraft could nearly immobilize them by forcing them to submerge. Until the aircraft had effective radars, U-boats were at risk from them only in daylight. Doenitz advocated night surface attacks by his U-boats because they could move freely within convoys, confusing the escorts, and because, having a shallow draft, they would not hit each other. Such tactics became much less effective as the British introduced effective surface search radars aboard escorts.

Detailed operational control was exercised from a control center ashore, most prominently BdU (Befehlshaber des U-boote) in Lorient, France. Local command was rejected, because any U-flagship might well be lost. Central control entailed extensive communication. U-boats had to be vectored to their targets. They had to report their status (number of torpedoes on board, fuel status, damage, etc.) so that the controllers could know which U-boats to send where. Doenitz thought that the new technologies of high frequency (HF) radio and the Enigma code machine (for messages to the U-boats) made communication safe.[4] Both assumptions failed. Shipboard HF/direction finding (DF) became an important sensor in the Battle of the Atlantic, exploiting the short-range surface wave that all HF transmitters inevitably produced, no matter how far away their sky wave signals were sent.[5] Convoy escorts could detect a U-boat trying to signal BdU. They could run down the resulting line of bearing, knowing that the transmitter was only about thirty miles away. (At longer ranges it would not have been heard.) Later in the war Doenitz tried to improve U-boat security by adopting the Kurier "squash" transmitter, whose messages were even shorter than those sent manually in the three-letter code.[6] For much of the war the Allies were able to read the Enigma messages Doenitz sent.[7]

The Germans needed large numbers of U-boats. Given limited resources, they concentrated on the small Type VIIC. Until the Germans reached the French and Norwegian coasts, these boats could not patrol the central Atlantic at all. Boats operating from France generally spent only sixteen to twenty days in the mid-Atlantic (thirty-two to thirty-six if refueled). Without vectoring, such short patrols were nearly pointless.

German attacks on transatlantic convoys became practicable once their forces reached the Atlantic in 1940. The same campaign badly stretched the Royal Navy, whose initial efforts to mass produce replacement escorts took time to mature.[8] Through 1940–41, the most successful British antisubmarine warfare (ASW) measure was evasion, based on intelligence (DF and radio fingerprinting). Evasion, in turn, was possible because the German U-boat building program also had not matured, although by 1941 they had enough to form patrol lines.[9] Evasion entailed communication between the British U-boat surveillance organization and the convoys; when it detected the formation or movement of U-boat patrol lines, the convoys were ordered to change course. Through mid-1943 the Germans read these rerouting messages on a more or less current basis.

By the end of 1941, thanks to code breaking, the Germans understood the general pattern of convoy runs across the Atlantic, both in terms of frequency and in general terms of routes. Without further specific intelligence the Germans could estimate convoy position on a given date.[10] The German Special Intelligence branch (X-B) supporting BdU computed areas of greatest probable convoy density, where convoys from opposite directions passed each other. At the height of the Battle of the Atlantic, BdU had two to six wolf packs (twenty to sixty U-boats) patrolling these areas in up to three lines: one running south from Iceland (near 25 degrees West), one nearly east-west from north of Newfoundland, and one running south-east from the tip of Greenland.[11] These lines were used through 1942–43, the patrol lines being lengthened as the Allies began using southerly routes.

By late 1941, a combination of improving British measures (including early surface-search radars) and evasion was reducing the effectiveness of the U-boat force. When the United States entered the war, the Germans found much easier hunting in U.S. coastal waters. Defenses had not been organized, and there was not even a serious effort to turn off coastal lights against which merchant ships trying to shelter could be seen and attacked. This "happy time" lasted into mid-1942.

A larger U-boat force then returned to the mid-Atlantic. Given a consistent pattern of convoy operations, with enough wolf packs the Germans could do a great deal even without current information. Consistency was enforced by factors such as the limited endurance of many escorts, which had to leave convoys to fuel in Iceland. Also, as the number of maritime patrol aircraft grew, the Allies tried to maintain them in stations over convoys (as they would hold down U-boats preparing to attack). As long as most such aircraft had limited range, convoys had to operate within a limited area.[12] This area initially sufficed for evasion, but once enough U-boats were at sea, evasion may have become almost unnoticeable.[13]

It is difficult to calculate the value of evasion; convoys escaped attack for many reasons, including a scarcity of U-boats in position. A British history of the effect of intelligence (such as code breaking) on the ASW war tabulated numbers of North Atlantic convoys and numbers of such convoys attacked at various times in the war:

TABLE 1. U-boat Attacks on North Atlantic Convoys

	Number of Convoys	Convoys with Losses
Sept 1939 – June 1940	375	11 (2.9 percent)
July 1940 – Dec 1941	489	87 (17.8)
Jan 1942 – May 1943	287	74 (25.8)
June 1943 – Jan 1944	110	6 (5.5)
Feb 1944 – May 1945	210	8 (3.8)

Numbers of convoys fell from June 1943 onward because convoy size increased dramatically. (It was found that large convoys were no easier for U-boats to find than smaller ones.) The sharp rise in 1942–43 presumably resulted from the loss of special intelligence. Other tables in this history show that north Russia convoys, whose routes were much more difficult to change, and which were more subject to air reconnaissance (so that German code breaking was not so important), suffered much higher attack rates: 37 percent in 1942–43 and 23 percent in the final phase of the war. The pattern for convoys from the UK to Gibraltar roughly mirrored that in the North Atlantic, but the percentages attacked were smaller (the peak rate was 15 percent).

The Atlantic had some respite when U-boats were repositioned after the invasion of North Africa. By early 1943 longer-range escorts were coming into service, tankers were fueling escorts at sea, and longer-range aircraft were available. Now evasion over wider areas was possible (based on German codes being read concurrently). In January 1943, U-boats began to miss planned attacks on convoys.[14] The burden shifted to German ocean surveillance and hence to code breaking. Overall, the BdU war diary shows considerable emphasis on code breaking.[15] Now the Allies were reading German messages, seeing how quickly the Germans reacted to changes in convoy routing. The German ability to read Allied codes was revealed.[16]

In early 1943 there were still not enough escorts, or at least not enough fully trained and equipped ones. In the spring of 1943, the Germans were still reading Allied convoy codes; their ocean surveillance system was still working. However, the convoys were much better protected, so the escorts began to win their battles.[17] Aircraft were increasingly effective, not only against U-boats trying to track and then to concentrate against convoys, but also against U-boats trying to reach their patrol areas from their French bases. U-boats found it difficult to transit even at night because the aircraft could detect them using radar. A U-boat could spend less and less of her limited endurance on patrol in the battle area. The Germans hoped U-tankers (refueling U-boats on the surface) would solve this problem. The fueling rendezvous had to be set up by radio—by mid-1943 the messages involved were being read.

In June 1943 the Allies changed to convoy codes the Germans never succeeded in breaking. German ocean surveillance collapsed. Allied successes traceable to the flood of new escorts made the collapse of German ocean surveillance less obvious. From mid-1943 on German messages were generally read within a day. This information was used both defensively and offensively. An early defensive example came on 24 May 1943. BdU ordered seventeen U-boats to form a patrol line 750 nautical miles southeast of the Azores to attack U.S.-Gibraltar convoys. The convoys were successfully diverted.

With pressure on convoys reduced, some forces could go hunting. Like Doenitz, the Allies could not pinpoint their targets on the basis of code breaking alone. Given an initial datum, they had to search. The best means of doing so was using aircraft. Escort carriers were reassigned from North Atlantic convoy cover to hunter-killer attacks. During July and August 1943, nearly forty attacks were conducted (thirteen U-boats sunk, five damaged) in a vast area (1,200 x 1,800 nautical miles) in which the average number of U-boats was only fourteen (and only ten during the latter part of July). Code breaking was used directly and indirectly: sometimes to vector attackers, sometimes to reveal a pattern of operations from which refueling rendezvous were predicted. Decryption of a U-boat position apparently doubled the chance that she would be sunk. The aircraft destroyed the special U-tankers. The British argued unsuccessfully that consistently finding and attacking U-boats in mid-ocean, for example, at fueling rendezvous, would raise German suspicions, just as German reactions to the rerouting of Convoy HX-229 had revealed German code-breaking successes a few months earlier. The Germans refused to believe that Enigma had been compromised.[18]

Allied ASW killed the most aggressive U-boat commanders and subjected others to stresses that dramatically reduced their effectiveness. As more operational boats were sunk, more new crews were needed, so a larger proportion of the entire U-boat force had to be devoted to training. In 1943 the Allied strategic air offensive gathered momentum. Its targets included cities like Hamburg, where U-boats were built. The Germans adopted prefabrication for their late-war submarines, so that they would spend little time on the slip. By that time, the stress of war was reducing quality control, and the modules were not fitting together well enough. These problems fatally delayed the Type XXI program.

Doenitz was forced to abandon the central Atlantic almost completely in favor of safer areas such as the Indian Ocean and the West African coast. He hoped the shift was temporary, and in October and November 1943 he sent his U-boats back to the North Atlantic. They failed again, and they were withdrawn. The last Atlantic wolf pack was disbanded in March 1944.

U-boats returned to the Eastern Atlantic in mid-1944, largely to help stop the imminent invasion of France and then to cut the vital supply line to Britain and thence to Europe. Without reconnaissance support, they reverted to pre-Doenitz tactics, lying in wait in focal areas (such as the Thames estuary) and in the Channel. Often they simply bottomed to await convoys, taking advantage of the difficult acoustic conditions of shallow water. Doenitz hoped that new technology would make it possible for the U-boats to work in such narrow waters despite the opposition being concentrated there. The snorkel (first used seriously after D-day) considerably reduced the value of ASW aircraft but not of the numerous surface ASW craft. Toward the end of the war, U-boats were deployed to North American coastal waters, such as the St. Lawrence estuary off Canada. Hunter-killer groups alerted and vectored by code breaking destroyed a group off the U.S. East Coast.[19]

In 1945 Doenitz hoped that his new "electro-U-boats" of Types XXI and XXIII could return to the offensive. One Type XXI reportedly conducted dummy attacks on a British cruiser without being detected. She could probably have survived in the open ocean. However, without effective ocean surveillance, it is not clear how effective small numbers would have been. The Germans still had to signal their defensive forces to help the U-boats get to sea, and decrypts would have cued using long-range aircraft armed with homing torpedoes. Wolf pack tactics, still essential to contact convoys, required more communications, which the Allies were well placed to exploit. The new U-boats would probably have been forced into focal areas and the approaches to ports. Allied ASW would probably have shifted toward tactics that had been secondary during earlier phases, such as mining and attacks on bases.

Given the use of ocean surveillance on both sides, the Battle of the Atlantic might be seen as the first "net versus net" war. The British, but not the Germans, understood what was happening. In a network war, information becomes a primary asset. The British practiced deception in the form of convoy evasion, but it does not seem that the Germans tried anything equivalent. Possibly the small size of the BdU staff precluded the analysis that might have encouraged such operational countermeasures.

To some extent the coastal forces battles in the Channel resembled the U-boat war on a small scale (alternatively, it was a scaled-up version of the World War I Flanders operation).[20] Like a U-boat, an S-boat had very limited night vision. S-boat groups were vectored by shore stations (using voice radio). The main surveillance measure was code breaking; even in 1944–45 the Germans were reading the low-level codes used for British east coast convoys. The British had a control room ashore (an AIO) that vectored their own destroyers and small combatants to intercept the S-boats (they also escorted the convoys). In 1944 they fitted out some frigates as small combatant command ships, using surface search radars and plot-like plan position indicator (PPI) displays.

Like the German U-boats, U.S. submarines in the Pacific relied on ocean surveillance through code breaking.[21] Like Doenitz, the U.S. submarine command ashore needed to know the status of submarines at sea. However, the U.S. Navy was under no illusion that HF was safe. Japanese operating practices solved the problem. Japanese convoys always broadcast a noon message giving their status and describing recent events, such as submarine attacks. Based on the broadcasts, U.S. submarine headquarters could guess how many torpedoes had been expended, how much fuel had been used—even whether submarines had been damaged during the attack. They sent new orders accordingly. Submarines did sometimes have to transmit, as when reporting scouting contacts, and that carried a risk. However, the U.S. equivalent to the Doenitz system was infinitely superior.

CHAPTER 4

Commanding the Fleet: Plotting

Tactical Plotting

T actical plots were the fleet equivalent of the war room plot Admiral Sir John Fisher invented in 1901. Like the large-scale plot, they provided a commander with the sort of situational awareness he needed to control a complicated situation, spread over an area too large for him to understand simply by looking around him. As in the case of the war room, tactical plots seem to have been adopted by the British Royal Navy and its allies, but not by the Germans.

In 1910 the Royal Navy began to experiment with divisional tactics, in which the battle line was split into smaller units maneuvering independently. That offered both flexibility and less vulnerability to the rising threat of long-range torpedo fire. The idea was rejected in 1910 and again in 1912, but it remained interesting. In May 1914 Grand Fleet gunnery officer Commander Frederic Dreyer suggested a solution. He had already devised a fire-control calculator based on plots of range and bearing versus time. Now he proposed a plot of the fleet's course (and relative positions of various units and of the enemy) to provide situational awareness. This was a a picture-centric approach to fleet command. Dreyer's was not the first such suggestion, but it seems to have been the first one adopted.[1] Fleet commander Admiral Sir John Jellicoe set up a plot on board his flagship HMS *Iron Duke* as a basis for tactical decisions. (Ironically, he never used it for the intended purpose of making divisional tactics possible.) At Jutland he used it to decide how to deploy his force against the approaching German fleet. He also used his plot to decide how to evade the threat of German torpedoes.

Despite its crudity, it gave him a considerable advantage over the German commander, who had no plot at all and thus did not understand the situation. Thus, several times Admiral Reinhard von Scheer blundered into the massed firepower of the Grand Fleet, saving himself only by extraordinary maneuvers like a fleet turn masked by smoke, torpedo fire, and the "death ride" of the German battle cruisers. Apparently Scheer had imagined that diagrams of fleet formations could be replicated in combat, and he had never reckoned with the smoke of battle, let alone North Sea fog. Jellicoe avoided any such blunders, although he also failed to achieve the decisive results some think he could have had.

Other Grand Fleet units, such as cruiser squadron flagships, maintained plots so that they could provide data, such as the course and speed of enemy units, for the flag plot. Unfortunately, the new picture-based operation was not well understood in Jellicoe's fleet. Prewar exercises showed that ships transmitting too freely could easily jam each other, so the rule was to limit message traffic. Yet, the tactical plot required freer, rather than more restricted, signaling. As in the December 1914 failure, commanding officers (COs) seem not to have realized that their ships were the sensors feeding the flag plot. British COs approved (perhaps even originated) all messages. A captain desperately fighting his ship was unlikely to stop every few minutes to write out a position or status report. Yet, without numerous reports, the flag plot could not reflect reality. Little thought seems to have been given to the need to control the fleet's radio traffic so that the few available channels would not be saturated. Much the same sort of problem can be seen in U.S. air defense exercises four decades later. Even limited numbers of signals interfered so badly that radio operators described pandemonium. The Germans used the same radio technology, so their signals could also be heard (but proved distinguishable). Little information got through.

Poor navigation made Jellicoe's plot less than realistic. Navigation and plotting were apparently particularly poor in the battle cruisers. Jellicoe relied on them to give him the German course and speed while the Germans and the battle cruisers were still well beyond the horizon. When the battle cruisers came into view, running from the German main body, their flagship could not tell Jellicoe the German course and speed, only where the Germans were currently bearing. Apparently the battle cruiser flagship was not maintaining a plot. At times Jellicoe's plot showed a cruiser apparently making three knots and a battle cruiser apparently making sixty. Even so, the value of plotting was obvious, and it was adopted throughout the Royal Navy. Plots made it possible to understand what was happening, even if parts of the battle area were invisible. Tracks on a plot showed not only where ships were at a given moment, but where they were going. Given that sort of situational awareness, tactical decisions could be made. Moreover, plotting made it possible to compare observations and to smooth estimates of trends to make up for errors.

The solution to the navigational problem was to make all reports in terms of a ship's own range and bearing from the flagship, rather than in terms of her latitude and longitude. That was difficult when ships were beyond the horizon from the fleet flagship. The British solution, developed in the 1920s, was acoustic/radio ranging. A ship dropped a practice depth bomb at the same time that she emitted a set radio signal. The receiving ship compared the delay in receiving the acoustic signal with the nearly instantaneous receipt of the radio message. This method seems to have been used through the 1930s. It inspired British work on the use of small explosives to indicate the positions of crashed airplanes in the Indian Ocean.

Plotting was so important that capital ships were modified postwar to provide larger spaces for it.[2] Ships needed both a large-scale ("strategical") plot and a smaller-scale tactical plot used for local situational awareness. The strategical plot was to be maintained from the moment of receiving the first enemy report (or even leaving harbor) to the end of an operation. It showed the relative position of the opposing fleets at any moment, tracks being plotted continuously by dead reckoning the ship's own track and based on all sources of information about the enemy. It also showed land and navigational dangers. This was the sort of plot Jellicoe used when he first deployed his fleet. The tactical plot was begun as soon as the enemy was sighted, to provide a view of the general tactical situation and the relative position of own-fleet units. It would show the fleet's exposure to enemy torpedo attack (particularly by destroyers) and also the potential vulnerability of the enemy to British torpedoes (particularly from destroyers in the van of the fleet). It would also show the position and extent of areas made dangerous by British torpedo fire, so that ships could avoid them.

The first standardized plotting instructions (August 1923) required strategical plots (ideally, five miles to the inch) in light cruisers and larger ships and, if possible, in flotilla leaders. (In smaller ships they could be combined with the usual navigational plot on a chart.) All capital ships and some light cruisers would maintain tactical plots (ideally, one inch to the mile). In some ships, the two plots were widely separated; some ships had viewing glasses to allow those at flag plot to see the tactical plot. This problem of keeping plots current and coherent became more acute when plotting was used to deal with aircraft and air attacks.

Detailed instructions for action plotting arrangements were issued in July 1924. Further plotting instructions were issued regularly, although no plotting handbook appeared until 1936.[3] Plotting became more important as the Royal Navy came to rely more on remote sources of information—on what might be called network-centric sources, particularly fleet aircraft. To handle this increased flow of information, more officers were assigned to plotting. Initially, they came from the Instructor Branch; after 1933 all of them underwent a special course given by the Royal Navy's navigation (later navigation and direction) school, HMS *Dryad*.[4]

By 1923 the British envisaged using a dead-reckoning table to keep track of own-ship position, other ships' positions being plotted relative to the moving light spot or pencil line representing own ship. The first such tables were issued for trials in 1928.[5] By September 1934, 194 tables had been allocated to specific ships, according to a list by serial number. (The list had grown to 232 by September 1937.) By 1939 destroyers and larger ships had automatic plotting tables. It turned out that such tables were necessary for antisubmarine warfare (ASW) ships using sonar and depth charges, so they were widely installed.

Plotting transformed the British attitude toward night fighting. Initially, it was feared because a night battle was expected to degenerate into a melee in which superior numbers would merely mean more friendly fire casualties. That might not be so bad if the problem was gunnery (the gun was considered a cumulative weapon), but the ideal night weapon was the torpedo, from which a single hit might be fatal. Through the 1920s, British tactical publications warned that night combat was to be avoided, although they began to add that combat need not necessarily end at nightfall, if the enemy was on the run. In 1934, however, the Admiralty's *Progress in Tactics* asserted that the British fleet should welcome night gunnery battle. The plot provided a sort of synthetic, albeit limited, night vision. For it to work, the fleet had to maneuver precisely, and reports from the fleet units had to be precise and frequent, so that what was reported to the flagship accurately reflected what was happening.

Given a picture of the situation, a fleet commander could order a destroyer to switch on a searchlight to illuminate an enemy ship for another of his ships to hit—as at the Battle of Matapan in 1941. This was a revolutionary way to fight. For the Italian victims of Matapan, suddenly being lit up and then hit was a terrible surprise. The British knew exactly where they were. The Italians, who had shown no great interest in night combat, had no idea that the British were anywhere nearby. This kind of tactical surprise is a hallmark of picture-centric warfare.

U.S. Navy

The pre-1914 U.S. Navy was far more interested in plotting than its British counterpart was, but as a way of estimating the course and speed of a target ship to support gunnery. The British rejected such plots because existing compasses were neither accurate enough nor capable of canceling out a ship's motion as she yawed back and forth around her nominal course. The U.S. Navy operated in calmer waters (so that it suffered less from yawing), and its Sperry was a superior gyrocompass. The U.S. Navy also probably relied on war gaming, which meant on the tactical board, more than any other navy. It was not a long jump from using the tactical board to learn how to maneuver a fleet to using a seaborne equivalent to visualize what was happening in combat. About 1914 American officers at the Naval War College began to see plots (synthetic situational awareness) as an essential tool for fleet command.[6] Although this idea was repeated in 1917, it seems not to have gained acceptance by the time the United States entered World War I and the U.S. Navy met the British Grand Fleet.

By that time the Sperry company had sold the Navy the mechanical Battle Tracer plotter. Its "bug" crawled across a chart, moving in response to gyro and log (ship speed) inputs. An arm represented a target ship. Although the U.S. Navy did not adopt the Battle Tracer as an input for fire control, it saw the device as a useful means of action plotting. The U.S. Ship Control Board specified it and a chart table with a universal drafting machine (a means of moving rulers over the chart table, to plot reported enemy or other positions relative to own-ship position) for post–World War I flag plots.[7] Although in theory plots were limited to designated flagship, plotting facilities were installed on board all major units, so that they could serve as alternative flagships. Destroyers used their wardrooms as plotting spaces. The most visible indication of U.S. adoption of plotting was that in the early 1920s U.S. battleships were all fitted with navigational range finders (plotting sensors for targets within visual range) and with spaces to house plots. Carriers maintained air plots, initially to vector offensive strikes, but later also for fighter direction. Because scouts flew far beyond the horizon, navigation and plotting (to arrange strikes) became key.

Control using a flag plot entailed much more communication than in the past. The radio problems the prewar and wartime Royal Navy had encountered were rediscovered. The first major U.S. postwar exercise, Fleet Problem One (1923), revealed an inadequate number of radio channels, resulting in clogged circuits. There was no way to prioritize messages, so relatively unimportant ones swamped essential ones (the Blue Fleet commander attached a copy of all messages sent to or from his flagship, with the comment that only six of them were vital). The commanding officer (CO) of USS *Delaware* reported an average of two hours to get a contact report through to its intended recipient. Delays caused great confusion. Presumably based on wartime experience, the opposing Black Fleet maintained radio silence, but it discovered that visual signals were not enough, for example, to coordinate the screen with the main body. It too experienced delays of two to three hours in transmission. In July 1923 chief of naval operations (CNO) Adm. Edward W. Eberle (who had commanded the Black Fleet during the fleet problem), appointed a special committee to improve fleet communications.[8] It proved possible to reduce transmission time dramatically.[9]

Plotting made it possible for the U.S. Navy to adopt new tactics. In 1923 a new kind of formation, in which outlying cruisers and destroyers formed circular screens around the battleships and other high-value units, was proposed.[10] It offered warning of attacks from any direction. That may have seemed particularly valuable as the U.S. Navy contemplated an advance across the Central Pacific toward Japan, the fleet passing through Japanese-held island chains en route. Previously the battleships steamed in line ahead, its cruisers and destroyers either in line ahead or in line abreast. Either formation was easy to understand and to maintain, and the layout of the fleet was fairly clear to the glance of the fleet commander. A screen ahead of the main body of the fleet could deal with submarines lying in wait, and it could find an enemy fleet toward which the fleet might be steaming. However, aircraft could approach from any direction, and it was not clear that the U.S. fleet would be steaming toward its enemy. The new formations were first tested in Fleet Problem Two (January 1924). They suffered from communications problems, which had not yet been resolved. Even so, their promise was evident, and they were adopted.

Plotting facilities presumably reflected World War I experience, mainly with the Royal Navy. Not surprisingly, U.S. officers complained that their own plotting facilities were grossly inadequate.[11] Probably the key problem was that space sufficed for only a single plot. Thus a fleet commander could either keep track of his own force, or he could view a larger-scale plot showing the approach of an enemy. The British were learning that two complementary plots were needed, but that required more space. After Fleet Problem Nine (1929), the two opposing fleet commanders both argued that the fleet commander should use a cruiser rather than a battleship because the cruiser need not be tied to the battle line and also because it could more easily be adapted to his plotting and staff needs.[12] A cruiser would also be fast enough to move around the fleet as required.

A lack of plotting space translated to poor overall situational awareness. In Battle Problem Nine, the carrier *Saratoga* made a spectacular attack on the Panama Canal. Then three opposing battleships intercepted and sank her. This was despite her fleet's innovation of placing intelligence officers on board their flagship specifically to intercept and decrypt enemy messages—that is, to conduct ocean surveillance. Thus *Saratoga*'s fleet should have known where the enemy battleships were (according to the exercise report, the opposing fleet lost all radio security). The fleet commander blamed poor use of tactical information (which meant poor plotting) for the failure to stop or evade the battleships, whose positions and tracks had been reported.[13]

Messages took far too long to pass from ship to flagship because decoding was laborious, even though the U.S. codes of the 1920s proved too easy to break. Delays were particularly intolerable in air operations, leading to the use of plain language. From the 1920s on, the U.S. Navy worked on automated code machines; by World War II, it had the very successful Electric Cypher Machine (ECM) Mk II.[14]

The fleet's radio signals were too easy to intercept. At least in theory a distant enemy could not intercept or direction find (DF) very high frequency (VHF) radio, which usually did not pass beyond the horizon. The Naval Research Laboratory began VHF experiments in 1925, and the first two sets went to sea in 1929. After difficulties, the first limited-production models (CXL) appeared in 1935. A few were tested during Fleet Problem Seventeen (1936). Unfortunately, the 60 MHz maximum frequency was not high enough. These sets could be heard beyond the horizon. Finally, a satisfactory "talk between ships" (TBS) (60–80 MHz) was introduced in 1939. It finally gave the fleet the flexible and secure tactical radio needed to execute the new tactics.[15]

The U.S. Navy sought to reduce the communication load by adopting standardized formations and basic tactics as a kind of playbook for the fleet.[16] In theory the playbook was flexible enough to leave space for subordinates' initiative but rigid enough to limit what a fleet commander had to transmit. The U.S. Navy also adopted the fleet broadcast.[17]

Like the Royal Navy, the U.S. Navy needed some means of locating a scout beyond the horizon. The U.S. solution was to have several ships within visual range of each other from a DF net to locate the transmitter.[18] Medium frequency direction finders became obsolete as navies, including the U.S. Navy, switched to HF radio in the late 1920s. In 1930 OpNav made development of a shipboard HF/DF a high priority, and experimental units were tested unsuccessfully in 1932–33. A few shipboard HF/DFs were installed for Fleet Problem Sixteen (1935), the carrier *Saratoga* using them particularly effectively. Tactical radio direction finding was considered so important in the late 1930s that special measures were taken to keep the antennas in question from being seen by unauthorized persons. For example, civilian photography of U.S. warships was largely prohibited. These pre–World War II units were not those used successfully by ASW ships during World War II; they were too massive for any but large ships. They also did not cover the high end of the HF spectrum. Shipboard units were limited to the ground wave, which propagates about 180 nautical miles from a source.

The value of HF/DF was limited because ships far enough apart to get usable cuts on a distant target were generally over each others' horizons, hence had to communicate using HF radio—which the enemy could exploit. When he became commander in chief (CinC) U.S. Fleet in June 1936, Adm. Arthur J. Hepburn suggested an alternative. A shore net of HF/DF stations could be linked together and to a tracking center. The product could be broadcast to the fleet. This was probably the origin of the Mid-Pacific Strategic HF/DF Net.

During the interwar period, the Battle Tracer gave way to the dead-reckoning tracer (DRT), which also used a mechanical "bug" crawling across a chart.[19] The

DRT was analogous to the contemporary British tactical table. It projected ahead a ship's position on the assumption that there was no current or wave action, that is, that the ship was really steaming in the direction indicated by the gyrocompass, at the speed over the ground indicated by the log. The dead-reckoned position was reasonably accurate over a few hours, but not over days. In combat, the DRT "bug" unfortunately tended to jump off the chart under the shock of gunfire. DRT failure helped make U.S. track charts of World War II actions less than reliable.

Plotting seems to have led the U.S. Navy to conclusions about night action similar to those of the British, involving elaborate night tactics that would have been impossible without coordinating plots. As with the British, success depended on how accurate the synthetic vision of the battle situation was; a fleet commander working from an erroneous plot would issue the wrong orders. In daylight individuals could correct for errors based on what they could see. At night, however, the only overall vision of the situation resided on the flagship. Because the flag plot could not be duplicated on other ships, none of the subordinate ships had a particularly good view of the overall situation. As long as the enemy was not very active, as at Matapan, this was no great problem. If, however, the enemy also had a night plot, *and* if subordinates were not careful, disaster could easily result. The night battle off Guadalcanal on 11–12 November 1942 is a case in point.[20]

U.S. commander Rear Adm. Daniel Callaghan formed his cruisers into line ahead, presumably because this formation was the easiest to follow and the safest, from a friendly fire point of view. Unfortunately, his best night sensor, an SG surface-search radar, was in the cruiser *Helena* rather than on board his flagship *San Francisco*. The flagship carried the plot on which Callaghan's fleet depended. *Helena* fed her SG data into that plot via voice radio. Unfortunately, it connected the flagship not with the radar plot on board *Helena*, but with her bridge. Errors crept in between plot and bridge. Because the situation developed rapidly, time lags further confused the flag plot (the basis for all orders) and thus corrupted the tactical decisions he made. When the line-ahead formation kinked, ships seen apparently moving through the formation (but actually merely turning out of line) were misidentified as Japanese. U.S. ships used fighting lights for night identification: turning them on attracted Japanese fire.

As the British had feared before World War I, a long straight line of ships made an ideal torpedo target. The U.S. Navy understood as much, but until early 1944 it had no idea of the range of Japanese torpedoes. Commanders mistakenly thought that they could use their own rapid-firing radar-controlled six-inch guns outside Japanese torpedo range.

Other Navies

In 1919 plotting was a new idea for other navies. French archives include a lengthy presentation by a staff officer arguing for plotting as an alternative to the traditional "seaman's eye" approach to command.[21] Because it survived among relatively few such papers, this one was presumably considered significant. Plotting was vital because ranges had grown to the point where a battle situation almost certainly would not be obvious to the commander's naked eye. Like the British, he argued for separate complementary strategic and tactical plots. The large-scale plot was essential if the fleet were to be served by a variety of scouts operating beyond the horizon. He valued the tactical plot mainly as a way of deciding how to maneuver to avoid long-range torpedoes. The most visible sign of tactical plotting on board interwar French warships was the proliferation of tactical range finders.

Having worked with the Royal Navy during World War I, the Imperial Japanese Navy also adopted plotting. The visible signs include special plotting spaces on board cruisers and battleships and dedicated tactical range finders. It is not clear whether the Japanese had a dead-reckoning tracer equivalent. As in the U.S. Navy, the Japanese found plotting a way of implementing complex tactics, particularly for night action.[22] Their equivalent to the stunning British night success at Matapan was the devastating attack at Savo Island in August 1942, when five Allied cruisers were sunk, at least one of them by friendly fire. The Japanese had a particularly apt weapon in their Type 93 ("Long Lance") long-range torpedo. The problem in night action is the sudden loss of situational awareness once action has been joined. The British solved it at Matapan by destroying the Italian ships very quickly, using concentrated gunfire. The Japanese solution was to run in, launch torpedoes, and then leave, so that the changing situation after firing was not too relevant. Ships could re-form outside the battle area, reload, and then make another pass. It helped that the Japanese had a superb night sensor in the form of large binoculars, so that they could maintain situational awareness better than other preradar navies. However, sustained contact, as at Guadalcanal in November 1942, destroyed Japanese situational awareness just as it did everyone else's. Despite their experience in tactical plotting, the Japanese never graduated to an equivalent to the Combat Information Center (CIC).

There was no way to duplicate the flag plot on other ships. Other units in a force maintained their own plots, but mainly to generate information to feed to the flag plot. However, there was insufficient communications capacity to make sure that plots matched. Thus the loss of a flagship—of her plot—might terminate an operation. A replacement flagship could start up a new plot—as long as the group was not engaged. This reality may help explain why Japanese admiral Takeo Kurita turned back at Samar in the face of desperate U.S. destroyer and air attacks, rather than carry out his mission of destroying invasion shipping at Leyte Gulf. His flagship, *Atago*, had been lost the previous day. When he transferred to the battleship *Yamato*, he lost some of his staff.[23]

It is not clear to what extent the Royal Italian Navy used tactical plotting. The Italians bought a pair of plotting tables from the British in 1931, when the two countries were still friendly. *Littorio*-class battleships had large tactical range finders supplementing their main battery units. However, other Italian warships do not show the secondary range finders that indicate tactical plotting in other navies.

The Germans apparently had nothing like the British tactical plots. Before World War I, they plotted gunnery practice as a way of scoring, but they did not use plots operationally during the war. Jutland was a case in point. Accounts of German fleet development in the late 1930s suggest that there was little interest in a classical battle fleet. Instead, German battleships and cruisers were intended to work in small battle groups that an admiral could easily coordinate based on what he could see from his bridge. The Germans had automatic plotting tables in their fire control centers (to estimate target course and speed as an input to fire control). It does not appear that they ever had British-style tactical plots.

Admiral Sir John Fisher's picture-centric operating concept vectored ships to distant operating areas. They had to be fast to take advantage of fleeting data. They also had to have long radio receiving range to take advantage of updated data, hence the combination of high speed and tall masts (for long radio range) in the battle cruisers. HMS *Inflexible* is shown in the North River (Hudson River), New York City, in 1910.

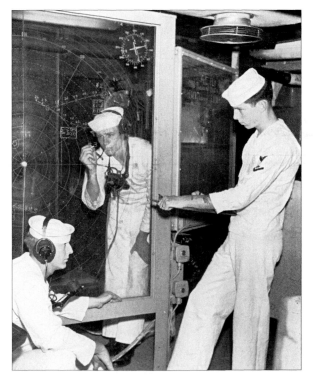

The key to creating a tactical picture is associating a series of observed target positions to form a track, which shows where that target is going. Here plotters aboard the radar picket USS *Sellstrom* (DER 255) create a track from the series of point detections indicated by the crosses on his vertical plot. The plotter behind the board registers the detections (the crosses). An evaluator in front of the board decided which plots were part of which track and drew in the tracks, which became the basis for tactical decisions. With more than one target present, it cannot always have been obvious which plot went with which target.

During World War I, the Royal Navy learned to use tactical and large-scale ("strategical") plots as a way of understanding a developing situation. Plotting required a ship to measure the ranges to many other ships she was not engaging, hence she had separate tactical range finders. In New York in the 1930s, the Australian heavy cruiser HMAS *Australia* shows one of her tactical range finders against her forefunnel.

By 1940 the Royal Navy had a network of land HF/DF stations using U-Adcock fixed antennas (two crossed pairs, with a sense antenna at their center). The U.S. Navy considered such Adcocks superior to its earlier trainable antennas and bought some from the British. In this station, a goniometer (a directional receiver) rotated between contacts to the two pairs of antennas. The operator measured the direction of a radio signal by seeking a minimum or zero signal. That indicated the direction opposite that from which the signal originated. (The operator could not be sure of the maximum, in the direction of the signal.) During World War II, the Allies discovered a better way to use such equipment, displaying signal strength versus bearing, so that the operator could easily find a maximum. The British did so by using the pair of antennas to drive a CRT. The U.S. alternative, developed by ITT's Alfred de Busignies in France, was to spin the goniometer at high speed, displaying its output on a screen. Both alternatives were well adapted to fixing short signals. The remaining problem, not solved until the 1960s, was that all of the stations in a net had to communicate in order to know that they were seeing the same signal. That communication took time. The solution this time was retrospective DF, recording signals as they came in for later comparison, using fingerprinting to know that two stations had seen the same signal. Because the antenna of this type of station was fixed, it could be larger than that in the earlier type of fully rotating direction finder, and hence could have greater gain (range against a weak signal). Even so, an Adcock was subject to serious inaccuracies when receiving sky waves because the waves might not approach vertically. (They might in effect be canted.) To some extent the Adcock limited the problem by receiving only the vertically polarized components of the sky waves, but even then it could be seriously inaccurate—in the worst case, according to a September 1945 German analysis, 90 degrees off. This Australian station was at Harman. Each "U" consisted of two of the four uprights connected by the ground. U.S. equivalents used wire stays rather than wooden towers to support their quad antennas. Because these antennas had to be calibrated, a set of them could handle only a limited frequency range, and a DF station normally used several sets. Postwar the U.S. Navy learned to use broadband antennas, and its GRD-6 had four pairs of such antennas spaced around a circle (without, apparently, any sense antenna in the center). The key difference from the later Wullenwebers was size: the spacing of the antennas was only a fraction of the wavelength handled by the system. *(RAN photo via Josef Straczek)*

The U.S. Navy became interested in land-based HF/DF in the 1930s, largely because its code breakers discovered that the Imperial Japanese Navy was already using this technique for ocean surveillance. The initial approach adopted by the Naval Research Laboratory was to swing the DF antenna. This prototype DT is shown in 1936. The production version moved the receiver down into a fixed hut. This type of receiver swung a single Adcock antenna (a pair of dipoles) rather than a goniometer. *(Courtesy of Naval Research Lab)*

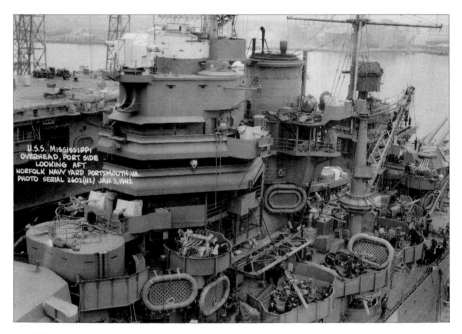

The U.S. Navy learned the value of plotting both from its own pre–World War I exercises and from its contact with the Royal Navy when U.S. battleships served with the Grand Fleet. U.S. warships of the interwar period generally had separate tactical range finders. Refitting at Portsmouth Navy Yard in January 1942, USS *Mississippi* shows her prominent shielded tactical rangefinder (apparently painted white) atop her bridge.

At least for the U.S. and Royal navies, the advent of automatic plotting tables made complex tactics practicable. In such tables a spot of light automatically traced the ship's position. Other ships' positions were plotted relative to this spot, so that their tracks could be deduced. Note the drafting device in the foreground, used to enter other ships' positions. This photograph is from a post–World War II edition of the *Bluejacket's Manual*, but tables like those shown entered service during the 1930s.

Plotting changed the significance of a flagship: she carried the fleet commander's tactical and wide-area pictures in a form difficult to duplicate on board any other ship. Before World War II, the U.S. Navy debated whether the flagship should be a major fleet unit, engaged in the fleet action, or a cruiser that could disengage, giving the admiral more flexibility. Adm. William F. Halsey chose a middle path in Third Fleet, making the battleship *New Jersey* (shown here off Korea) rather than a carrier his flagship. His choice of the battleship suggests that he considered his battle line integral with his carrier force, hence would have been unlikely to detach it (as many have supposed) to deal with the Japanese surface threat at Leyte Gulf. In a preplotting world, the fleet commander in effect carried the situation in his head, so it was enough for him to move from ship to ship. Plotting was needed because the battle area extended over so great an area that a fleet commander could not possibly see the whole situation. The wider-area plot was needed because, once aircraft were a major factor in naval warfare, the fleet commander had to take a far larger area into account.

A plot on board his flagship enabled a fleet commander to envisage and control complex all-arms tactics. Thus plots became vital when fleets first combined guns and long-range torpedoes on board both capital ships and lesser craft. The French fleet included battleships, cruisers, large destroyers (contre-torpilleurs), and destroyers (torpilleurs), all with different roles. The contre-torpilleurs, like the three ships in the foreground, were conceived to deal with Italian surface strike forces directed at French commerce in the Mediterranean. A group of three such ships could, it was thought, overwhelm a cruiser. The countersurface role in turn required central direction, the ships being vectored to intercept the enemy force. Behind the three contre-torpilleurs are three Marseillaise-class light cruisers and, in the background, three Bretagne-class battleships. The pre–World War II French fleet also included a single aircraft carrier, but the bulk of its airpower, including long-range torpedo bombers, was based ashore, on the northern and southern shores of the Mediterranean.

Although not conceived as such, convoy was an antisurveillance measure. As a U-boat commander in the Mediterranean in 1918, Admiral Karl Doenitz noticed that once convoys were formed, the sea was swept nearly clear of Allied shipping.

Any U-boat that did encounter a convoy could not handle the mass of targets it presented. Thus, the advent of convoys focused Doenitz on the ocean surveillance problem, which he solved mainly by code breaking and then by forming patrol lines of U-boats (wolf packs) that could make up for the imprecision of code-breaking data on convoy routes and positions. Even when signals did not give warning of the position of a particular convoy, the information about convoy routes provided by code breaking made it possible to position U-boats—until circumstances allowed the Allies to reroute convoys radically. This convoy was photographed in November 1942.

Intelligence-based ocean surveillance could be used for offensive action. Here aircraft from the escort carrier USS *Card* attack U-66 and U-117 (which was sunk), August 1943, based on Ultra information. Aggressive U.S. use of such data worried the Royal Navy, which feared that the Germans would deduce that their code had been broken.

The advent of new types of U-boats in 1945 would have changed ASW; the threat that the Soviets would copy and mass produce such submarines shaped postwar Western naval development. When World War II ended, the Germans had numerous Type XXI U-boats in various stages of construction, but only one was operational. Type XXIs are shown under construction in Bremen, 5 May 1945.

The radar input area of a precomputer carrier CIC shows a row of radar consoles. Console operators detected targets, i.e., decided that particular blips represented real targets. Then the talker behind the row of consoles reported them verbally so that they could be plotted. These separate steps imposed time lags. This photograph was taken in February 1958.

In a precomputer CIC, the tactical picture—the basis for decision—was formed by plotters, like the one in the middle of this photograph, entering data received by sound-powered phone. The tracks actually used as the basis for decision were created by an evaluator in effect connecting the points plotted on the board. The vertical plot in this

photograph is flanked by status boards. The officer in the foreground seems to be operating an analog fighter intercept computer, several types of which were tested in the 1950s. The process of plotting imposed significant time lags (latencies), which made for inaccuracy. As the plotter handled more and more targets, the latencies became worse and worse, until the picture in CIC was no longer good enough to support fighter control. To some extent the officer in the foreground could compare the picture on the vertical plot with what he could see via the radar display (indicated by the rubber hood to the left of the status board writer on the right).

The process of plotting to create a usable tactical picture imposed time lags, which made fighter control difficult. The solution was a screen that projected the radar picture onto what amounted to a plotting board, so that it could be used directly. These fighter controllers on board USS *Ticonderoga* (CV14) off Formosa in January 1945 are working directly on the plotting screen, a device the U.S. Navy called a VG. (The British called it a Skiatron.)

With a big APS-20 radar and its operator replacing the usual torpedo, radioman, and gunner, a TBM-3 Avenger became Cadillac, the first airborne early warning radar airplane. The radar picture was provided to the ship via a dedicated link, appearing on a radar scope in the ship's CIC, just like any of the ship's own radars.

The step beyond the Avenger was an airborne CIC using the APS-20 radar: Cadillac II, using a B-17G bomber (designated PB-1W in Navy service). This VW-1 aircraft was photographed at Barbers Point in 1952.

The operational descendant of Cadillac II was the WV-2 Warning Star (designated EC-121 by the Air Force, and then by the Navy under the unified 1962 designation series), a modified Super Constellation airliner. It had an APS-20 search radar under its belly, with an enlarged antenna, and an APS-45 height finder on top. The height finder was limited in that the airplane had to turn toward the target to use it. Originally, this large airplane was valued because it had sufficient endurance to spend several hours above a deployed task force. However, the Warning Star was most important as a means of extending U.S. continental radar coverage out to sea, in conjunction with lines of picket ships. The aircraft in effect contributed to the tactical picture used by North American Air Defense, with its SAGE automated picture system. The U.S. Navy was authorized to develop a computer tactical system specifically to connect to the shore air defense net, but the radar picket aircraft and ships were never automated: they transmitted their data via conventional radio. When the North American air defense mission was abandoned, many of these aircraft were used in Vietnam for electronic surveillance.

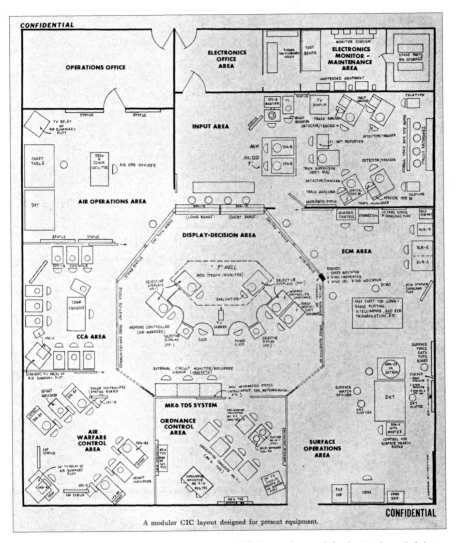

A modular CIC layout designed for present equipment.

As more and more CIC functions were added, it became more difficult to see the central plot showing the tactical picture. The modular CIC was a precomputer solution: a television camera was trained on the main plot (in the display/decision area),and its picture shown in each functional area of CIC. That could not be entirely satisfactory because what happened in each separate functional area affected the perceived tactical picture. OpNav saw the modular CIC as a way station toward a computerized CIC. This diagram is from an article on the Modular CIC in the January–March 1959 issue of the the formerly classified OpNav magazine *Combat Readiness*, which explained to the fleet the reason why only computers could cure the existing CIC problems.

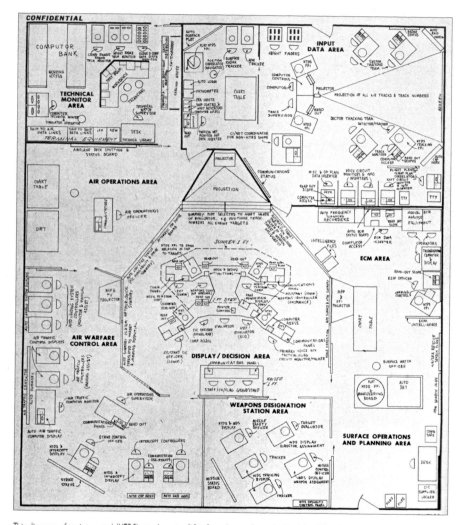

This diagram of an integrated (NTDS) attack carrier CIC is from the article on the Modular CIC in the January–March 1959 issue of *Combat Readiness*. The great change was that the picture displayed at the center of CIC was also carried, in effect, by the ship's NTDS computer system, so that its elements could be displayed anywhere in CIC—and actions taken in various areas of CIC could be entered automatically in the picture, and hence in the central display. Although plans called for installing NTDS in all U.S. combatants, it was accepted that the process might be lengthy, so special provision had to be made for communication with non-NTDS ships. Ultimately that meant Link 14—and, ironically, there were protracted efforts to use the Link 14 teletype message to drive a computerized tactical display on board non-NTDS ships.

The NTDS CIC on board the nuclear carrier *Enterprise* is shown in March 1967, with a standard NTDS console at left. The central computer created the graphics for all the system consoles, in effect broadcasting video to them. Thus, operators could tell that a system was overloaded when the video did not refresh often enough, so that symbols on their screens seemed to blink. *(PH1 Strickland, USN)*

NTDS made it possible for a ship in the Tonkin Gulf to control the complex air traffic over the gulf and also over North Vietnam. Such ships could arrange the interception of North Vietnamese MiGs (an enlisted controller aboard the cruiser *Chicago* was decorated for twelve kills achieved in this way). The computerized CIC of the missile cruiser *Wainright* is shown in September 1968. Note that, because each console had access to the picture held in the ship's computer, there was no longer any need for all the operators to be able to see a central display. Consoles could be arranged in rows, to fit the small deckhouse available on board this ship.

To exploit the power of a computerized tactical picture required a means of automatically vectoring aircraft: a data link from the tactical computer on board a ship (or in a land-air control center) to the fighter that would intercept the enemy aircraft. The U.S. Navy first decided to buy such links because some of its fighters were always assigned to North American Air Defense, hence to control by the Air Force's SAGE system. Once it had adopted this Link 4, it realized that, among other things, it could be used for carrier-controlled (night and bad-weather) landings, as part of the Automatic Carrier Landing System. By 1959 Link 4 was planned for the new fleet fighter, the F-4 (then designated F4H) Phantom II. In fact, the first Phantoms with data links were twelve F-4Gs converted from standard F-4Bs in 1963. (They received the new designation the following year.) F-4Gs had the two-way ASW-21 data link that reported back to the carrier the airplane's fuel, oxygen, and weapon status. But the ASW-25 link installed on board F-4Bs was one-way (carrying commands for interception and for automatic landing). Feedback was verbal rather than digital, perhaps reflecting the limited capacity of the controlling computer system on board ships. The F-4J shown had an improved link (ASW-25A) and a new pulse-Doppler radar (APG-59) feeding a digital (AWG-10) weapon system. Unlike the AWG-9 of the F-14 Tomcat, AWG-10 could not track multiple targets simultaneously, a limitation presumably accepted because the airplane could not engage more than one target at a time with its semiactive Sparrow III missiles. An F-4J of VF-96 is shown taking off from the carrier *Constellation* in the South China Sea, July 1974.

Computers and their associated data links made it possible to create a unified air defense system. Here its airborne CIC element (on board an E-2C Hawkeye) is flanked by the associated Tomcat (F-14) fighters. The E-2C could automatically command the fighters to engage targets it detected, and it could also see targets they detected. The E-2C was also connected to surface forces via the battle group–wide Link 11. That is, the carrier and the E-2C—and, to some extent, the F-14s—created the tactical picture, on the basis of which the F-14s attacked enemy aircraft.

In the late 1950s it suddenly seemed that computers could go aboard aircraft. Grumman's A-6 Intruder (in the background) was one of the first U.S. naval aircraft to benefit from the new kind of electronics, which could automatically create (in effect) a viable tactical picture from a radar. The A-6 was intended to use its radar picture for precision navigation, for terrain avoidance, and for fire control. Roughly parallel to this bomber project was a planned interceptor, Missileer, which was to have used a computer to create a tactical picture allowing it to engage multiple targets simultaneously. For reasons unconnected with the computer-missile concept, Missileer was delayed by about a decade, finally emerging as the F-14 Tomcat in the foreground. The F-14's AWG-9 missile control system could create up to twenty-four tracks, engaging six targets with long-range Phoenix missiles. These two aircraft are shown aboard USS *Enterprise* in March 1975. The missile under the Tomcat's wing is a Sparrow III.

PART 2 | The Radar Era

Just as radio made it possible for a remote commander to maintain a more or less real-time picture of events at sea, radar made it possible for a commander to see what was happening in a broad battle space. Moreover, the radar on each ship provided something approaching an accurate real-time plot, with minimal manual plotting. This new capability was particularly important as aircraft shrank the time scale and expanded the range scale of naval warfare, but it also had vital implications for surface warfare.

CHAPTER 5

Picture-Centric Air Defense

R adar is always remembered as the key to British survival in the face of German air attacks in 1940. What really mattered was the way in which information from radar and from other sources, such as signals intelligence, was used. British air defense was picture-centric. The land-based system inspired the approach to radar adopted by the Royal Navy. This was not the only way to organize a radar air defense system. The British system really was special. Its basic concept dated back to World War I and to defense against German bombers. Its core was a filter center that combined available information to create a usable picture of the air situation. The word filter is a reminder that such a center must not only merge useful information, but that it must also recognize and reject bad data.

When the German raids began in 1915, British home air defense (by aircraft) was the responsibility of the Royal Naval Air Service. By that time the Royal Navy was using plots for situational awareness. The centralized London Air Defence Area (LADA) was developed during the war around a master filter room or plot at Horse Guards, London.[1] Early warning was provided by radio intelligence: the Germans had virtually no radio discipline in the air as at sea. However, they tended not to transmit once well away from their bases. LADA used other sources of information, such as spotters (including those on ships offshore), to report attackers as they approached London. As at sea, action was based on tracks that enabled the system to predict where attackers were going. At its peak in 1918, LADA used twenty-five regional subcontrol centers, which coordinated information to form initial plots. At each a "teller" read plots for replotting at Horse Guards, each of whose ten plotters had headphones. Horse Guards fed its filtered raid tracks back to the subcenters. Vectoring was essential, particularly once the Germans shifted from day to night raids, and the individual fighter pilot might find it difficult to find them at all. The best hope seems to have been to trigger searchlights to illuminate attackers against clouds. By April 1918 some of the fighters Horse Guards controlled had radiotelephones. LADA was completed in September 1918, too late to see action. (The Germans had switched to more tactical targets.) Its commander, artillery Brig. Gen. E. B. "Splash" Ashmore, thought that the central organization quadrupled the chance of successful interception. During a night battle, he would stand on a balcony looking down on the plot to assess the course of the attack in order to plan the defense.

Once radar emerged, British air defense was modeled on LADA; the first filter room was set up in 1937.[2] Like LADA's Horse Guards center, each filter room was built around a large horizontal table. Hockey pucks on the table represented friendly and enemy aircraft. The table became the system display—and memory. A filter room fused information from multiple sources: various radars, but they might also be radio direction finders or even observers on the ground. Information might be supplemented by code breaking. Data fusion was possible because all of the information was in compatible form: a bomber was detected at such and such a place and then again at another place, so its course and speed (its track) could be calculated. Given tracks, interceptors could be vectored to deal with the incoming bombers. The system had to track both enemy and friendly aircraft, to keep from vectoring friendly aircraft to intercept other friendly aircraft. "Identification of friend or foe" (IFF) was in its infancy, so identification was mainly by tracking.

The filter room converted radars (and other sources of air defense information) into a unified track-while-scan system that could handle the multiple raids visible on its big horizontal plot more or less simultaneously. Like any track-while-scan system, the filter room had limits. There were time lags between a report and the placement of a puck and the assignment of a fighter to a target. As the number of targets mounted, the plot would fall farther and farther behind reality. Lateness was reflected in vectoring errors. It could be tolerated up to a point because a fighter pilot placed anywhere near the target could see it, and if he was not too far away, he was fast enough to make up the vectoring error. As bombers became faster, the tolerable error level shrank. Vectoring was always somewhat imprecise, not least because British radars had wide beams. Because there was no alternative, the British seem not to have tried to estimate the point at which a given filter room would collapse. The system was useless at night unless the fighter had radar, and even then radar detection range was generally considerably less than eyeball range.

It was impossible to cover the whole country, or even the whole of southern England, with a single filter room. The Royal Air Force (RAF) set up multiple rooms, but there was no way to link them automatically. The system lost efficiency when targets crossed from one filter room area to an adjacent one. If that happened only rarely or slowly, phone calls sufficed for coordination.

The wartime German approach to radar air defense shows how unique the British filter-room approach was. Like the British, the Germans had long-range early warning radar, but they did not send its information to filter rooms. Instead, they used early warning to trigger individual fighter-control cells in a system they called Himmelbet, or "Sky Bed." In each cell, one radar tracked a bomber and the other a fighter. Like a command-guided missile system, the command linking the two ordered the fighter into position to deal with the bomber. The system was practical because the German radars were technically superior to the British, with the narrower beams needed for tracking and fighter control. Compared to the networked British approach, the German approach offered much greater precision, but it could not handle large numbers of attackers.[3]

By 1942 RAF Bomber Command realized that the German system could be saturated.[4] To do that, it adopted stream tactics, rushing each control box with as many bombers as possible in the shortest possible time. Then, when it raided Hamburg in July 1943, it added chaff (Window), which neutralized the control radars. The Germans had to decentralize.

One alternative was to accept that radar was useless for anything but overall raid warning. Once a night raid was in progress, bombers were often lit up against clouds, either by searchlights or even by the flames of the city they were attacking. Day fighters could attack; such practices were called Wilde Sau (Wild Boar).[5] Another approach (Tame Boar) was to feed long-range night fighters into the stream of bombers as it crossed the European coast. Control was limited to a broadcast describing the general course of the bombers, based on early warning radars.[6] The mass of bombers was so dense that a fighter would almost inevitably find targets. This theme of decentralization to handle saturation can be seen in the carrier air defense tactics of the 1950s. In each case, the British adopted counter-countermeasures. For example, they dealt with Tame Boar by broadcasting noise (often amplified engine sounds) on the controllers' frequencies. The Germans responded by using music, which was easier to recognize through jamming, to indicate which major city the RAF was attacking. All of these measures were means of preserving or destroying the information crucial to the defense. The RAF also learned to make decoy attacks, in hopes of forcing the Germans to commit the bulk of their fighters before the main attack began. Again, this was an information war tactic. Presumably it would have been far more difficult to deceive a British-style filter plot, which could develop a more complex tactical picture.

CHAPTER 6

The Experience with Radar

The British Experience: The AIO

Initially, the Royal Navy saw radar as one more sensor contributing to its existing plots. HMS *Valiant* seems to have been the first British warship to maintain a separate air plot on her bridge (based on lookout information) to designate targets for her antiaircraft guns. The plot was operational during the Norwegian campaign of April–June 1940. Other ships maintained a separate visual plot based on lookout data. It was easily adapted to radar plotting.[1] In HMS *Rodney*, radar data were added to the ship's tactical plot.[2] Also during the Norwegian campaign, HMS *Ark Royal* became the first British warship to use radar data to control fighters. As she had no radar of her own, she relied on those of the cruiser in company, HMS *Sheffield* or HMS *Curlew*.[3] The Royal Navy was obsessed with radio silence, so it limited radar emissions and even used flags rather than radio to pass radar information.[4]

During the *Bismarck* chase, the cruiser HMS *Suffolk* relied on a radar plot to estimate the course of the German battleship despite her zigzagging. The battleship HMS *Prince of Wales* used the cruiser's reports to track *Bismarck* without breaking radar silence—an example of net centricity. Two and a half years later HMS *Duke of York* and her cruiser consort HMS *Jamaica* relied entirely on the reports of the shadowing cruisers (led by HMS *Belfast*) to intercept and sink the German battleship *Scharnhorst*. The navigating officer of HMS *Sheffield* later said that "one of the most dramatic experiences with radar of the whole Naval War was the moment when *Duke of York* appeared on the cruisers' radar displays, due south of *Scharnhorst* and in a perfect position to intercept her," having been navigated into position on the basis of various ships' plots.[5]

The Royal Navy combined filter center and navigational plot into what it called an Action Information Centre (AIC) operated by the Action Information Organization

(AIO). Compared to the filter center, the AIO was much more platform-centric; it concentrated on the outputs of radars and other sensors on board the ship it served. It accepted radioed data from centers on board other ships, but there was no question of using their radar data directly. Time delays and uncertainties about the relative locations of ships would have introduced gross errors into its plots. The AIO also used other new sensors such as sonar (for antisubmarine warfare [ASW]), radio direction finding, and radio intercepts ("Y").

Through mid-1943 the Admiralty received numerous reports from ships at sea describing their home-grown plotting arrangements and advocating standardized ones. Apparently no one on the naval staff realized that all were describing a common, and very serious, problem. Then the commanding officer of the small destroyer HMS *Cleveland*, having proposed a standardized AIO was promoted to captain and assigned to the Admiralty. He found his own proposal on his desk for comment. He soon pushed through a standard policy.[6] On board a major warship the Action Information Centre comprised an Operations Room, an Air (or Aircraft) Direction Room (initially the Fighter Direction Room), a Target Indication Room (TIR, to direct a ship's antiaircraft battery), and, in carriers, an Air Operations Room. The Operations Room provided the Command with a more-or-less current picture of the situation. It maintained both the general operations plot and the local operations plot. As an indication of the areas involved, on board the battleship HMS *Valiant* in 1945, the local plot extended out to thirty nautical miles from the ship and was plotted at a scale of two nautical miles to the inch; the general plot was run at ten nautical miles to the inch, which implied that it covered the area out to 150 nautical miles. The Aircraft Direction Room (ADR) maintained an overall air situation plot. The object was to display the air situation for decision making, including—but not limited to—fighter direction. Close collaboration between the U.S. and Royal navies ensured that both used much the same technologies and procedures for air tracking and fighter control.[7]

By 1945 the Royal Navy wanted more plots. For example, ideally in a large ship the Command needed simplified (filtered) local and general plots in a separate Bridge Plotting Room, away from the complexity and activity of the Operations Room. The Flag had his own plot. A new Radar Display Room (RDR) was conceived as a filter room that would meld radar data into a single stream before it was plotted elsewhere. It appeared in the Pacific at the end of the war but was not used in combat. In each room plotters marked boards with grease pencils, using the same stream of data—but that did not guarantee that the tactical pictures on all the boards matched. In 1945 the most difficult plotting targets were aircraft. As they gained speed, the differences and time lags inherent in the system became more significant.

Radar and the AIO radically changed British naval air defense. In the mid-1930s, when war in the Mediterranean loomed, it was assumed that fighters could not defend the fleet because they could not be launched (and vectored) in time. The Royal Navy therefore designed carriers with armored hangars (usually described incorrectly as armored decks). That drastically limited aircraft capacity; the ships were expected to accommodate strike but not fighter aircraft. If air attack was imminent, they would strike their aircraft below to ride out the attack in relative safety. Ironically, radar was invented just as these *Illustrious*-class carriers were being designed. Although British naval fighters had only limited performance, in 1940 the combination of radar and AIO made it possible for them to intercept and drive off approaching Italian bombers.

AIOs and their tactical pictures gave weaker forces important advantages. The Battle of the Barents Sea (31 December 1942) was a case in point. Convoy JW51B, from Britain to Russia, was escorted by six destroyers, five corvettes, and a minesweeper, with the light cruisers *Jamaica* and *Sheffield* in support. The German attacking force consisted of the pocket battleship *Lutzow*, the heavy cruiser *Admiral Hipper*, and six large destroyers. The British destroyers managed to hold the heavy German ships at bay, partly by threatening them with torpedo attack, but also because the Germans seem to have found it difficult to understand the complex tactical situation under conditions of poor visibility; clearly they were unable to use radar to create situational awareness. Another mark of poor situational awareness was that, as in the U.S. fleet in the Solomons, they were unwilling to allow their destroyers to act independently, presumably for fear of hitting them with their heavy ships' shellfire (or of having destroyers accidentally torpedo the heavy ships). A third mark was that the two British cruisers achieved complete tactical surprise when they appeared, firing at the cruiser *Hipper*. Those on *Hipper* were concentrating on their tactical target (the convoy). They lacked the "track while scan" capability conferred by a plot or an AIO.[8]

The Germans' problem was symbolized by the fact that they had only a single radar, which they used primarily for fire control rather than for surface search. Major British ships typically had separate surface search (feeding an AIO) and fire-control sets. When the British cruisers fatally hit one of the German destroyers, her commander plaintively radioed that his own cruiser, which he thought was firing, was hitting him by mistake. He was entirely unaware that British cruisers were present. The British won the day; the convoy escaped unscathed, and their losses were limited to a destroyer and a minesweeper. The far more powerful German surface force lost a destroyer, and the cruiser *Hipper* was badly, nearly fatally, damaged.[9] The Germans had placed great hope in this Operation Regenbogen, and when it failed, Hitler ordered his heavy ships laid up. (German naval chief Admiral Karl Raeder resigned in protest.)

Unlike the U.S. Navy, the Royal Navy often had to coordinate land-based tactical aircraft with its ships. As at sea, an AIO—which it called a Maritime Headquarters (MHQ) could solve the problem.[10] Similarly, a shore AIO could direct coastal forces, just as an AIO directed fighters (the Royal Navy also tried using frigate AIOs for this purpose). When the North Atlantic Treaty Organization (NATO) was formed, many of its maritime commands, such as those in the Baltic and on the North Sea coast, controlled coastal strike aircraft as well as ships, so they used British MHQ techniques. Plots and an overall picture made it easier to keep friendly strike aircraft from attacking friendly ships. In the 1960s and 1970s, the manual MHQs gave way to automated ones, important examples being the German MHQ at Murwick and the British MHQ (operating on a much larger scale) at Northwood.

The U.S. Experience: The CIC

The U.S. Navy tested its first radars in a 1939 fleet exercise. As in the Royal Navy, the new sensor naturally fitted into the existing system of plots, including air plots and antiaircraft (Sky Control) plots. The first step was to add a radar plot.[11] The commanding officer of USS *Yorktown*, the first U.S. carrier with a radar, formally proposed a radar plot after a March 1941 exercise.[12] Approved by the secretary of the Navy in July 1941, the first was installed on board the new carrier *Hornet*, in her island near her radar control room, before she was completed in October 1941.[13] Typically, the radar plot occupied a corner of the air plot. Two plotters using a large vertical board were supervised by an officer (evaluator) who resolved issues such as track ambiguities. One fighter direction officer used the plot.[14] The British were clearly leaders in radar plotting, so the first class of U.S. Navy fighter director officers was trained in August 1941 by the Royal Canadian Air Force, which used British radar techniques.

The single air search radar set itself was too massive—and generated too much heat—to go into the plot, and there were no radar repeaters.[15] Radar plot—and all other plots that needed radar information—thus relied on reports of target range and bearing via sound-powered phone or voice pipe. When PPI (plan position indicator, i.e., map-like) displays appeared, some ships had paper tracings of the blips on their faces messengered to users. Those at the different plots using this data to create tactical pictures could never refer back to what the scope showed. These limitations help explain why, a year later, radar reports from the bridge of the cruiser *Helena* at Guadalcanal did not quite match what was seen in her radar plot.

The U.S. Navy first used its radar fighter-control system during a 31 January 1942 raid on the Japanese-occupied Gilbert Islands. The carrier *Enterprise* detected five Japanese bombers, and her Combat Air Patrol (CAP) shot them down. Her consort, *Yorktown*, had only two contacts, and the one she intercepted dropped its bombs before being shot down.[16] The system showed its limits under heavier Japanese attack during the Battle of the Coral Sea (May 1942). *Lexington* was hit after having been shadowed by undetected snoopers. (One was shot down after having been spotted visually.) The fighter director had placed his CAP too close to the bogey, so without some kind of "identification of friend or foe" (IFF) he was unable to distinguish the two. Later radar detected four contacts at a range of eighty-two nautical miles, but the CAP was already busy with other contacts; the ship's defense was, in effect, saturated. Without a height-finding radar, the altitude of the raiders was incorrectly estimated. Fighters from *Yorktown* were unable to intercept because they were below the raiders. Both carriers were damaged. *Lexington* had to be scuttled after suffering an aviation gasoline explosion.

Midway showed much the same problems as Coral Sea. The first Japanese raid was detected at forty-five nautical miles, but interception was not even ordered until they were twenty-five nautical miles out. Much of CAP was distracted by non-targets, apparently because of confusion caused by IFF failure. Even so, only seven of thirty-six Japanese aircraft survived to attack the carrier *Yorktown*. A second raid, detected at forty-five-nautical-mile range, was intercepted by two of six CAP fighters. The other U.S. fighters were too high to join the battle. *Yorktown* was hit again, and she was abandoned. Again, failed height finding was the problem. The solution was to break CAP into sections stacked in altitude.[17]

After Coral Sea the CO of *Yorktown* blamed poor performance partly on interference between radar and air plots, which were in the same space. He wanted the search plot (the overall tactical picture) separated from the fighter-control plot. The separate radar plot became the Combat Information Center (CIC). Fortunately, radar repeaters were soon perfected. Now the radar picture, rather than a more-or-less accurate report of that picture, could be seen in radar plot. An operator at a repeater could concentrate on detecting targets and reporting them directly to the plotters, rather than on keeping the radar operating. He could estimate raid course and speed directly from his scope, by grease-penciling detections on successive radar sweeps and connecting the dots. It was even possible to control an interception directly from a repeater, rather than from a plot.

Radar plot became Consolidated Radar Plot (using multiple radars), then Combat Operations Center (COC, November 1942), and finally CIC (Combat *Information* Center), because COC implied a command function, which some thought was more properly exercised from a ship's bridge. Its core was the new

British vertical plot, adopted after one was seen aboard HMS *Victorious*, under repair at Norfolk Navy Yard in 1943.[18] In turn, the Royal Navy apparently adopted U.S. CIC arrangements for its carriers after U.S. specifications were provided to British liaison officers at Pearl Harbor in the summer of 1943.[19]

CIC technology triumphed at the Battle of the Philippine Sea in June 1944. Although the Japanese found the American carriers first, the CICs of the U.S. fleet vectored defending fighters so effectively that they massacred the Japanese naval air arm. Four major attacks were all intercepted fifty to sixty nautical miles from the carriers; no raiders got through. An attempted low-level torpedo attack was also intercepted. The "Turkey Shoot" killed the pilots the Japanese had laboriously trained since the disasters in the Solomons in 1942–43. The significance of this success was not realized at the time, probably because the U.S. Navy was producing so many replacement pilots; it was not understood that the Japanese had not streamlined their own pilot-training process.

Then the Japanese discovered that a CIC could be saturated when they introduced kamikazes late in 1944 in the Philippines. It was not that they fielded more aircraft, but that the kamikazes flew in smaller groups, hence created more distinct targets. Conventional attackers bunched to saturate terminal defenses, and the hit probability per airplane was small because of the deterrent effect of heavy antiaircraft fire. A dedicated kamikaze pilot intentionally steering for the most intense fire had a much better chance of hitting, so there was much less need to bunch. (There was some attempt to group aircraft to complicate antiaircraft defense.) The number of distinct targets multiplied dramatically. The Japanese further complicated the problem by flying either very low (so that they could not be detected until they were close to their targets) or very high (in effect, above radar beams until they came very close).

Saturation meant that the picture in the CIC fell too far behind reality to be useful: some attackers were never intercepted. The processes of spotting a target on a repeater, then calling out its position (with inevitable errors because the blip on the repeater had a finite size), and then plotting on the vertical board all involved small delays (latencies). The more targets, the more the delays would add up. Postwar experiments showed that those in a CIC could never tell how badly they were falling behind. British trials on board the carrier HMS *Illustrious* (1948) showed that a conventional CIC could handle no more than twelve raids per hour by World War II aircraft; the situation would be far worse for the fast jets just entering service.

Just as the Germans had found with British stream raids, the only instant solution was to decentralize control. Off Okinawa in April 1945, the U.S. Navy deployed radar picket destroyers with sophisticated radars and enlarged CICs. Each was assigned a section of fighters. In effect, the CIC task was split up so that the load on each ship was reduced. The Japanese saw the pickets as a barrier they had to breach in order to get to the targets they wanted, so they hit each with multiple kamikazes. However, the idea of splitting up the CIC load was considered a success; the postwar U.S. Navy used radar picket destroyers and even radar picket submarines (which had been planned late in the war for the invasion of Japan).

Individual ships were saturated. They found it impossible to use their CICs to designate targets to their antiaircraft guns. In 1945 the U.S. Navy distributed simple directors around its ships, so that when CIC control broke down, they could divide up their batteries. Contemporary accounts mention observers on ships' bridges assigning targets to individual weapons. This was analogous to the Germans' Wild Boars.

The kamikazes seemed to foretell a postwar threat, the antiship guided missile, early versions of which the Germans had developed. Missiles would hardly fly in formation, so they would present numerous targets that might well saturate defenses. In 1945 both the U.S. and Royal navies knew that the CIC was key to most kinds of naval operation. Neither could abandon this networked tactical picture, which was needed to make efficient use of limited resources. Both therefore sought new technology that could speed CIC operation: computers.

CICs in Surface Warfare

CICs changed surface warfare, particularly at night. With a radar giving ship positions and a plotter easily turning that data into tracks, each ship in a group had much of the information required for a full surface plot. In the past, it had been impossible to approximate the same plot on multiple ships. Too much information was involved. Now the task was reduced largely to identifying the different tracks each plotter created. Each ship in a group, even at night, now had much the same situational awareness. With much less information to send back and forth, a commanding officer no longer had to rely on rigid formations. Tactics could become much suppler. Also, because CIC identified the ships in the plot, friendly fire became far less problematic. CICs were considered so important for surface warfare that some destroyers surrendered antiaircraft guns to accommodate them. As U.S. cruisers and destroyers in the South Pacific were fitted with CICs, U.S. tactics became more flexible. Even though ships still fought within the range of Japanese torpedoes, they could maneuver freely, making hits much less likely. After mid-1943, U.S. cruisers began to win the night battles.

The CIC concept extended to amphibious command and control. By the end of World War II, U.S. amphibious flagships had both fighter-direction CICs (to control defending fighters operating from ashore, but as yet without air control centers ashore) and Supporting Arms Coordination Centers (SACCs), in effect fire support CICs. They also had planning centers analogous to ground-forces head-quarters, which had some CIC-like functions. These ships also directed the boats landing troops in real time.

Airborne Early Warning

Airborne early warning began as a way of transmitting ships' radar pictures to detect surface ships beyond a ship's horizon—as a way of giving a CIC a longer-range sensor. By March 1944 it was airborne early warning Project Cadillac—primarily to detect aircraft. By late 1944 it was a high priority way of detecting low-flying kamikaze planes.[20] Cadillac was supposedly named after the Maine mountain where the radar relay was first tested, but the cost of the system suggests that the developers had the expensive car in mind. A specially developed APS-20 S-band radar was mounted in the belly of a modified TBM-3 Avenger torpedo bomber. Its picture was beamed down to a ship (not necessarily the carrier) via a new link. The airborne radar became, in effect, another of the ship's air search sets. Its picture appeared on a repeater in CIC, so its targets could be handled in standard fashion by the vertical plot. The ship controlled the radar. She carried a beacon that the radar used as a reference point. Cadillac was operationally tested on board the carrier *Ranger* between 23 May and 8 June 1945. Adding Cadillac to the carrier or to a naval formation was a network-centric step. The project enjoyed high priority postwar, detachments of TBM-3Ws and their successor AD-5Ws being assigned to carriers.

Cadillac II added a CIC to the airplane, for quicker interception, but retained the link to a ship. That was too much for a carrier airplane. Engineering tests to install the radar on board a B-17G led to a decision to convert several such aircraft and to install airborne CICs on board.[21] Longer-range aircraft with sufficient endurance could loiter over a fleet, extending its horizon. They could also provide warning overland during an amphibious landing even if fast carriers were not present. The first squadron of such aircraft (redesignated PB-1W) was formed on 20 July 1945 (the first fully equipped airplane was delivered 5 January 1946). The results were impressive, particularly when a height-finding radar was added. Some PB-1Ws remained in Navy service through the Korean War. The ultimate Cadillac II was the Lockheed Super Constellation (WV-2, later redesignated EC-121). Unlike the small carrier aircraft, it had both a long-range search radar (APS-20, in a belly radome) and a height finder (in a big dorsal fin). The airplane turned to bring the height finder to bear on a selected target. These aircraft were built in numbers, primarily to support North American Air Defense. They demonstrated the value of airborne fighter control, and thus contributed to the development of the future E-2 Hawkeye.

The big APS-20 proved an excellent surface-search radar capable of detecting small objects such as submarine periscopes and snorkels. After war broke out in Korea, carrier early warning aircraft vectored strike aircraft, their radars recognizing particular parts of the coastline. British airborne early warning Gannets using this radar later guided antiship strikes in exercises. Some postwar antisubmarine warfare (ASW) aircraft, such as the Neptune, received APS-20, not for airborne early warning, but for ASW search sensor. In the Falklands an Argentine Neptune used her APS-20 to guide the Super Etendard that hit HMS *Sheffield* with an Exocet missile.[22]

PART 3

The Computer Era

Computers answered the saturation problem: they could organize data far more rapidly than humans could. They could also transmit and receive data much more rapidly, so that plots could be spread instantly around a force. A third essential factor is Moore's Law, expressed in 1964 by computer executive Gerald Moore: the unit price of computing halves every eighteen months. That is often taken to mean that computer capacity (or speed) doubles every eighteen months. Thus, although in 1964 usable computers were too massive and expensive for anything but a fleet flagship, a decade later a heavy fighter (the F-14) could be designed around a tactical computer, and two decades later virtually all Western fighters had mission computers. These three facts of life made modern network-centric warfare conceivable.

Moore's Law said little about how many advanced computers might be built. In the early 1950s virtually all digital computers were handmade. Despite the limitations of their electronics industry, the Soviets were probably about as advanced as the West. In the West, however, a vibrant civilian electronics industry made mass production possible. At least in the United States, mass production of military computers created an industry that then sought civilian markets—and which added enormous production capacity. The Soviets had no equivalent production base. Despite the civilian industry, until sometime in the 1970s, the U.S. military dominated the high-end computer market. Relatively slow procurement policies gave it machines that often underperformed Moore's Law. Then commercial machines caught up. Their cost fell so dramatically that it was impossible to justify new military-only machines. This is the current world of commercial-off-the-shelf (COTS) hardware. The great question is whether Moore's Law will continue, or whether economic or other factors will slow computer development. No other form of technology has escaped the usual S-shaped pattern, in which an apparently exponential rate of improvement (as in Moore's Law) levels off.

CHAPTER 7

The Birth of Tactical Automation: The Fleet Air Defense Crisis

n 1945 both the U.S. Navy and the Royal Navy realized that manual Combat Information Centers (CICs) could not cope with the new threats of jet aircraft (compressing available time) and guided missiles; aircraft speeds roughly doubled.[1] Bombers would probably be armed with standoff missiles (and nuclear bombs could be tossed at a fleet from standoff), so the minimum acceptable interception range increased. It also seemed that the World War II tactic of orbiting Combat Air Patrols (CAPs) would have to be abandoned because jets lacked the endurance of propeller aircraft. The wartime practice of close control (one controller handling one fighter) had to be abandoned because no human controller could handle more than two interceptions. (The U.S. Navy hoped for a time that this function could be automated.)[2] The Royal Navy adopted the late wartime German solution: broadcast control. A fighter knowing where it was and where the bomber was could navigate itself into position.[3] Broadcast control explains the emergence of the tactical air navigation (TACAN) beacon in the 1950s, both at sea and, later, on land, as a navigational aid. It provided each fighter with its own position; using a simple analog computer or even a plotting board, the fighter could compute its intercept vector.

Sixth Fleet exercises in 1951–56 showed that the situation was grim.[4] In the language of the time, a target was detected when someone in a CIC decided that a blip was a real target. It became a numbered bogey, which had to be identified either as friendly or as a bandit. A fighter section assigned to intercept the bandit was said to tallyho it when the fighter leader first spotted it. Minimum Sixth Fleet requirements about 1953 were to detect incomers seventy-five nautical miles from task force center, to tallyho at fifty nautical miles, and to intercept (first effective fighter gun run completed) at thirty-five nautical miles—that is, at about estimated Soviet missile standoff range. Radars common to all the ships in the force could detect 75 percent of all aircraft at a median range of fifty-three nautical miles. Airborne early warning (AEW) aircraft could detect over half beyond fifty nautical miles (in practice, at least 20 percent at a range somewhat over forty nautical miles).

In 1952–53 exercises, Sixth Fleet first detected "enemy" aircraft at an average range of sixty nautical miles if they were flying above four thousand feet. Altitude was not measured on over a third of the raids, and 15 percent of raids were not detected at all. Airborne early warning and pickets contributed little or nothing to fleet air defense. Many friendly aircraft were misdesignated as raids, and investigating them tied up CAP for an average of five minutes each. In gunnery exercises, about a quarter of the raids were never acquired by even one fire control system. The Operational Evaluation Group (OEG) concluded that an enemy might have inflicted unacceptable losses on U.S. forces even using conventional weapons. If ten raids were mounted, three would inflict maximum damage without loss, four would inflict heavy damage but suffer heavy losses, and three would inflict minor damage but suffer badly. OEG blamed poor training of CIC personnel—failures of the combat direction system—partly as a result of excessive turnover. Comparison with World War II data showed that wartime CIC crews would have done better. It also suggested exploiting electronic countermeasures (ECM) and tactical deception.[5]

The situation deteriorated as airplane performance improved. By 1956 even more attackers (20 percent) were never detected at all.[6] Of the bandits that were detected, the main body picked up half at eighty nautical miles and 65 percent beyond fifty-five nautical miles (as it happened, roughly the standoff range of the missiles the Russians were about to introduce). This was a considerable improvement: average range to detect half of the bandits was forty nautical miles in 1951 and sixty nautical miles in 1951–52. Airborne early warning aircraft detected about a fifth of the bandits. Picket ship radar had a median range of fifty nautical miles, and they detected half of all raids. Overall detection improvement was ascribed mainly to the use of pickets—which raised the issue of how well they could communicate what they discovered back to the carrier so that she could direct her fighters.

Detection was only the beginning. Most aircraft were friendlies (typically 69 percent; another 13 percent were typically transients not involved in the exercise at all), but identification was so slow that about as large a proportion of CAP was assigned to friendlies as to real attackers (about 75 percent in each case).[7] The load was so great and communication so slow that half of all bandits closed seventeen nautical miles or more between being detected and having CAP assigned. Delays in the arrival of CAP further reduced defense effectiveness, so that in the end, three-quarters of all raids arrived at the force completely unopposed by fighters. OEG calculated optimum task force performance against a mixture of high-flying jets (at over 20,000 feet) and low-flying propeller aircraft (below 1,000 feet). At best, carrier-based early warning aircraft, spaced perhaps fifty nautical miles from task force center, could detect over half of incoming aircraft at a fifty nautical-mile range. Picket destroyers at similar distance should detect about 75 percent at a similar range, as would the main body. Overall, 10 percent of jets at extreme altitude would get through, but all other aircraft would be detected. The fleet's antiaircraft guns and the antiaircraft missiles that would soon enter service would have to deal with the jets (or with whatever missiles they launched). It would take new radars (the UHF SPS-17, which entered service as SPS-29 and, in improved forms, as SPS-37 and -43) to achieve significantly better ranges; OEG expected aircraft to be detected within twenty to forty nautical miles of crossing the two hundred nautical-mile horizon defined by such sets. That would buy considerable time.

How close the task force could come to such performance depended on how its command and control worked. The worst problem was misassignment of resources to friendlies. OEG suggested what might now be called Blue force tracking would solve the problem of wasting scarce resources on friendlies. Once TACAN entered service, each friendly aircraft could regularly report its position. A ship could be assigned specifically to handle this information, in effect subtracting the friendlies from the air defense picture. Because they would be identified virtually as soon as they were detected, bogeys would close only five to ten nautical miles before CAP was assigned (rather than the usual twenty nautical miles for a bogey detected at seventy-five nautical miles). Thus, 85 percent of bogeys would have CAP assigned to them. To make this concept work, however, the identification ship needed some way of rapidly transmitting its plot data to the carrier.

Using this kind of analysis, Sixth Fleet improved its performance, so that by the last quarter of FY55, it was assigning CAP to 90 percent of bandits. However, CAP was often misassigned: the wrong fighters were chosen, and they could not reach their targets. Information was transferred too slowly from main plot to fighter control. More than half the time altitude was misread, mainly because the separate radar used for height finding was pointed at the wrong target. OEG estimated that eliminating gross altitude errors, or stacking CAP in altitude, would cut tallyho failures by a quarter. Ultimately 90 percent of raids might be tallyho'ed. If two CAP stations were assigned to each, and if each fighter got two firing runs, 90 percent of tallyho'ed raiders might be splashed.

Sixth Fleet transferred control of surface and air pickets to sector air defense ships. Instead of initiating interceptions, the sector ship decided only when to veto interceptions ordered by the pickets. Radar coverage improved because each picket concentrated on a narrower sector. The formerly saturated radio control nets could operate more effectively. This sort of decentralization had been envisaged by 1954, the master air defense ship at task force center being responsible mainly for targets crossing from sector to sector, or approaching on the line between sectors. Decentralization made it easier to disperse the fleet, both to protect against H-bomb attack and to make it more difficult for approaching enemy bombers to decide which was the high-value target.[8] It could not be effective unless the air picture could easily be transferred between ships.

CDS

The British were the first to try automation. Beginning about 1947, Dr. Ralph Benjamin of the Admiralty Signal Establishment sought a way of duplicating plots at various shipboard stations and of passing plot information automatically between ships. Sufficient digital computer technology did not yet exist, so he developed an analog Comprehensive Display System (CDS).[9] It was built around a stack of separate analog dead-reckoning computers, each of which handled the track of a single aircraft. Because the tracks were held in electronic memories, any plot in a ship could share the same readout of target tracks, without any delay caused by copying them from some other plot. The great difference from the later Naval Tactical Data System (NTDS) and other digital systems was that, because each track was handled separately, CDS could not compare tracks to decide which targets were most threatening or which could or could not be intercepted using available resources. That function fell to an officer observing the display, which showed all of the tracks.[10] About 1952, versions of CDS were planned to handle twenty-four, forty-eight, or ninety-six tracks (the two smaller versions were for ships). CDS was associated with a huge three-dimensional (altitude as well as range and bearing) Type 984 radar.

Because only a few ships could accommodate CDS, Benjamin proposed a link between it and a display system for smaller ships. Canadian work on Digital Automatic Tracking and Remoting (DATAR) (see "DATAR—The First Digital System" section below) seems to have convinced the British to make the link digital, presumably for better immunity to noise. By 1956 the British planned to place this digital plot transmission (DPT) link on board all new-generation frigates and destroyers. That solved a major problem. The new "Country" class missile destroyers needed three-dimensional radar to support their Seaslug missile, but they could not accommodate Type 984 without surrendering their 4.5-inch guns—which the British considered essential for the important power projection (Commonwealth policing) role. Using DPT, the carrier could provide her screening destroyers with three-dimensional radar data.[11]

The Royal Navy considered cooperative attacks the only way to deal with the new fast submarines. All platforms involved should contribute to a single merged antisubmarine warfare (ASW) plot; it was likely contact by any one of them would be fleeting. Attacks would be based on joint tracks. To support this kind of tactic, CDS technology was applied to a multitarget mechanized plotting table, or ASW tactical table, initially called the automatic surface plot (ASP) and then CAMBRIA.[12] In addition to keeping track of target and pursuing ships, ASP would show weapon danger spaces, for example, shock damage zones associated with heavy depth charges. As in CDS, the system had a central memory supporting multiple displays. Initially, ASP would have used three tactical tables: one for the local-area operational plot (LOP), one for the usual antisubmarine (A/S) plot (smaller scale, showing ships' maneuvers), and one very small scale, to gauge submarine maneuvers. The concept was formulated about 1948, and a staff requirement was written in 1950. CAMBRIA was to have been associated with an analog data link. Design and construction of a prototype began about August 1951; it was delivered on 17 February 1953.[13] By that time the very small scale table had been eliminated, and the system was expected to display raw radar video from two plan position indicators (PPIs) in geographic format (i.e., moving with the ship). The tables would also show eight electronic markers, which could be bearing lines or position dots. CAMBRIA apparently entered service as the ASP of the late 1950s, an electronic plotting table with six uncoded markers for plotting own-ship detection data. Versions were designed for both large ships and for destroyers/frigates.[14] The Canadian NC-2, which the U.S. Navy ultimately adopted, was comparable.

U.S. Analog Approaches

Irvin L. McNally was responsible for the U.S. Navy's leap into digital command systems. In 1949 Lieutenant Commander McNally moved from the Bureau of Ships (BuShips) radar branch to become chief of the Naval Electronics Laboratory (NEL) in San Diego. Like Benjamin, he understood that much of the lag time in a CIC could be ascribed to the steps between an operator's recognition that a blip was a target and a notation on the vertical plot. He ordered development of Coordinated Display Equipment. When an operator tagged a blip and then another blip representing the same target on another radar sweep, the device automatically computed its course and speed. It then projected ahead (dead reckoned) target position, so that the operator could see whether the target was still moving along its estimated course at its estimated speed. McNally was apparently inspired by an existing NEL radar simulator, which displayed raw radar video and symbology simultaneously. Coordinated Display Equipment was much like Benjamin's CDS, but NEL engineers opted for digital rather than analog target tracking, to avoid the wear and tear associated with scanning switches. In 1951 NEL demonstrated its new

Semi-Automatic Digital Analyzer and Computer (SADZAC) magnetic-drum digital computer, with analog-to-digital converters to enter data into memory and digital-to-analog to read it back into a form representable on their analog display. BuShips was sufficiently impressed to let a contract to a small computer firm, the Teleregister Company, for a development it called the Semi-Automatic Air Intercept Control System (SAAICS), an automated plotting and vector computing aid for fighter interception. It was never completed, but the experience convinced McNally that an automated air defense computer was practicable. He took that knowledge with him to the triservice LAMPLIGHT symposium in 1954.

The other U.S. equivalent to CDS was the Naval Research Laboratory's Electronic Display System (EDS).[15] It shows how interested the pre-NTDS U.S. Navy was in combat system automation.

DATAR—The First Digital System

Two Canadians, Stanley F. Knights (a Canadian Marconi communications engineer) and Lieutenant (L) James Belyea, seem to have been the first to argue that the future lay with digital rather than analog technology.[16] In 1948 Belyea was a research officer in the Royal Canadian Navy research laboratory in Ottawa, interested in a naval tactical system. He was already convinced that it would have to be digital: digital techniques could avoid ambiguities caused when targets were close to each other. Unlike analog systems, digital ones did not have to be tuned constantly. Both men envisaged a system in which a ship's sensors would feed data into a plot. A digital link would connect the systems aboard ships operating together. These were extremely advanced ideas in a world in which there were probably many fewer than a hundred digital computers, none of which operated in what would now be called real time. Belyea thought Ferranti Canada might develop the necessary system. That October officials from Ferranti Canada and its parent British firm met with the Canadian Defence Research Board. Ferranti was interested in digital computers; it offered to set up a Canadian digital electronics team. The board refused to fund a project it thought could not be commercially viable. Instead of abandoning the project, Ferranti decided to go ahead on its own.

The Canadian government let two contracts as components of the same project: one for a tactical data management system and one for a tactical trainer. In theory, the tactical trainer would be a simulator to test techniques required for the tactical data system. Unfortunately, this idea was discarded; the initial simulator contract went for an analog system. However, in 1951 Ferranti Canada received a contract for the digital tactical system, Digital Automatic Tracking and Remoting. Remoting referred to the data link; by mid-1950 Ferranti had transmitted radar data in digital form via radio. Stanley Knights became technical manager. A DATAR policy committee was chaired by the scientific adviser to the chief of naval staff. DATAR took off when Canada began to rearm for the Korean War; $1.9 million went into the project.

The Canadians hoped to interest the U.S. Navy and the Royal Navy in the project. The DATAR link successfully carried data digitally generated in Toronto to a six-by-six-foot vertical display in Ottawa. That convinced the Canadian Navy and the Royal Navy. The U.S. Navy already assumed that a digital tactical data link would soon be in service.[17] However, U.S. and British observers considered the associated digital tactical data handling too complex for shipboard use.

The next test (August–September 1953) used two Canadian minesweepers (*Digby* and *Granby*) linked to each other and to a Canadian National Research Council facility at Scarborough, Ontario. The shore station included a sonar simulator, a U.S. Navy multitarget radar simulator, and a DATAR display and control console. Data were inserted via a new "ball tracker" (the now-familiar trackball). The system could handle sixty-four targets in an eighty-by-eighty-nautical-mile tactical area. Forty observers, including many U.S. and British officers, were suitably impressed. The only major problems came from the system's vacuum-tube electronics.

The Canadians had proved the concept of a digital tactical data system. Unfortunately, Ferranti failed to convince the Canadian government to fund a solid-state operational version. However, in 1954–55, when the U.S. Navy participated in Project LAMPLIGHT (see the "Sage" section below), DATAR was the world's only naval digital combat direction system. The LAMPLIGHT project report recommended that the U.S. Navy adopt just such a system beginning with six DATARs. Knights, DATAR's guiding genius, became an important consultant to the U.S. NTDS program. At the commissioning of the first U.S. NTDS ship, the missile "frigate" (DLG) *King*, he was acclaimed by the U.S. Navy as "the father of Naval Tactical Data Systems."[18] The NTDS link, moreover, was an adaptation of the Canadian DATAR link concept. Because of DATAR, Canada was brought into U.S.-British discussion of naval data links.

SAGE

The U.S. Semi-Automatic Ground Environment (SAGE) national air defense system was why LAMPLIGHT wanted the U.S. Navy to go digital. SAGE was the solution to what seemed, until 1953, to be the impossible problem of strategic air defense—an urgent issue once the Soviets exploded an atomic bomb in 1949. The key was an unusual kind of digital computer, Whirlwind. It began at MIT in 1944 as a Navy flight simulator. Project manager Jay M. Forrester soon realized that only a digital computer would be flexible enough for what he had in mind. To simulate an airplane, Whirlwind reacted in real time to pilot inputs. Existing computers ran on a batch basis handling data input at one time according to a fixed program. Real-time intervention proved extremely difficult to implement. By 1949 the Office of Naval Research (ONR) could no longer afford escalating costs.

Responding to the new Soviet threat, in January 1950 the Air Force set up a Government Air Defense System Engineering Committee, chaired by MIT physicist George E. Valley—who met Forrester. He saw Whirlwind as the basis for an air defense system in which computers would collect radar data, evaluate threats, assign interceptors, even guide the interceptors to their targets. In effect Forrester had already solved the worst technical problem Valley faced. In March 1950 the Air Force contracted MIT for a prototype air defense system. Its computer was operating by March 1951, and by April it was receiving data from a prototype Microwave Early Warning (MEW) radar. On 20 April 1951, it demonstrated that it could vector a fighter into a collision intercept course. Work soon began on a prototype operational site at Cape Cod.

By this time the Air Force was interested in the British CDS, which was being used in the British national air defense system. It decided that the new digital system was much more promising. When the National Security Council learned about the new system late in 1953, it approved a nation-wide digital system, SAGE.[19] The system's remote radar stations fed data into SAGE computer centers, which created tracks (up to three hundred of them) to form the tactical picture for the local air defense commander. On this basis he could allocate his forces and, he hoped, overcome deception raids (a successful Allied World War II tactic). Given the picture inside it, the computer could control fighters via a digital link to their autopilots (later called Link 4). Thus, the specialized F-106 SAGE interceptor was sometimes described as a "missile with a man in it," whose pilot was needed only for takeoff and landing. Pilots disliked full control, preferring a mode in which a cockpit display (a pair of needles) indicated desired turns and the weapon release point. Because the U.S. Navy contributed interceptors to North American Air Defense, it adapted its aircraft to the SAGE link, which became Link 4. The SAGE project developed the ball-tab device (later used in Naval Tactical Data System [NTDS]) by which a radar operator translated the position of a blip on his screen into target coordinates, which could be transmitted down a telephone line to the SAGE center.

No single center could handle the whole country, so SAGE decentralized into regional (sector) computer centers. To handle tracks crossing sector boundaries, it had a digital point-to-point link carrying computer commands and data words. A computer receiving such a Link 1 message automatically updated its track file to match. Eventually, twenty-seven SAGE centers, one of them underground in

Canada, were built, the last entering service in 1963.[20] SAGE made the sky over North America a single battlespace in which long-range fighters and missiles could be targeted as needed, rather than being wastefully concentrated around particular potential targets.

SAGE proved that computer-controlled air defense would work. From a technology point of view, SAGE was premature. Designs had to be frozen too early; the computers used vacuum-tube technology, which made them unreliable. The money spent on those computers financed initial work on the far more reliable solid-state machines that powered NTDS, the naval offshoot of SAGE. SAGE, in turn, became a model for other national air defense systems, which helped start national computer industries: STRIDA in France, STRADA in Italy, NATO's NADGE, Japan's BADGE. The Swedish STRIL, which led to some Nordic coast defense systems, was inspired by the British equivalent SAGE.

The initial SAGE radars blocked the Soviet bomber route over Canada. In 1954 MIT, which was developing SAGE, held the triservice LAMPLIGHT conference to examine ways of extending it, for example, to preclude end runs over the sea. The conference proposed modifying the existing Navy picket ships so that, like digitized radars ashore, they could enter data directly into SAGE computers. That entailed digital data handling on board the ships and a digital link from ship to shore.[21]

The U.S. Navy delegate to the conference was Commander McNally, who had been trying to develop a tactical system at NEL. In SAGE he saw the beginnings of a fully digital solution. Perhaps prodded by McNally, the conference recommended that the Navy automate its CICs so that ships at sea could connect with SAGE. The civilian character of the conference shows in its idea that carrier task forces would contribute to North American air defense. The conference recommended deploying the analog EDS the navy was then developing as an interim measure, followed by a fully digital system. The conference rejected any analog alternative: expanding something like CDS to handle hundreds of targets would be astronomically expensive. Although the conference recommended that the Navy buy six DATARs, it understood that they were only a first step, incapable of handling the sheer numbers of targets—perhaps a thousand aircraft—which might be involved.

During the conference, McNally began to develop his own idea of what the Navy needed not just for pickets but for the fleet as a whole. He imagined a scalable system for installation on board many kinds of ships, its computers exchanging data automatically. Airborne early warning aircraft would participate in McNally's net (and, indeed, in the offshore net LAMPLIGHT envisaged). If ships were no more than about twenty nautical miles apart, they might use the new line-of-sight ultrahigh frequency (UHF) radios then being introduced for ship-to-air communication. They offered the high data rates McNally knew he would need. Given new radars looking out 250 or even 300 nautical miles, McNally estimated that each ship might have to handle up to 1,000 tracks (including ships and submarines, friendly and enemy), which might be derived not only from radar data but also from alternatives such as "identification of friend or foe" (IFF) trackers, electronic warfare (EW) sensors, and sonars.[22]

Dr. Jerrold Zacharias, the senior MIT member of the committee, told McNally that his idea was a fantasy; transistorized computers barely existed in prototype form. A representative of IBM, which was building the SAGE computers, was more encouraging, even though the huge SAGE computers were only entering production. He told McNally to write a formal proposal for his naval system.[23] McNally submitted it to the Office of Naval Research.

McNally's idea was an alternative to a proposal by the CORNFIELD group developing SAGE interceptor control: simply take a SAGE center to sea aboard a large ship. It appears that plans to convert the large cruiser *Hawaii* to a fleet command ship built around the huge SPS-2 three-dimensional radar reflect the CORNFIELD idea. The conversion died in 1955, as McNally's idea gained acceptance.

CHAPTER 8

The Naval Tactical Data System

I rvin L. McNally had to convince senior officers that his idea was important and that it would work. Because he had been Navy delegate to LAMPLIGHT, he had the opportunity to speak early in 1955 at the headquarters of the Atlantic destroyer force linked with Semi-Automatic Ground Environment (SAGE). (The first pickets were converted destroyer escorts.)[1] This force was closely associated with radical ongoing changes such as arming destroyers with antiaircraft missiles. It would soon urge the Navy to build nuclear-powered destroyers even though large nuclear cruisers seemed barely practical. In the audience was Adm. Arleigh A. Burke, who would become chief of naval operations (CNO) that August. A former gunnery officer and a survivor of kamikaze attacks, he had headed the July–August 1945 anti-kamikaze experiments in Casco Bay, Maine. Kamikazes produced the sort of saturation the Naval Tactical Data System (NTDS) was intended to overcome. Burke was willing to take technological gambles such as adopting the Fleet Ballistic Missile (Polaris) and an all-nuclear submarine fleet. His enthusiastic support for McNally's ideas proved crucial.

Fortunately Lt. Cdr. Edward C. Svendsen, head of the Bureau of Ships (BuShips) Special Applications Branch, was developing the kind of transistorized computer McNally needed. He joined McNally's project to write a Tentative Operational Requirement (TOR) for a digital combat data system, which beat out several alternatives.[2] An Office of Naval Research (ONR) committee endorsed it in the summer of 1955, and the CNO tentatively approved it that fall. It was so important that it was assigned a short five-year schedule. The TOR formally approved on 24 April 1956 envisaged automated data systems aboard ships, aboard an airborne Combat Information Center (CIC) aircraft (ultimately the Hawkeye), and for Marine Corps air defense. The Naval Electronics Laboratory (NEL) was made prime contractor, partly to ensure fleet involvement with the technology. An NTDS Project Office was formed within the BuShips. McNally retired in June 1956, leaving Svendsen in charge of the project. McNally envisaged the Electronic Display System (EDS) then under development, like LAMPLIGHT, as an interim replacement for manual combat direction. It proved disappointing, and computers developed surprisingly quickly, so that few ships ever had EDS.

Existing CICs were obviously badly overloaded. Unlike the Royal Navy, the U.S. Navy had never endorsed the idea of multiple plots. All users needed access to the single vertical plot. CIC became a tangle of operators trailing the wires of sound-powered phones and somehow ignoring extraneous information coming from loudspeakers overhead. One official writer observed that the 1955 CIC was so overloaded with functions that, however many men worked in it, it was almost as impotent as a pre-CIC ship had been in, say, 1941. However, many officers saw the new system as an attempt to take over their functions, as in Admiral Sir John Fisher's day. The Office of the Chief of Naval Operations (OpNav) tried to make the case, for example, with a series of articles in its quarterly journal, *Combat Readiness*.[3] It also ordered CICs rebuilt so that NTDS would be easier to install.[4] Once in service, it became obvious that NTDS automated the more mechanical elements of a CIC, not the key decision-making parts—and that NTDS ships clearly outperformed noncomputer ships.

To provide growth potential, Svendsen and McNally decided to use general-purpose rather than special-purpose (i.e., hard-wired or fixed-program) computers, even though at the time it seemed that only the latter would be fast enough. Different types of ships would have different numbers of standard computers and consoles. The minimum was two computers, to provide a fallback in the event of computer failure. In larger versions, separate computers would perform different functions, exchanging data on a memory-to-memory basis. In 1955 these concepts were radical. (The distributed architecture was not realized.)

No U.S. company had yet built the required compact transistorized computer. Univac won the contract. Its computer designer, Seymour Cray, later famous for supercomputers, conceived the time-sharing architecture. The computer shifted programs in and out of memory, storing intermediate data in special stacks so that it could later resume the earlier task. Time-sharing made possible a modular program, only some modules of which were loaded at any one time. Cray wanted to use the same thirty-two-bit words as SAGE but found that transistors limited him to thirty. Svendsen estimated that each of the two computers in the minimum version would need 20,000 words of memory, but opted for 24,000 to allow for growth. Cray argued that memory was becoming cheaper, so he chose 32,000. McNally had to scale down his requirements to some extent. Instead of 1,000 tracks, the large-ship version could handle 256 and the small ship, 128.

Radar operators entered data into their own ship's system by moving cursors at their consoles, much as in EDS or the Comprehensive Display System (CDS). They automatically measured target range and bearing by "hooking" its blip. Hooking the same target on three successive radar scans entered it (with three successive positions) into the computer's track file. Much as in CDS, the computer automatically deduced target course and speed and then dead reckoned (and displayed updated target positions) until the operator decided that the target had changed course or speed. Because he could enter a target quickly, an operator could shift attention to other targets. Unlike CDS, NTDS carried all its tracks in the same memory. They could be compared, for example, to decide which targets should be engaged most urgently. The computer could decide whether a given target could be engaged, and it could choose which weapon should be assigned (paired with) which target. To do that with airborne interceptors, it had to keep track of their changing fuel and weapon status (at least on an estimated basis). It also had to keep track of special points (such as Formation Center), fixed or slaved to another point or track or moving at a speed set by an operator.

McNally saw his system as an aid to human judgment, not a replacement. It recommended action and it carried out ordered operations, but it did not initiate them automatically. SAGE was semiautomatic for much the same reason. Also, NTDS was the creature of BuShips, but weapons were the responsibility of the separate Bureau of Ordnance (BuOrd). McNally saw NTDS as a picture keeper that would pass targets to a separate BuOrd system. That made for duplication because by this time BuOrd was developing Weapon Designation Systems (WDS) like small-scale picture keepers, storing targets so that missile systems could switch rapidly from target to target. Initially the WDS was an analog system. By 1960 work was proceeding to digitize the WDS and fold it into NTDS. The main virtue of separating NTDS and WDS was that a ship could keep fighting even if her NTDS computers crashed. That reflected the more general idea that, because NTDS supported rather than replaced decision makers, its failure could not cripple a ship altogether.

In an NTDS net, a master ship called the roll, the pickets responding with their information. When a ship first detected a target, it assigned a track number. A second ship assigned its own track number. To avoid flooding the group with data, the system constantly compared new tracks with those already in memory (correlation: cancelation of double-counted tracks). That was possible because all tracks were in the same digital memory. Starting from an empty picture, the ships in a net all built up their pictures in parallel. Any ship might miss the occasional message. However, ships constantly reported what they were detecting. Data would be redundant enough to ensure that pictures would match. Each ship's data terminal carried all addresses in the net. If the master ship were sunk or disabled, another ship in the net could replace her. The old problem of losing the flagship and the flag plot was solved.

As McNally developed his system, the U.S. Navy adopted dispersed formations, so that a single H-bomb could not wipe out more than one carrier. The primary ("A," later Link 11) computer-to-computer link had to operate at high frequency (HF), to reach beyond the horizon. Link messages consisted of computer commands (in machine language) and data. Some commands added or updated a track. Others were orders, for example, to engage a given target. When the "A: link was exported, governments objected that they did not want their ships taking commands from other navies' ships. Computers on allied ships had some "A" link commands disabled. It appeared that most ships would not have computers. McNally proposed that the computer generate formatted teletype messages for them (the "B" link, later Link 14). The TOR envisaged a simplified ultrahigh frequency (UHF) ship-to-ship link ("C" link). Limited to line-of-sight range, it never entered service. A fourth link (later Link 4) controlled aircraft, as in SAGE.

Design Problems

As in any other netted system, all ships in an NTDS net had to share the same system of coordinates. To use those common coordinates, each ship had to recalculate (transform) ranges and bearings of targets centered on herself into terms of the common grid—which required her to know her own position in that grid. Unless their supposed positions matched the grid properly, two ships tracking the same target would report it as two distinct targets. Aggravating the situation, NTDS used flat coordinates on a curved earth. Corrections for curvature were imprecise because the earth is not perfectly round. To work in dispersed formations, NTDS demanded precision navigation, generally using the new Ships Inertial Navigation System (SINS). Making sure that ships' coordinates matched was called gridlocking. With the advent of a third-generation NTDS computer (UYK-43, in the 1980s), it finally became possible to solve the problem self-consistently. Each ship's system pulled coordinates back and forth until each ship's picture of the locations of the others in a group matched what they reported.

There was a major human engineering failure: NTDS designers misestimated the abilities of the operators entering data into the system. In 1967 ships were equipped with Model 2, which in theory could handle ninety-six local and ninety-six remote tracks. NTDS developers had imagined that the limit was the time it took an operator to decide that a blip on a radar scope was a real target, worth entering into the system. They found that monitoring the picture was another limiting factor. Early Vietnam experience showed that an operator could handle only five tracks at a time, so a typical frigate (DLG) with four input consoles was limited to twenty tracks. The quick solution in Vietnam, where most of the aircraft in sight were American, was to automate "identification of friend or foe" (IFF) detection using beacon video processing (BVP).[5] CNO made BVP a high priority project in October 1966. The engineering development version was successfully tested on board USS *Belknap* in the Tonkin Gulf in the fall of 1967, and BVP was service approved in November 1968. What the experience really showed was that all targets had to be detected automatically, by the operator monitoring the system. Radar video processing (RVP) was more difficult, but Moore's Law made it practicable in the 1970s. The Royal Australian Navy installed the first U.S. RVP in 1975. A broader lesson was that systems as complicated as NTDS needed full-scale tests before they went to sea.

NTDS had a vocabulary shaped by its Cold War origins. For example, it categorized objects as friendly, enemy, or unknown (assumed enemy). The software translated such identifications into symbols on a screen. Combat decisions were made based on the picture on the screen—including the symbols. By the 1980s the U.S. Navy often found itself monitoring situations in which categories were more complicated. It suffered two disasters. In 1987 the missile frigate *Stark* was operating in the Gulf. An Iraqi Mirage F1 was detected by a Saudi Airborne Warning and Control System (AWACS) aircraft. This information was passed to the frigate via her NTDS link. To the Saudis, the Iraqi was friendly, and it was so categorized. Actually, its intent was more ambiguous. NTDS was designed not to engage friendly aircraft. The tactical action officer in the ship's CIC could not stand back and say, "it is supposed to be friendly, but perhaps not." To do that might have slowed his reactions fatally. In this case it was the other way around: the Iraqi flew toward the ship and fired two Exocet missiles. Two decades later it is not clear whether the attack was intentional.

The next year USS *Vincennes* mistakenly shot down an Iranian Airbus, killing all of those on board. This seems to have been another case of unexpected consequences of basic system design. She and the frigate *Sides* were operating together. *Sides* detected the Airbus first and automatically assigned it a track number. *Vincennes* assigned a different number. Her combat system soon realized that she and the frigate were seeing the same airplane, so it switched numbers. Unfortunately, those in the *Vincennes* CIC did not realize that the number had been changed. When they wanted to know what the unknown airplane was doing, they asked their computer about the original track number. (Their display did not show which track number was assigned to which symbol.) It happened that another group, about a hundred miles away (hence within HF radio range) had assigned the same track number to an airplane landing on the carrier *Saratoga*.

That was not supposed to happen; different NTDS nets were supposed to use different blocks of track numbers. *Vincennes* had been sent to the Gulf specifically to clean up sloppy NTDS practice. This sort of problem would not have arisen in the scenario for which NTDS was conceived, in which one battle group fought more or less in isolation. In this case, the two HF nets, for *Vincennes* and *Sides* and for the *Saratoga* battle group, merged without anyone realizing it. As the "unknown, possibly hostile" symbol moved down the Gulf toward *Vincennes*, an officer in her CIC queried its altitude. (Her display was limited to two dimensions.) Using the wrong track number, he received information that it was diving—toward a landing on the carrier. Diving meant a possible kamikaze attack, for which intelligence had primed the ship—so she shot back. An entirely innocent airliner was shot down.

A contributing factor was the limited power of the UYK-7 computer that created the display. It showed only the centerline of the airliner corridor. The Airbus happened to be slightly off center, but still within the corridor. Those in CIC knew that they had an incomplete picture, but as tension mounted, they could not focus on anything but what they saw: an unknown aircraft approaching them apparently outside the no-fire zone. It did not help that the airliner pilot never answered their urgent queries; later it emerged that such pilots do not normally listen to the channel involved. The pilot was probably completing his paperwork for landing on the other side of the Gulf, having completed his climb out, when the missile destroyed his airplane. To those on the ship, who saw a threatening airplane, the pilot's innocent silence seemed ominous.

NTDS was no mistake; manual CICs would have done even worse. The problems showed that what might seem to be abstract software design choices, such as the way in which data are represented on a screen, had real consequences. It mattered that the NTDS vocabulary was so limited, which in turn was a consequence of limited computer capacity. It mattered that, both because of the limited computer power and of a desire to simplify displays, the screen never showed track numbers alongside symbols for targets. It mattered how the software correlated onboard and off-board tracks.

Picture-centric warfare means exactly that: the ship is fought on the basis of what those in CIC (or its equivalent) see on their screens. They may know that the situation is actually more complicated, but what they see is paramount. Modern networked systems are far more complex, but in the end they still produce a picture that a commander uses as the basis for action. The picture is built up out of information from many sources. Some years ago the Naval War College began using a "knowledge wall" to present the mass of information. A commander could always query it, drilling down to find the sources of information so that he could evaluate them. The human reality is that, as action became more urgent, he would rely more and more on what he could see. As in *Stark*, what he had in the back of his head might have no effect at all. As in *Vincennes*, the subtleties of the system, which might have been brought out in school, also would not matter. Moreover, disasters resulting from relatively minor cases of bad data tend to destroy the commander's faith in the entire system.

The NTDS Fleet

In 1959, well before the NTDS system had been tested, OpNav decided to install it on board all combatants large enough to take it: all carriers, all missile cruisers, all heavy cruisers (presumably because they were used as flagships), all missile "frigates" (DLG/DLGN, later reclassified as cruisers and missile destroyers), and all missile destroyers (DDG).[6] Later amphibious flagships, existing and planned, were added. Through FY62 the program included the carriers *Enterprise* and *America*, the nuclear cruiser *Long Beach*, the three *Chicago*-class cruisers (CG 10–12), the two nuclear-powered "frigates" *Bainbridge* and *Truxtun*, and the *Belknap*-class "frigates" (DLG 26–34).[7] *Enterprise* and *Long Beach* were included because their electronically scanned radars already required so much digital computer processing. FY61 money also paid for the conversion of two "frigates" for a service test (the accompanying carrier conversion was paid for by research, development, testing, and evaluation [RDT&E] funds). In 1962, before NTDS had been tested at sea, it became clear that it was too massive for DDGs, so a smaller DDG system was envisaged.

As of July 1964, half the NTDS funding was in place, for a program to be completed in 1972. Then costs escalated and funds dried up, probably largely because of the war in Vietnam. All of the large carriers received NTDS, although by 1962 planned conversions of smaller *Essex*-class ships were abandoned. The program was reviewed in 1967. By this time Secretary of Defense Robert McNamara planned a new class of destroyers (DX/DXG, built as the *Spruance* class), which could be completed as either antisubmarine warfare (ASW) or missile ships. He used the prospect of these ships to justify killing NTDS on board the two remaining *Cleveland*-class missile cruisers. Of the other three missile cruisers, *Albany* was already being converted. Conversion of the other two, planned for FY67 and FY69, was rescheduled to FY70 and FY73, after the cost per ship rose from $27 to $96 million. The last ship, *Columbus*, was dropped. As a measure of what was involved, with NTDS *Albany* could handle 128 local and 128 remote tracks.[8] An unmodified ship handled only twenty-four. DLG conversions survived because they offered more AAW firepower six years earlier than the projected DXG (which materialized only in the form of four *Kidd*-class ships begun for Iran). The fit in the *Leahy* and

Belknap classes (in a deckhouse) was apparently quite tight: as much as six years after completion there was still talk of how difficult the project had been.

Service Test

The service test was assigned to the Pacific Fleet. It required a carrier and surface ships. The carrier *Oriskany* was chosen because she was the only Pacific Fleet carrier with a large modular CIC, hence she was suited to NTDS installation. Two large DLGs had construction schedules matching those of the project: USS *King* and USS *Mahan*. Because they were being built in naval shipyards, such last-minute modifications were relatively inexpensive. All had Model 1 systems with the same USQ-20 computer as the final shore prototype (Model 0): three for the carrier, two for the DLGs. Their new software was divided along major functional lines but was not modular. It could operate in specific modes, such as antiair warfare (AAW) and ASW for the DLGs. Link 11 was updated, and the surface-to-air Link 4 added. Model 1 passed its operational test and was approved for service in 1963.

After operational evaluation, commander, Carrier Division ONE wrote on 31 December 1962 that "NTDS should be installed in as many ships as rapidly as availability of funds and schedules permit, with priority to the CVAs [attack carriers]."[9] In July 1964 OpNav answered the question of whether NTDS was worth its high cost: "[It] has given us effective AAW, a capability that has proven most illusive [sic] for too many years, as you and I well know." Relative to the weapon system, NTDS was no more costly than the World War II CIC: about 1.5 percent of total carrier task force cost versus about 1 percent for conventional CICs. The commander of Pacific naval air forces (NavAirPac) wrote that "NTDS permits the CVA to operate in effective emission control (EMCON) conditions and still detect, engage, and destroy a higher percentage of targets at significantly greater ranges than conventional forces." Seventh Fleet estimated that an NTDS CVA group (one CVA, 2 DLG) with existing radars could detect and engage twice as many raids at eighty to one hundred nautical miles as a conventional force could at twenty to fifty nautical miles from fleet center.

Development

Model 2, which equipped all but the five test ships, entered service in 1964. It introduced modular software: a core program plus separate modules for particular applications, which could be shifted into and out of active operation as needed, reducing the load on the computer. This version added an interface to the digital underwater fire control system (Mk 111), again updated Link 11, and it began a change to the upgraded CP-642A computer, which was easier to maintain.

Introduced in 1967, Model 3 reflected early Vietnam lessons, with Link filtering and later with Ships Anti-Missile Integrated Defense (SAMID) fixes and automatic IFF interrogation (BVP). Its CP-642B computer was twice as fast as CP-642A, albeit with the same storage capacity, 32,000 words. Dynamic Modular Replacement (DMR) made for quicker insertion of program modules while the system was running. Link 11 was again updated. Ultimately, an additional computer was needed to accommodate new self-defense software. This was the version in the two new *Blue Ridge*–class amphibious flagships.

In Model 3 the analog WDS was replaced by extra consoles and software embedded in the new computers. Development of this WDS Mk 11 began in 1960. Associated with it was the SPS-48 stacked-beam scanning radar, the first U.S. digital radar. Instead of showing an operator a blip, it automatically detected a target and produced target coordinates.[10] Replacement of the analog system saved seven thousand pounds and two crewmen. The stage beyond was to digitize the fire-control systems controlled by the WDS. Given a digital fire-control computer, all of the ship's weapons could be connected simultaneously to the combat direction system. Because all of the ship's systems were controlled by software, which could be replaced, digitized weapon systems could be upgraded far more easily than their analog forebears, a dramatic example being the New Threat Upgrade program of the 1980s.

In 1966 work began on a thirty-two-bit UYK-7 computer. About a quarter the size of CP-642B, it had more than twice as many instructions, and it was 2.5 times as fast. Its modular design could support up to 262,000 words of memory. The prototype was delivered in April 1969, and deliveries began in 1970. UYK-7 occasioned a new Model 4 version of the NTDS software, which was compatible with both it and existing (CP-642B) computers. It entered service in 1974. This version was adapted to the digital SPS-48 radar, to digital air traffic control, to digital ship's inertial navigation, and to digital ESM. A fighter could transmit its tactical data to the ship controlling it via a new two-way version of Link 4, acting, to some extent, as one of the ship's sensors. In carriers, Model 4 was directly connected to the new ASW module then being designed to support carrier ASW aircraft (S-3As). Model 4 was intended to be compatible with the planned JTIDS (Link 16) data link.

UYK-7 and Model 4 were associated with the DX/DXG destroyer, which could be completed in either ASW or AAW version: the *Spruance* class and the *Kidd* class; the nuclear version of the AAW version was the *Virginia* class. In 1969 it was decided that they would have all-digital weapons. The *Virginias* became the first all-digital ships in the U.S. fleet. The DX/DXG concept required that one core

NTDS system be adaptable to either ASW or AAW; digitizing all weapons helped. A central computer complex was responsible for all combat functions, including fire control. That made for fewer computers, fewer consoles, and faster exchange of data among weapon systems for, it was hoped, faster response. The associated WDS Mk 13 could accept ten targets from the ship's combat direction system. It could transfer targets both to missiles and to the ship's Mk 86 gunfire control system. There was also a digital interface between the ship's sonar (SQS-53A) and her underwater fire control system (Mk 116), which in turn had a digital connection to the ship's combat direction system. The standardized computers could switch roles. For example, the underwater fire-control computer could be used as the WDS computer, the WDS computer could control the gun, and the sonar could be connected directly to the combat direction system computer, rather than through the Mk 116 fire control system. Digitization probably explains why it proved relatively easy to upgrade the *Spruance*-class destroyers throughout their lives. Trials showed that the behavior of so complicated a system was difficult to predict. Reportedly early trials of USS *Virginia* were disastrous. The U.S. Navy learned to set up a full-scale land-based test site.

The Model 4 UYK-7 combination equipped early Aegis ships, *Tarawa*-class amphibious carriers, and modernized *Adams*-class missile destroyers. In Aegis ships it changed sufficiently that NTDS became the CDS (combat direction system), but the software continued the same Model series.

To accommodate Model 4, in existing ships all system computers (three in a cruiser, four in a carrier) shared an extended memory control unit (EMCU), with 262,144 words. With the extra capacity, NTDS could accommodate all modules simultaneously rather than move them in and out of memory. To reduce the load on the main computers, when WDS Mk 14 was introduced, it ran on a separate UYK-20 (the smaller companion to UYK-7). About 1980 a *Leahy*-class missile cruiser (ex-DLG) with Model 4.0 could handle a total of 256 tracks, typically 128 local and 128 remote. An upgrade made it possible for the ship to engage forty quick-reaction (QR) targets. As an indication of the importance of EMCU, with it a *Mahan*-class missile destroyer could handle 256 system tracks, but without EMCU it was reduced to 64 (with no remote tracks). In antiship missile defense (ASMD) mode, EMCU doubled the number of tracks (from twenty to forty). Model 3 ships not yet converted to Model 4 received separate UYK-20 computers to translate the new version of Link 11. Even so, by the mid-1970s all NTDS systems were badly overloaded.

Extending NTDS to Smaller Ships

In 1959 a CANUS (Canadian-U.S.) Working Party developed characteristics for a destroyer-frigate combat direction system, which would draw on Canadian experience. It may have originated with a two-month study conducted at NEL in 1959 by Stan Knights and Lieutenant Commander Bryan Judd, data link project officer at Canadian naval headquarters. In March 1960, before NTDS had been tested aboard ship, NEL began working on a Small Ship Combat Direction System (SSCDS) project.[11] The U.S. Navy seems to have hoped that the ASW-oriented SSCDS would bring NATO navies into the new world of NTDS. SSCDS was reoriented in 1961 as a "common design" ASW combat system for NATO navies, then again in 1962 as the Small Ship Combat Data System (also SSCDS) within the Anti-Submarine Development and Experimental Center (ASDEC) at NEL.[12]

NEL hoped to cut NTDS to fit by reducing it to a single computer. Much of one of the two NTDS computers was needed to handle the complex Link 11.[13] SSCDS would substitute a simple line-of-sight UHF link (later NEL realized that Link 11 could be accommodated if the system handled fewer tracks: ASW involved fewer targets, and they moved much more slowly than aircraft). For tests, the fixed NTDS installation at NEL was to have been linked with SSCDS on board: a modified Canadian *St. Laurent*-class frigate and on board a U.S. Fleet Rehabilitation and Modernisation program (FRAM I) destroyer. The NEL station incorporated an experimental Signal Processor and Display Equipment (SPADE) processor intended to filter, detect, and track sonar targets from SQS-26 and SQQ-23 sonars then in development. Canadian involvement reflected the key roles played by Knights and Judd in the development process.

As SSCDS matured in 1964, a new OpNav ASW office, Op-95, was created. SSCDS became the ASW Ship Command and Control System (ASWSCCS), the Specific Operational Requirement (SOR) for which was signed in September 1964. ASWSCCS became part of the larger Sea Hawk project to develop a new-generation ASW ship.[14] The binational test was shelved, but the U.S. Navy asked the Canadian programmers who had headed the project to remain. The Royal Canadian Navy used what had been learned in the next purely Canadian system, CCS 280 for the Tribal class.

ASWSCCS would tie together an ASW carrier (CVS) and her escorts. Roughly contemporary with Model 3, ASWSCCS would have the same new CP-642B computer (the test installation would have had a 642A). The carrier version would have two computers, the escort one (plus an EMCU). Because the main underwater sensor was active sonar, ASWSCCS was not too different from the radar-oriented NTDS. Unlike NTDS, ASWSCCS had to maintain track histories over the wide area that might be swept by the carrier's aircraft and by Link 11–equipped P-3s. The carrier version incorporated a disk memory specifically to store contact and track history. Unlike more elaborate forms of NTDS, ASWSCCS lacked automatic threat evaluation, on the theory that the surface warfare coordinator would have sufficient time to do so himself. Capacity was 160 system tracks (preset as 64 local and 96 remote), 4 active contacts for handover, 20 sonobuoys, 4 ESM fixes, 4 acoustic fixes, 8 acoustic lines of bearing, and 24 tracked aircraft (12 local, 12 remote). The ship's Link 11 system could accommodate twenty participants, and it offered twenty command messages. The preset split between local and remote tracks was unusual in U.S. NTDS systems. Software was not modular: computer memory could hold all functions simultaneously. Different capability packages were loaded for particular missions. On board a frigate, the system would be connected to the standard Mk 114 analog surface ASW fire-control system, which might be likened to a WDS–missile control combination.

Tests using the carrier *Wasp* (fitted during a 1967 refit) and the new frigates *Voge* and *Koelsch* were conducted successfully in March–April 1968.[15] The program then died, presumably a victim of the escalating cost of the Vietnam War. (Sea Hawk was already dead.) It did leave some hardware used in other NTDS systems: the EMCU (which made a single-computer system practicable) and a twenty-two-inch operations summary console (OSC) for the commanding officer. It was equivalent to the horizontal multioperator displays that some foreign developers (particularly Dutch and Italian) were using. Other new features applicable to NTDS integrated-circuit UYA-4 consoles, which could be used either for input or for control; a switchboard that could handle up to eleven different sensors; and a lightweight Link 11 radio system.

By this time, Moore's Law had produced the much more compact UYK-7 computer, which might well fit on board a missile destroyer or a destroyer escort. The sacrifices inherent in ASWSCCS might not be necessary. In 1969 SOR 35-18 established a new JTDS, for "Jeep" or "Junior" Tactical Data System program.[16] Adding a data link made it JPTDS, the *P* indicating participating (in a net). By this time it was clear that manually controlled combat systems could not react quickly enough to a growing antiship missile threat. "Jeep" was part of the ASMD program described in chapter 12. Like early versions of NTDS, Jeep would concentrate on creating and maintaining a tactical picture, communicating with existing analog weapon systems (such as the WDS on board a missile destroyer) via digital-to-analog converters. The system was so simple that it could be installed during a regular overhaul (ROH) rather than a major refit. Unlike NTDS, Jeep could not transmit on Link 14 or Link 4.

Four ships received JPTDS under the FY71 and FY72 ASMD programs: DDG-15, 9, 12, and 20. System capacity was about half that of a missile cruiser: 128 system tracks, 64 local and 64 remote, plus 10 track histories. Because of its ASMD origin, the system incorporated the quick-reaction (QR) feature. The ships could recognize (and react to) three preprogrammed threats. The electronic support measures (ESM) system was not connected directly with the ship's combat system, but its operator could enter tracks and parameters either at a display console or at an electronic warfare keyset panel.

After the first four conversions, the program stalled, as the Navy lost funding after the end of the Vietnam War. Awareness of the program was so low that few documents distinguished the four JPTDS ships from their much less capable analog sisters. Thus, when the Greek navy obtained ex-U.S. *Adams*-class destroyers, it seems to have made no impression that one of the four was a JPTDS ship.

Australia adopted JPTDS to upgrade three *Adams*-class destroyers built in the United States. By 1969 the Australians were planning to build small destroyers, which they designated DDL. As part of the process of selecting a design and a weapon system, they investigated the state of the art in digital combat direction. This effort apparently brought them into contact with the JPTDS program.

Despite curtailing JPTDS, the U.S. Navy urgently wanted to extend Link 11 through the fleet. In January 1974 deputy chief of naval operations (DCNO) (Surface Warfare) circulated a series of papers to support programs for the coming five years, through FY80 (as part the POM-76 process). One called for development of a low-cost version of Link 11. It seemed that cost could be at least halved. Plans already called for installation in 169 ships and 287 aircraft over the next seven years. Unless costs could be slashed, it would be impossible to install Link 11 in low-end ships, more of which were being built (mainly frigates). In 1973 three new classes (the sea control ship [SCS] operating short takeoff and vertical landing [STOVL] aircraft, the patrol frigate [PF, later the *Perry* class], and a missile hydrofoil [PHM]) were in prospect. The Navy was particularly interested in the coming Harpoon anti-ship missile. To fire it beyond a ship's horizon would require that the ship receive and display a wide-area tactical picture, hence that it had to be able to use Link 11. DCNO warned that weapons like Harpoon might be canceled if the link they depended on proved unaffordable. At this time the SCS and the new frigate were expected to have JPTDS, but only space and weight reservation for Link 11. No combat system at all was planned for the PHM.[17]

DCNO wanted automated combat systems for both the new ships and for the many surface combatants that still relied on World War II–style manual plots. They included nineteen or twenty-three *Adams*-class missile destroyers and all six *Brooke*-class missile frigates, plus all the modern ASW frigates (forty-six *Knox*, ten *Garcia*, and two *Bronstein* class). A frigate version of JPTDS had been under development since at least 1970. It was apparently rejected as too expensive for existing ships, but a reduced version was proposed for the remaining missile destroyers. The DCNO wanted something less expensive, which in the end meant something built around the most important new computer, UYK-20, a sixteen-bit machine used as an auxiliary to UYK-7: an OpNav Composite Combat System that could apparently be built in modular form or a UYK-20 Radar Graphics system with optional Link 11.[18] These less-expensive systems were considered adequate for frigates.

DCNO (Surface) liked the composite system, which used existing hardware in tailored combinations (one for DDG and DEG, one for the others). It also offered reduced cost through commonality. It does not seem that those evaluating the systems were aware that, whatever the commonality in hardware, the Composite system would need entirely new software. Funding was tight, and nothing was done. Navy plans continued to show installation of JPTDS on board the missile destroyers, but it was delayed again and again.[19] The new *Perry*-class frigates did receive JPTDS (but under another name), but the planned SCS died, and the PHMs never got an elaborate system.[20] A few *Knox*-class frigates received a system built around a computerized plotting table, designed primarily to handle their sonar data.

Lessons?

In 1960 many naval officers must have wondered whether NTDS was worthwhile. A decade later the question was how to achieve full automation at a reasonable cost. Conversely, NTDS also showed that computers had definite limits. Some were obvious to operators, in forms such as flickering displays and buttons that did not produce the desired results in time. Others, like the paucity of vocabulary (*Stark*) and limits on the questions the system could answer unambiguously (*Vincennes*), were subtler. Increasing the sheer capacity of combat direction systems was essentially an engineering problem. The human problems are far thornier, not least because it is difficult to say exactly what tactical assumptions go into the design of any combat system.

Note: NATO Digital Data Links

It seems convenient to summarize U.S./North Atlantic Treaty Organization (NATO) naval data link development (NATO is taken to include Australia, New Zealand, and Japan). Because in the 1960s and even the 1970s the main links (Link 11 and even Link 10) exacted a considerable price, different navies' willingness to invest in links gives an idea of their enthusiasm for netted operation. Conversely, by the 1980s it was impossible to imagine a NATO naval formation not connected by Link 11: the data link became, in effect, the price of admission to an important club. Now wideband (usually satellite) communication using unformatted types of message are nearly the rule.

In 1954 the U.S., Canadian, and Royal navies met to discuss data links, which were then imagined largely as a means of connecting analog systems (digital transmission offered reliability). Then the meetings focused on the NTDS "A" link. It used the HF surface wave, which has a range of about 180 nautical miles. HF signals bouncing off the ionosphere interfere with the surface wave. The longer the symbols (the ones and zeroes of digital code), the better they resist interference. In the 1950s it was accepted that the maximum rate was seventy-five symbols/second. Early estimates showed that NTDS required about 1,125 bits/second—fifteen normal HF channels. This figure was doubled to provide overhead, for example, for control and management and for error correction, for a total of about 2,250 bits/second. This considerable data rate gave NTDS and Link 11 enough growth potential to survive for the next forty years. To transmit enough data, Collins Radio used fifteen different frequencies (tones) in parallel and both possible polarizations for each. It took a computer to disentangle such a signal. Because the original NTDS computer used thirty-bit words, the link used words of the same length (of which six bits were error-correcting code, the remaining twenty-four carrying messages). Word length limited the precision of the data the system could transmit. Details of the NTDS "A" link were probably settled by about 1958.

A Canadian wag called the link TIDE—Tactical Information Distribution Equipment—after the detergent, as TIDE would clean up one's tactical picture.[21] It was included in the British Action Data Automation (ADA) system and Action Data Automation Weapon System (ADAWS). The Royal Navy's existing digital plot transmission (DPT) link became Link I, so the "A" link became Link II. By 1962 NATO needed a common nomenclature for its digital air defense links. The SAGE point-to-point link (also used in European systems) became Link 1 because it was so important. The NTDS "A" link became Link 11 to avoid confusion between Link I, Link 1, and Link II. Thus the alternative UHF link became Link 12, an abortive simplified UHF link became Link 13, and the "B" link became Link 14. A proposed simplified HF link became Link 15.

The SAGE surface-to-air link, which the U.S. Navy agreed to adopt in 1955, became Link 4, presumably because it was the fourth link in the NTDS system.[22] It used the UHF radio band recently adopted for aircraft control, with seventy-bit words. The Navy became particularly interested in Link 4 because it could command an airplane to maneuver all the way to a blind landing on board a carrier. It could also be used to control strikes (see chapter 14). Link 4A, implemented beginning in 1962, existed in both one-way and two-way versions.[23] The latter required a computer on board the fighter (this version was designed for the F-14A).[24]

Unfortunately, Link 4A was not encrypted. A 1979 report on U.S. Navy command and control pointed out that "because certain Link 4A technical documents were downgraded to unclassified and then reclassified, it can be assumed that all messages and message formats are known to the enemy. Further, since all Link 4A messages are transmitted in the clear, an enemy who monitors the Link 4A net would have an excellent tactical picture of U.S. operations. In addition, Link 4A is susceptible to intrusion, with potentially serious consequences." Spoofing Link 4A messages coordinated with tactical air navigation (TACAN) beacon signals could change the displays in the F-14 fighter. Flipping a single bit in the right message would change target classification from hostile to friendly. An enemy could vector an F-14 almost at will. A single bit was used to order bomb release, so an enemy could insert such a bit to cause an airplane to bomb U.S. troops. Finally, since Link 4A used aircraft tail numbers for identification, monitoring Link 4A could provide an enemy with details of the U.S. force.[25] It was no surprise that the replacement Link 16 was badly wanted.

Links 11 and 14 had their own problems. Both were easily jammed. Even in the absence of jamming, both were often unreliable because their designs offered little natural noise immunity. This situation improved as new HF radio technology incorporating computers (to solve multipath problems) appeared in the 1980s. The 1979 report claimed seventy-six different implementations of Link 11; generally "the capability of one Link 11 net member to transmit data does not match the capability of another to receive it. . . . For example, if there are 10 different Link 11 implementations within a Battle Group, 45 unique two-party states of interoperability will result. Each state is defined in terms of the implementation or non-implementation of hundreds of different information elements."

Beginning in the fall of 1963 the U.S. Navy tried to convince NATO to adopt Link 11.[26] The NATO 3G Committee on this subject collapsed in 1967, but the French, German, and Italian navies had already decided to buy NTDS technology and Link 11, including the computer needed to disentangle the parallel tones. As in the U.S. SSCDS, the way to less-expensive combat data automation was to eliminate the computer handling Link 11. UHF could carry the Link 11 message load on a single channel because it operated at a much higher frequency and did not suffer from multipath interference. In 1962 the Dutch Philips company built six prototypes of a version of Link 13. Work stopped when the Royal Navy adopted Link 11 (TIDE).

In 1967 the Royal Navy became interested in the austere link for its new Computer Assisted Action Information System (CAAIS) low-cost frigate combat system, the link processor of which was to account for less than a fifth of total system cost. Given the origins of the term TIDE, the British may have taken the name of the new link from the usual detergent commercial, in which the advertised brand beats "Brand X."[27] In effect, the British were saying that for many purposes Brand X—Link X—was good enough. Because the British used twenty-four-bit computers, their Link X used twenty-four-bit words. For broad compatibility with the thirty-bit Link 11, it spread its messages over pairs of words (data rate was about half of that for Link 11). Link X messages used Link 11 coding but were largely limited to position (including track) data. A parallel voice circuit carried information such as that for track management or weapons control. In 1970 it was estimated that to use all Link X messages required about 2,500 words of core, compared to about 10,000 (minimum 5,000) for Link 11.

The Dutch argued that Link X was joint Dutch/British naval property, because it used features they had developed for the abortive Link 13. (They proposed an austere Link C at the same time the British began work on Link X.) Link X (later naturally called Link 10) was adopted by the Royal Navy, the Royal Netherlands Navy, the Royal Norwegian Navy, and the Turkish navy. Like Link 11, it was not adopted across NATO. Its existence raised compatibility issues. Both the Royal Navy and the Royal Netherlands Navy equipped some major units as gateways, capable of handling both links.

Until the Falklands, the British maintained their long-standing policy preferring radio silence. They abhorred data links that might transmit automatically. They rejected the U.S. view that the risk of detection was worthwhile. In the Falklands, Link X proved its worth. For example, HMS *Sheffield* was hit by the fatal Exocet when her radar warning receiver was turned off. (It would have been triggered by the sidelobes of her satellite transmitter.) Based on prewar practice, the ship's tactical action officer imagined that when the ship's sensors were off, she could not fight, so he left CIC for coffee. In the linked world, that was not the case; he received warning via Link X. He could have saved his ship. Having become convinced that links were well worthwhile, the British adopted Link 11 throughout their fleet after the war.

Link X is historically significant because, unlike Link 11, it could be exported, becoming the first data link that many navies used. The export version was usually called Link Y. When the Argentines bought British Type 42 missile destroyers, which used Link YA, they bought a compatible CAAIS system for their carrier, so that she and the destroyers could form a tactical unit. Egypt bought Link Y to connect radar-equipped aircraft with missile boats. However, when the Brazilians bought their Mk 10 frigate, which had CAAIS and Link YB, they did not buy any automated combat system or link for their carrier. (Ultimately it received a Brazilian-built system developed by the local joint venture set up initially by Ferranti.) Navies that bought Dutch Signaal combat direction systems generally received Link Y as part of the package. It survives in some navies. Signaal later marketed a more sophisticated

Link Y Mk 2, which uses a computer to overcome HF multipath problems, and hence offers Link 11 data rate.

Only navies that bought British or Dutch export ships (or combat systems) adopted Link Y. The Italian navy bought Signaal's Link 11, and it made no attempt to develop an export equivalent to Link Y. The navies that bought Italian systems had no digital links. The other main purveyors of export warships in the 1970s and 1980s, the French, produced their own Link 11 hardware. They developed an export Link W (for Project SaWari, the sale of frigates and other hardware to Saudi Arabia). A form of Link W may later have been exported to the PRC as part of a combat system deal; possibly it went to Taiwan as part of a frigate export deal. Apparently, navies outside NATO generally bought data links only when they were part of combat system packages; they had little interest in computer connectivity. That seems to have changed only in the 1990s.

Link 14 proved a poor substitute for Link 11. Received by teletype, its content had to be plotted manually. That might be fast enough for ASW, but not for anything else. From the 1960s on there were attempts to use the small new tactical computers to turn those messages back into an automated plot. None was successful enough to be adopted by the U.S. Navy.[28] However, the Japanese Maritime Self-Defense Force bought a Link 14 decoder. As late as 1997, Japanese escort squadrons had a flagship fitted for Link 11 and subordinate ships using Link 14 in automated form.

U.S. interest in Link 14 translators declined as Moore's Law made it possible to package Link 11 receivers compactly and cheaply (ultimately, on single computer cards). In the 1980s the U.S. Navy planned to install Receive-Only Link Eleven (ROLE) aboard all ships, including combat auxiliaries. However, Moore's Law outpaced ROLE; by the late 1980s, ships were receiving two-way Link 11, albeit without any corresponding combat direction system, for example, as part of the Radar Data Distribution System (RADDS) radar coordination system.

By this time a new biservice Link 16 was coming, in effect merging Link 4 and Link 11. It began with time-difference navigation. If the time at which a station transmitted were known, the measured time difference at the receiver indicated distance. Given multiple transmitters, a receiver might triangulate. The Bureau of Aeronautics (BuAer) was developing this idea at the same time as Gordon Welchman, working at MITRE on close air support for the Air Force.[29] Welchman realized that the timed net would show all friendly aircraft transmitting on it: it would function as a Blue-force tracker. Instead of carrying only timing messages, the transmissions could be used as a data link, so that system integrated communication, navigation, and identification (CNI). For any such system, messages had to be precisely timed, which meant that they could be encoded efficiently. The Air Force and the Navy emphasized different possibilities. The Air Force was interested mainly in data transmission when it proposed the SEEK BUS link (derived from an earlier PLRACTA link) in 1974, specifically for its new AWACS radar aircraft. The Navy was more interested in navigation (for broadcast control) than in information rate.[30] About 1970 Naval Air Systems Command (NAVAIR) began an Integrated Tactical Navigation System (ITNS) program. Both services used the same L-band part of the specturm, which was already used by TACAN and by IFF. The Integrated Tactical Air Control System (ITACS) coordinated CNI functions and developed an ITNS waveform that would minimize interference with them. Both services planned to use seventy-bit message words, as in Link 4, presumably because existing airborne computers were already adapted to that message length.

Short of money, the Defense Directorate for Research and Engineering (DDR&E) decided to merge the two services' programs to create Joint Tactical Information Distribution System (JTIDS), or Link 16, which is based on the simpler Air Force system.[31] Compared to Link 11, Link 16 offered a richer vocabulary, greater precision, and much larger track files. Ideally, it should have fed into a new combat system, but it also had to serve ships with NTDS computers meeting Link 11 data standards. They were given gateways, in the form of C2 Processors (C2Ps), which create common streams of messages from Link 11 and Link 16. Much was lost in translation, but to rewrite existing software was unthinkably expensive.

Like Link 11, Link 16 needed a separate computer to maintain its tactical picture, this time the one implicit in the times of arrival of messages. The heavy first-generation computer for ships and aircraft was called the JTIDS terminal. A lighter computer suitable for the F/A-18 and comparable aircraft was called MIDS (Miniature Information Distribution System). Although it would not enter service on board airplanes for some years, as early as 1979 there were studies of using JTIDS to navigate weapons to their targets

Link 16 inspired a new NILE (NATO Improved Link Eleven, also known as Link 22), which used Link 16 messages on Link 11 media. Link 16 is a line-of-sight system because it was conceived for aircraft, not ships. NILE is a beyond-line-of-sight (BLOS) equivalent to Link 16 because the HF Link 11 is a BLOS system. The alternative is a satellite version of Link 16. The U.S. Navy has pursued satellite Link 16 (because the fleet is getting more and more satellite capacity for other reasons and because satellite links are inherently covert), while the NATO partners are pursuing NILE.

CHAPTER 9

Another Path to Automation: Weapons Control

T he Combat Information Center (CIC) and its relatives were not the only path to automated situational awareness (i.e., picture-centric practices). Once one target had been hit, a fire-control system had to switch quickly to another. It needed an existing track that could quickly be refined to fire-control quality. Thus it needed a track-while-scan memory—a picture of the tactical situation. The British were the first to understand the need for this alternative path to situational awareness. Their broad-beam World War II air search radars created a picture too diffuse for gun target designation. They therefore interposed a layer of tracking between the Action Information Organization (AIO) and fire control: Target Indication. The plot in a Target Indication Room was based on a narrow-beam Target Indication Radar. Targets were designated from this plot (picture) to an even narrower-beam single-target fire-control radar.

How badly the intermediate level was needed depended on how precise the target track was in AIO because that decided how long a fire-control tracker had to search before locking onto the target (and, if targets were numerous, the chance that it would lock onto the wrong target). For most of World War II, the U.S. Navy saw no need for the intermediate British picture. Its search radars had narrower beams, so its CIC pictures were precise enough for gun target designation. Late in World War II, however, the U.S. Navy faced saturation by kamikazes. Acceptable CIC pictures could not be maintained at short range.

Bell Labs, then the most advanced U.S. computing research organization, received a contract to develop a solution, Fire Control System Mk 65, which soon became Target Designation Equipments Mk 2 and Mk 3.[1] They were the first U.S. approach to automated situational awareness. Like the British Comprehensive Display System (CDS) conceived at about the same time, they had a separate analog memory for each target. Because it worked with narrow-beam radars at short range,

Mk 2 did not track each target; it merely entered current target range, bearing, and elevation into its system. Mk 3 uniquely tried to automate target evaluation and weapon assignment (TEWA) using preset rules, even though each targets was held in a separate memory. Mk 2 and Mk 3 were installed only on board the command cruiser *Northampton* (in effect a command and control experimental ship).[2]

Early postwar U.S. missile air defense systems needed the intermediate picture Mk 3 provided. Their Weapon Designation Equipment (WDE) or Systems (WDS) were similar analog track keepers.[3] They displayed their track data—their short-range air pictures—to an officer who performed TEWA. The associated radar was SPS-39, the first U.S. electronically scanned radar. Picture keeping was good enough that when the Naval Tactical Data System (NTDS) was canceled for the missile cruiser *Columbus,* her ship's force turned her digital (but hard-wired) track-keeping computer into a "Poor Man's NTDS."[4]

What limited the capacity of an air defense system? Was it the number of targets in the intermediate picture, which was set by electronic technology? Or was it the number of directors that controlled the missile? In the 1950s the U.S. Navy developed parallel missile systems for short, medium, and long ranges. Both the short- and medium-range missiles (Tartar and Terrier) required guidance by a dedicated radar director (pointed at the moving target) throughout the missile's flight.[5] The longer-range Talos was different. For most of its flight, it was command guided on the basis of the picture in the system's WDE. Only in the last phase of its flight did it home on radar energy reflected from the target. This technique had been adopted because the Talos range was so great that a missile on the rail was most unlikely to detect radar reflected from a distant target. However, it offered interesting advantages. The missile could take a more energy-efficient path (e.g., up and over). One missile could be guided in midcourse while another switched to terminal homing. Unlike its two siblings, Talos was guided (not merely designated) on the basis of the short-range picture in the WDE.

Typhon and Eagle

The great question was whether the emerging fleet air defense system could be saturated. Each ship could engage only a few targets at a time. If the defending missiles were much faster than the attackers, they might pick them off one at a time. In 1955 the Applied Physics Laboratory (APL) at Johns Hopkins University, the Navy's antiair studies organization, pointed out that low-flying bombers could not be engaged one by one at long ranges because they would not be seen; they could saturate a system. Another future threat, a submarine-launched pop-up missile (which would materialize in about a decade), demanded much faster reaction.

In 1957, while the three existing systems were still being developed, APL offered a solution. Midcourse command guidance could be exercised through an autopilot in the missile, instead of through a big missile director on deck. If it could be exercised intermittently, multiple missiles could time share the same command channel. The picture in the WDE, the basis for commands, would be the main limit on system firepower. It would not be precise enough for the whole engagement. Toward the end the missile would home on the target, probably semiactively. However, the more accurate the WDE picture, the less illumination time. Illuminators could be time shared. This kind of guidance also offered faster reaction because it eliminated the usual shifts from target designators to missile control.

This was as much picture-centric warfare as Admiral Sir John Fisher's vectored battle cruisers. In effect, the intercepting missiles would be sent to specific addresses in the air.

Existing radars could not create a precise enough tactical picture, which had to encompass both targets and defending missiles. APL proposed an electronically scanned track-while-scan radar plus illuminators for terminal guidance. The massive antennas of conventional radars could not scan quickly enough to revisit the positions of fast targets often enough to create useful tracks. That was no problem for an electronically scanned radar. Only electronic scanning could combine the necessary agility with high enough power to see small targets or to burn through jamming.

For electronic scanning, a radar creates numerous broad beams, applying different phases so that they add into a single movable beam. A modern radar like the SPY-1 of the Aegis system uses a digital computer to calculate the required phases fast enough to make the radar's concentrated beam move as desired. No such computer existed in 1957. APL chose the analog Luneberg Lens. The lens translates a directional beam from one side into the corresponding wide beams, with the appropriate phases. APL planned to place its lens deep in the ship. The single beam carrying the pulsed radar signal was passed through it, the individual properly phased beams amplified separately, and the results emitted at the right places in a spherical transmitting antenna. Three Luneberg lenses spaced around the base of the transmitting antenna were used for reception. This approach required large numbers of perfectly tuned amplifiers, and very precise alignments: in a cruiser, 10,800 beamformer elements, 2,700 amplifiers, and 10,200 transmitting antenna elements.

APL proposed both short- and long-range versions, using, respectively, a modified Tartar and a new ramjet missile. In 1960 both were renamed Typhon, after a mythical creature with a hundred heads. Although testing was only beginning, Typhon was so promising that a planned FY62 Talos missile ship conversion was canceled in favor of a Typhon ship to be built under the next year's program.

Meanwhile the Bureau of Aeronautics (BuAer) sought a new fighter missile for fleet air defense. Like Tartar, its first-generation Sparrow missile homed semi-actively: the fighter launching it could engage only one target at a time. Performance was concentrated in the fighter. Beginning in 1955, a series of studies suggested that it might be more efficient to concentrate performance mainly in the missile.[6] BuAer held a competition for the missile, not the fighter. A Bendix-Grumman team won (announced 2 January 1959). Its great advantage was the projected electronic counter-countermeasures (ECCM) capability of its Eagle missile. The missile had a commandable autopilot and a terminal seeker. Like Typhon, the new system created a tactical picture (of up to six targets) in a computer. It could deal with some forms of jamming by dead-reckoning targets the jammers covered, flying its missile toward their predicted positions. Unlike Typhon, it had a terminal-active seeker because the fighter used the same radar to track all its targets; it could not devote that radar to illumination. The six-target capacity was nothing like what Typhon offered, but a carrier could keep several Missileer fighters in the air simultaneously.

Typhon and Eagle-Missileer were parts of the same fleet defense force. Typhon was the most efficient counter to the low-altitude and pop-up threats. Eagle-Missileer was probably best against massed bomber raids, snoopers, and long-range weapons. Each offered far more than existing systems.

When the new John F. Kennedy administration entered office in 1961, Typhon was much further advanced than Eagle-Missileer, and hence was eating much more money. Perhaps not surprisingly, Typhon was canceled in November 1962. The rationale was that it was pointless to buy a new missile system when existing ones did not yet work. Only the Typhon prototype system, for the experimental ship *Norton Sound*, survived. Secretary of Defense Robert S. McNamara seems to have been unaware of serious problems already plaguing the SPG-59 Typhon radar. That several other major programs were killed at about the same time suggests that this choice was financial rather than technical. Given the justification cited, in 1964 McNamara ordered a "get well" program for the three existing surface missile systems, so that they could achieve their design performance on a regular basis. Tartar (and the Tartar-like upper stage of later Terriers) was replaced by a new, far-more-reliable Standard Missile. It was derived from the Tartar-like short range missile of the Typhon system and thus had provision for a digital up-link to its autopilot. It was thus adaptable to the Aegis system, which eventually realized the promise of Typhon.

The Eagle-Missileer contracts were canceled, but McNamara reaffirmed the idea, which was adapted to the new biservice TFX tactical aircraft he ordered. Because it could not have accommodated the systems already designed, a new competition was held. This time Hughes won with what became the Phoenix missile.

The Navy version of TFX gave way to the F-14 Tomcat described in chapter 14. Although apparently much less mature than Typhon in 1960, the Eagle successor beat the Typhon successor (Aegis) into service by about nine years. Both became practicable thanks to Moore's Law.

Aegis

When he killed Typhon, Secretary McNamara established an Advanced Surface Ship Missile System (ASMS). In mid-May 1965 a special assessment group (the Withington Committee) affirmed the basic Typhon concept but proposed that the analog electronically scanned radar be replaced by a digital alternative. The Bureau of Ships (BuShips) radar branch head was the group's radar and command panel chief. Reportedly, he argued that the same radar should control both fighters and missiles, that is, that the command and decision element of the new system be an outgrowth of NTDS. Fighter control required a radar range of about 250 nautical miles, rather than the roughly 150 nautical miles of the Typhon system. Even so, the new system was more an upgraded WDS than a modified combat data system. RCA received the system contract on 1 December 1969. ASMS was renamed Aegis.

RCA built its system around a flat-array SPY-1 radar-exploiting cheap, new digitally controlled phase shifters (to create radar beams). Its SM-2 missile was an improved version of the SM-1 Standard Missile developed under the get-well program, with the commandable autopilot. The picture created by SPY-1 was so precise that Aegis illuminators could simply be slaved to it and snapped on only at the last moment. Radar tests began in 1973, about a decade after the demise of Typhon. Entry into service was delayed by problems in choosing a platform, but by 1983 Aegis was at sea on board the cruiser *Ticonderoga*.[7]

The Aegis picture was so good that Aegis ships were often used to support surveillance operations. For example, in 1985 an Aegis ship disentangled the complex air situation over the central Mediterranean well enough for F-14s to be directed to intercept an airliner carrying Arab terrorists. The F-14s forced it down in Italy.

Aegis was built around two closely integrated elements, a Command and Decision (C&D) System, and a Weapon Control System (WCS). C&D formed and displayed the tactical picture. It performed all the old WDS functions, including threat evaluation and weapon assignment. A ship's commanding officer (CO) could choose between automatic operation, relying on C&D to know what to do, and semiautomatic operation in which he decided which targets on his screen were to be engaged. One irony of the *Vincennes* incident was that the ship was in semiautomatic mode. It might well have rejected the Airbus the ship shot down had it been in automatic mode. This degree of automation was probably adopted for quick reactions against pop-up threats; it mirrored contemporary work on antiship missile defense.

C&D added something new: it incorporated tactical doctrine, which could be adjusted as needed aboard ship. For example, that doctrine might filter out slow-moving objects seen on the radar because they were unlikely to be threats. That made for an embarrassing incident off Lebanon in which an Aegis ship repeatedly rejected a radar target detected by a conventional missile cruiser. Finally, the target—a Cessna—came into view. The moral, in a world of terrorists using unconventional weapons, was that such cutoffs could be dangerous. Conversely, ships off Lebanon often saw what they thought were aircraft heading toward them at moderate speed, then vanishing. Later they discovered that they were watching cars on a mountain road. That was not obvious in ships' CICs because their displays showed no details of the geography ashore (the computers involved were not powerful enough).

Close-coupling to the WCS made for extremely quick reactions. When the Cold War ended, the ability to deal with saturation raids was no longer so important, but close coupling offered the ability to deal with the new threat of small numbers of missiles launched from a hostile coast (or from missile boats) at relatively short ranges, giving little warning. In some scenarios Aegis was the only system capable of defending itself.

Aegis concepts were applied to existing missile ships. No conventional air search radar could match SPY-1. However, an NTDS track picture could define homing baskets, albeit much larger than those Aegis used. On that basis, uplinks could provide midcourse guidance. There was no question of slaving illuminators, but, as in Aegis, illumination would be needed only near the target. Illuminators could be time-shared. Missile range was boosted (roughly doubled) because the missile could fly most of the way along an energy-efficient path under autopilot control. Hybrid replacements for the existing Tartar and Terrier systems were fielded about 1980 as the new threat upgrade (NTU).[8] In a Terrier ship, such as a *Leahy-* or *Belknap*-class cruiser, each missile battery (two or one, respectively) was served by a new WDS Mk 14, which used a pair of UYK-20 computers. One pair could accept twenty tracks from the ship's combat direction system (thirty for two batteries). Tracks could also be taken from the ship's gunfire-control system (Mk 68, when fitted). Threats were engaged in priority order. Each missile fire-control system could control up to four SM-2 missiles in flight.

Other countries adopted the Aegis idea, that a fire-control level tactical picture could overcome saturation. The most prominent example is the European PAAMS/LAMS system, adopted by the British, French, Italian, Saudi, and Singaporean navies. The South African Umkhonto system (adopted by Finland and Sweden) applies the same idea to a missile with an infrared terminal seeker. The U.S. Army's Patriot applied this idea to a missile with a hybrid semiactive seeker, and U.S. ballistic missile defense weapons use a similar concept of operation. This concept also applies to the Enhanced Sea Sparrow Missile, which is carried by some Aegis ships as a shorter-range supplement to SM-2 and its successors. Ships carrying Enhanced Sea Sparrow, but using less elaborate radars than SPY-1, correspond to Cold War New Threat Upgrade ships.

Cooperative Engagement Capability

When Aegis was conceived, its tactical picture came from the ship's SPY-1 radar, but the Applied Physics Lab realized that it could come from anywhere else, as long as the source was good enough. Several ships could pool their data. Compared to NTDS and Link 11, any such pooled system had to transmit data on a far-timelier basis, with far greater precision. APL created just such a system as the Cooperative Engagement Capability (CEC). It sought a great increase in the number of engagement channels in a fleet. If a ship ran out of ammunition or suffered launcher or radar damage, she could still contribute to battle force firepower. In effect, NTDS and Link 11 (or 16) transmitted vectors that could be used for decision making but not for fire control. CEC transmitted individual radar plots, which each ship's system could assemble into a tactical and fire-control picture. That picture could be passed on to ships with less-capable systems.

Using several radars cooperatively made for much better target tracking and for a much clearer overall tactical picture, as a target maneuvering too violently for any one radar to handle it could not evade several, which were not synchronized. Compared to NTDS, CEC dramatically reduced double counting of targets.[9] CEC could overcome stealth, which generally is not total. Typically a stealthy aircraft is intermittently detected by any given radar, but the combination of detections is not enough to generate a usable target track. Adding up intermittent detections by multiple radars might well be, particularly since many stealthy aircraft and missiles trade maneuverability for low radar cross section.[10] Ships could hit targets invisible to their own radars.[11] If ships operated inshore, the fleet as a whole could overcome blocking by terrain. One ship could provide terminal illumination for another ship's missiles. Once E-2 Hawkeyes were brought into the system, it could see far beyond a ship's horizon, and the E-2 could illuminate targets. CEC became the basis for a version of the Standard Missile (SM) with an active seeker, directing the missile into a "basket," where it could effectively engage a target out of sight of a fleet's illuminators.

Work on CEC began in 1985 as Battle-Group antiair warfare (AAW Coordination).[12] E-Systems received a contract for the data link in 1988.[13] It carried far more data than Link 11 or Link 16, and it had to indicate the positions of the ships precisely. It did so using what amounted to a secondary C-band radar (distance-measuring transponder) with the first active array in U.S. service. The array determined the bearing of the ship at the other end of the link. Each ship in the net added its data to the flow around the net (data mounted in proportion to the square of the number of users). Despite its megabits/second throughput, the link could handle only about twenty participants.

CEC was first demonstrated, using vans, in August 1990 off Newport News, Virginia, aboard the Aegis cruisers *San Jacinto* (CG 56) and *Leyte Gulf* (CG 55) in August 1990, including integration of Marine Corps ground assets. In September 1993 there were successful four-mode tests between *Kidd* and three CEC shore sites: the Aegis Combat Systems Center (ACSC), Wallops Island, Virginia, and the Fleet Combat Direction Systems Support Activity (FCDISSA) Dam Neck. In 1994 CEC was installed on board three ships of the *Eisenhower* battle group and on board the large amphibious ship *Wasp*. In a summer 1994 test, the battle group tracked a Sergeant rocket fired from Wallops Island to an apogee of 580,000 feet (108 nautical miles) and successfully transmitted the CEC picture to a Patriot battery ashore and to an air force control and reporting center (which would normally control tactical aircraft) via a commercial Inmarsat. Launch and predicted impact points were transmitted within seconds of launch. This was the first time official Washington had realized the connection between CEC and theater ballistic missile defense. Secretary of Defense William S. Perry was so impressed that he ordered the program accelerated as much as technically possible. In January 1996, in the "Mountain Top" Advanced Concept Technology Demonstration (ACTD), CEC was key in the first demonstration of over-the-horizon engagement of cruise missiles. CEC (USG-2) on board *Hue City* and *Vicksburg* was certified, in accordance with congressional direction, as having attained initial operating capability on 30 September 1996. Low-rate initial production (Milestone III) was scheduled for 1997.

Then the system ran into trouble. APL had imagined that a group of ships with the same SPY-1 radars and with the same CEC software and hardware could automatically create the joint picture. The system embodied a threat evaluation and weapon assignment (TEWA) element, which APL assumed would assign the right ship to each target, automatically launching weapons as needed. In fact, the situation turned out to be more complicated. Ships in different positions saw targets slightly differently. A ship had to be assigned to decide whether particular targets were friend or foe, as otherwise different ships made different choices. (The "identification friend or foe" [IFF] transponder on an airplane could not answer all queries simultaneously.) No one really liked the automatic engagement feature of the system TEWA. The problems emerged in a 1996 test. Thus it was not until September and December 2000 that integration of CEC ships into a mixed group was finally demonstrated; CEC was successfully operationally evaluated in May and June 2001 using six CEC-equipped ships: the carrier *John F. Kennedy*, the large amphibious ship *Wasp*, and the cruisers *Anzio*, *Cape St. George*, *Hue City*, and *Vicksburg*, supported by a CEC-equipped E-2C. The first operational deployment came in January 2002 with the *John F. Kennedy* battle group, including the cruisers *Hue City* and *Vicksburg*, and the destroyer *The Sullivans*, all with Baseline 2.0 software.

As in so many other systems, the key to CEC was Moore's Law. CEC became practicable with the advent of the PowerPC processor, conceived for the Mac computer. The system's first parallel processor used thirty of these chips on a bus.

Submarine Tactical Data Systems

Like Aegis, U.S. submarine combat (situational awareness) systems grew from fire-control systems. Torpedoes had such short ranges that it was easy to separate wide-area situational awareness (represented by a plot) from the approach and attack. The pre–World War II U.S. Navy was quite advanced in using an analog Torpedo Direction Computer (TDC) to deduce target course and speed from a series of observations. Once that problem had been solved, the same computer passed the data to a position keeper, which projected ahead target position so that torpedoes could be aimed (using their gyros, which steered them after they emerged from torpedo tubes). At least in theory, the TDC made it possible to aim the torpedoes rather than the submarine, and thus to fire both bow and stern tubes at the same target (in practice submarine commanders tended to close in to fire, and they did not use the full capability designed into the TDC). Typically, the system handled only one target at a time, but it had the potential to shift rapidly from target to target in a complex situation. It was at the edge of what we might call situational awareness. The TDC shaped postwar submariners' expectations of future fire-control systems.

As the U.S. and Royal navies became interested in using submarines for ASW after World War II, they developed Target Motion Analysis (TMA); a submarine's position, course, and speed could be deduced from the way her direction (bearing) changed over time. TMA was based on the assumption that, unaware that it was being tracked, the target would maintain course and speed. TMA techniques amounted to guessing a solution and then seeing whether that solution corresponded to further target bearings and bearing rates. In theory, TMA could have provided a submarine with situational awareness, but in the 1950s it was a lengthy

manual process. Submariners generally handled one TMA solution at a time, pass-
ing a good solution into their fire-control systems as they approached the target.
Given their speed, nuclear (but not diesel) submarines could obtain complete
TMA solutions by maneuvering between bearing measurements.[14]

When the *Thresher* class was conceived in 1957, the submariners needed something fundamentally new. The submarine was designed around a big BQS-6 spherical bow sonar capable of detecting enemy submarines at much longer ranges. The
associated weapon was the nuclear submarine rocket (SUBROC), with a range of
thirty-five nautical miles. After emerging from a submarine torpedo tube, its rocket
engine ignited, and it burst through the surface to follow a ballistic trajectory until
it struck the water, to explode underwater near its target. SUBROC needed a passive (TMA) target solution because, as long as the target submarine was unaware it
was being tracked, the noise of the igniting motor gave too little warning for her to
escape the lethal radius of the bomb. SUBROC would be fired on the basis of a single
confirming sonar ping (which, like motor ignition, was too late to warn the target).

The big new sonar in *Thresher* offered much more precise bearings at long
range. Given a string of bearings, a special-purpose digital computer could calculate a TMA solution that might be accurate enough not to need the usual lengthy
process of refinement using further data. That was what SUBROC needed, to strike
before the enemy submarine passed out of range. The designers saw the new Mk
113 fire-control system as more.[15] It could handle four solutions simultaneously (in
separate memories, sharing a common calculating core). The prototype on board
Thresher (completed in 1961) could display all four as dead-reckoned tracks, to
provide situational awareness at a summary display the designers hoped would be
the preferred battle station of the submarine commander. Commanders tended
not to use this display, and later versions of Mk 113 were limited to the pair of targets of earlier analog systems.

One reason for displaying so complex an underwater situation was the hope
that submarines would work together using an underwater data link. *Thresher's*
prototype link failed, and the U.S. Navy also dropped ideas of submarine direct
support of surface ships (the British persisted).[16] The Russians seem to have been
far more successful in developing and using such links, probably because they did
not try to send complex messages.[17]

General-purpose computers offered better situational awareness, including
awareness of the acoustic environment, which might make it easier for the new
strategic submarines to evade pursuit. It took a computer to translate a mass of
oceanographic information into usable recommendations. The main studies were
CSED, Fast-Reaction Submarine Control (FRISCO), and Submarine Integrated
Control (SUBIC).[18] By 1965 BuShips was interested in something like a submarine

NTDS.[19] The British had similar plans, well known to U.S. developers, for their first production nuclear submarine (HMS *Valiant*). They were particularly interested in situational awareness for direct support (the system was a variant of the Action Data Automation [ADA] surface ship system). The U.S. and British projects all incorporated computer display systems, computer sonar environmental prediction, and the ability to display predictions about own ship, target, and weapons. And they all involved alternative (which would now be called photonic) or relocated periscopes. All but CSED had a separate CO display. The British system was probably the most ambitious because it was intended to integrate all shipboard sensors (including electronic support measures [ESM]), accept data by link, and send data to consorts by link. The British program was badly delayed, not least by the effort to build four strategic submarines, but it survived.

Under a SUBIC program, Arma developed a Submarine Safety Monitoring System (SSMS) for the small research submarine *Dolphin*. At the time it was the only general-purpose digital computer system on board a U.S. submarine. Its central computer integrated data from sensors throughout the submarine, displaying the results on several computer screens. However, it could also be used as a test bed. For a follow-on contract to develop a tactical display, Arma integrated SSMS with an attack teacher (for the Mk 106 analog fire-control system) to evaluate a tactical display during the approach to a target. Another experiment evaluated tactics prior to the approach. Arma concluded that an Integrated Conn Complex should be installed in the submarine's attack and control center, with summary displays showing ship dynamics and safety, the overall geographical situation affecting tactical decisions, and ship operating and engineering status. Under battle conditions, the geographical situation would involve mainly detection and environmental sensors, fire control, and ship control. Otherwise it would use the same sensors and ship control but would add navigational data.[20]

It was not altogether clear that the new digital computer technology was mature.[21] Early solid-state computers were proving difficult to maintain (as in the case of the DIANE system in the A-6 Intruder). Sometimes the Navy retreated from digital to less flexible but more reliable analog technology. For example, the digital Mk 111 underwater fire-control system (for surface ships) was succeeded by the analog Mk 114. One application that had seemed essential was assistance with ship control. It seemed that a fast nuclear submarine could respond in unexpected ways (such as snap-roll) to steering and depth commands. Surely a computer could provide the helmsman and planesman with vital advice. It turned out that the software in their heads more than sufficed (the "road in the sea" display notoriously induced sleep).

In 1965 another possibility opened. U.S. interest in direct support—the use of a submarine to protect a surface force—revived, as it became clear that Soviet nuclear attack submarines were operational.[22] This role required a much faster nuclear submarine (the existing *Sturgeon* was limited to twenty-six knots, hence could not keep up with a carrier). The solution advanced by Adm. Hyman Rickover's Nuclear Reactors branch was simple: install a destroyer reactor (twice the power of the *Sturgeon* reactor). The question was whether the existing manual command and control system could successfully support the new mission. Those responsible for surface command and control (NTDS) thought not. The new submarine was called AGSSN (a nuclear test submarine).[23]

The Navships Electronics Branch, which had developed NTDS, selected RCA to explore the command and control requirements of the new mission. The company argued that existing manual systems were grossly inadequate. It wanted something like NTDS (in this case, capable of tracking and displaying twelve targets simultaneously).[24] A submarine in direct support had to know where friendly forces were. She might often vector aircraft to attack the enemy submarines she spotted, so she had to know where they were, too. Moreover, a submarine tied to a fast carrier might close an incoming enemy submarine so rapidly that her CO would need far more automated support than before. To further complicate matters, both submarines might be armed with long-range missiles comparable to the new SUBROC. At this time it seemed likely that the AGSSN would be built under the FY69 program (i.e., the program beginning 30 June 1968, hence requiring a mature design early in 1967). The first *Los Angeles*–class submarine was built under the FY70 program.

Without an automated plot, existing submarines could not effectively vector aircraft or surface ships to distant targets her sonar detected. Nor could they get the most out of their sonars. The CO used a look-up table to predict sonar range at his operating depth. That was confusing and time-consuming, so he could not quickly choose optimum depth and speed. Nor could he quickly choose optimum sonar mode. Submarines could not correlate targets detected by their own targets' different sonars (let alone those detected by both the submarine and surface consorts). The passive ranging sonar (PUFFS) lacked range (it was calibrated to 20,000 yards), and it often broke down. The passive classification sonar had a limited range of frequencies. There was no means of acoustic identification (i.e., a signature library). The DUUG sonar intercept set picking up an enemy submarine's pings did not measure target frequency, nor did it have a wide enough frequency range. The big active sonar could not use the acoustic short-pulse echo classification technique (ASPECT) short-pulse classification technique (often giving target speed and course) that some more primitive sonars used. There was no way to determine the depth of a distant target.

The plot providing the CO's tactical picture was not close enough to the CO, and he lacked speed, depth, rudder angle, and trim indicators. As he decided what action to take, nothing provided answers to his what-if questions. The intelligence information he might have used was spread throughout the submarine in reference publications, not arranged for quick access. The CO could not easily evaluate the threat of multiple targets or estimate kill or survival probabilities if he attacked them. Once the submarine fired, the CO had no indicator of point of impact (for SUBROC) or torpedo path (including the path of a wire-guided torpedo), yet both would certainly shape what he decided to do. Even the periscope was a problem because the entire attack center had to be darkened or red-lit so that it could be used in the dark. Many of these problems would be solved by a submarine equivalent of NTDS.

RCA proposed a picture keeper like NTDS, controlling weapons through the existing Mk 113 system.[25] It would classify targets (approach, retreat, submarine, or nonsubmarine) and identify them using a signature library and perhaps underwater IFF. For TMA, the system would keep track of own-ship course. The concept included long-range acoustic and radio links. For example, surface ships contacted acoustically might act as radio links to aircraft and to more-distant surface ships. It was not entirely clear that existing technology could meet RCA's requirements.

By late 1966 the idea of extending NTDS to the AGSSN was apparently dead. The main remaining attack submarine digital computer project was the integrated digital New Sub Sonar/Fire Control (which would certainly figure in the next attack submarine) under development by Navships and Navord. It was intended, among other things, to increase the number of targets the sonar/fire-control combination could handle. The big bow sphere in *Thresher* was connected to three analog trackers, each, in effect, a small replica of the sphere; it could track three targets. The new digital sonar would use preformed beams; it would register which of many beams an incoming signal occupied. A computer would assemble successive signals into tracks. The limit on the number of tracks was the number of beams. The specification called twelve targets, but that later increased dramatically.

In connection with this project the Naval Underwater Systems Center (NUSC) at New London rethought TMA. It saw the CHURN technique for automatic submarine tactical data calculation as the starting point, rather than the end point, of a TMA solution. A digital computer could project ahead a TMA solution for comparison with new data. It could display the effect of changes an operator made in a trial solution while retaining the data: an operator could keep adjusting a solution until it tallied with the new data. This was much better than the usual manual procedure because the computer could do projections much more quickly and also because it could combine different TMA techniques. Instead of a fire-control party taking hours to work out a solution, a single operator could develop one in a few minutes.[26]

An operator detected and fixed a target not too differently from the way an operator at a CIC console detected a target in NTDS. Just as in NTDS, once the system had target position, course, and speed, it could estimate future target position. The operator had only to check periodically to be sure that the target had not changed course. How many targets one operator could handle depended on how quickly solutions could be obtained and also on how often target motion had to be reviewed—in effect, on how much deviation from the earlier solution could be accepted before the target solution had to be redone.

There were some important differences from AAW practice. In NTDS, an operator monitoring a particular sensor, such as a long-range radar, was responsible for a target that particular sensor had picked up. In a submarine the sonar operator assigned a tracker (analog or digital) to a chosen target; the system then passed a string of bearings automatically to the fire control system One consequence of adopting digital sonars was that data from different sonars could be merged before being fed in. The string of bearings became the basis for a TMA solution.

NUSC's system represented observations (bearings of a particular target) as dots grouped around a vertical line. Their distances from the line represented deviations from a TMA solution. As an operator turned dials representing quantities such as target speed and course, the dots moved to show how close the modified solution might be. When they were all on the vertical line ("stacked"), the solution was correct. Dot-stacking was called manually aided target evaluation (MATE).[27] Typically, it began with a crude estimate, for example, range fifteen thousand yards, speed fifteen knots, course reciprocal of the bearing. A Kalman filter-based system smoothed the string of bearings for use by the operator (the system was called Kalman Assisted Tracking [KAST]). Ekelund ranging (using the target bearing rate and own ship's speed across the line of sight) provided an estimated range once enough data had been collected and the ship maneuvered to resolve ambiguities. Proponents claimed that a single operator could handle twenty targets under average conditions, but in reality a good operator would find it difficult to keep loose track of ten. None would be good enough for fire control, but once a target of interest was chosen, the solution could quickly be refined to that point. Thus, Mod 9, the first application of MATE, was generally credited with an effective capacity of ten or fewer. The number of tracks a submarine could handle was determined by how many tracking consoles she had. With all the tracks in one computer, they could be compared and engaged just as in Aegis or NTDS. Once one target had been chosen for engagement, its track was passed to the fire-control portion of the system. Instead of a fire-control system focusing on a single target, NUSC had the germ of a passive submarine situational awareness system, a kind of underwater NTDS. Nothing of that sort had been imagined before.

MATE was tested at sea aboard an attack submarine in 1968. Strategic submarines already had digital computers for missile control, introduced with the Polaris A3 missile. When not calculating fire-control information for the missiles, they were used for submarine fire control, replacing the hard-wired computer in the Mk 113 system.[28] When U.S. strategic submarines were refitted with MIRVed (multiple independently targetable reentry vehicle) Poseidon missiles, they received a more powerful Mk 88 missile control computer. In the Mod 9 system, it offered NUSC enough power to implement MATE. This was the first U.S. submarine fire-control computer with a CRT (graphic) display, in a redesigned Mk 78 analyzer. Apparently there was no interest in actually displaying all the targets together to show the underwater situation: like its predecessors, Mod 9 could show only two tracks, albeit on a single display rather than on two separate ones.[29]

Mod 9 was being developed early in 1968 just as two studies of what became the *Los Angeles*–class submarine were conducted. One examined the overall configuration that had already been developed by Newport News. The other developed requirements for the ship's weapon system—which had not yet been developed at all. Those writing the second report wanted an equivalent to Mod 9, which might finally realize the promise of TMA. Thus far long-range TMA had been disappointing because existing gyrocompasses (to measure target bearing) and the Ships Inertial Navigation System (SINS) were not accurate enough. Both were needed because TMA was based on comparison of a string of observations. For each, the submarine had to know where it had been and where its sensors had been pointing. Computer TMA seemed vastly preferable to manual TMA, which was credited with a 10 to 15 percent range error, hence required occasional pinging to confirm target position.

The tactical picture-keeping requirements RCA had envisaged were still valid, but in theory AGSSN was a prototype. It was not worth developing a new version of NTDS for a single ship. At this time BuShips, responsible for NTDS, was working on what it thought would be the next attack submarine, CONFORM. AGSSN was very much the child of Admiral Rickover's Naval Reactors branch. Even so, it clearly needed a fire-control system. Mod 9 showed that a fire-control system could expand into an NTDS-like situational awareness system simply by displaying the full tactical situation. The tactical decision aids elements of the RCA system did have to be omitted or folded into the sonar system.

Money was too tight to develop the ideal all-new digital system. Alan Marins, a civilian with the Naval Ordnance Systems Command, realized that Mod 9 could be the basis for a step-by-step transition to the desired future system. He created an attack submarine system based on Mod 9. In this Mod 10, a single-bay UYK-7 computer, far more powerful than the Mk 88, was combined with two consoles (Mk 81, which could show the dots or the situation or the dials).[30] As initially envisaged, each of two Mk 81s would track two targets and engage one. The system would offer three times the effectiveness of a *Sturgeon* system. As built, Mod 10 also provided a display panel at the CO's battle station alongside the periscopes. It equipped the last two *Sturgeon*-class submarines and the first few of the new *Los Angeles* class. It was a true situational-awareness system. Mod 10 retained the old pair of Mk 75 analog attack directors, which, as in the past, translated target data into fire-control terms. Overall, it was a digital system saddled with a great deal of analog-to-digital and digital-to-analog hardware.

It was not too difficult to take the next step to a fully digital fire-control system. Development was greatly simplified because, unlike the plans of the past, there was no attempt to integrate sonar and fire control. Each remained separate. The sonar simply sent a stream of bearings (in digital form) to the fire-control system. Marins replaced the single-bay UYK-7 with a two-bay version, and the two Mk 75s with two Mk 81 weapon control consoles for MATE. A third Mk 81 served as commander's console.

This time the system could display the underwater situation (as one of several possible modes on the commander's console). The analog BQQ-2 sonar gave way to a digital BQQ-5.[31] Given two MATE consoles, the system could handle about twenty-four targets. Reportedly, sensor tracker capability and man-machine interface (presumably MATE stations) limited Mk 117 to less than a fifth of its theoretical track capacity. That suggests an ultimate capacity of about 120 tracks. Because the system dealt in tracks rather than in data from any particular sensor, some of those tracks could be provided by accompanying ships and aircraft via a special version of Link 11. (Similarly, the submarine could provide data to an accompanying surface force via Link 11.) Although sonar was the main attack sensor, the system could also accept periscope bearings. Formal development began in 1971. This Mk 117 system was tested on board USS *Narwhal* (SSN 671), first installed on board USS *Dallas* (SSN 700), and then retrofitted to earlier submarines, including the *Permit* and *Sturgeon* classes. Mk 117 was initially called the All-Digital Attack Center (ADAC).

None of this worked entirely as expected. Submarine commanders continued to use alternatives alongside the new automated TMA. Thus, the *Los Angeles* had an automated plotter for manual TMA and to help maintain a picture of the tactical situation during an attack. Commanders often preferred to watch the changing plot rather than rely entirely on their electronic displays. They had additional ways of estimating target range, not least as a check on the computer (which sometimes made serious mistakes). Thus, they typically used Range of the Day (i.e., current sound conditions), signal-to-noise ratio (given target identification), and the elevation or depression angle from which sound was heard, assuming that they bounced off bottom or surface. The expanded situational awareness inherent in Mk 117 was not fully exploited because the close-in direct support role was little exercised. At least until the advent of the BSY-2 system in the *Seawolf* class, COs continued to rely heavily on plots, particularly the geoplot (geographical situation) and the contact evaluation plot. However, automation did eliminate the manual time-range and time-frequency plots.

The advent of submarine-launched antiship missiles—the medium-range Harpoon and the long-range Tomahawk—changed the situation. Harpoon was included in the initial version of the system, although it was probably not envisaged when Mk 117 was conceived. Given the flexibility of a digital computer, Mk 117 could be adapted to handle Tomahawk (treated as a longer-range Harpoon). Neither missile could be used effectively without reference to a tactical picture, as targets had to be sorted from nontargets. Harpoon range was at the limit of the submarine's own sensors, but it could benefit from Link 11. For Tomahawk, the submarine relied on externally supplied data, provided mainly via Submarine Data Exchange System (SSIXS) and other satellite links. (See the discussion in chapter 18 on over-the-horizon [OTH] targeting.) Key was that the ship's fire-control system was adapted to using a picture, not the products of particular sensors. An additional computer and another Mk 81 console were added to handle that picture, but its product was connected to Mk 117 for fire control. A precomputer submarine would have required an entire additional fire-control system, for which there might not even have been space. Recent Russian problems integrating the Klub missile (comparable to antiship Tomahawk) into Indian Navy "Kilo"-class submarines suggest that this was not a trivial proposition. The new Combat Control System (CCS) Mk 1 was approved for service use in July 1980, work having begun in FY73.

Further systems adopted very different architectures and more-automated approaches to TMA, which gave them the ability to handle many more targets. However, Mk 117 had established the key idea that a submarine system should be built around a tactical picture rather than tied to particular sensors. That made it possible to accept remote data, via sources such as Link 11 and SSIXS. After the Cold War, the picture-centric system could accept information from all sorts of other sources, such as unmanned vehicles. The picture, moreover, could be sent to others via new high-speed satellite links. The submarine could be a node in a netted wide-area system because its own information-handling system was built around an abstract picture that could be created by many different kinds of sensors.

CHAPTER 10

Spreading CIC Automation

The U.S. Navy was the first to adopt a digital CIC system, but it was not unique. The extent to which other navies took the same expensive step gives some idea of how universal the netting concept was—and thus of how widely the more generalized ideas of network-centric warfare are likely to spread.

Large-Ship Automation in the Royal Navy

Dr. Ralph Benjamin saw his Comprehensive Display System (CDS) as a first step toward a digital system. Work on the system and on its electronically scanned Type 985 radar began in 1957. System design included automatic radar target detection. The radar proved too ambitious, but the digital system became Action Data Automation (ADA). Using twenty-four-bit Ferranti computers, it was adapted to the existing Type 984 radar on board the carrier *Eagle*. Apparently ADA was seen as CDS with a digital memory, a relatively simple step forward. Later the British admitted that they should have built a development model for shore testing and that they should not have omitted manual radar tracking.

Because they were interested in direct support, the British envisaged a submarine version of ADA for their first production nuclear submarines (*Valiant* class). Development took much longer than expected, and this system was ready in 1970; it was installed in 1972 on board the first next-generation submarine, HMS *Swiftsure*.[1] Thus, it was slightly later than its U.S. equivalent, Mk 113 Mod 10, but unlike the U.S. system, it was connected to an underwater data link.

Like the CDS carrier, an ADA carrier would work with County-class missile destroyers. ADA was compact enough to fit them. The destroyer version added a second computer for missile control, so it was designated Action Data Automation Weapon System (ADAWS). It became the British equivalent to Naval Tactical Data

System (NTDS). Development of the initial version took four and a half years. Functions included threat evaluation and weapon assignment, which the British called Computer-Assisted Target Evaluation (CATE). Operators came to mistrust CATE as too complex. Second-generation versions were designed for the abortive 1965 attack carrier CVA 01 (Mk 3) and for its *Bristol*-class consort (Mk 2). In both ships, ADAWS was associated with a new three-dimensional Anglo-Dutch Type 988 (Broomstick) radar, which was needed for fighter control rather than for missile control. Both ships would have been armed with the Ikara antisubmarine missile, which outranged existing sonars. Data linking allowed it to exploit sonar data from other ships: it was an inherently networked weapon. *Bristol* also had the Sea Dart antiaircraft missile. When the British government canceled the carrier, the Royal Navy canceled all but the first *Bristol*-class destroyer. The Anglo-Dutch radar project had already been abandoned. ADAWS survived for simplified successor ships.[2] Simplification included eliminating Link 11 in favor of Link X. (See chapter 8.) Just as the U.S. Navy abandoned plans to put NTDS on missile destroyers as unaffordable, the British gave up plans for a version of ADAWS on board *Leander*-class frigates. Further versions of ADAWS were designed into the 1980s.[3]

The submarine equivalent of ADAWS, equivalent to the U.S. Mk 117, was DCB. The British were particularly interested in software for fire control because World War II had taught them that they might have to rely on U.S.-supplied weapons once they ran out of British ones. The U.S. Navy also had some weapons they lacked, most important the SUBROC missile. Although the Royal Navy never adopted SUBROC, its digital weapon system made adoption of the U.S. Sub-Harpoon missile relatively easy.

Automating Destroyers and Frigates

As a first step in its campaign to spread NTDS, the U.S. Navy encouraged France and Germany to form NATO Committee B2 to develop a destroyer-sized version. Like the Small Ship Combat Direction System (SSCDS), it was cut down to a single computer. Maintaining full Link 11 capability cut capacity to sixteen tracks. Like NTDS, the B2 system did not control weapons—different NATO navies used very different weapon systems. In 1964 the British considered adopting the B2 system for low-end frigates, but in the end no NATO navy adopted the system. The B2 program collapsed in 1966.

The British were still interested in automating frigates, not least because any Ikara ship in a formation needed their sonar data. In 1966 it was estimated that ADA for a *Leander* would cost £300,000, slightly over twice as much as the existing analog command and control system. The cost target for the new Computer

Assisted Action Information System (CAAIS) frigate system was £100,000 (plus £20,000 for a data link). It was conceived as a parallel to the central tactical system of the new Nimrod maritime patrol aircraft, using the same Elliott 920C computer. (By about 1968 the Royal Navy wanted the Ferranti computer it was using in ADAWS.) Moore's Law made such smaller-ship systems possible. Also, unlike ADAWS (but like NTDS), CAAIS was a picture keeper that fed tracks to separate weapon systems corresponding crudely to a U.S. Weapon Designation Systems (WDS).[4] Unlike NTDS, CAAIS transmitted tracks only at operator discretion; that may have reflected the British preference for radio silence. The system's antisubmarine warfare (ASW) orientation showed in its displays of sonar tracks and electronic emitters. Given CAAIS, a *Leander*-class frigate could send data from her sonar to an Ikara ship. The ASW plotting function included target indication for a shipboard helicopter-control system (MATCH) and for an ASW mortar (Limbo).

CAAIS became the standard combat direction system of both modernized and new (Types 21 and 22) British frigates of the 1970s. It was also installed on board British mine hunters, which had no real-time data link. Instead they transferred electronic charts of mine hunting operations from ship to ship, or from a ship to a command center.

A private-venture version of CAAIS was exported, but not the Royal Navy version (except on board exported former Royal Navy ships).[5] The associated digital weapon control system built for Type 21 frigates became the basis of export small-ship combat direction systems, beginning with Marconi's Sapphire.[6]

France

Unlike the British, the French were not initially interested in netting. They were driven to automation by the sheer mass of data produced by the big stacked-beam DRBI 23 radars on board their two *Suffren*-class missile frigates (actually small cruisers like U.S. "frigates" [DLGs] of this period). Initially, the French simply provided sufficient computer capacity for later installation.[7] The link became necessary when they decided to install the missile, but not the radar, on board the existing cruiser *Colbert*. As in the British County class, the link provided the ship with three-dimensional data. The French computer industry could not have supplied a system quickly enough, so the French bought as much as they could of what they considered the only acceptable system, NTDS.[8] Probably the deal to buy hardware and some core software was complete by the end of 1961. The French navy set up an organization to develop the rest of the required software. Work on what they called Systeme d'Exploitation Navale des Informations Tactiques (SENIT 1) formally began in 1962.

Encouraged by Project B2, beginning in 1965 the French and the Germans developed a destroyer-sized SENIT 2, using NTDS computers and displays but their own software. Only the French adopted it. A single-computer radar picket or ASW version was installed on board *Surcouf*-class radar picket destroyers and the ASW destroyer *Duperre*. A three-computer version was installed on board *Surcouf*-class destroyers rearmed with U.S. Tartar missiles. Like its U.S. equivalents, this system could maintain 128 tracks.

Once the French combined the software they had written for SENIT with their own hardware (in SENIT 4), they had exportable systems comparable to the British CAAIS.[9] Unlike the British, they were not exporting warships large enough to use it. Instead, they built a series of small-ship systems using the same computers the French navy was then using for gun fire control. The associated track-while-scan memory became the basis of the Vega small-ship computer combat system. The more powerful Vega III equipped Saudi frigates and was probably sold to China.[10]

Germany

The Germans wanted a tactical data system for the *Adams*-class destroyers they acquired in the 1970s. Plans initially called for six ships, all to be built in Germany with German-built equipment (hence probably with SENIT 2). When the program was cut to three, it was decided that all would be built in the United States, hence would have U.S.-supplied hardware.[11] The German officer in charge of building them was favorably impressed with the NTDS system then being developed for the *Belknap* class. Like others who adopted U.S. hardware, German officers wrote the software for the system, SATIR (System zur Auswertung Taktischer Informationen auf Raketenzerstoren [System for Processing Tactical Information on Missile Destroyers]), at the U.S. naval programming center at San Diego. Like SENIT 2, SATIR initially used the USQ-20B computer (later it was upgraded with UYK-7). In 1969 the Germans opened their own programming center. It developed a version for their next surface combatants, the *Bremen*-class frigates (equivalent to the Dutch "standard" class). Unlike the French and the Italians, the Germans continued to use U.S. computers for their next classes of surface combatants, the last being SATIR III, in the *Brandenburg* (F123) class, using UYK-43, the last of the U.S. shipboard mil-spec computers. Their SATIR-1 data link was Link 11.

Unlike the United States, Britain, or France, Germany was concerned mainly with antiship warfare in narrow seas. How could missile boats work with larger ships there, without risking mutual destruction? The solution had to be a shared tactical picture. The Germans automated their MHQ at Murwik. Work began in 1972, and the basic system was ready in 1980. It could handle forty plots per second.

Sources for its picture included shore radars, aircraft, and ships. Beside ships, Murwick controlled Tornado strike aircraft. It was up to Murwik to ensure that they attacked the right targets. Murwick controlled deployed strike boats via a special lightweight Link 11 terminal ("Mickey Link") developed specially by Collins Radio (the Link 11 equipment maker) for German small attack craft using aircraft radio technology. When it entered service in 1976, few of the world's frigates had computer combat direction systems.

Moore's Law helped. A powerful new AYK-10 (Univac 1830) computer, which was being adopted for the S-3 antisubmarine airplane, could fit on board a missile attack boat. It could receive and display the tactical picture developed at Murwick. Flotilla leaders had full two-way Link 11 capability, in a three-computer system (Link 11, tactical picture keeping, and weapon control) called AGIS (Automatische Gefechts und Informations-system Schnellboote [Automatic Combat Evaluation and Weapons-control System]). Lesser units received the one-way PALIS (Passiv-Aktiv-Link-Lage-Informationssystem [Passive-Active Link Information System]). Beside fast attack craft, PALIS was installed on board older German destroyers (*Hamburg* class) and in mine craft.

Italy

The Italian derivative of NTDS was SADOC (Systema Dirizione della Operazioni di Combattimento [System for Combat Direction]), for *Andrea Doria*–class missile cruisers roughly equivalent to the U.S. *Leahy* class. NTDS systems for these cruisers were developed in the early 1960s. Installation of SADOC may explain why these ships, laid down in 1958, were completed only in 1964. Like the French, the Italians then developed a version using their own hardware, including a new picture-keeping computer comparable to, but slightly faster than, the U.S. UYK-7 used in second-generation NTDS systems. This SADOC 2 used a second computer for digital weapon direction. The picture was displayed on a unique three-operator horizontal command (summary) console. It was used to designate targets and for navigation, maneuvering, and ASW operations. SADOC 2 was first installed on board two upgraded *Impavido*-class missile destroyers, under the 1974–75 and 1976–77 budgets. It was also installed on board Italian *Lupo*- and *Maestrale*-class frigates in 1978—and on board *Lupo*-class frigates and *Wadi Mragh*–class corvettes exported to Ecuador, Iraq (which never used them), Peru, and Venezuela. The system was also sold to China, India, and Taiwan.[12]

Other NTDS-like Systems: Japan and Spain

NTDS hardware and concepts were exported to Japan at about the same time as to major European allies. The Japanese began with an integrated data system (NYYA-1), built around a single U.S.-type CP-642B computer, which was probably comparable to SSCDS. The successor weapons-entry system (OYQ-1 and 2) added an auxiliary UYK-20 computer, presumably as a WDS equivalent. A helicopter destroyer system (OYQ-3) added Link 11, using an additional UYK-20 computer. It was described as a tactical data processing system (TDPS). Japan adopted a rough equivalent of the U.S. Junior Participating Tactical Data System (OYQ-4) for missile destroyers completed from 1982 on, that is, somewhat later than the U.S. system. This system used a separate computer for missile fire control. Like JPTDS, it did not handle underwater warfare. Roughly parallel to OYQ-4 was a simple track keeper (OYQ-5) to replace NYYA-1 on board nonmissile ships. OYQ-7, a full combat direction system integrating track keeping and weapon control, finally appeared in 1987 aboard modernized helicopter destroyers and new destroyers and frigates. Follow-on systems introduced a few years later finally replaced the UYK-7 computer of OYQ-4 with the last U.S. mil-spec naval computer, UYK-43, supplemented by the UYK-44 minicomputer. All of these developments roughly paralleled those in the U.S. Navy, but all were several years later. OYQ-8 was the Japanese equivalent to the U.S. Aegis system with the newer computer.

Spain developed an NTDS equivalent under the designation Tritan specifically for the carrier *Principe de Asturias* (a version of the abortive U.S. Sea Control Ship) and her consorts, the *Baleares*-class missile frigates. The frigates had been built without digital combat systems. Tritan-1, for the *Baleares* class, uses the UYK-20 minicomputer and can handle sixty-four tracks. Tritan-2, for the carrier and the last two *Perry*-class frigates (*Santa Maria* class), uses a UYK-7 and has greater capacity. Both systems can handle Link 11, as can the system on board Spanish *Perry*-class frigates.

Canada

Canadian government dithering wiped out the lead created in the early 1950s. Thus 1955 plans for a follow-on to the Digital Automatic Tracking and Remoting (DATAR) system for the new *St. Laurent* (DDE 205)–class frigates were abandoned as unaffordable; better to rely on U.S. or British developments. In 1960 the Canadian naval staff rejected a proposal to develop an automated tactical data system for the follow-on *Restigouche* (DDE-257) class.[13] Instead, the Canadians joined the SSCDS project in 1961. They were unhappy with the U.S. approach, arguing that an ASW system should generate search and attack plans and screening recommendations. The U.S. developers considered computer capacity insufficient for that, and the Canadians dropped out.[14] Another opportunity for a new Canadian system died in 1964 with a proposed general purpose frigate, which would have been armed with Tartar. In 1970 a Canadian commented that its command system probably would have failed because its computer would have had only 32,000 words of memory.[15]

Canadians advocating a home-grown command system were rewarded in 1965 with a study contract to develop a command system for the projected FHE-400 hydrofoil escort. Its prototype was demonstrated in 1967 and delivered in 1968 as the Marine Tactical Data System (MARTADS) trainer.[16] This project placed Litton Industries Data Systems Division in position to win the 1966 contract to develop the CCS-280 command system for the "Tribal" class. Its L-304F central computer was used in the U.S. E-2C radar airplane, but not in any version of NTDS. Litton had not been involved in either ADAWS or in NTDS. However, Stanley Knights, the veteran of DATAR and NTDS, was very much involved in CCS-280. It could store 60 real tracks (30 internally generated), 140 artificial tracks (lines, reference points, etc.), and history points on 60 tracks. Functions included the tactical advice (e.g., suggested submarine searches and helicopter flight patterns) the Canadians had wanted in 1960. CCS-280 supported Links 11 and 14, so the ships could operate with their U.S. counterparts. More important, CCS-280 convinced the Canadians that they could (and perhaps should) develop their own combat direction systems. The next Canadian system, the revolutionary Shipboard Integrated Processing and Display System (SHINPADS), will be discussed in chapter 13.

In the 1970s the Canadians had four linkable "Tribals" and a mass of modern frigates without command systems, hence without data links. The same applied to the new *Protecteur*-class replenishment ships, which might have a command role. However, existing ships were not worth tearing apart to install major command systems. Moore's Law solved the problem. Litton developed a simple Advanced Data Link Information Processing System (ADLIPS) computer track keeper, which could receive and display Link 11 data, so that they could work effectively with other ships. ADLIPS did not handle weaponry. It attracted no customers outside Canada, even after the United States began transferring non-NTDS *Knox*-class frigates to foreign customers who presumably might have wanted some data link capability in their ships. Probably these navies did not appreciate the value of tactical networking.

The Netherlands

The Royal Navy brought the Dutch into the computer combat direction world. About 1962 the British hoped the Dutch would join them to develop a next-generation ADAWS, using the new Dutch Broomstick radar to control their Sea Dart missile. The connection with the British convinced the Dutch to adopt twenty-four-bit computers. A few HSA (Signaal) personnel were placed at the British ASWE establishment developing ADA (1963–67). In 1963 the Royal Netherlands Navy (RNLN) assigned two officers to the NATO B2 project. The Dutch became interested in Link 13 as a less expensive alternative to Link 11.

The connection began to collapse in 1964. The Dutch decided to adopt the U.S. Tartar missile instead of Sea Dart, and the British dropped Broomstick. The Dutch began to develop their own *Tromp*-class missile frigate, for which they wanted a fully Dutch system. To support that project, in 1967 the RNLN sent two of its personnel to the NTDS Programming Course for training. (They switched to the German NTDS course when that was set up in 1969.) These trainees were intended as the core of a Dutch naval programming center.

The *Tromp* system was called SEWACO (Sensor, Weapon, Control). Like the French ships with powerful three-dimensional radars, it had to detect targets automatically to cope with a flood of data. As developer, Signaal apparently had an export version in mind from the beginning. It already supplied many navies with radar fire-control systems. Thus, SEWACO was built around a common core (about 75 percent of software modules and tactical-picture elements). Common software made for compatible performance: all versions had a capacity of 225 point tracks (objects whose range and bearing were both known) and thirty bearing tracks electronic support measures (ESM, passive sonar, and visual bearings). All versions used one of two variants of the same basic computer, SMR or the smaller SMR-S. The *Tromp*-class had gateways between Link X and Link 11.[17]

Systems Derived from Weapon Control

Weapon control systems became short-range combat systems when their surface search radars were upgraded to track-while-scan by adding a digital memory. The U.S. example was Mk 86. European equivalents were developed by Signaal in the Netherlands (the W20 "egg"), by Thomson-CSF in France (the Vega small-ship system by Selenia in Italy (NA 10), by Philips in Sweden (9LV), by Oerlikon in Switzerland (Sea Hunter), and by Marconi in the United Kingdom (Sapphire). Moore's Law made it virtually inevitable that navies would receive digital track keepers. It was not at all inevitable that they would take the next step and link ships digitally.

The Dutch developed a Mini-Combat System, apparently specifically for German missile boats, using a standard SEWACO horizontal tactical display showing mainly surface contacts. Fire control and track management shared a SEWACO-type central computer in a weapons control console. In the expanded (Compact) version, the computer fed two or three horizontal displays.[18]

The Italians never exported a small-ship combat system. However, NA-10 was probably the basis of the Israeli Gabriel missile fire-control system and thus of the initial combat system of Israeli missile boats. First-generation Israeli boats (Sa'ar 2 and 3 types) apparently had a three-man combat system console but no separate digital combat direction system. Then the Israelis added a separate Automatic Tracking Computer (ATC) that could, among other things, maintain twenty tracks, ten of them from the boat's own search radar. A second computer could service a data link. This combination probably incorporated some NA-10 technology, such as the plot extractor/tracker and the multiweapon calculator. The next step was to supplement the three-man combat system console with a four-man electronic warfare (EW) console, a search radar operator's console, and a manual surface plotting table. The follow-on Naval Tactical Command and Control System (NTCCS) probably appeared in the late 1970s. Reportedly, it was originally built around a U.S. UYK-20 computer, which received digital radar data and was connected to a separate data link unit (SACU). Later versions have considerably more powerful computers, but they still reflect their missile boat origins. The *Eilat* (Sa'ar 5) class introduced a completely new combat system using a distributed architecture, unrelated to the earlier fire-control systems.

The Swiss system was bought only for four Iranian frigates, controlling the Sea Killer antiship missile.

STRIL and Nordic Coast Defense

Sweden developed another kind of system, centered on coast defense. Neutrality required that major systems be developed at home, so Swedish technology could be exported relatively freely to countries such as Yugoslavia, with ambivalent Cold War status. About 1962 the Royal Swedish Air Force fielded a version of its J-35 Draken interceptor, which was said to be integrated with its STRIL national air defense command and control system (broadly equivalent to SAGE), presumably meaning that it had the requisite data link. Roughly contemporary with STRIL was the STRIKA national coast defense command and control system. Given the STRIL philosophy, STRIKA envisaged using a combination of fixed defenses (mainly guns, but some missiles) and mobile interceptors (missile boats) cued by data links. Given the rudimentary character of the link, and navigational inaccuracies in a pre-Global Position System (GPS) age, STRIKA did not support true over-the-horizon targeting. The shipboard receiving end of the system was a combat system built up from a digital version of the 9LV fire-control system designed to meet a 1968 Royal Swedish Navy requirement. Mk 1 was hardwired; Mk 2 was a programmable digital system equivalent to the Dutch WM series. Parallel to the fire-control system was an electronic plotting system (EPLO), which in minimum form was built around a horizontal display similar to that of the Dutch minicombat systems. Both 9LV200 Mk 1 and EPLO entered service in 1973 on board the Swedish *Norkopping* class.[19] The next generation Command Electronic Plotting System (CEPLO) was announced in 1975. The *C* prefix probably indicated a data link.[20]

The STRIKA data link was also used in the Philips system of air traffic control at Stockholm Airport (the Swedes sold the system to the Soviets for use in Leningrad). Danes used to joke that the Soviets would have no trouble with the unencrypted Swedish link in wartime; they could read it themselves. (Their own link was an encrypted version.)

Missile boats the Swedes sold for export probably incorporated data links integrating them with larger coast defense systems modeled on STRIKA.[21] Unfortunately, sales of coast defense systems (as opposed to particular weapons) are poorly documented. The obvious candidate is Yugoslavia because it bought not only Swedish boats but also land-based Swedish RBS 15 missiles, which would have been part of a larger coast defense system—a category of military technology the Yugoslavs had embraced in the past.

Denmark bought CEPLO and probably also STRIKA. There was no attempt to integrate the Danish system with the German one at Murwick across the Baltic (or, for that matter, with the Swedish system across the Sound). Instead, the German tactical picture was passed by land line to Danish naval headquarters for further transmission via Danish links. Denmark did not buy Link 11 until the Royal Danish Navy was assigned to work with the U.S. and other NATO navies in the course of the 1990–91 Gulf crisis and war.

What Did It Mean?

There is a radical difference between a networked attack against a nonnetworked enemy and net-on-net combat. Clearly major NATO navies understood the value of computer combat systems. Most of them also understood the value of data links. As for the others, by 1970 not only was it relatively easy to computerize ships, but also virtually all frigates on offer for export embodied computer combat systems. After 1971 only one major Western-oriented navy, the Chilean, seems to have been willing to buy nonautomated frigates (Chilean *Leanders*). At least one company,

Plessey, developed its own system, Nautis, to service the demand it expected. Ferranti, which was responsible for British naval systems, set up joint ventures in both Brazil and Chile to develop semi-indigenous systems, both of which became operational. The message that a ship's own systems had to be netted seems to have been understood fairly widely.

The other message, that ships should be netted to each other, seems not to have sold nearly as well. During the early 1990s, the U.S. Navy sponsored development of a one-way equivalent to Link 11 called Link America, which could run on a computer equivalent to an IBM PC. The hope was that Latin American navies that had joined the U.S. Navy in the war against drugs would share the U.S.-supplied tactical picture. To American surprise, the navies in question rejected Link America in favor of a much simpler high-interest target (HITS) technique, in which a central control indicated which ships to board. From a netted perspective, Link America should have been preferable; it would have allowed a ship's commander to know, for example, which of three adjacent ships to board. HITS would not even indicate that there were three ships among which to choose. It is also suggestive that only in about 2003 did the Indian navy, which had long used computer tactical data systems, seek a ship-to-ship net.

CHAPTER 11

Fleet Netting in Action: Vietnam and After

The Vietnam War, particularly the carrier air war conducted off the coast of North Vietnam (and over that country), was the first test of the new digital command and control technology. It demonstrated both the power of the new ideas and their unsuspected limitations. About four decades later, these operations are still the most difficult U.S. aircraft have faced, in terms of the numbers involved and the intensity of the combat. The Vietnam experience shaped the further development of automated combat systems.

Positive Identification Radar Advisory Zone

Vietnam was a confusing new kind of war, fought in the presence of large numbers of neutrals. For example, airliners regularly flew over the Tonkin Gulf en route between major Asian capitals. How could a fleet preserve its ability to fend off air attack without risking attacks on the airliners? Most of the airplanes over the Gulf of Tonkin at any one time were friendly, so the problem of disentangling the air picture merged with that of avoiding attacks on airliners.[1] As the fleet moved north to launch strikes against North Vietnam, it moved closer to possible air attack. Possible warning time shortened. Yet the fleet could not maintain large numbers of interceptors on station, where they would not contribute to the war against North Vietnam. It was also vital to keep China out of the war. Given their limited navigational capabilities, aircraft needed ship control to keep them out of no-fly zones.

All of these roles translated into the need for a good-enough air picture—a classic radar picket role. Having considered the problem from April 1966 on, on 16 July 1966, Pacific Fleet set up a Positive Identification Radar Advisory Zone (PIRAZ) in the Tonkin Gulf, centered on a picket ship.[2] From 7 November all U.S. aircraft operating over the Gulf were subject to PIRAZ procedures. The name indicated a zone in which aircraft were positively identified and, to an extent, controlled ("radar advisory zone"). To support fleet air defense for Task Force 77, all aircraft in the PIRAZ zone had to be identified and continuously tracked. Given the experience of intense kamikaze attacks off Okinawa in 1945, it was understood that the picket needed adequate antiaircraft armament. Later it turned out that the more significant threat was surface attack, and ships on PIRAZ duty were generally accompanied by a destroyer with a five-inch battery.[3]

PIRAZ was both a ship and a geographical reference point (indicated by a radar buoy) in the Tonkin Gulf; sometimes it was referred to by its Red Crown call sign. Each carrier strike passed over the PIRAZ ship. The ship identified each aircraft in the strike, assigned it a track number, and tracked it to the target and back. That prevented the North Vietnamese from inserting their own aircraft into or near a returning formation. When the Japanese tried to do that late in World War II, special U.S. fighter units ("Tomcats") were assigned to examine returning strikes visually to pick off intruders. In the Gulf there were far too few aircraft to provide such services, but the PIRAZ ship could distinguish the strike aircraft she had been tracking from intruders. Having identified a questionable contact, the ship could vector a fighter to it. Also, because she was tracking each airplane separately, the PIRAZ ship was aware of the position at which it might have ditched, and hence could vector rescue helicopters. Through 1967 the potential of the PIRAZ ship came to be appreciated more and more. Additional services were requested. For example, Seventh Air Force wanted the ship to take control of tankers over the Gulf. Seventh Fleet refused: the ships' Combat Information Centers (CICs) were already heavily loaded.[4]

When the non-Naval Tactical Data System (NTDS) cruiser *Topeka* was tested in a proto-PIRAZ role in April 1966, her CIC was quickly saturated: NTDS was a prerequisite. Unfortunately, Seventh Fleet had only two NTDS ships, the cruiser *Chicago* and the missile "frigate" (large destroyer, DLG) *King*. *Chicago* became the first PIRAZ ship.

North Vietnamese air activity increased sharply in mid-April 1967. The PIRAZ ship was well placed to listen to North Vietnamese communications and thus to warn U.S. aircraft; on average she handled thirty-five MiG warnings each week. To ease the load, the cruiser *Long Beach* tested a concept in which a second NTDS ship, the strike support ship (SSS), well to the north of the PIRAZ ship, provided warning and control and controlled tankers joining U.S. Navy aircraft. That freed the PIRAZ ship for surveillance and early warning and also for services required by the Air Force. The SSS ship also served as backup for the PIRAZ ship. Tested from June through September 1967, SSS was permanently established on 10 October. It became feasible as the number of Seventh Fleet NTDS ships grew. In November 1967 CinCPacFleet asked chief of naval operations (CNO) to maintain four PIRAZ/

SSS-capable ships in the Western Pacific at all times. Requirements included automatic "identification of friend or foe" (IFF) interrogation.

By February 1967 merely controlling air traffic over an increasingly congested Gulf was becoming a serious problem. Ships lacked the communication capacity to maintain en route traffic control. A Joint Chiefs of Staff (JCS) team visiting Vietnam in 1967 concluded that if the three services' air control nets could be combined, commanders would have an air picture covering the whole area of operations. The JCS ordered the necessary gateways created on a crash basis. The Naval Electronics Command (NELC) was assigned to develop the necessary communications buffer. The Marines already operated the Beach Relay buffer to connect their land system and NTDS. Now a connection with the Air Force serial link was added. Beach Relay translated the Air Force picture into Link 11 format, and vice versa. Some netting predated the JCS decision. Beginning on 23 February 1967 the PIRAZ ship was connected to the Air Force's Big Eye airborne control aircraft via an encrypted ultrahigh frequency (UHF) voice circuit. The existing Marine air-control facility (Monkey Mountain, Danang) joined the Tonkin Gulf Link 11 net on 12 July 1967. The interface between the Air Force SEEK DAWN radar net and the Link 11 created the Southeast Asia Tactical Data System (SEATDS). By 1969 there were also special intelligence nets. The nets in the Gulf were coordinated by an encrypted UHF voice circuit, "Air Force Green," relayed by an Air Force KC-135 flying over the Gulf. This circuit connected the watch officer on board every picket or search and rescue (SAR) unit in the Gulf with the watch officer on board the Yankee Station flagship, so that any emergency situation could receive immediate command attention. Tonkin Gulf air control was probably the first U.S. example of operational network-centric warfare.

Air search radar on ships in the Gulf saw deep into North Vietnam. Such radar could, for example, track North Vietnamese fighters trying to intercept American bombers. Because NTDS had been conceived for fighter control, the system could vector U.S. fighters against the North Vietnamese. The first success came on 9 October 1966, when USS King vectored an F-8E from Oriskany to shoot down a MiG-21, the first such aircraft shot down by a U.S. Navy fighter. One enlisted air controller on the cruiser USS Chicago, Senior Chief Radarman Larry B. Novell, received a Distinguished Service Medal (DSM) for arranging twelve "kills" in this way.

The ships also used their own missiles. USS Long Beach shot down two MiGs with her Talos missiles while on PIRAZ duty. Successes came despite fear that the tactical picture used by the missile shooters was unreliable; they might well shoot down U.S. aircraft, particularly if most aircraft in the air at any one time were friendly.[5] There was also fear that firing weapons into North Vietnam might compromise missile system technology.[6] By 1972 the combination of long-range radar, computer, and missiles was considered so reliable that USS *Chicago* was primary protector of carrier aircraft mining Haiphong Harbor. Her tactical picture was considered reliable enough that she would surely destroy MiGs trying to interfere rather than aircraft laying mines.[7]

When the United States resumed large-scale air raids against the North in April 1972, the PIRAZ ships were far better prepared than they had been in 1967–68. They proved quite successful. They warned of MiG attacks (PIRAZ was responsible for more than half the thirty-four Air Force MiG kills in April–September 1972), controlled CAP, and joined escorts to strikes as required. PIRAZ also supported Air Force B-52 strikes.

Netted Intelligence

The Vietnam experience seems to have caused a drastic change in the way signal intelligence (SIGINT) was treated by the U.S. Navy. By the 1960s, SIGINT detachments on ships were considered primarily a way of collecting sensitive information for later analysis and to build capabilities that might much later have operational value. Each detachment also supported the ship's commander. For example, the detachment aboard the destroyer *Maddox* warned that North Vietnamese torpedo boats were about to attack during the 1964 Tonkin Gulf incident. That was a distinctly secondary role.[8]

As the British Y-Service experience in World War II showed, correlating a wide range of enemy emissions offered important tactical warnings, such as indicating that air attacks were imminent. By 1969 SIGINT officers in the fleet were well aware of this possibility, but they also knew that the few operators on any individual ship could not possibly monitor enough North Vietnamese circuits to provide such information. There was neither space nor personnel on any one ship to do more. Based on a suggestion from one of the detachments at sea, Pacific Fleet ordered the detachments on different ships linked, so that together they could monitor enough circuits: [typically, two carriers, PIRAZ, and a destroyer or DLG on SAR duty in the Tonkin Gulf.] Combining their detachments quadrupled coverage. It made sense to add an airborne SIGINT collector (Big Look). The airplane had to be modified with a new covered circuit compatible with those on board the ships. Big Look offered an unexpected advantage: now the network could simultaneously observe the interior of North Vietnam and the coast in real time. To keep linkage timely, new covered voice circuits were added. Ultimately the net included in-country radar; mixing active and passive and electronic intelligence (ELINT) sensors. The naval net exchanged tracks with a parallel Air Force net, presumably created at about the same time. The net could make intelligent use of information already collected by

SIGINT systems, and it could make those controlling national SIGINT systems aware of the fleet's needs.

Results were spectacular. For example, the net provided B-52s with warning that MiGs were flying to intercept them. The great lesson was that the fruits of SIGINT collation could be used tactically without compromising SIGINT itself. In the past, SIGINT information had rarely been used operationally for fear of compromising that very special source, which the enemy could shut down. Using the sanitized product of a mass of different SIGINT sources was a very different proposition. The enemy could not backtrack to identify any one U.S. action with a particular source.

This successful experiment illustrated a key network-centric principle. Often the information that commanders need has already been collected for some other purpose. The real problem may be to unearth it, rather than to develop some new way of reacquiring it. To do that, it is necessary to change the way in which information is structured. Information is typically categorized by the way it is collected, for example, ELINT using some particular system, bought to support some large-scale program—and not for the particular tactical requirement at hand. The Vietnam experiment showed that combining the fruits of stovepiped programs could produce valuable tactical intelligence. Ideally, the larger-scale systems should be steerable to meet the needs of the tactical commander. Tactical situations are far too fluid to use the preprogramming typically associated with large intelligence-gathering systems.

The Vietnam experience was apparently influential. In about 1973–74 Sixth Fleet adopted a similar concept for operational management of signals exploitation assets: they were all controlled and coordinated in real time. That made it possible to assign limited SIGINT collection facilities to the highest priority targets in real time to avoid duplication, assuring broad cover of Soviet C3.[9] SIGINT became a fleet *operational* sensor, on a fleet-wide netted basis.

CHAPTER 12

Intraship Netting: ASMD

y the early 1960s, U.S. warships faced the threat of low-flying missiles, which
might not be detected at all until they crossed the horizon less than twenty
nautical miles from a ship. Warning time might be as long as about four
minutes—or as short as about thirty seconds. Reaction time became far more
important. Would system operators have enough time to decide to fire? It seemed
likely that the Soviets would provide antiship missiles for North Vietnamese coast
defense. The Office of the Chief of Naval Operations (OpNav) established an ad hoc
committee in 1966.[1] A Fleet Anti-Missile Defense Executive Committee followed in
June 1967 to establish both immediate and long-term programs. Its work became
even more urgent when the Israeli destroyer *Eilat* was sunk by Soviet-supplied
Egyptian missiles in October 1967. These committees were the first to realize that
existing manual command systems could not react quickly enough. What could
be done with ships too small for the Naval Tactical Data System (NTDS)? A Ships
Anti-Missile Integrated Defense (SAMID) office was established in July 1967.[2]
Note that all of this came before Egyptian missile boats sank the Israeli destroyer
Eilat with Soviet-supplied Styx missiles, in the first such attack. The following year
the secretary of the Navy's Office of Program Appraisal produced a formal study
of antiship missile defense (ASMD) weapons, tactics, and combat direction. Initial
tactical trials were conducted by Cruiser-Destroyer Flotilla Eleven.[3]

An incoming missile was a difficult target with a very small radar cross section.
A conventional system handed a target from a search radar to a narrower-beam
tracker, which searched again to acquire it. The new idea was to net all radars on
a ship together, so that if any of them detected the target, the system could react
immediately. Thus missile control radar (SPG-51 and 55) was given horizon search/
sector scan capability. System developers also thought that humans would react
too slowly, so they reversed the NTDS philosophy. Instead of initiating reaction, a

human decision maker would be limited to vetoing what the system began doing. Human operators disliked this idea, so commanding officers tended not to operate their systems in automatic mode. (The designers had to provide a semiautomatic, that is, human-initiated, option.)

SAMID devised what amounted to a combat direction system tailored to short-range missile engagements. The three main sources of information were the fire-control system(s) scanning the horizon and two electronic warfare (EW) elements, a specialized threat receiver (to recognize preset threats) and the SLD-1 EW direction finder.[4] Presetting was possible because the system was designed to deal with only three threats: the Soviet-made Styx (SS-N-2), Samlet (SS-C-1), and Shaddock (SS-N-3). Styx was the boat-launched antiship missile (Soviet P-15). Samlet was a standard coast defense missile, the surface-launched equivalent of the air-launched AS-1. Shaddock was the major Soviet long-range antiship missile, but it was also used for coast defense. Thus SAMID converted electronic support measures (ESM, passive monitoring of enemy radar emissions) into a search sensor capable of triggering reactions. Alternatives to electronic warfare identification were evaluation of a radar track to meet criteria established by the ship's evaluator console operator. Alternatively, the operator might designate tracks as antiship cruise missiles.

The core of the system was an evaluator station linked to a weapon control station in the Combat Information Center (CIC) Display and Decision area. It received sensor data and could directly activate passive electronic search sensors to amplify other data. It could directly activate the ship's jammer, and it could fire weapons and chaff via the ship's existing weapons control station in CIC. Electronic countermeasures (ECM) were now considered coequal with hard kill, so chaff launchers and jammers were functionally integrated with missile and gun fire-control systems. All of this required a digital computer. For non-NTDS ships (Fleet Rehabilitation and Modernisation program FRAM Is and *Adams*-class missile destroyers), that was the Digital Data Correlation and Transfer System (DATACORTS) built around a CP-967 digital computer, made possible by Moore's Law. It was impractical to tear up ships to create integrated digital systems, so the system sent information mainly via synchros (for bearing) and discrete signals setting relays that turned on lights on panels. That was good enough to perform fire control against particular types of missiles headed directly at a ship.

For a single attacker, the system was expected to cut reaction time from a hundred to about twenty-five seconds. A manual system would be swamped by two attackers, but DATACORTS would probably manage about a twenty-eight-second reaction time against five simultaneous attackers. It could handle up to fifty targets, about a fifth of NTDS capacity. DATACORTS could automatically accept and use Link 14 data, but it offered no digital link to other ships. The system was conceived to exploit existing analog sensor and fire-control systems aboard the FRAM I and *Adams* classes. For a DDG, DATACORTS in effect competed with the Junior Participating Tactical Data System (JPTDS) already developed but not funded for production. FRAM *Gearings* had the stations installed in modularized form because they lacked CIC volume.

The evaluator console operator set the level of automation to manual, semi-automatic (ship weapons control [SWC] center accepts or rejects designation), or fully automatic (QR, Quick Response). The SAMID evaluator also set ASMD zones, which helped the system decide whether an incoming target should be engaged.[5] In fully automatic mode, the system reacted automatically (reflexively) to ESM identifying a particular threat: the ESM station would alert (with designated bearing) fire control, chaff launcher, and jammer. Fire-control systems would begin sector search around the designated bearing, to lock on and react. If the system was being saturated, the command had to decide whether to switch weapon or chaff or jammer to the new threat.

NTDS ships already had evaluation and weapon-control stations. They gained a third NTDS computer that could run the SAMID program module (AMW, anti-missile warfare) whatever else their NTDS systems were doing. *Sterrett* was the first ship with the additional computer. In AMW mode the combat system limited itself to two weapon systems: missiles and electronic warfare. It automatically assigned weapons, decoys, and jammers to targets.[6] Each potential sensor station was fitted with an audio-visual alarm panel (AVAP) with which ASMD-related functions could be activated: each target designation transmitter (TDT), each fire-control system station, and the ASW sensor space (sonar became an ASMD sensor). The Mk 68 gun fire-control system was modified so that it could generate an ASCM alert and provide a target position to the combat direction system. Replacing its analog computer with a digital unit added guns to the AMW system.

As in the non-NTDS ships, missile-control radar was given quick-detection search modes.[7] Clutter suppression improved surface search radar low-altitude performance. It was given an automatic audible alarm and a bearing strobe to indicate targets with specific parameters. Ships were fitted with a new ESM set.[8] It could automatically detect, analyze, and classify a series of predefined missile threats.[9] A new Comprehensive Display System (CDS)/EW interface rapidly transferred data from the combat direction system to the EW system, automatically controlling that system and designating threats to it. However, ships fitted with the later SLQ-32 instead of the earlier ULQ-6 jammer had no rapid-transfer interface and lacked the automatic designation feature.

Sonar was recognized as a potential ASMD sensor because it could detect missile-shooting craft beyond the ship's horizon ("under the horizon"). Thus a new director data interface connected the ASW system and the combat direction system. Some cruisers had an improved sonar system (PAIR) offering computer-assisted digital processing, integrating active and passive detection, and connecting to the Mk 111 or Mk 114 underwater battery fire-control system and to the combat direction system. The combat direction system could provide the sonar operator with up to eight tracks, allowing him to pay more attention to hostile targets otherwise unavailable to the combat direction system. In turn, the sonar operator could provide up to four tracks to the combat direction system.

By mid-1968 plans called for one missile ship and two *Gearing* packages per month beginning in January 1969, for a total of twenty: four *Belknap*, three later (DDG 15) *Adams*, and thirteen FRAM *Gearings*, the worst-protected of all. All three versions were tested between October 1968 and February 1969, using jet aircraft and small craft to simulate missiles and Soviet-supplied KOMAR-type missile boats. Dramatic improvements were claimed, both in detection time (using search and fire-control radar as well as ESM) and in overall reaction time.[10] *Jouett* (DLG, later CG, 29) the NTDS prototype, completed her tests on 1 March 1969, well ahead of schedule. Her fire-control radar was modified for both horizon scan/sector search mode and for boat track mode (to track a small missile boat). The manager of the ship's Terrier missile system planned additional modifications to improve short-range performance (Project Custer).[11]

Given test results, in 1970 the SAMID office announced a more sophisticated near-term package for the 1970, 1971, and 1972 programs, to handle a wider variety of threats, and to protect a wider variety of ships. Thus the nine-ship 1970 program included two non-NTDS carriers; the 1971 program added seventeen more. Plans for modifying 250 ships by FY77 were dropped at the end of the war.[12] ASMD money financed at least two of four DDG JPTDS installations: quick responses required a high degree of combat system integration.

Ironically, it is not clear that the Soviets had ever supplied antiship missiles to the North Vietnamese before 1972. The major example of damage they inflicted on a U.S. warship offshore was a bomb dropped by a MiG on the destroyer *Higbee* (which was a SAMID ship, as it happened).

CHAPTER 13

Crisis and Transformation

The Naval Tactical Data System (NTDS) was a victim of its own success. As more and more functions were added, the system ran slower and slower, to the point where the picture on its computers was no longer close enough to reality. If you have a home computer, you have some idea of what happened. You may remember a time when you ran one program at a time: a word processor, perhaps, or a spreadsheet. All the power of your computer was concentrated on it. Then you found that you had to run several programs at the same time: one in the foreground, others in the background so that they could be called up as needed. Although it seemed that you now had several computers running at once, every so often it became obvious that one central processing unit (CPU) was doing only one job at a time, switching quickly between jobs. Sometimes the computer took a noticeable time to respond because it was doing something it could not instantly quit so that it could switch to another task. Waiting a bit for an image to form on the screen or for a different document to pop up may be annoying, but it is not fatal. Waiting for a computer to switch from receiving a Link 11 message to designating weapons to engage a rapidly closing missile was another matter altogether—but it had the same cause. That single computer was trying to do too many things at once.

NTDS continuously ran base functions (tracking, Link 11, and display). Meanwhile, it switched others in temporarily for particular purposes (e.g., antisubmarine warfare [ASW], electronic countermeasures [ECM], naval gunfire support [NGS], Air Control, intercept profile, Link 14). The modular structure of the software made it easy to modify. By 1970 ships' commanders normally ordered development of new modules.[1] Some argued that the resulting variety would make it more difficult for an enemy to predict U.S. tactics. Only one function could run at a time. The more modules running, the longer the time between repeats of any one function. That was unavoidable as long as computers were too massive and too expensive to be installed in such numbers that each would carry out only a few functions. For NTDS to work, local tracks had to be refreshed ten times each second. Target evaluation and weapon assignment (TEWA) had to be conducted six to twelve times per second.

For operators, the most obvious sign of overload was a flickering display because the displays showed only what the central computer broadcast to them (and had to refresh them fifteen to twenty times each second to avoid flickering). The system could register a button push for only part of its time-sharing cycle. Unless it was in the mode when it was open to console action, the system ignored whatever an operator did. Between openings, the system cycled through its modules. The heavier its load, the slower the cycle. Operators sensed the problem as the system's inability to register the operators' actions (such as the movement of a ball tab to position a cursor on the screen). For example, normally it took about three seconds to roll the ball tab from the center of the display to its edge, an example of an action required to register a target position in the computer memory. A single action could cover only a quarter of the distance, so the full movement required four cycles. In the worst case, the system might allow operator action only once every four seconds, so the full stroke from center to edge might take a totally unacceptable sixteen seconds. By the time the computer registered the motion of the ball tab and moved the cursor in response, the blip might be somewhere else. It became difficult for an operator to "hook" a target using the bell tab. Some important functions (such as Quick Reaction) required double button pushes. Again, unless the system was open to button pushes, it would ignore them. If the operator depressed the "QR" button more than once during a cycle, only the first push counted. Often operators did not realize that the second push had not registered. They kept pushing buttons in hopes that some pushes would register. Each push that got through took up CPU time and further slowed the system. Tests showed delays as long as sixty-eight seconds for button actions, such as engage missile or engage interceptor. The system was designed to handle ten operator actions per second, with 100 microseconds between interrogations. Although that was insufficient for real-time operation (fifteen to twenty were desirable), it could not be achieved. A solution (circa 1970) was to draw out the effect of pushing a button so that it might coincide with a button-receiving cycle. Unfortunately, some operations required sequences of button pushes. Sometimes the computer did not notice that the sequence was wrong because it did not distinguish the two pushes.

Possibly because the system did not respond properly to operator inputs, tracking was often poor. In 1973–74 tests, 18 to 46 percent of hostiles detected by radar (which detected 90 percent of potential targets) were not entered into the NTDS computer—which was still significantly better than for non-NTDS ships. At any one time, 15 to 25 percent of NTDS symbols (indicating where the computer thought targets were) did not correspond to target video, that is, were at least five nautical miles from the locations indicated by the video. On average, symbols were four nautical miles from the corresponding video (i.e., from what radar saw). The average delay from the first appearance of a target on video to a firm track was 3.3 minutes. The average time a target was *not* tracked (from detection to when it flew overhead or was successfully engaged) was 3.2 minutes. In tests, as the track load increased, console actions actually tailed off because operators could not get their actions through to the computer any faster.

By the late 1970s, it seemed that NTDS had reached its limit. It was plagued by navigational errors (gridlock errors). Units that misreported their positions in the force grid reported tracks that did not correspond to those seen by other ships, so many targets were double counted. A single ship could generate double tracks when she lost and reacquired a target owing to either a radar fade or a computer crash. Misaligned sensors on board a ship (an example cited was the beacon video processor and the automatically detecting SPS-48 radar) caused similar double counts. The fairly ancient system computers (CP-642) were already badly overloaded; the more tracks they carried, the slower they ran.[2] New automatic detection radars (on board ships and on board the E-2C) could not be used fully because other net members would have been swamped by the data they produced.

Worse, NTDS had to deal with more, not less, complicated situations. Operating in places like the Gulf and the Indian Ocean, the U.S. Navy had to deal with neutrals and a host of semineutrals or semihostiles. The automatic "identification of friend or foe" (IFF) tracking that had reduced the operator load in the Tonkin Gulf was nearly useless. Meanwhile, ships were receiving new systems, such as an Antisubmarine Warfare Control System (ASWCS) and the LAMPS III helicopter, whose radar and electronic support measures (ESM) systems were intended to feed directly onto a ship via data link. The coming Tomahawk missile required a Common Weapon Control System (CWCS) taking data both from a satellite link and from NTDS. The situation would become more confusing if, as proposed, CWCS also controlled the Harpoon missile. There was continuing interest in automatic electronic warfare interfaces, mainly for SLQ-32 and Outboard (a new form of high frequency/direction finder [HF/DF]). In the *Spruance* class, SLQ-32 was connected directly into an input/output channel for the electronic warfare (EW) supervisor, but in other ships data were entered manually. The more complex the tactical situation, the less acceptable such an arrangement. As an over-the-horizon (OTH) sensor, Outboard was a natural candidate for integration, particularly for a ship armed with antiship missiles. Its data were sanitized semiautomatically before being fed into NTDS. To what extent would NTDS be integrated with the coming higher-level Tactical Flag Command Centers (TFCC) system?

The personal computer world gives some idea of the Navy's options. One was simply to install a better computer, analogous to the CPU in a personal computer. Running faster, the new computer might be able to reduce delays sufficiently to keep the system running. In the late 1970s, Moore's Law was about to provide the U.S. Navy with a new family of mil-spec computers, UYK-43, to replace the UYK-7, introduced a decade earlier, and UYK-44, to replace the UYK-20 minicomputer. A new UYQ-21 series of consoles incorporated display processors that could reduce the load on the central computer. In the mid-1970s, an NTDS replacement was envisaged, using the new computers and displays plus new software: the Advanced Combat Display System (ACDS).

A second solution was to rewrite the system software in a more rational, or more modular, way. Microsoft found that it had to do just that when it replaced the Windows XP operating system with Windows Vista. The old software included a great deal of code that was no longer needed, but that slowed machines down. Microsoft system designers discovered that they could no longer improve performance by modifying what they had. Instead, they had to restructure their software and make it modular so that the machine could run only what it needed to run. The process was difficult but necessary. In 1977 the Navy announced that it would rewrite NTDS as Restructured Naval Tactical Data System (RNTDS), or Model 4.1. All modules would be standardized, communicating with the ship via an executive module, to which all other programs would connect in a standardized way. Only the executive module would be tailored to a particular ship. This approach unfortunately required still more computer capacity. Although announced in 1977, it was not completed before the introduction of UYK-43/44 computers.

The basic design of NTDS also imposed limits that no longer seemed acceptable. The 512 x 512 nautical mile display space no longer seemed adequate in the face of faster longer-ranged threats (the demand was for at least 2,000 x 2,000 nautical miles). Because the gridlock problem had not been solved, the value of netting was limited. Different sensors were difficult to align. Autotracking quality was poor, and the diverse characteristics of different autotracks made it difficult to integrate them. Link 11 no longer seemed sufficient. By 1980 it was widely agreed that the link could easily be jammed. If they were not carefully synchronized, net units could jam themselves. Switching frequencies to evade jamming might take one to eight minutes, beginning with the recognition (which was unlikely) that Link 11 was being jammed in the first place. In a 1979 exercise, 83 percent of participants received data at least once per minute, which was better than in previous exercises, but altogether unsatisfactory for combat coordination. Link performance improved when ships operated together for a protracted period, sometimes reaching 95 percent. The anti-jam Link 16 became attractive—but it needed more computer power.

With money tight in the mid-1970s and with no single organization responsible for combat direction systems, ACDS development was deferred in favor of new platforms and sensors, such as the F-14/Phoenix combination, Aegis, advanced towed arrays, and *Los Angeles*–class submarine. Few seem to have realized that the failure of core command/control would drastically reduce the value of the new systems. There may have been a feeling that better command/control could always be inserted, but that opportunities to buy the platforms would vanish.

At the end of 1979, however, the C3 Sub-Panel of the chief of naval operation's Executive Panel requested an emergency study of NTDS problems. Without any parent, there was no formal Top Level Requirement (TLR) for combat direction; no one was in charge of architecture or configuration. No one correlated changing C3 architecture with NTDS capabilities and development. New tasks were not screened to see whether they could be accommodated because no one had ever counted the cost of adding tasks. This "free lunch" attitude had ruined the system. NTDS began with fifteen functions, two data links, and a missile. In 1980 it had twenty-seven functions (added, the report said, "Band-Aid by Band-Aid"), three data links, three-dimensional radar, the beacon video processor, the ASW Module (for carriers), NATO Sea Sparrow, and the carrier air traffic control center (CATCC). As modules proliferated, computer capacity did not grow to match them. Only some of the modules aboard a ship at any given time could be run simultaneously.[2] The solution was Dynamic Modular Replacement (DMR).[3] This was the predisk era; the modules were all held on tape. The display operator called for various modules to replace those currently stored in core. The computer indicated which modules were in core and how much core remained for further ones. Programs in core could be reshuffled to leave one continuous area of memory for an incoming module. The process took seven to seventeen seconds. The more modules, the slower the system ran. Tests showed that carrier and cruiser systems running about sixty local and sixty remote (linked) tracks, about half rated capacity, with antiair warfare (AAW) functions only, were no longer quick enough.

The existing system represented so vast a sunk cost that no one was willing to redesign it. Instead, NTDS was developed to death, to meet new requirements such as Positive Identification Radar Advisory Zone (PIRAZ) and automatic detection and tracking (ADT) radar, with no effort to conduct a top-down review. The closest the Navy had come to such a review had been as part of the initial ACDS project, which had just been zeroed for FY81 and the out years. It was vital now to establish NTDS requirements for the 1985–90 time period.

The panel urged that ACDS be developed on an urgent basis and that the Joint Tactical Information Distribution System (JTIDS; Link 16) replace Link 11. It also suggested decentralizing the system to reduce the load on the central picture-keeping computer. That computer's functions should be limited functions as tightly as possible. NTDS problems came from trying to do too much with one central computer complex because it had been conceived when computers were so expensive that even a major warship could afford only one or two. For example, why maintain a file of EW parameters in the central complex? That should reside in the ship's EW system computer. Correlation of air tracks, based on dissimilar sources, would certainly be a central computer function. However, correlation of same-source tracks could be removed. (Ships were being fitted with SYS systems for this purpose.) Status reporting should be a central computer function because it would be necessary for several different functions. However, weapon status could be handled at a weapon-control console, with its own computer. Data link communication could be moved to a separate computer. Smart displays could handle user interface processing. This reduction in the load on the central computer might clear the way for some important functions that had not yet been implemented at all, such as automatic application of tactical doctrine to the tactical situation (as in the Aegis Command and Decision [C&D] computer).

Early in 1981 the improvement plan, particularly ACDS, was tentatively approved. One by-product was a regularly revised ship combat system master plan describing existing combat system deficiencies and illustrating the systems aboard each ship (with planned improvements in two time periods, the next five years and the five years after that). ACDS would begin with standard hardware (UYK-43/44, UYQ-21) and blocks of progressively improved software. Block 0, to enter service in 1986–91, would run the Restructured Naval Tactical Data System (Model 4.1) and would have new interfaces to shipboard systems. It would communicate with other ships via Link 11. Block 1 (1991–96) would begin a transition, demanded by OSD, to a new standard Defense Department programming language. It would also use Link 16. Block 2 would introduce new hardware running upgraded software (ADA).

Plans rarely go as expected. ACDS encountered severe developmental problems exacerbated by the crash in funding at the end of the Cold War. To make matters worse, the U.S. government decided to shift from using the Navy as prime contractor to using private contractors. Block contractors were chosen separately: Unisys (responsible for NTDS computers but not their software) for Block 0 and Hughes Ground Systems for Block 1. Block 0 entered service in FY87. By 1998 it was on board twelve aircraft carriers, four *Wasp* (LHD-1)-class and two *Tarawa* (LHA-1)-class amphibious assault ships. Block 0 had also been installed on board several missile cruisers and the *Kidd*-class destroyers, which had been discarded by then. By 2001 all of the major amphibious ships had Block 0. Some of the carriers retained modular NTDS software, which they ran on UYK-43 computers. Although this system was called Block 0, it had nothing in common with the RNTDS version.

Link operation was removed to a separate C2P (command and control processing) computer adapted to the new Link 16.[4] Link 16 uses different (North Atlantic Treaty Organization) target categories than Link 11, yet the same C2P must prepare information from both for insertion into the picture-keeping computer. As gateway between the Link 16 receiver and a tactical system adapted to Link 11, C2P reduced the detail offered by Link 16 to the level of Link 11 that NTDS software running on the central computer could handle. Using C2P so reduced the load on the main computer that it quadrupled track capacity and effective surveillance range; it also increased the target-insertion rate.

The more complex Block 1 (CDS software Model 5) was intended to break the centralization of the earlier NTDS systems, which ultimately limited their growth potential. It introduced the Aegis concept in which a separate command and decision processor applies decision-making (doctrinal) rules—which can be changed on board ship—to the tactical picture in the main computer. Software-embodied doctrine decides how to combine different sources of data, including OTH data, to identify tracks. The basic C&D software was a version of the Aegis Tactical Executive System (ATES). Block 1 represented the first use of artificial intelligence (in the C&D computer) to analyze the tactical situation, heightening a crew's situational awareness.

Block 1 introduced real-time distributed software, which made it possible to employ 8 tightly coupled and 248 loosely coupled nodes. Presumably the tightly coupled nodes included the main and C&D computers. Reportedly, the system tracked three times as many targets as any previous shipboard combat direction system. It had the first full implementation of Link 16 on a surface ship. It covered an unprecedentedly large operational area (4,000 x 4,000 nautical miles theater surveillance area). It was also the first U.S combat direction system to use color symbology. Compared to Block 0, Block 1 was said to offer eight times the track capacity and four times the range. However, Block 1 was still a time-shared central-computer system, with the same basic problems as NTDS.

A second important change was direct connection to over-the-horizon data, which initially meant to TFCC. (See chapter 17.) Information from over-the-horizon systems, including tactical decision aids, could not really be separated from own-ship data. For example, electronic intelligence (ELINT) data in over-the-horizon files can dramatically improve identification performance. Probably the advent of antiship Tomahawk was a major impetus in this direction. This apparently minor change was profound because Block 1 development paralleled the shift in over-the-horizon systems to common operating pictures (COPS), in the form of Joint Operational Tactical System (JOTS) and its successors. The latter were acceptable as long as they could not control weapons. Block 1 integrated them with the ship's command system.

Development was ordered on 15 December 1988, and the Block 1 Decision Coordinating Paper issued 22 August 1989. Given development problems, in 1991 Block 1 was divided into levels, Level 0 having the least over-the-horizon extension. Level 1 was coupled directly into GCCS-M (Navy element of Global Command and Control System; successor to JOTS, giving the OTH picture) via an open gateway. It required about 10 percent more software, including automatic EW correlation (of local and remote tracks). The lead Block 1 ship was the carrier *Constellation* (CV 64). Her new system (with the accompanying carrier ASW Module Model 5.1) was delivered in December 1992 for demonstration tests between November 1993 and April 1994. Because computer capacity was barely adequate, the system often crashed. Without any real alternative, development continued. Block 0 replacements by Block 1 began in FY96 with USS *Eisenhower* (CVN-69) and *Wasp* (LHD-1). However, Block 1 failed its February 1998 operational evaluation (OPEVAL). It was neither survivable nor reliable enough. Software crashed too often, and could not be restarted quickly ("warm started") after a crash. Block 1 did not work effectively with Cooperative Engagement Capability (CEC) (then under development), producing extraneous tracks that saturated a fleet air defense picture. Operator workloads increased. The operational evaluators scored the system unsatisfactory in own-ship mission management, composite warfare command management, and doctrine management. Because these problems remained as late as 2001, installation stopped with five ships: the carriers *John F. Kennedy*, *Nimitz*, and *Dwight D. Eisenhower*, and the amphibious assault ships *Wasp* and *Iwo Jima*. Attention shifted to an altogether different fully decentralized Surface Ship Self Defense (SSDS).

Decentralization

The alternative approach, distributing all functions among separate computers, had been actively promoted since the 1970s, initially by Honeywell. It was possible, thanks to Moore's Law: once computers were compact and relatively inexpensive, even a small ship could accommodate several. Like several European companies, Honeywell built its system up from a digital fire-control system, in its case the H930 developed from the Mk 93 optical fire-control system announced in 1975 for coastal craft. H930 entered Korean service in November 1978 aboard PSMM Mk 5 patrol boats. It employed a pair of minicomputers in a local network. One dealt with air targets and one with surface targets, but these functions were interchangeable. Mod 1 (1976) was a large-ship equivalent, using five UYK-19 computers on a bus, with two operator consoles and a command console. Installed on board thirteen modernized Taiwanese *Gearing*-class destroyers (Wu-Jinn I program), it seems to have been the first distributed-architecture combat direction system in the world. Capacity was far more limited than that of NTDS, but the ships could not possibly have accommodated NTDS. Using two consoles, the system could handle up to eight tracks. Given one track, it took four seconds to evaluate a second track, to decide whether it was more threatening. If that was the case, it took ten to eighteen seconds to slue a director onto the new target. Such figures were spectacularly better than what the Taiwanese could get with manual systems, but they did not approach Junior Participating Tactical Data System (JPTDS) performance. Further versions were for small boats.[5]

The Office of Naval Research (ONR) funded Honeywell to the point where part of its system went to sea for a time on board a *Spruance*-class destroyer. However, just as there was no money for ACDS, there was no money to tear up the enormous NTDS investment in favor of a completely new approach that would have nothing in common with existing systems. The Taiwanese encouraged the company to develop H930 into the Modular Combat System (MCS), which equipped the remaining Taiwanese destroyers (Wu-Jinn III program). With four consoles, capacity grew to twenty-four tracks (including underwater); four targets could be engaged simultaneously. Because MCS was modular, Honeywell was able to sell reduced versions for special purposes.[6]

The Canadians took the step to a full-capability system. In 1974 they chose a distributed architecture for their projected frigates, which materialized as the "City" class. Among the organizations they visited before making this choice was Honeywell, which was then developing H930 and trying to interest the U.S. Navy in a fully distributed system. The Canadian Shipboard Integrated Processing and Display System (SHINPADS) has a central database (tactical picture), divided into two elements, with primary and backup storage. All users have access to the entire database. Like ACDS (and presumably inspired by the demands of defense against pop-up antiship missiles) the system has an automatic mode (the command can control engagements by veto) in addition to the usual semiautomatic one and a fallback manual mode (the operator assigns weapons, begins engagements, and reconfigures the system to account for failures or damage to its components). They are supported by thirty-three minicomputers (sixteen-bit UYK-507s). Like NTDS, SHINPADS handles 256 local tracks. Largely because of the lengthy process of acquiring the "City" class, SHINPADS was not operational until 1987. Efforts to export it proved fruitless because by then the Dutch, the French, and the Italians were producing their own modular systems: the Dutch Tactical Information and Command System (TACTICOS), the later versions of the French Systeme d'Exploitation Navale des Informations Tactiques (SENIT) and Traitment Automatique et Visualisation Tactique (TAVITAC), and the later versions of the Italian Systema Dirizione della Operazioni di Combattimento (SADOC). In each case the fully distributed version was preceded by a federated version that retained a picture-keeping computer but moved all other functions out, so that there was no time sharing.[7]

The British experience was more interesting. In 1977 the main combat direction system contractor, Ferranti, proposed a new Computer-Assisted Command System (CACS) as a midlife replacement for the Computer Assisted Action Information System (CAAIS) on board relatively simple Type 21 frigates. CACS was adopted instead for the more demanding Type 22 Batch 2. It was the first British command system intended to handle passive ESM and passive sonar data. Passive sonar would be used to control ASW aircraft, so the frigate had to maintain an air picture. CACS was also the first Royal Navy system for which Ferranti, rather than the Royal Navy, was entirely responsible. (Ferranti had developed export systems.) Unlike CAAIS, CACS was a full command system, including its own AAW system computer (like the Action Data Automation Weapon System [ADAWS]). Much as JPTDS was not given an NTDS designation, CACS was not given the ADAWS-series designation it should have had, probably to avoid admitting how complex the frigates had become. Its two computers shared a common memory (mainly the tactical picture). The second computer is sometimes described as a running spare. A third (auxiliary) computer handled long-range sonar and ESM pictures. Although it was installed in 1984–86, CACS 1 did not become fully operational until 1991. CACS 3 was to have replaced ADAWS in the missile destroyers, and CACS 4 would control Type 23 frigates.

CACS 5 was a relatively simple modification of CACS 1 for Type 22 Batch 3 frigates, the major change being addition of a 4.5-inch gun—which would be controlled through the combat direction system. Ferranti told its customer that it was time to switch to a decentralized, distributed system.[8] The Royal Navy wanted to continue using proven software associated with a central computer. It feared the nightmare of developing and testing entirely new software. Ferranti went so far as to develop its own distributed System 500 but had no luck selling it. CACS 5 worked, but the system had no further growth potential.

Before any Type 23s had been completed, the Royal Navy admitted that their planned CACS 4 system would never work. With the system canceled, eight new frigates were commissioned without command/control systems. Despite official claims that the ships were usable, they could not be deployed anywhere they might meet even modest opposition. Given an upper limit on the number of destroyers and frigates in the Royal Navy, earlier ships that were actually more effective could not be retained until the command system problem had been solved. Ships that did have usable command systems had to spend more of their time deployed abroad, with predictable effects on morale. The lack of public outcry says much for how invisible command systems are.

The distributed Surface Ship Command System (SSCS) won the competition for a replacement. It seems to have been successful, despite early rumors that system reaction time was excessive, possibly because each processor had to spend too much of its time maintaining interfaces with other elements of the system. Rumor also had it that this problem was cured by Moore's Law: later and much faster versions of the microprocessors involved were installed. That worked because the developers were lucky: they had an upgrade path. SSCS used Pentium processors. Other developers were not so lucky. The U.S.-built system for Australian *Collins*-class submarines used Motorola 68000-series chips, as in Mac computers. Macs were popular, and Motorola was not about to go out of business. However, Motorola and Apple shifted to PowerPC chips, and the simple upgrade path disappeared. The *Collins*-class system was judged a disastrous failure because it was visibly slow in a crucial tactical application. The Australians ended up buying the U.S. open-architecture BYG-2 system, one benefit of which was that it had a much more robust upgrade path. In addition to the Royal Navy, Korea bought SSCS for the new KDX-class destroyer, and it is the basis for the command system in the new *Daring* class. British submarines are being fitted with a version of SSCS.

A private British system developer, Plessey, announced a distributed Naval Autonomous Information System (NAUTIS) in 1983, well before the Type 23 fiasco. Each console carries a full copy of the tactical picture: at least two hundred tracks (radar and sonar). That a company regarded such a system as a viable product, even without official backing, suggests that by this time any navy buying new ships would demand automated combat direction. Conversely, the first version of NAUTIS was developed for a British warship, the single-role mine hunter (*Sandown* class). NAUTIS may therefore have been conceived as a CAAIS replacement. It has enjoyed considerable commercial success.[9]

RAIDS into SSDS

The U.S. Navy followed the same path as the British, but it began with antiship-missile defense. Interest revived when USS *Stark* was almost sunk by Exocet missiles in 1987. Repeated false alarms had blunted *Stark*'s alertness. Her command assumed that Iran presented the only threat to a U.S. ship, although the situation in the Gulf that night was ambiguous—and although an approaching pilot might be entirely unable to identify the blip on his radar as a U.S. ship rather than as a viable target. The ship's ESM operator seems to have misidentified the signal received from the Iraqi attacker's Agave radar. The ship reacted too slowly. Even if she had tried to react, there was no useful guide to the sort of integrated maneuver and chaff-launching reaction that was needed. Appropriate maneuvers depend on too many variables to be extemporized. As Ships Anti-Missile Integrated Defense (SAMID) had realized two decades earlier, success demanded a small-ship combat direction system. This time Congress mandated a self-defense program to extend beyond automated surface combatants to classes such as major amphibious ships.

A new emergency program began. Early in FY88 the Naval Surface Weapons Center (NSWC) started the Rapid Anti-Ship Missile Integrated Defense System (RAIDS) to supplement existing combat systems. Like SAMID, it would better integrate the information already available aboard ship to use hard- and soft-kill defenses. That meant merging data from all available sensors: search radars, fire-control radars, and ESM. By this time all of them automatically detected targets, so their target data could easily be combined. RAIDS fed data from all sensors into its Ethernet local area network (data bus). The ship's NTDS was counted as one sensor, creating search radar tracks. As tested on board a *Spruance*-class destroyer, the sensors were the ship's combat system itself, the ship's ECM system, and the precision radars of her two Phalanx guns.

The system's software "tactical engine" was an intelligent track manager that reduced the usual false-alarm rate by associating search radar tracks formed in NTDS with particular emitters, using both apparent target behavior (range/range rate) and emitter character. Some missiles did not emit. To deal with them, RAIDS guessed the most likely identity of the launch platform and created a missile track, calculating estimated impact time. Like Aegis, RAIDS used programmable criteria to rank threats. Given the tactical picture it created, RAIDS issued maneuver and other recommendations. Like the Digital Data Correlation and Transfer System (DATACORTS) twenty years earlier, RAIDS *was* a combat direction system in its own right, creating a tactical picture and coordinating reactions based on it. From a programmatic point of view, it survived because it did not compete with Aegis and ACDS.

RAIDS ran *Spruance*-class operational trials in January–March 1993. Having completed operational evaluation in July 1993, it was important enough to be approved for production a month later. By 1996 it was on board *Spruance*-class destroyers and was scheduled for installation on board *Perry*-class frigates—to supplement existing combat direction systems.

RAIDS did not fire weapons, but a Phase 2 version was intended to do so. It was redesignated SSDS System Mk 1. RAIDS became SSDS Mk 0. The SSDS mission need statement (MNS) was submitted in August 1991. RAIDS used rule-based reactive planning, but SSDS used a degree of artificial intelligence. It incorporated work done by NSWC in the mid-1990s on a Tactical Response Planner (TRIP) that would constantly plan an optimum route for a ship while minimizing exposure to known or projected threats. TRIP would manage a ship's sensors, looking for data to allow the tactical action officer to anticipate and potentially avoid problems.

RAIDS and SSDS reportedly benefited heavily from the abortive NATO frigate project of the 1980s. It included national antiaircraft systems designated NAAWS (NATO Antiair Warfare [AAW] System). A major object of U.S. participation in the program was to transmit Aegis or Aegis-like technology to NATO allies. U.S. competitors for NAAWS developed weapons-system-oriented combat direction systems ("cores"). Like the Aegis CDS, they were weapons-direction systems grown up to handle further combat direction tasks. The rules of the NAAWS competition required companies to develop Aegis-like cores without the associated radars. Such systems required the C&D-like element used in RAIDS and in SSDS.

The congressional mandate placed SSDS on board ships that had no other kind of combat direction system, such as many large amphibious units. They needed the services that combat direction normally provides, so SSDS grew into that role. By 1996 the typical three-operator SSDS console had five screens and drove a pair of large-scale display screens. It was described as Aegis for amphibious ships. Growth was relatively easy because the system was conceived in distributed form. Putting all sensor data on a common bus made new sensor/weapon combinations natural. For example, for some time General Dynamics, which made the Phalanx close-in defensive weapon, proposed that the Phalanx search radar (which normally triggers the gun) trigger the Rolling Airframe Missile (RAM) fire-and-forget missile. The same bus and the same computer could accept other kinds of data, for example, from an infrared (IR) search/track device or from ESM. SSDS Mk 1 was defined as a combination of RAM, Phalanx, and available sensors with the appropriate command/control elements. An alternative stripped-down version was developed for *Perry*-class frigates and *Wasp*-class amphibious ships, which already had combat direction systems.

The preprototype SSDS Mk 1 was installed in USS *Whidbey Island* (LSD 41) rather than on board a frigate. Tests were successfully completed on 5 June 1993. One showed that the system could blend the outputs of multiple sensors (ESM, search radar, and Phalanx radar) to form a composite track of fire-control quality. In another, the system engaged two targets simultaneously, using both its weapons. Full-rate production was approved in 1997, and SSDS Mk 1 was installed in all twelve *Whidbey Island* (LSD-41) class amphibious ships, the principal noncombat direction major amphibious units.

SSDS Mk 2 was intended for major warships: the *Nimitz, Spruance, Wasp* (LHD 1), and AOE 6 classes. It would use more sensors, and its weapon would be the Evolved Sea Sparrow missile. A Mk 3 version would be integrated with ACDS and with CEC. These versions died.

As ACDS died, something remarkable happened. The small-scale SSDS became the core of a replacement carrier combat direction system. Like some of the earlier weapon direction systems, SSDS was scaled up, its functions fully distributed among multiple computers—none of which time shared to slow it down. The database—the files that amount to situational awareness—is spread among them, kept up to date as they communicate. The demonstrated ability to integrate a wide range of sensor inputs suggested that SSDS was compatible with the new CEC. Other forms of integration, for example, with off-board sources of information (for strike operations) were becoming more important. Mk 2 Mod 0 was installed on board the carrier *Nimitz* in 2001. The first Mod 1, successfully tested in 2002, equips USS *Ronald Reagan*. The system will equip the *Wasp* class and the new *San Antonio* (LPD 17)-class amphibious ship. In *Wasp*, as in the carriers, SSDS replaces ACDS.

Was decentralization always the answer? All of the system's computers have to share information. If each transmits at will, messages collide and are lost. Above a fairly low utilization rate, the system has to control each of its central processors tightly enough to avoid such interference, each computer sending its messages in turn. In that case routine traffic may block high-priority messages (such as "a missile is coming"). How smart can the net controller become? Attempts to decentralize Aegis have often been mandated but generally failed miserably. The problem was reaction time. Ultimately, it depends on access to the tactical picture. Many system functions update that picture periodically. Because Aegis has only one tactical picture, whatever function consulted it was seeing the very latest picture. It could not change during consultation. In a distributed system, each computer carries its own version of the picture. The versions cannot be updated simultaneously; some of the computers are responsible for updating. What happens when the version in a computer ordering action is a few beats out of date? If the action of one computer affects the part of the picture on which another is basing decisions? The Aegis developers were not quite able to solve these problems and yet retain the very quick reactions that were the objective of the system. At best they could unload some functions, but even that presented problems. Success in developing Aegis into a distributed system was reported in 2007, but that has often been claimed before.

For the U.S. Navy, the long-range Talos missile system was the beginning of picture-centric combat. For most of its flight, the missile was guided on the basis of target position revealed not by special tracking radars, but rather by the ship's search radars—by her tactical picture. Only in the terminal phase was a tracking radar used, to illuminate the target for semiactive homing. In this 1966 photo of the after end of the nuclear cruiser *Long Beach*, the two big  objects are the SPG-49 directors that generated the beam along which the missile flew. They were controlled on the basis of search radar data—in effect, on the basis of a tactical picture. The small dishes above and below them are the illuminators used for terminal guidance. The conceptual difference between Talos and its successor, Aegis, is that the SM-2 (and later) missiles of the Aegis system have a programmable autopilot, hence can respond to commands rather than follow a mechanically controlled beam generator. Aegis also uses a far more precise electronically scanned search radar to create its tactical picture, and hence can place its missiles much closer to their targets before illumination is needed.

The most visible feature of the Aegis system is the SPY-1 electronically steered radar, one antenna of which is visible here. However, the key to the system is the picture it creates in its computer, on the basis of which missiles are fired. The picture and the way in which it is used to direct missiles are why Aegis could be adapted for ballistic missile defense—in which the picture is generated by external sources of data almost as much as by the ship's own radar. Here USS *Shihloh* fires a Tomahawk cruise missile from her forward vertical launcher. One great advantage of the vertical launcher is that it is impossible to tell externally whether a ship is carrying land-attack missiles. During the Cold War, this sort of ambiguity was a countermeasure to the Soviet Ocean Surveillance System. The development of the antiship version of Tomahawk helped drive U.S. Navy interest in a picture-centric style of operation. This particular shot was part of a fourteen-missile attack mounted on 3 September 1996 to retaliate against an Iraqi offensive into Kurdish areas.

The U.S. Navy encouraged Allied navies to adopt NTDS-like computerization. Italy and France began with NTDS hardware and some related software, then developed their own systems—which became eligible for export. The Italian system employed this characteristic three-operator conference console, which is used, among other things, to designate targets. It was widely exported; this example was photographed aboard the Peruvian frigate *Villencio* in July 2003. Many Chinese photographs of their automated CICs show similar consoles, probably based on a prototype provided during the period of NATO assistance to China during the Cold War. *(USN photo by PH1 Marthaellen L. Ball)*

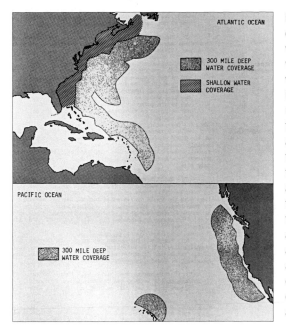

In effect, SOSUS promised to restore to Western ASW the sort of wide-area surveillance which HF/DF and code breaking had provided during World War II. Ocean surveillance was so important to World War II ASW that its loss, presumably with the end of enemy use of breakable machine ciphers, made for a sense of desperation in early postwar analyses. The Soviets apparently did use HF far too freely in the early postwar period, so for well over a decade HF/DF (ashore and at sea) remained a valuable surveillance tool. Even then it was clear that SOSUS was far more likely to be durable, despite scares about probable Soviet silencing. The priority afforded SOSUS is obvious from the coverage achieved as early as 1958, as shown in a declassified map from the 1977 Cross Report on the history of airborne ASW. (SOSUS was a primary sensor for U.S. air ASW forces.)

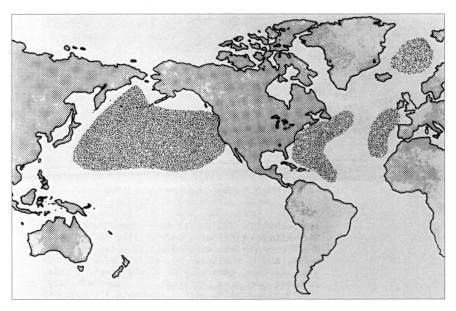

SOSUS made possible a picture-centric approach to ASW. This declassified map, originally published in the 1977 Cross Report on the history of airborne ASW (a copy of which is in the U.S. Navy Operational Archives), shows SOSUS coverage in 1970.

The P-3C Orion was conceived to exploit SOSUS coverage. Although always described as a patrol airplane, in fact it was an interceptor vectored on the basis of a tactical picture of Soviet submarine activity. SOSUS was one of several sources that created the picture. The P-3C exploited new computer technology. Like the contemporary E-2C, it used its onboard computer to create a tactical picture, on the basis of which it could attack. This cutaway view shows the two sensor operators facing to port, each at a console used to interpret sonobuoy data. Computer integration is reflected in the position of the Tactical Coordinator (TACCO), at a separate console, facing forward. In earlier versions of the airplane, the sensor operator stations were not too different, but the TACCO had to stand behind them, trying to visualize the consequences of what the sensor operators were detecting. That is why the sensor operator stations were located as they were. In this version, the sensor operators' conclusions were fed into the airplane's mission computer. The TACCO used the resulting integrated picture to choose tactics (asking what-if questions systematically). The result was considered many times as effective as the earlier versions of the same airplane, occupying visually almost identical airframes. The computer also made it far easier to integrate sonobuoy data with data from the airplane's other sensors—and from sources outside the airplane.

Big circularly disposed antenna arrays (Wullenwebers) were the workhorses of ocean surveillance, both West and East, during more than the first quarter-century of the Cold War. These arrays are sometimes called elephant cages. This type of array was developed during World War II by a group led by Dr. Hans Rindfleisch of the German naval communications research command. (Wullenweber was a cover name.) It was seen as a logical follow-on to a straight-line wide-aperture array (i.e., with dimensions of multiple wavelengths, where an Adcock was typically a quarter- or half-wavelength across). A prototype was built at Skisby, Denmark, late in World War II. A Wullenweber array is a circle of monopole antennas backed by a reflecting screen. The prototype used forty dipoles in a 120-meter circle, each backed by a reflector monopole. Unlike a U-Adcock, which has two receiving beams at right angles, a Wullenweber can form numerous beams using a network of

delay lines; it is analogous to a cylindrical array sonar. Because the beams are narrow, the array can be much more sensitive than a conventional one. The Germans claimed that it was inherently far superior to an Adcock when using sky waves (i.e., when operating at long range) because it was far less likely to be confused by waves approaching at an angle to the vertical. The German array was intended as a radio receiver. However, the array of narrow beams can also be used for radio direction finding, which is why Wullenwebers became an important ocean surveillance sensor. Both the Allies and the Soviets captured the technology and some of the developers at the end of World War II. The Soviets seem to have been the first to deploy Wullenwebers for this purpose, under the designation Krug; one Krug antenna was a kilometer across (larger diameter made for narrower beams). All used the German forty-dipole configuration, although diameter varied. At least thirty such arrays were erected in the Soviet Union and its allies. They were apparently operated by Soviet military intelligence (GRU) rather than by the Soviet navy; for example, they were used to track early Sputniks and reentry vehicles. The British studied the Skisby array before destroying it. During the war Telefunken built a second array at its own expense at Langenargen/Bodensee. It was brought to the United States and reassembled at the University of Illinois, where it became known as the Wullenweber. The university then built a 120-monopole array at Bondville, with a 1,000-foot diameter circular screen of vertical wires, operating at 2 to 20 MHz. A beam was formed by combining inputs from forty contiguous monopoles; circuits swept the beam at high speed by switching different monopoles in and out and by changing phase relationships among them. (Presumably later versions were equivalent to preformed-beam sonars, with multiple beams listening simultaneously, hence able to pick up very short signals.) The U.S. Naval Research Laboratory sponsored this work; it released its first report on array direction finders in December 1947. In effect NRL repeated the German straight-line experiment with a 1952 array of loops 1,100 feet long, which managed to focus on a transmitter 1,200 miles away, achieving a bearing accuracy of 0.25 deg. Its sensitivity (because of its narrow beam widths) enabled it to detect and DF short burst transmissions such as those Soviet submarines could be expected to produce. NRL's next step was a 400-foot diameter precision array (shown here) at Hybla Valley, Virginia, which determined the orbit of the first Soviet Sputnik satellite in 1957. NRL claimed that its circular array was the first to achieve high bearing accuracy. In 1959 the U.S. Navy let a contract to ITT Federal Systems to build the Classic Bullseye network of 800-foot diameter FRD-10 arrays based on the Bondville array, the first being installed at NSGA Hanza, Okinawa, in 1962. The last of eleven more was completed in 1967 at NSGA Imperial Beach, California. Others were operated by the Canadian Forces, the last being installed in 1971 at Gander and at Masset, British Columbia. During the 1970s Japan installed two similar arrays at Chitose and Miho, and probably other governments have also installed such arrays. In addition, a pair of FRD-10s not equipped for direction finding was installed in 1969 at Sugar Grove for radio reception, working with the station at Cheltenham, Maryland. The U.S. Air Force used a larger-diameter FLR-9 array built by GTE Sylvania Electronic Systems (now General Dynamics Advanced Information Systems). The Army used a version of FLR-9 with a different beam-forming network. Plessey (now Roke Manor Research Ltd) developed a 400-foot diameter Pusher array in the 1970s, designed FRD-13 or AX-16. This is NRL's 400-foot array. *(Courtesy NRL)*

In the early 1970s it seemed to the U.S. Navy that an airplane carrying a radar and ESM would be needed to maintain a usable surface picture in the Mediterranean. This was a May 1971 proposal for an Ocean Surveillance System Aircraft (OSSA). A U-2 was tested in this role. The great surprise was that intelligence-driven ocean surveillance information, collated in the form of OSIS, was a viable substitute.

The form of ocean surveillance used by the U.S. Navy depends heavily on emissions by the ships being tracked. To form usable tracks, the system must distinguish ships of the same class, based on the details of their emitters. That requires aircraft that can analyze signals and confirm that they come from a particular ship. The U.S. Navy began to operate EP-3 Orions like this one as it developed OSIS on the basis of passive surveillance. This is the first EP-3E converted by the L-3 company from a P-3C, therefore benefitting from the latter's mission computer (March 2006).

The RA-5C Vigilante was conceived as a supersonic strategic bomber, but it was also chosen as the platform for a new reconnaissance package. The package in turn was so powerful that the carrier intelligence center it fed had to be automated in order to exploit its product. In effect, the new automated center created a tactical picture out of intelligence, and that picture was timely enough to be used during the Vietnam War to reroute strike groups already airborne. These two Vigilantes were photographed on board USS *America*, 16 January 1973.

Computer links made it possible for a picture-keeping airplane like an E-2C to cue attack aircraft. Using Link 4, an E-2C could point the electro-optical turret under the nose of this A-6E TRAM prototype, photographed in November 1976. The same E-2C could control a strike by several attack aircraft against a surface target, an increasingly important capability when the U.S. Navy contemplated attacks against heavily armed Soviet surface combatants in what it called War at Sea (WAS, as opposed to ASW).

The most powerful force in modern command and control is Moore's Law: computers keep shrinking and becoming more powerful. The F/A-18 Hornet was conceived as a lightweight fighter, an inexpensive supplement to the F-14 Tomcat. However, its computer was far more powerful, and it conferred a remarkable flexibility on the airplane, reflected in its F/A designation. The Hornet, which is far less expensive to operate, is now the sole carrier-based fighter and the sole carrier-based attack airplane—admittedly at a cost in range and payload. Here two F/A-18F Super Hornets of VFA-32 fly above the carrier *Harry S. Truman* in the Persian Gulf, April 2008.

Moore's Law gave the A-7E Corsair II a mission computer, hence some of the capabilities of the A-6E. In particular, the computer could receive and carry out commands transmitted via Link 4 from a ship or an E-2C Hawkeye. Moreover, because it had a data bus extending into its weapon pylons, it could connect its computer (hence the other platforms) to pods such as the electro-optical one visible beneath the wing of this VA-76 aircraft operating from the carrier *Dwight D. Eisenhower* in November 1987. Computer mission planning, which produced plans insertable directly into the mission computer, still lay in the future.

Western navies saw the results of Soviet Ocean Surveillance System operation, but not primary elements such as Krug arrays and processing centers. The element they most often saw was the intelligence-gathering ship (AGI, in Western parlance): a relatively slow but long-endurance ship laden with intercept gear (and, usually, with a MI-110K nonacoustic submarine detector), loitering off a base or near a choke point. Here the intelligence ship *Gidrofon* shadows the U.S. carrier *Franklin D. Roosevelt* in the Tonkin Gulf during the Vietnam War, 28 October 1969. *Gidrofon* was a Mayak (Project 502)–class small intelligence-gathering ship, one of several built at Volgograd between 1965 and 1970.

U.S. analysts saw larger AGIs as seagoing centers for intelligence concentration (from smaller AGIs), evaluation, and onward transmission to SOSS centers. They had more radomes (for both sensors and for transmitters), and much more enclosed space—and, apparently, intelligence-gathering combat systems. Here a 3,100-ton Balzam-class (Project 1826) AGI observes the U.S. helicopter carrier *Iwo Jima* during Ocean Venture 84, in the spring of 1984.

During the Cold War carriers and other high-value targets were often shadowed by "tattletales." It was tempting, but wrong, to consider them the fast equivalents of AGIs. Rather, they were a means of confirming to Soviet strike forces the position of the high-value unit within a formation. Unless missiles were concentrated on the right target, it was unlikely that enough of them would hit. The visual clue to this role was the ships' aft-facing antiship missiles. Just before the attack, the tattletale would steam away, so that she would not attract missiles and thus dilute the attack. That meant turning 180 degrees—and bringing the aft-firing missiles to bear. Here a Modified Kashin-class missile destroyer shadows the carrier *Saratoga* in 1979. When the U.S. Navy adopted a network-centric (or picture-centric) method of targeting Tomahawk antiship missiles, its greatest problem was exactly what the Soviets faced: how to make sure that the missiles would find the right target in a group of ships—which, in the Mediterranean, might well include merchant ships that were not even being tracked. The principal U.S. solution was to equip the missile with a passive radar detector, which it hoped would pick up radar unique to high-value Soviet warships.

For much of the Cold War, the greatest Soviet threat to U.S. carrier strike forces was missile-carrying bombers like this Badger (Tu-16), which carries a supersonic AS-6 (KSR-5) under one wing. Soviet strike tactics involved jammers and also aircraft laying chaff corridors down which aircraft were expected to fly, shielded from radars to either side. These tactics required that the Soviet Ocean Surveillance System locate the targets, since any formation merely searching for a target would itself be vulnerable. Countering the Soviet tactics required the U.S. force to create a tactical picture, using sensors so distributed that they could see around the chaff and the main jamming beams. The U.S. Navy also developed deception and jamming tactics to force the Soviets to search rather than attack from a distance. Although AS-6 had a long theoretical range, it could not be fired until the airplane carrying it locked it onto a target. For example, by operating in a fjord, a carrier could make such a lock-on impossible until the missile was at nearly its minimum range—and the bomber was vulnerable to land-based fighters as it searched. Other counters were EA-6Bs jamming the Badger's attack radar, and decoys, such as "rubber ducks," which could confuse the approaching bomber. After the Cold War it became clear that the Soviets also wanted visual confirmation of the position of the high-value target within a group, hence assigned pilots to fly into U.S. formations at low altitude. Even practicing such tactics could be dangerous—a Badger probably doing that cartwheeled into the sea after making a low pass over USS *Essex* in 1968.

When the supersonic Backfire (Tu-22M3) replaced the Badger, the U.S. Navy was faced with an additional problem: now the bombers could approach over a much more varied route. Its solution was network-centric; carriers would be given an over-the-horizon picture of approaching bombers, using a wide variety of sensors, even including satellites. After the Cold War, it became clear that Backfires were an even more serious threat because they could launch their missiles without locking them on. The missiles had data links back to the firing aircraft. Conversely, the Soviets failed to develop a jammer version of Backfire, so they were reduced to supporting attacking Backfires with subsonic Badger jammers, dramatically reducing their tactical flexibility. (The jammer problem was solved only at the end of the Cold War.)

The Soviet long-range missile attack system was ultimately platform centric: each shooter was responsible for his own attacks, and he had to lock his missiles onto the right target. To that end, the Soviets developed a long-range airborne surface-search radar, which NATO nicknamed Big Bulge. As in the APS-20 system, its video was sent down to a shooter, such as a Kynda-class missile cruiser or an Echo-class submarine, and on its basis the cruiser or submarine set up its attack. After the airplane departed, missiles were fired. As they approached the target, they sent their own radar video back to the firing ship, the shipboard operator locking the missile onto a target he selected. In effect an airplane carrying Big Bulge was doing what the U.S. Navy originally planned to do with its Cadillac airborne radar: seeing beyond the horizon. Because missile ships could not fire until after they had the sort of data Big Bulge provided, the airplane carrying it offered tactical warning: a popular saying was "Bears in the morning, missiles in the afternoon." Big Bulge occupies the belly radome of this Bear D (Tu-95RTs), being escorted by an F-14 of VF-84 (from USS *Nimitz*) about September 1980. A smaller version of Big Bulge—equipped cruiser-borne helicopters, providing them with a measure of self-sufficient targeting. One tactical defect of the system was that the firing ship had to remain in contact with the missiles as they approached their target. Until the missiles were locked on, any attack on the firing ship or submarine might well abort the missile strike. To some extent the Soviet radar ocean reconnaissance satellite (RORSAT to Western navies) reduced the tactical warning drawback associated with the Bear/Big Bulge combination: satellites passed overhead periodically, and it was unlikely that they would support an attack on each pass. However, the downlink associated with the satellite (and ordered from Moscow) certainly was an attack warning.

From the late 1950s on, the Soviets deployed large numbers of missile boats like this Osa, armed with Styx antiship missiles. These weapons were first demonstrated against the Israeli destroyer *Eilat* in October 1967. The boats were not intended to operate independently. Rather, they were part of an integrated coast-defense system based on a tactical picture generated at a regional command center. Soviet coastal ASW used a similar command system based on the same kind of regional center. Such coastal systems determine the value of the fast missile attack craft and other coastal defenses that many countries deploy. For example, much depends on whether the system can distinguish approaching warships from the mass of coastal traffic. Much also depends on whether the system is precise enough for fire control, in which case an attacking boat will not reveal its intentions by switching on a fire control radar. Unfortunately, coastal systems are generally little known, compared to their shipboard and airborne equivalents.

Bazalt (P-500, NATO SS-N-12) was the ultimate development of the series of missiles locked on by the firing ship, i.e., linked to the ship after launch. The Soviet designation indicated a radical improvement of the original P-5 (Shaddock: NATO SS-N-3) submarine-launched antiship missile. Bazalt used its radar at high altitude. Once the operator designated a target, it dove nearly to the sea surface, turning off its search radar and even stowing the antenna to reduce its radar cross section. During its initial radar observation of the target formation, it computed target course and speed, so that it could estimate the appropriate point at which to turn on its radar for terminal homing. In effect it was creating a tactical picture for itself, probably based on its knowledge of its own position and motion, using inertial guidance. This sort of sensing might well make chaff and other static decoys ineffective, unless they were deployed just before a missile reached a ship. The tactical drawback of requiring a postlaunch link with a launching submarine was probably tolerated because this air-breathing missile could not be launched submerged, so the submarine had to expose herself when firing.

With Granit (P-700, NATO SS-N-19) the Mashinostroyeniye design bureau (responsible for SS-N-3 and 12) finally solved the problem of launching an air-breathing missile underwater. Once that could be done, the postlaunch link with a launching submarine was no longer acceptable. Conversely, as the U.S. Navy deployed nuclear Tomahawks on board surface warships, it was no longer clear that missiles should always be concentrated on a single high-value target. As before, the submarine acquired an initial picture of the target formation using either satellite or aircraft radar data, satellites being preferred. When a salvo of Granits was fired, one missile (the "scout") flew high to see the target formation. It communicated with the other missiles to distribute their fire. There may have been some selection on the basis of which radars targets appeared to be using. The trick Mashinostroyeniye used was to cap the air intake with a head containing solid-fuel rocket motors, which pulled the missile out of the water. Once airborne, the missile discarded this element and started up its (dry) jet engine. A similar device was developed for the smaller Yakhont, a development of which was adopted by the Indian navy as BrahMos. Without such a device, submarines were limited to short-range submerged-launch missiles powered by rockets, or to surface-launched long-range missiles.

Once the Soviets developed missiles that could fly beyond the horizon, they needed some means of targeting. One possibility was a shipboard over-the-horizon radar—a totally platform-centric concept. The big "Band Stand" radome visible forward of the bridge of this *Sovremennyy*-class destroyer contains the ultimate Soviet solution, Mineral—two antennas back to back. One is a troposcatter radar with a range of about 100 to 180 kilometers, corresponding to the range of the ship's SS-N-22 Moskit missiles, which occupy the big tubes near the radome. Backing it is an X-band ducting radar with a range of up to 100 kilometers. The system also incorporates a passive element and a data link. Nanuchka-class missile boats had an earlier system using the same radome; Soviet Tarantuls had another system in the same family. In addition, many Soviet missile boats, such as Tarantuls, had X-band radars adapted for ducting operation, so that their range was roughly that of the missiles on board the boats. Mineral has been exported to China; it is both aboard Russian-built *Sovremennyy*-class destroyers and aboard Chinese-built ships. Several other navies have deployed ducting radars, which exploit conditions specific to areas such as the South China Sea and the Eastern Baltic—and the Gulf. The troposcatter radar idea seems to have been unique to the Soviet Union, and apparently it was unsuspected in the West until the Russians published an account in 1996. The Western assumption had been that any Soviet surface warship with an over-the-horizon weapon had to rely entirely on some external means for targeting, hence that "Band Stand" housed some kind of data link. This perception was not entirely inaccurate because the troposcatter radar probably cannot be used for efficient search. Rather, it is the final stage of a cueing process in which other sources indicate that a target is nearby, and the shooter uses its sensors to establish fire-control parameters. *(Alexandre Sheldon-Duplaix)*

The U.S. Navy deployed the Tomahawk cruise missile on board its surface combatants at least partly to saturate the Soviet Ocean Surveillance System: instead of tracking a few carriers and major amphibious ships, the Soviets had to track every U.S. ship that could fire nuclear Tomahawks. The nuclear cruiser *Virginia* shows characteristic Tomahawk armored box launchers aft.

In contrast to the Soviet Navy, the U.S. Navy adopted a network-centric or intelligence-driven approach to targeting its long-range antiship missile, a version of Tomahawk. It had no equivalent to the Bear D or to tattletales, hence nothing to warn any particular Soviet ship of impending attack. Instead, it maintained continuous track of most Soviet warships, to a quality sufficient to support missile strikes. Any attacks on Soviet warships would have been surprises. Such unexpected attacks should be a hallmark of network-centric operations, and the impact of surprise after surprise may be the most  valuable contribution of this style of warfare. Unfortunately, such psychological impacts, which are often decisive, are nearly impossible to model and hence impossible to compare with more conventional approaches to war. Given the network character of the U.S. fleet, for a missile-armed ship like the destroyer *Fletcher*, the most important supporting devices were satellite reception antennas, not her own sensors. They supported the ship's wide-area picture. However, the ship also had the Classic Outboard tactical HF/DF system, some of whose antennas are barely visible near the top of her foremast. Note the open missile cell covers on her sixty-one-cell vertical launcher, installed specifically to accommodate Tomahawks (it replaced her ASROC). *Fletcher* is shown in March 2003, supporting Operation Iraqi Freedom. *(USN photo by Chief Journalist Alan J. Baribeau)*

CHAPTER 14

Extending Combat System Automation: Aircraft

Perhaps the most spectacular application of Moore's Law was to aircraft. Computers became compact enough first for large aircraft (E-2, P-3C), then for large fighters and attack aircraft (A-6 and F-14), and then for smaller fighters and attack bombers. The possibility that the pilot of an attack bomber could have a tactical picture, and thus could plan his attack with a precision weapon, seems to have inspired Adm. Arthur K. Cebrowski's vision of network-centric warfare. Perhaps the most interesting development of all was the almost accidental creation of a network that used computer flight planning and a data link to redirect attack aircraft already in the air, in what is now called either Retargeting in the Cockpit (RTIC) or Real Time in the Cockpit.

The Airborne CIC: ATDS

McNally's Naval Tactical Data System (NTDS) concept included a computerized airborne Combat Information Center (CIC) data-linked to the shipboard CIC, both controlling fighters via Link 4. Like the modular CIC, there was an interim carrier-based analog airborne CIC, on board the Grumman E-1B.[1] The E-2A (Airborne Tactical Data System [ATDS] platform) flew in October 1960. When it was tested in October 1964, its reliability and maintainability were so poor that the airplane was impossible to evaluate. Planned FY65 purchases were canceled and a get-well program was begun.[2] It succeeded well enough that the Office of the Secretary of Defense (OSD) approved FY66 purchases and development of an improved E-2B. Vietnam experience showed a need for new capabilities, such as detecting aircraft overland. The original hardwired computer was replaced by a programmable unit. Capacity fell to thirty tracks (all of which could be designated for interception). The requirement had been 256 tracks (as in NTDS) and support of ten simultaneous interceptions. The modernized E-2A was redesignated E-2B, and a new version with a new computer and a new radar was developed into the current E-2C. The effect of Moore's Law shows in growth from capacity projected about 1968 of 150 targets (75 interceptions) to the 650 tracks (300 from own sensors, 350 from external sources) of 1974. Given the computer, other sensors could be integrated with the radar: a passive detection system (electronic support measures [ESM]) and the ALQ-108 extended electronic countermeasures (ECM) system to track Soviet targets by triggering their two standard "identification of friend and foe" (IFF) transponders, Type 2 (ships and most aircraft) and the newer Type 9 (aircraft only). ALQ-108 exploited tight Soviet control policy using IFF. (This capability was so important—but so vulnerable if compromised—that its use was barred except in wartime.)[3] Improved versions of the E-2C are still in production more than forty years after the airplane first flew.

A-NEW: The P-3C

On board the large antisubmarine warfare (ASW) aircraft of the 1950s, tactical coordinators (TACCOs) plotted sonobuoy data to create a tactical picture, on the basis of which they ordered more sonobuoys laid or else ordered an attack. In effect they were carrying out CIC functions, although that may not have been immediately obvious. Thus broadly paralleling ATDS was a digital airborne CIC for antisubmarine warfare, developed under the A-NEW (literally a new ASW weapon system) program. A-NEW was conceived in July 1960 at the Naval Air Development Center (NADC) at Johnsville, Pennsylvania. The contract for the first (analog) version of the Orion, which it would replace, was not let until that October. ASW aircraft were already, in effect, CICs. Instead of radar plan position indicators (PPIs), they had sonobuoy processors, each with its own operator. The TACCO merged sonobuoy detections to create a kind of tactical picture, on the basis of which he directed the pilot to drop further buoys or to make a low pass and drop a torpedo (based on further sensing, e.g., with the airplane's magnetic anomaly detector). Like NTDS, a mission computer could help the TACCO visualize the situation and plan further moves. It could answer what-if questions (equivalent to weapon engagement analysis in NTDS), and thus materially improve tactics. Such comparisons had not normally been done because evaluation of each alternative entailed so much calculation. Linked to the airplane's autopilot, the mission computer could direct the crew to lay more complex sonobuoy patterns—and it could help draw conclusions more quickly from their output. Automation made for both more extensive and faster searches, so it was more likely that the airplane would find a submarine even after a longer flight out to the search area.

The A-NEW airplane was the P-3C Orion, one of the first two maritime-patrol aircraft to have a computer tactical data system. The other was the British Nimrod. In 1967 it was officially estimated that automation would make the P-3C two to three times as effective as its predecessor P-3B. Automation brought complexity; it was said that one P-3C had as many electronic parts as all 144 P-3Bs. However, reliability did not suffer badly because the new electronics was generally solid state. As the manufacturer of the P-3C, Lockheed became system integrator. The Mod 1 version was flight tested on board a P-3A early in 1964. It was reportedly so successful that the fleet tried to bring this interim version into production. The P-3C (Mod 3.2) was approved for production in August 1967, and the prototype flew on 18 September 1968. The P-3C entered service in 1969.

A-NEW had a mission computer connected to an acoustic processor, to an automated navigation system, and to other aircraft sensors such as radar and ESM. The capacities of the acoustic processor and its associated radio determined how many sonobuoys (and of what type) the airplane could handle at the same time; the mission computer maintained the tactical picture. As sonobuoys developed and the Soviets silenced their submarines, the acoustic processors were upgraded to match. Much less had to be done to modernize the mission computer, although eventually it was replaced.[4] The presence of a powerful new mission computer made it relatively easy to adapt the P-3C to the anti–surface ship warfare (ASUW) role in the ASUW Improvement Program (AIP). Originally, the emphasis was on passing targets the airplane detected into a network used to direct over-the-horizon attacks. However, the computer could also connect new sensors (such as electro-optical/infrared [IR] cameras), to new downlinks used by ground forces. AIP aircraft were valued in Afghanistan because they could work directly with ground forces, providing them with images of what was happening just over the horizon so that they could ambush enemy forces. Conceptually, this was not so very different from providing sonobuoy data to a surface ASW unit via Link 11.

A-NEW envisaged computerized Tactical Support Centers (later renamed ASW Operations Centers) to program P-3Cs for their missions and play back the data they brought back. Its relation to the airplane was not different from the relation between a carrier's CIC and the E-2C. The airplane could transmit data in flight, using a dedicated high frequency (HF) link (used for Link 11 when not transmitting raw acoustic data). To do this the Antisubmarine Operations Center (ASWOC) contained a P-3C-type computer and acoustic analyzer. It had the Antisubmarine Warfare Center Command and Control System (ASWCCS) to exchange data with other ASWOCs and with fleet commanders in chief (CinCs). Playback made the P-3C an ocean surveillance sensor because the ASWOC could feed played-back data into the ocean surveillance system (which normally cued the airplane). Also, playback might reveal targets missed in flight. By 1980 typical ASWOC capacity was 2,600 tracks, 100 messages, and 1,200 acoustic signatures.

Moore's Law made it possible to shrink the P-3C system so that it could go aboard a carrier airplane. Work began on this Mod 4 (ground prototype) with first contracts awarded during FY66. Mod 5 was the airborne prototype. To make the carrier system more compact, the analog sonobuoy analyzers of the P-3C were replaced by fully digital (paperless) units that could time-share buoys among fewer crew members. The resulting S-3A Viking worked with a carrier equivalent to the ASWOC, the CV-ASWM (ASW Carrier Module). It could receive data from ASWOCs (i.e., from the shore ocean surveillance system). The module was also connected to the ship's NTDS and to ASW-related ship spaces.

Bombers

As long as a bomber could fly high, its ground-mapping radar could take it to the target. Once bombers had to fly under enemy radar, navigation became more complicated. Computers could help. Thus the first U.S. airplane with an onboard digital computer was the North American A-5 (originally A3J) Vigilante strategic bomber. It had alternative high-altitude supersonic and low-level subsonic approaches to a target. The A-5 was proposed in 1953 as North American was completing development of the long-range inertially guided Navaho cruise missile. An inertial system taken from the missile made the bomber an effective low-level attacker. The bomber popped up near an enemy coast so that its ground-mapping radar could locate a starting point for its inertial guidance system. Diving to low altitude, the pilot relied on the inertial system, which communicated with him via a head-up display, the first to enter production. It was also connected to a fly-by-wire control system, and to a bombing system. The bombing system was needed because the new bomber would toss its bomb at the target to give itself time to escape the bomb's shock wave. The maneuver demanded a complex calculation. The system was also adapted to the alternative approach, at high speed and high altitude. Although it was not very successful as a bomber, the A-5 became an important reconnaissance aircraft, intimately connected with the Integrated Operational Intelligence System (IOIS) described in chapter 16, which in turn had important implications for air attack planning and for other system developments.

Much of the logic driving the A-5 also applied to tactical attack bombers. In 1955 an operational requirement was written for a new all-weather tactical bomber. The following year Grumman won the design competition with the A-6 Intruder, which was built around a powerful radar, an inertial navigation system, and a general-purpose programmable computer. Thus it conceived the airplane as an integrated weapon system. The company's system experience in turn probably helped gain it contracts for other airborne systems, the E-2 Hawkeye and the closely related F-14 Tomcat. Litton developed the onboard computer, and that experience was significant for the later Missileer project. It is not clear whether the A-5 concept influenced those proposing the A-6.

The A-6 would fly lower than the A-5, so it needed to avoid ground obstacles. Computers were far too unreliable for automatic evasion. The airplane's forward-looking radar produced images of a series of slices of the terrain.[5] The computer assembled those slices into a usable picture for the pilot. Given its limitations, the computer produced a wholly artificial display, resembling a road in the sky, much as NTDS transformed a tactical picture into an artificial set of symbols. In the initial version of the A-6, a second radar tracked the target on the ground so that the airplane's bombing system could aim a bomb at it. The appropriate moment of release depended on bomb ballistics and on the airplane's path. The idea of aiming the airplane to aim the bomb it dropped or threw was hardly new, but the general-purpose digital computer offered much greater flexibility. Earlier analog bombing computers embodied the ballistics of particular weapons. As the variety of weapons grew, such computers could not keep up. The digital computer in the A-6 had limited capacity, but it could be reprogrammed. The computer offered an additional possibility. Many targets were indistinct on a radar scope. The A-6 system could be programmed to drop weapons at a specified range and bearing (an offset) from a radar beacon or an object visible on radar; the computer could, in effect, visualize target location. It could practice a kind of picture-centric warfare, in the sense that the attacking airplane never saw the target directly. This was not a new idea, but the A-6A was particularly well adapted to such tactics. When the A-6A entered combat in Vietnam, its greatest problem turned out to be that targets were often difficult to distinguish on radar.[6]

The system made it possible for the airplane to hit accurately even when flying relatively low. Otherwise the only really accurate mode of delivery was dive or glide bombing, in which the pilot aimed the airplane at the target. He had to approach relatively high, hence was relatively vulnerable to antiaircraft fire. There was a low-altitude toss-bombing technique, but it was relatively inaccurate, and it was intended mainly to deliver nuclear weapons. The A-6A system automatically released the bomb based on sensed aircraft motion and bomb ballistics. Dive-bombing was less affected by details of bomb ballistics, since the bomb continued in more or less the same direction as the airplane.

The same mission computer navigated the airplane, using an inertial system set up at launch time on the basis of the carrier's known position. Generally, the pilot planned a mission in terms of waypoints and preplanned turns. They were inserted into his mission computer and also written on his kneepad. The A-6 had no data link, and mission planning was entirely manual. Planning low-altitude flights was a lengthy process, taking into account factors such as enemy radar cover and weapons, the terrain itself (a pilot might plan to fly up a valley, only to discover that there was no way out of it), and even fuel consumption en route. It was impossible to replan quickly to take account of new targets or new circumstances.

All of this came at a cost in complexity. Aircraft like the A-6 represented an enormous jump in capability, but maintenance was far more difficult than in the past.[7] Between December 1967 and January 1968, the A-6 managed 0.81 sorties per aircraft per day. The simpler day attack bombers (A-4 and A-7) managed, respectively, 1.28 and 1.13 during a period when all of these aircraft were used under similar conditions. (After January 1968, the A-6 was used mainly at night or in bad weather, so statistics were no longer comparable.)

The Intruder was vastly more complicated than existing light attack aircraft. When it entered service, the standard such airplane was the A-4 Skyhawk, conceived for day delivery of a single nuclear bomb. A comparative table of avionics in the two airplanes showed almost nothing at all for the Skyhawk: only IFF, an ultrahigh frequency (UHF) radio receiver, and a tactical air navigation (TACAN) receiver (for navigation), plus whatever avionics or ordnance equipment were needed for a specific mission. Much less could go wrong. However, a Skyhawk could hardly attack at night or in bad weather. (But an A-6A without its ballistic computer was nearly a longer-range Skyhawk carrying much more ordnance but also slower and less maneuverable.) As it became obvious that naval aircraft would deliver conventional rather than nuclear weapons, the Navy sought a larger but still simple light bomber. The A-7A Corsair II entered combat in November 1967. Compared to the Skyhawk, its most important piece of new avionics was a ranging radar in its nose linked to a bombing computer (APQ-116/CP-741). The radar fed slant range to the target into the computer during a dive, so the pilot did not have to roll in to a fixed set of delivery conditions. (The same computer had been used in some versions of the A-4, but with inaccurate or unreliable radars.) This new device seemed to work so well that pilots preferred it to manual bombing. Tests suggested a circular error probable (CEP) of 100 feet, which was better than the A-6A had done in trials. However, this was still a daylight system; the pilot designated the target to the radar. The A-7A also carried onboard ECM.[8] As might be expected, it was about as reliable as its predecessor, the A-4C. It could carry much more ordnance, of greater variety, and it had much longer endurance.

Given Moore's Law and the success of the A-6, Naval Air Systems Command (NAVAIR) sought a computer system for light attack aircraft. This Integrated Light Attack Avionics System (ILAAS) project was envisaged in two phases. Phase I placed

ILAAS aboard a new version of the existing A-7 light attack airplane (the A-7E).[9] It entered combat in May 1970. Phase II would develop an optimum version for later installation. Presumably, it was embodied in the next major project, which became the F/A-18. Like the A-6, the A-7E had a central computer that navigated it to the target and back, as well as performing bomb and missile fire control. Also like the A-6, it had an inertial navigation unit and a Doppler radar. The new APQ-126 radar offered multiple operating modes, including ranging, ground mapping (for navigation near the target), terrain avoidance, and air refueling rendezvous. In theory, ILAAS gave the A-7E night and bad-weather attack capability, making level attacks like those typical of the A-6. However, pilots much preferred visual dive-bombing (using flares at night). The Center for Naval Analyses (CNA) commented that "unlike the A-6A, the A-7E is a single-place aircraft, and the pilot must function as both pilot and bombardier-navigator. His workload during night and all-weather attack missions has reached the saturation point, and only highly trained pilots should be expected to deliver ordnance within the system's potential." The main attempts to simplify the pilot's workload were a new heads-up display driven by the central computer and a moving-map display. ILAAS provided the A-7E with significantly better delivery accuracy than the A-7A/B and less sophisticated aircraft, as well as with greater freedom to choose different tactics (level, dive, and dive-toss, plus loft and high-angle with some weapons) without compromising that accuracy. Dive-bombing accuracy was 9.17 mils (45-degree dive), which meant about 45 feet from 5,000 feet—half of what the A-7A had achieved three years earlier. Overall, the A-7E could expect a CEP of less than ten mils. Corresponding figures for earlier and simpler aircraft were thirty mils for the A-4, twenty-six mils for the A-7A/B, and twenty-nine mils for the F-4, all using the same CP-741 computer (the A-7E used a CP-841 for computed dive delivery).

The A-6 and A-7 were stand-alone systems. However, both had Link 4 for automatic carrier landing. That connection could be used in other ways. The Marines were the first to grasp this possibility. They saw their attack aircraft as extensions of Marine Corps artillery, which was controlled on the basis of maps showing friendly and enemy positions. After World War II, the Marines sought to push this sort of control further so that their aircraft could provide close support even at night or in bad weather. They created a control center containing the MPQ-14 ground-controlled radar bombing system. It tracked the incoming bomber and commanded it to drop a bomb. However, it was no simple matter to ensure that a bomb dropped on command would hit the desired target. MPQ-14 entered combat in Korea in September 1951, and was formally approved for close air support in the summer of 1952, having proved its effectiveness.

Given this heritage, Link 4 offered an obvious advantage. A link that could direct a fighter could also direct a bomber. By about 1965, the Marines were experimentally using Link 4 to control tactical strike aircraft in conjunction with their TPQ-10 radar bomb director and a high-powered UHF radio. TPQ-10 could control properly equipped aircraft, even dropping their weapons without intervention by the pilot. In one series of tests, the system apparently flew aircraft over and down a mountain before bombs were to be released. Pilots were less than impressed. They had a switch allowing them to drop the bomb and in effect opt out of control, which they tended to do.

Link control made it possible to direct aircraft against targets relatively close to Marines; the TPQ-10 operator maintained a current picture of both Marine positions and of the incoming airplane, which he would pick up and direct. Computer control was sometimes ineffective, and often voice had to be used. TPQ-10 and Link 4 were used in Vietnam, to control not only Navy and Marine Corps aircraft, but also B-52s making Arc Light strikes. TPQ-10 was also used to control helicopters, for example, in Army operations. It was regarded as the most precise bombing aid available in Vietnam. Between 1966 and 1971 Air Support Radar Teams of Marine Air Support Squadron 3 controlled more than 38,010 TPQ-10 missions, directing more than 121,000 tons of ordnance onto 56,753 targets.

The A-6E target recognition and attack multisensor (TRAM), production of which began in 1978, had a passive narrow-beam forward-looking infrared (FLIR) sensor, which it could use in support of an attack on a surface target. The same year the A-7E was modified to carry an underwing FLIR. Normally these aircraft used their own radars to cue their FLIRs, but doing that exposed them to detection and destruction. Using Link 4, an E-2C could cue the FLIRs remotely on the basis of its own radar picture. This was a net-centric solution.[10]

Fighters: Phoenix and the F-14

Relatively immature in 1961, the Eagle-Missileer combination was further delayed because incoming Secretary of Defense Robert S. McNamara insisted on amalgamating Missileer with the projected high performance Air Force TFX. One reason the project failed was that it was impossible to provide anything like TFX performance in an airplane carrying the heavy computer the missile system demanded. However, within a few years Moore's Law had made it possible to build a higher-performance Navy fighter, the F-14 Tomcat, with much the system performance envisaged for Eagle-Missileeer, using a new Hughes Phoenix missile. Phoenix was lighter and more compact, and it added a post midcourse phase using intermittent semiactive homing. (Terminal homing was active, as in Eagle.) Like an SM-2,

Phoenix could fly an energy-efficient path that gave it extra range; it did not have to pick up energy reflected from the target until it came fairly close. Fired at a long-range target, Phoenix climbed almost vertically while its engine fired, then glided down toward the target. This initial maneuver created a column of smoke that, it was later understood, warned the target airplane to evade. Evasion was possible because the Phoenix missile motor was exhausted by the time it neared the target. The U.S. Navy later became interested in missiles that would be powered in their terminal phase, using either rocket ramjets or multipulse rockets.

Phoenix was enough like Aegis that in the mid-1970s there were serious proposals that it replace the more massive shipboard system. It would fit on board smaller, less-expensive ships. However, the AWG-9 developed for the F-14 could track only twenty-four targets, a fraction of what Aegis could do. Moreover, in ship-launched form, the missile would have had a much shorter range. The proposals died.

Moore's Law affected both the F-14 and its missile. When the F/A-18 was conceived about a decade after the F-14 first flew, its much smaller airframe could accommodate computers that, like those in the F-14, made a multimode radar possible and maintained a useful tactical picture using its output. The system was also powerful enough to be operated on a single-seat basis. Similarly, a much smaller missile, Raytheon's Advanced Medium-Range Air-to-Air Missile (AMRAAM), could be used for the sort of multiple engagements for which the F-14 had been conceived. Like Phoenix, it had a programmable autopilot connected to the airplane by an uplink, plus an active seeker. Because AMRAAM was designed for much shorter ranges, it lacked the intermediate semiactive feature of the Phoenix. (Many argued that, because of the smoke column, Phoenix was not really useful at anything like its maximum range.)

Moore's Law could not turn a lightweight F/A-18 into an F-14; it could not make up for the smaller airplane's shorter range, for example. However, it went quite far to provide the sort of weapon system performance for which the far more expensive F-14 had been built. Moreover, the F/A-18 could also function effectively as a bomber, so it could replace both the F-14 and the A-7 light attack bomber. By the early 1990s, the sheer cost of running carriers militated in favor of standardization. The F-14 was retired and an enlarged version of the F/A-18 (E/F version) adopted. AMRAAM was an acceptable replacement for Phoenix (and for larger missiles contemplated in the 1980s) because, with the demise of the Soviet Union, the long-range standoff threats that had justified the F-14 in the first place were gone.

Carrier Strike Planning: TAMPS and RTIC

Until the 1980s, the strike plans in the mission computers of A-6 and A-7E bombers were developed laboriously by hand. As in other warfare areas, a manual system could handle only a limited number of operations, developing about one plan per attack group per day. That was acceptable because it took all or most of the carrier's aircraft to attack each target, ensuring that enough bombs would be dropped to do the desired damage. The carrier's intelligence center provided the necessary information about the target area and enemy defenses, based both on the carrier's own reconnaissance aircraft and preloaded information from other carriers and from other intelligence systems. In effect, the intelligence center was the carrier's strike CIC, forming a kind of tactical picture. It paired weapons (strikes) with targets, and it developed strike plans (equivalent, in a sense, to the fire-control function of a CIC). The strike aircraft themselves corresponded to the weapons a CIC wielded.

By about 1970 the strike planning process began when the flag or commanding officer of the carrier listed targets and gave the desired level of damage or probability of destruction for each.[11] Other factors set at this time were rules of engagement, time over target, available forces, command and control constraints, and reconnaissance requirements. All of this information was given to a Strike Board composed of representatives from Strike Operations, Weapons, Air Intelligence, Navigation, CIC, and the flag officer. They decided first whether to launch a single mass strike or a series of strikes. At this stage factors like terrain and enemy defenses were taken into account. The Joint Munitions Effectiveness Manuals were used to decide how many weapons of which types were needed, taking into account what was available on board the ship and also whether delivering some kinds of weapons might be impractical. Unfortunately, the manuals were not well designed to help choose the mix of weapons.

The flight to the target and back was planned in segments, required fuel being calculated for each. Planners (for a group strike) guessed which approach to the target would be best, taking into account factors that included enemy defenses. The process was iterative, as alternatives were tried and rejected. Even so, it was unlikely that the plan selected was the best possible. That was particularly the case when terrain was complex. For example, it might be difficult to guess how terrain would affect enemy radar performance. Once drawn up, the plan was reviewed by the Strike Board and then by the officer in tactical command. Ultimately, the product of mission planning was a track chart the pilot mounted on a board strapped to his knee. With the advent of "smart" bombs, sometimes a single airplane could destroy a target, so individual pilots rather than teams created separate plans. That was certainly true for lone-attack aircraft such as A-6 Intruders.

Surely computers could try more alternatives, taking so many factors into account, and thus could help produce better plans. About 1974 ONR began to sponsor studies of computer strike planning aids: the Air Strike Timing Decision Aid (ASTDA), the Air Strike Outcome Calculator, and the Route Planning Aid.[12] They seem to have attracted little interest from the fleet.

It took a disaster to show that the existing system was inadequate. On 4 December 1983, as retaliation for the murder of U.S. Marines in Beirut, U.S. Navy attack aircraft struck Syrian positions in Lebanon. The attack proved unexpectedly difficult, in part because of delays. It had been designed to come out of the sun at dawn, but by the time the aircraft arrived over target, it was about noon. Given the complexity of the planning process, there was no way to revise plans quickly to take account of the delays.[13] An A-6E and an A-7 were shot down, the first U.S. naval air losses since Vietnam. One captured pilot was paraded through a street. To Secretary of the Navy John Lehman, this was unacceptable proof that the Navy's most important limited-war offensive arm, its carrier-based attack aircraft, was not operating effectively. He analogized their problem to that of the Navy's fighters during the Vietnam War: it was time to create an attack equivalent to the fighters' Top Gun training course. That became "Strike U" at NAS Fallon. The same examination also revealed that lengthy strike planning made for inflexibility.

Strike planning had to be automated. Fortunately, such planning was already being demonstrated for the new Tomahawk cruise missile. Tomahawk was a small low-flying airplane much like an attack bomber, except that it crashed into the target rather than dropping its bombs and returning. It needed the same sort of preplanned course to the target that a bomber used. The most important difference was that, because it could not see ahead, the missile needed a much more carefully planned flight path; any obstacle more than fifty feet high would stop it. Its planners certainly had to take enemy defenses and radar coverage into account. Without dedicated reconnaissance support, Tomahawk relied on national sensors, particularly satellites. Like air strike flight planning, Tomahawk planning was iterative. Tomahawk Missile Programming Centers (TMPCs) with access to national-level data were created at Norfolk and in Hawaii. They produced packages of flight plans in the form of data transfer devices (DTDs) that Tomahawk-shooting ships took to sea—a display system that showed which missions were in the DTD. The ships could not produce new flight plans, although they could modify the end points of missions.

When the Navy opened competition for the desired attack mission planner, McDonnell Douglas won with a system derived from the one it had developed for Tomahawk: Tactical Automated Mission Planning System (TAMPS).[14] Moore's Law made it possible for TAMPS to fit aboard ship and to develop plans more rapidly. TAMPS entered service in 1986. Initially it generated the same sort of paper kneeboard maps pilots had used in the past. The maps reflected better mission planning, but the airplane's computer was still set manually. That was slow and vulnerable to error. Conversely, the new electronic mission plans could be fed into a new mission-rehearsal system, TOPSCENE. It used the plan to create images similar to what a pilot executing it could expect to see as he approached the target. Pilots who had rehearsed their missions found it easier to orient themselves. Faster orientation undoubtedly made it easier for the pilot to penetrate enemy air defenses. Images of the target itself made it far easier to deliver weapons accurately.

Putting It Together: The F/A-18 and RTIC

The F-14 Tomcat was designed in the mid- to late-1960s. About a decade after the F-14, the Department of Defense sought a simpler and less-expensive fighter, and the Navy chose the twin-engine F-17. It wanted two follow-on airplanes, a fighter (F-18) and a light attack bomber (A-18, to replace the A-7). They needed different radars and fire controls. The fighter needed a pulse-Doppler radar for air-to-air combat. The bomber needed a ranging radar for bomb and missile fire control. Moore's Law offered the sort of computer power the F-14 had enjoyed on board this much smaller airplane. The F-14 needed a multiwaveform radar merely to control its Phoenix air-to-air missile. That capability was provided by using a computer to generate the waveform. The same computer could generate the waveform needed for air-to-ground operation. Since the F-18 would have a similar radar and a similar computer, it, too, could have both air-to-air and air-to-ground waveforms. There was no need for two separate airplanes, so the new tactical aircraft was designated F/A-18. That was much appreciated: carrier deck space was limited.

U.S. F/A-18s proved they really were dual purpose during the 1991 Gulf War. Two aircraft on a bombing mission encountered Iraqi fighters. The pilots switched radar modes, shot down the Iraqis, then switched back and completed their mission. Nothing like that had ever been done before.

Beginning with Lot 12, F/A-18s gained a digital connection to flight planning systems: a digital storage unit (DSU) plugged into the airplane to load its mission computer. Data include weapon programming and vital settings such as Link 16 slot timing and IFF codes. Loading and programming on the flight deck take only eight seconds. Conceived as a fleet air defense fighter, the F/A-18 has Link 16 (early ones have Link 4). Like other data links, this one sends information to the fighter by changing the data in its mission computer.

The combination of automated mission planning, a mission computer, and a data link opened an unexpected possibility. The same system that developed mission plans for a carrier's fighters could, in effect, dead reckon those aircraft once they had been launched, assuming they followed their plans. Using Link 16, it could redirect an airplane in flight, fully aware of the airplane's fuel status, hence its ability to reach some alternative target. Instead of the fairly static preplanned air operations of the past, this sort of automation offered dynamic control to deal with a rapidly changing situation.

The need to attack pop-ups probably became clear after the 1991 Gulf War. At that time all Coalition air strikes on targets deep in Iraq were coordinated via an Air Tasking Order that took about twenty-four or forty-eight hours to build. It was, in effect, a survival of earlier mainly Air Force ideas in which the proper role of air-power was to deal with fixed targets of enduring (strategic) significance. Somehow the Iraqis realized that it took substantial time for their enemy to react to whatever they did. They discovered that the Coalition was unable to hunt down and kill their mobile Scud launchers. When they moved aircraft around their cities (on a time scale shorter than twenty-four hours), the aircraft were not hit.

No slow planning technique could deal with fleeting or time-urgent targets. In the third world, few fixed targets were really important. Nearly all the targets worth hitting were mobile or relocatable. It might not even be possible to decide in advance which were important. The usual solution was forward air control, the controller in effect modifying the airplane's mission at its end. Deep in enemy territory, traditional kinds of forward air control might be impossible. However, unmanned aircraft (UAVs) could report back to air control centers via satellite links. The new strike planning systems gave these centers the kind of tactical picture of their own aircraft that allowed them to select the ones to hit the pop-up or opportunistic targets found by UAVs in real time. The existing planning software could be extended to "autoroute" (automatically route) an airplane as needed. Rerouting was simplified under conditions of air superiority, in which an airplane did not have to fly a complex low-altitude path. The new route could automatically be inserted into the airplane's mission computer via Link 16.

Typically, a forward air controller cued a pilot using a stereotyped ("nine line") targeting message. It turned out that a pilot needed a large-scale image of the target area to orient himself, then a smaller-scale image showing roughly where the target was, and then the sort of target image a UAV might produce. Given the location of the UAV, the control center could find the orienting image in its files. It could mark up the closer-in image, and it could retransmit whatever the UAV found. Link 16 could provide both the nine-line message and the three images. Generally precise target location could not be deduced from the image a UAV produced, but, given target images, a pilot could make up for that.

These elements were first put together late in the NATO war in Bosnia. The new concept was called Real Time in the Cockpit or Retargeting in the Cockpit. It could be extended to a target whose coordinates were known exactly. Link 16 could both reroute the strike aircraft and provide its Global Position System (GPS)–guided bomb with the appropriate coordinates. The pilot would need no visual cues at all. This possibility suggests the potential of future unmanned attacks. The U.S. Navy demonstrated a GPS attack on a pop-up target during 2002.

CHAPTER 15

U.S. Ocean Surveillance after 1945

Network-Centric ASW: SOSUS and HF/DF

After World War II the Western allies assumed that the Soviets, who had had the world's most numerous submarine fleet before World War II, would rebuild it postwar with something like the German Type XXI submarine introduced late in the war. They would surely use it against the vital NATO supply route across the Atlantic. A Navy study estimated that it would take six hundred escorts to maintain convoys. Wartime production had left about that many ships, but most of them could hardly deal with the new fast submarines. That would take far more expensive ships, and there was little reason to imagine that NATO could afford sufficient numbers. This was the sort of problem the British faced in 1904.

World War II demonstrated how powerful picture-based antisubmarine warfare (ASW) could be. It seemed unlikely that Allied code-breaking success would be repeated against the Soviets. High frequency direction finding (HF/DF) remained because the Soviets would have to rely on HF for long-haul communication. The HF/DF net built up during World War II was modernized. Short-range HF/DF sets were installed on board modernized or converted ASW ships. However, the future looked so grim that the U.S. Navy planned to base aircraft searches on reports of merchant ship sinkings ("flaming datums"). U.S. merchant shipowners were subsidized to install emergency radios in their ships' uptake casings, so that they would keep transmitting as a ship sank.

Fortunately, a technological solution appeared: Sound Surveillance System (SOSUS).[1] Suddenly a wide-area picture-based approach became possible. As early as 1947, the U.S. Navy found that low frequency sound traveled remarkable distances through the ocean. Based on earlier research into human speech, Bell Labs suggested analyzing the sound spectrum produced by a submarine. It turned out that submarines had distinct signatures. Woods Hole Oceanographic Institution discovered that their low frequency part could be heard, largely undistorted and thus recognizable, at great distances. The LOFAR (a made-up word, intended to sound like RADAR and SONAR) narrow-band analysis technique became the basis of U.S. and British ASW, its meaning secret until about 1973. In 1950 Bell Laboratories conceived a long-range fixed low frequency sound receiver, and successful tests soon led to a decision to build a SOSUS network of sensor arrays, the first being completed in 1954. That each submarine had a specific signature made it possible for SOSUS to place particular submarines at particular places at particular times. Such data could be strung together to form tracks: SOSUS could predict submarine position and cue interceptors.

Detections were by no means continuous. For example, a snorkeling diesel-electric submarine became effectively invisible once on batteries. The other main source of information, HF/DF, was also intermittent, as a submarine communicated only from time to time. Thus, the submarine surveillance system often worked with somewhat time-late information. SOSUS placed a submarine within a SOSUS Probability Area (SSPA), typically many tens of square miles. The further the area from the array (i.e., from a coast), the larger the SSPA. The search area, initially defined by SOSUS beamwidth, expanded as time elapsed. Typically, the interceptor was an ASW patrol airplane, flying from a carrier or from a land base. Ideally, the airplane could search the expanding SSPA rapidly enough to have a good chance of finding a submarine. It helped that its Jezebel sonobuoys used the same LOFAR sound analysis technique as SOSUS.[2] The U.S. Navy developed special radio links specifically to transmit LOFAR signatures so that, for example, those on board an airplane could know that they were detecting the submarine seen by SOSUS in the SSPA.[3] In the early 1960s, both the Atlantic and the Pacific fleets became interested in creating ASW Classification and Analysis Centers (ASCACs). An ASCAC translated raw LOFAR data into specific-submarine detections, which could be inserted into a track database.[4]

SOSUS and HF/DF became the basis of a network-centric ASW system. These remote sensors fed data fusion centers (Evaluation Centers), which created a picture for ASW Operations Centers (ASWOCs) and for the Atlantic and Pacific fleet command centers. ASWOCs controlled the aircraft that intercepted the submarines. Picture formation was cooperative: the ASWOCs fed back information brought back by their maritime patrol aircraft. Eventually the system also fed submarine command centers (Submarine Operating Authorities), which cued U.S. submarines (particularly for ASW), much as Pacific Fleet ocean surveillance had cued submarines assigned to attack Japanese ships. Thus, SOSUS justified maintenance of a shore-to-submarine command link that later became Submarine Data Exchange

System (SSIXS) and was vital for missile targeting. Cueing might have justified high submarine speed, much as it justified the speed of pre-1914 British battle cruisers, but apparently this argument was never used. SOSUS detected surface ships as well as submarines, but until about 1970 that information was considered noise rather than a contribution to ocean surveillance.

SOSUS seemed too good to be true. In the 1950s the Royal Navy discovered that it could silence even a snorkeling diesel submarine. Surely the Soviets could do what they had done. SOSUS would be obsolete just when all the stations were ready. The U.S. Navy tried massive active sound sources as an alternative. Existing SOSUS stations would be the receivers. This project was abandoned because the Soviets failed to silence their fleet. When they introduced nuclear submarines, they also failed to silence them. SOSUS was more effective against nuclear than diesel submarines because a nuclear submarine runs its noise-making machinery continuously: it cannot turn off its reactor. Even more remarkably, second-generation Soviet nuclear submarines had machinery with more stable—hence more detectable—noise characteristics than the first generation. Only in the late second-generation submarines (Victor III [Project 671RTM]) did the Soviets carry out the long-predicted silencing program. Silencing affected sonobuoys more than the big SOSUS arrays. Had the Cold War continued, the SOSUS arrays, whose listening beams fanned out through the oceans, would have been replaced or at least complemented by Fixed Distributed System (FDS) upward-looking arrays detecting submarines as they passed over. Submarine course and speed would have been measured by a series of lines laid on the ocean bottom.

SOSUS and the interceptors it cued would have had enormous psychological effects on Soviet submarine commanders. It would be one thing to steel oneself up to attack a convoy because between convoys the commander and crew could relax. It would be quite another to know that, whatever the submarine did, one day a P-3 could appear out of nowhere and sink it. The submarine might escape, but only at the price of heightened vigilance, which in turn would take a toll during any prolonged antiship battle. SOSUS would have ground down the Soviet submarine fleet. In 1960 the U.S. Navy estimated that three months of grinding would destroy that force altogether.[5] During those three months, submarines that were not destroyed would sink about three hundred merchant ships, which seemed an acceptable price.

NATO and the U.S. Navy never relied entirely on SOSUS, but it dramatically reduced the number of ASW ships required, to the point where NATO navies could build escorts of sufficient quality to face modern submarines. NATO benefitted heavily from geography: it planned to block the choke points through which Soviet submarines had to pass to reach the shipping lanes. That was much what the British relied on in 1939–40, when U-boats had to pass around Scotland or through the Channel en route to patrol areas. It was subject to the same possibility that military action ashore would reverse favorable geography. Even so, while the choke points stood, they would have exacted a considerable toll, not only in submarines going out to attack, but also in those returning to rearm. (Soviet submarines, like all others, had limited weapon loads.)

Initially, SOSUS was mainly a way to locate submarines so that convoys could avoid them, but its picture of Soviet underwater activity offered much more. At least as early as 1957 the picture was seen as a strategic warning indicator: surely the Soviets would surge their submarines into the Atlantic before starting a war.[6] As long as Soviet strategic submarines operated within SOSUS detection range, the picture was valued for strategic defense.[7] It also supported battle groups trying to evade submarines. Such roles justified investment that dramatically improved SOSUS coverage over time.[8]

At the outset, SOSUS was very secret. For example, during the 1950s the U.S. Navy experimented with carrier-centered ASW task forces that recalled World War II hunter-killer (HUK) groups prosecuting wide-area intelligence and HF/DF data. Critics argued that HUK operation was pointless; money should go to convoys. They seem not to have guessed that somehow the wartime wide-area techniques were being revived (by this time HF/DF but not code breaking were reasonably well-known). In the mid-1960s, Defense Secretary Robert S. McNamara's annual defense budget reports mentioned SOSUS for the first time and associated it with P-3 maritime patrol aircraft. No details were given. By this time the Soviets were probably aware of the system. In the late 1950s, their trawlers reportedly tore up U.S. undersea cables, which were probably part of SOSUS. Remarkably, no one seems to have associated SOSUS with the sudden appearance of naval cable-laying ships in the U.S. Navy and in some NATO navies. SOSUS was probably compromised by the Walker spy ring, as one of its members was an ASW officer instructor and John Walker himself was a watch keeper in the Atlantic Fleet submarine plot. To the extent that Walker reported where the U.S. Navy thought Soviet submarines were, the Soviets could find areas of better or worse SOSUS coverage. Walker's reports also probably brought home to the Soviets just how detectable their submarines were and thus helped trigger the fairly successful silencing program of the 1980s.

The Walker ring may help explain why system performance began to decline about 1971–72. The Soviets were making their submarines quieter because they were patrolling further from U.S. shores and because they were moving their patrol areas to areas of poor acoustic conditions. Even so, in 1976 SOSUS deployed on Soviet egress/ingress routes was detecting first- and second-generation Soviet nuclear submarines making better than ten knots.[9] The system was encountering problems once the submarines reached their patrol areas and ran at lower speeds. The U.S. Navy was working on ways to redress the balance.[10] By that time, too, the U.S. Navy was deploying towed-array surveillance ships, in effect mobile SOSUS arrays, which changed the configuration of the system.[11]

As in so many other contexts, Moore's Law affected this one. The first stage was in signal processing. In 1954 it took a massive shore installation to do LOFAR processing. Less than a decade later a LOFAR processor could fit on board an airplane, but SOSUS shore stations could still conduct more sensitive processing, and thus could detect targets hundreds or even thousands of miles away. The tactical towed arrays introduced about a decade later were, in effect, miniature SOSUS stations.

After the Cold War, the U.S. Navy expected to fight local or expeditionary wars, which erupted several times in the former Yugoslavia (which had submarines), in Afghanistan, and in Iraq. Could the Cold War form of networked ASW be transplanted? One solution was a bistatic version of the Cold War towed surveillance array, a single ship towing the array far aft and suspending a powerful pinger beneath her hull. A very different multistatic technique was developed to solve the difficult problem of detecting a bottomed submarine—which makes no noise, hence cannot be detected passively. Sound echoes off the bottom—and off the submarine. In the mid-1990s, a Defense Advanced Research Projects Agency (DARPA)–sponsored Distant Thunder project showed that when a point charge was exploded, processing the outputs of an array of passive sonobuoys could generate a detailed map of the bottom—including the submarine. The key was sufficient bandwidth to pass detailed signals to the single processor. The sonobuoys combine their information, looking at the same scene from many different viewpoints. In the mid-1990s, a shoebox-sized processor could find the submarine within twenty minutes. That is almost ten Moore's Law generations ago.[12]

Passive techniques could be transformed to solve the difficult problem of detecting submarines in shallow water. The key was to focus on a picture of underwater activity rather than on a particular submarine. Even a quiet submarine radiates noise as she moves, and an upward-looking bottom array can hear her. It can tell where the submarine crosses the array (in effect an underwater fence). A series of such crossings reveals the submarine's course and speed, which can be projected ahead so accurately that that a helicopter can be vectored to the submarine's position, to drop an ultra-lightweight homing torpedo. Because sensing is passive, the submarine cannot be aware that it has been detected and tracked. This idea has been called precision ASW, in much the same way that network-centric warfare is sometimes called precision warfare. As in SOSUS, the important unstated virtue of such a technique is that the submarine commander cannot be sure he is safe.

The Surface Picture: Merchant Ships

U.S. post–World War II surface surveillance began with fears that the Soviets might bring a nuclear bomb into a U.S. port aboard a merchant ship. This idea figured in several National Security Council meetings, all of which concluded that it would be difficult to detect such a weapon. (The same meetings ordered radiation detectors placed on bridges and in tunnels, for example, leading to Manhattan.) Hence the LAMPLIGHT recommendation that the U.S. Navy track merchant ships around the world. In 1955 the National Security Council ordered the U.S. Navy to track non-Soviet merchant shipping, the assumption presumably being that the Soviets would not use one of their own relatively few merchant ships for the purpose.

Khrushchev soon began to use Soviet merchant ships to supply arms to client states, such as Egypt, and to Third World revolutionaries. The Office of Naval Intelligence (ONI) began to track them, too. Like submarine movements, it seemed that Soviet merchant ship movements might be a war warning. It was generally assumed that the Soviet merchant ships would all be withdrawn to port just before the outbreak of war. Skeptics suggested that, instead, the merchant ships would be used to cover naval movements, for example, by turning on warship-mimicking emitters. Soviet surface warships were of less interest because until 1967 they stayed almost entirely in home waters.

Tracking was predictive: as in Admiral Sir John Fisher's day, the U.S. Navy relied on unclassified sources of data, assuming that ships followed their planned routes. There was no systematic means of covering the vast oceans. In January 1961 Portuguese rebels seized the liner *Santa Maria* as a protest against their country's colonial policies. They cut off all communication, so in effect the ship disappeared in the South Atlantic. She was not found for days, to considerable U.S. embarrassment. Many in the U.S. government had no idea of how trackless the sea was.

WWMCCS and Command Automation

At about the same time, in 1961, the incoming Kennedy administration sought to centralize control of the U.S. military—which required more-or-less current pictures of the locations of U.S. and foreign forces. There was already interest, formalized by the Joint Chiefs of Staff in 1959, in greater centralization as a way of ensuring that U.S. nuclear forces could respond quickly to a Soviet attack. The Kennedy administration added a further justification for centralized control and, therefore, picture keeping. It imagined both that a nuclear war (or escalation) could and should be controlled once it began and that blunders by low-level officers might ignite it. Such views differed profoundly from those of its predecessor. President Dwight D. Eisenhower doubted that, once begun, a nuclear war was controllable. However, he doubted that anyone was foolish enough to risk nuclear war. Almost nothing that a local military commander could do would ignite one. Even if a local commander used tactical weapons, no one was likely to escalate to nuclear holocaust.

Thus, the new administration created a centralized World-Wide Military Command and Control System (WWMCCS).[13] It required data that only computers could assemble. By 1961 the U.S. Navy was already arguing that fixed land headquarters might be destroyed at the outset and that control of U.S. nuclear weapons might quickly devolve to senior commanders afloat—who would need similar amounts of data in order to make their decisions. WWMCCS envisaged a flow of information up from the services and from the intelligence agencies, and a flow of commands down into the services. It needed, for example, a more-or-less current picture of all surface activity, U.S. and foreign, and that, in turn, led the U.S. Navy to create a formal Ocean Surveillance Information System (OSIS).

For the Navy, this was the heady time after it seemed clear that the Naval Tactical Data System (NTDS) would succeed but before its limitations became obvious. The Navy's response to WWMCCS was a program to automate its own major command facilities (in a kind of super-NTDS net) so that they could feed data to the projected automated national headquarters, initially envisaged as a Washington command center, a reserve center to be used if Washington were obliterated, an airborne command center, and a seaborne center linked to the land centers by high-capacity radio equivalent to high-capacity land lines. In effect, OSIS was the sensor feeding the projected automated naval command system.

The Navy headquarters in the Pentagon was connected to the shore command centers of the three named fleets (Atlantic, European, and Pacific). Each named fleet commanded numbered fleets, each of which had an afloat flagship (as did major task forces). For example, CinCUSNAVEUR (at the fixed fleet level) communicated with Sixth Fleet, which in turn communicated with Task Force Commander (CTF) 60 on board a carrier in the Mediterranean. The automation plan envisaged a major operations control center data system serving the Pentagon headquarters and the two named fleets. They would be linked to the Fleet Flagship Data Display System (FDDS) and the Tactical Flag Data System (TFDS).

By the mid-1960s, the information, in the form of computer disks, came together in the Navy Information Center (NAVIC) in Washington. It provided daily locations for the chief of naval operations' flag plot and passed its information to WWMCCS. NAVIC was updated only periodically, and its plot seems not to have been dead reckoned to simulate a real-time picture. U.S. Navy data came from the Movement Reports Control Center (MRCC), which received regular movement reports via dedicated hundred-word-a-minute teletype lines. It also fed regional Movement Report Centers. Because computers were scarce, MRCC translated what it received into both hard copy *and* punched tape. Tapes were hand carried three times a day to NAVIC, where their data were transferred to magnetic tape for entry into its computer. Unfortunately, about half of all movement reports were automatically rejected because of formatting and similar problems. NAVIC's printout of accepted and rejected data was hand-carried to MRCC, where rejected records were hand-corrected. This processing made it difficult to meet the desired update rate of once every eight hours. MRCC also handled merchant ships, using sources such as Lloyd's List and weather reports.

ONI brought together its foreign data at the Naval Intelligence Processing Support Center (NIPSSA) at Suitland, Maryland. It worked with a smaller organization run by J-2 (intelligence) at CinCLANTFLEET (Norfolk, Virginia). NIPSSA fed its data into NAVIC to form the other half of the overall picture desired for WWMCCS. The ONI Ocean Surveillance Branch merged data from its main sources, SOSUS and signals intelligence (SIGINT) (mainly HF/DF).[14] SIGINT data were collated by the ONI Naval Field Operational Intelligence Office (NFOIO) at Fort Meade, the descendant of World War II code breakers. NFOIO also reported Soviet merchant and fishing vessels and other Communist bloc ships when they were outside home waters and conducted surveillance of Soviet aircraft over international waters. Automation was complicated because the special information used to track the Soviet navy could not be shared outside the intelligence community, which used manual techniques for analysis. Its conclusions apparently generally were not track data easily inserted into a dead-reckoning computer.

ONI also had three Fleet Intelligence Centers (FICs): FICEUR, LANTINTCEN, and FICPAC. (Ultimately the European center moved to Mayport, Florida.) They provided the fleet with detailed operational information, and they collected the information the fleet's sensors picked up. At this time they were probably most important as a means of supporting carrier operations against shore targets and were not primary elements in ocean surveillance. Experience in Vietnam showed how important forward facilities were. FICPAC in Hawaii could not service the fleet thousands of miles away; a forward facility built in the Philippines was not nearly large enough. Once the Soviets became active in the Mediterranean, the fleet intelligence role shifted more toward surveillance and warning of Soviet action. Hence a small intelligence detachment was created at Rota to serve the Sixth Fleet.[15]

Unfortunately, NAVIC could not share its plots with operational commands, which maintained their own forms of ocean surveillance. For example, at Norfolk each of four separate major commands had its own operations control center: CinCLANTFLT, ComASWForLant, ComSubLant, and ComOceanSysLant.

Fortunately, all were in the same building, where all surveillance activity except that conducted by the Naval Security Group (communications intelligence) was concentrated.

By this time ONI was interested in converting much of its information into computer form suitable for insertion into NTDS, to feed the system's estimates of target priority and engageability and also to provide it with electronic support measures (ESM) data. Navy electronic reconnaissance squadrons (VQ) were already collecting their data on foreign emitters in computer-readable form, using some of the first computers ever used by naval intelligence, IBM 650s. In June 1959, as part of an appeal for resources, ONI asked—and this time received—help from other naval agencies to design and then to develop the sort of automated data handling systems it needed.[16] In 1962 it developed a formal automation proposal. Some information, such as order of battle and electronic parameters, would be digitized directly. Other information would be reduced to microfilm and catalogued electronically. Both kinds of information would become much easier to transfer and to handle, with immediate impact on carrier intelligence centers. (See chapter 21.) The automation projects were formalized in November 1963. Research had begun the previous year with a contract to IBM for computer support of the Fleet Intelligence Centers.

The information storage and retrieval element was intended as the core of a future Naval Intelligence Processing System (NIPS). It could be compared to NTDS. Instead of the operators entering blips into a computer it had a coordination and control element, which logged incoming material. The equivalent of the track-keeping computer and the associated tactical display was the store/receive element, which produced reports and maintained files. Instead of the element that assigned targets to weapons, deciding whether engagement was possible, NIPS had an image information element with imagery interpretation facilities, as well as the ability to produce graphic products such as maps and sets of photographs. Because these were such general functions, it was easy to imagine extending the NIPS to very different roles. In addition to its naval functions, NIPS was intended to exchange information with other automated intelligence organizations. It was formally announced in 1967.[17]

ONI's computers were batch processors, essentially a means of filing the growing mass of available information rather than of creating an operational picture. However, NTDS had shown that much more could be done: a computer could dead reckon to translate a database into a reasonably accurate current picture. A Specific Operational Requirement (SOR) for a ship-tracking data system was issued in 1964.[18] It envisaged tracking systems at places like SOSUS centers and (U.S. Navy) Movement Reporting Centers feeding into the command data systems. This SOR probably accounted for the computer at Atlantic Fleet headquarters, which dead reckoned ahead the positions of merchant ships so that they could be reported on a daily basis.[19] The SOR envisaged more-or-less real-time links between ship trackers spread over the world, but existing radios could not have carried that sort of load. Nor were existing computers designed to exchange data on anything like a real-time basis. On 6 May 1965 the Office of the Chief of Naval Operations (OpNav) issued a formal General Operational Requirement (GOR 35) for ocean surveillance. It seems not to have had a particularly high priority at first, but eventually it led, in a circuitous way, to the creation of the OSIS system, which in turn was used not merely to form a tactical picture but also for missile targeting—a truly network-centric concept.

As an example of current practice in 1966, CinCLant had an Operations Control Center with a computer complex, an Indications Center (supported by the Intelligence Support System [ISS] computer), and Movement Reporting Center (MRC) Norfolk. The Operations Control Center (the "main floor system") was built around a massive new FYK-1 computer.[20] It dead reckoned the ships in its memory, and positions could be adjusted as new information was received. Unfortunately, computers were in scarce supply, so this one could not be dedicated to ocean surveillance. Nor, despite expectations, could it handle special intelligence alongside its normal classified content. The requirement to sanitize by hand any all-source information it used cut the flood of such information to a drip. The machine was effectively limited to tracking merchant ships. All other computers used for ocean surveillance were batch processors updated periodically, which could provide lists of current positions. They had very limited core memory (typically 32,000 words) and could not accept all-source information. Security may explain why ONI envisaged separate systems to track Communist naval forces, Communist and foreign civilian shipping, and U.S. shipping.

CinCUSNAVEUR in London had another FYK-1 with a similar dead-reckoning program. It also had a high-speed telephone connection to the global AUTODIN net. However, the next level down, Sixth Fleet on board the cruiser *Little Rock*, had neither a dead-reckoning computer nor a high-speed link. The three FICs were not involved in ocean surveillance at all. A prototype FDDS may have been installed on board the Sixth Fleet flagship *Springfield* during her 1970 refit, the sole afloat survivor of the super-NTDS plan. It is possible that the initial U.S. Navy satellite communication program, which provided terminals on board flagships, was intended to support the linkage envisaged in the super-NTDS plan.

A 1971 WWMCCS modernization program created the computers used in the Navy FICs that figured prominently in the creation of its modern ocean surveillance system. By 1976 WWMCCS had thirty-five computers around the world organizing its information. However, they were not yet netted together (at that time full netting was a 1980 goal, attainable in theory because all used common hardware and software). Without interconnection, computer data had to be transported physically, in tape or disk form, for insertion into other computers. Different computers in different places could not compare their data. Even so, WWMCCS requirements became a reason for agencies like ONI to convert their manual files so that they could readily be entered into WWMCCS computers. Moreover, the existence of WWMCCS encouraged NATO to create a comparable system. The automated British naval command center at Northwood was associated with this program.

WWMCCS itself is interesting from a picture-centric point of view because its developers, who were well funded, spent their money mainly on communications. As late as the early 1980s it relied for nuclear warning—for its picture of a developing Soviet attack, which should have been the basis for U.S. action—on an array of sensing systems built for different purposes and never very well integrated. Tests showed that different systems produced different reports of test data fed into them, although all of them were well adjusted to avoid false alarms. The picture was not cleaned up until it became important for national ballistic missile defense. The moral is unpleasant. The picture is what determines whether a command and control system can support operations. If it is no good, the best communications in the world are worthless. Yet, it is much easier to buy better communications links, and their capabilities are also easier to quantify. A detailed account of WWMCCS written for the Naval War College in 1976, recently declassified, did not even address the question of how good or bad the WWMCCS picture was.

Because WWMCCS was oriented toward nuclear war, it was poorly equipped to handle the complexity of a sustained conventional war like Vietnam, and the kinds of decisions it could convey were limited at best. Particularly once the 1971 modernization program began, and once extensive satellite communications became available, it seemed that WWMCCS could indeed connect the National Command Authority directly with local forces in limited emergencies. During the 1973 Middle East War, the White House reportedly gave detailed orders to the Sixth Fleet, but apparently their scope was limited. Two years later the *Mayaguez* incident was hailed as the first case of full connection down to the local level. It is a matter of opinion whether such control was particularly successful. High-level control may have helped ruin the 1980 attempt to rescue the U.S. hostages in Tehran. Many in the military considered the fear of accidental nuclear war through blunder ridiculous, and high-level interference (as encouraged by WWMCCS) a recipe for disaster. The U.S. military saw President Ronald Reagan's refusal to intervene when Navy fighters shot down Libyan fighters in 1981 as a breath of fresh air. He understood that small incidents were most unlikely to have enormous consequences. He could have intervened—but he chose not to. The picture-centric system enables central-ization, but it need not cause it.

Surface Surveillance in Action: The Cuban Embargo

The Cuban Missile Crisis of 1962 was the first real test of the new kind of surveil-lance.[21] The system in the Operational Control Center of CinCLANTFLT became operational in 1962, just before the crisis. Its sources were a voluntary merchant ship movement reporting system (the American Vessel Reports, AMVER), reports of planned U.S. naval ship movements (Movement Reports, MOVREPS), and selected intelligence reports. The system produced Predicted Ship Listings (PSLs) showing which merchant ships patrol aircraft could expect to encounter in their operating areas. PSLs were generated at 2200 each night by a batch computer run in Norfolk, and they were limited to six Atlantic Ocean rectangles corresponding to particular ASW areas of responsibility.[22] The sources were too limited to create anything like the full picture desired by the Kennedy administration during the crisis. (A 1964 report estimated that they covered about 26 percent of shipping.) Other sources, which were tapped later, included ships' weather messages (which indicated ship positions) and Lloyd's List data on sailings and destinations. At this time it was understood that a full ocean surveillance system would also use HF/DF and SOSUS data, but they were handled on a different security basis.

Because intelligence-based surveillance was still so limited, the Cuban quar-antine was enforced in a more-or-less classical (ship- and airplane-intensive) way, with ships spaced about every fourteen miles along surface barriers. Patrol aircraft overhead picked up merchant ships and identified them visually ("rigging" them). The result was the largest naval deployment since the Korean War.[23] The administra-tion's particular requirements made the embargo more difficult to set up. It wanted all merchant traffic (not only Soviet bloc) between European and Mediterranean waters and the Caribbean and the Gulf of Mexico located, identified, and photo-graphed. Initially it also wanted all suspect ships intercepted five hundred miles from Cuba (this figure was later reduced).[24] Soviet bloc ships had to be met at sea and visibly shadowed by U.S. warships, both to pressure the Soviets to back down and to demonstrate U.S. will. Sixteen Soviet ships stopped at sea and turned back. It was important to be sure that those that did not turn back were not carrying weap-ons. (Presumably it was assumed that missiles were too large to be stowed invis-ibly below decks.) It was also necessary to shadow the Soviet ships that eventually removed missiles and bombers from Cuba. Conversely, the Kennedy administra-tion thought that the movements of Soviet bloc ships might indicate larger Soviet intentions. No intelligence-based system could have met these requirements. Later it was estimated that about 86 percent of ships bound for Gulf and Caribbean ports from Europe, and about 72 percent from North America, were identified.

A postembargo analysis estimated that political and military considerations increased the force required by a factor of at least six. Surveillance of all shipping, not only that bound for Cuba, greatly increased the load on the embargo force. For example, barriers from Puerto Rico and Bermuda would have been about twice as effective had they been allowed to concentrate only on westbound traffic. Patrol aircraft flying in daylight made over half the identifications (carrier aircraft were relatively ineffective in this role), and the long range of the new P-3 Orion helped enormously. It could concentrate on tracking ships of particular interest. Concentration on ships of special interest consumed about 16 percent of the air and about 9 percent of the cruiser-destroyer effort. The load on the Navy was increased because it was also conducting intensive ASW operations (this was the first real test of SOSUS) and it was preparing to invade Cuba if ordered to do so. These other roles inevitably conflicted somewhat with the embargo because they involved the same types of ships and aircraft.

Lessons of the Cuban quarantine seem to have included the inadequacy of the sources the initial ocean surveillance system used. Much more was available. Examples included the lists of port clearances and destinations maintained by Lloyd's of London (in a way, the lineal descendant of the reports British consuls had been making nearly a century earlier), as well as the weather reports that many ships made daily as a contribution to world weather reporting. Probably such data were fed in as they became available in machine-readable form. By 1970 NIPSSA was using more than twenty sources, which varied enormously in format, accuracy, medium, content, reliability, security classification, and transmission delay. It was handling 14,000 to 16,000 pieces of information each day, providing regular reports to twenty users.

The Ocean Surveillance Information System

When the GOR was issued, the U.S. Navy had elements that could be developed into an ocean surveillance system, but they had not been designed to work together. After a 1966 Center for Naval Analyses (CNA) study of measures of effectiveness, a Tentative Specific Operational Requirement (TSOR) for an integrated all-source information processing and display system for ocean surveillance was issued on 3 February 1967. That month development was assigned to the Naval Electronics Laboratory (NEL) already responsible for NTDS, which could be imagined as a small-scale equivalent operating on a more urgent basis.

Events now made ocean surveillance important. After the June 1967 Six Days' War, a substantial Soviet surface fleet moved into the Mediterranean. For the first time since 1945 there was a real possibility that the U.S. Navy would fight fleet on fleet. Meanwhile, Communist-bloc shipping was supplying North Vietnam, although the U.S. government was not yet willing to try to intercept that shipping. With the Soviets active in the Mediterranean, in 1968 the U.S. government asked NATO governments to support a new intelligence center specifically intended to track the Soviet fleet. Joint Chiefs of Staff (JCS) Memorandum 701-68, tasking the CNO to maintain aggressive ocean surveillance, was later cited as the basis for Ocean Surveillance Information System (OSIS) development. Progress seems to have been slow, possibly because the ongoing war in Vietnam drained available funds. The Defense Intelligence Agency made OSIS an evolutionary development of existing systems rather than a justification for new dedicated ones. CNA was assigned to analyze existing resources to see how they might be integrated.

CNA envisaged a kind of super-NTDS for ocean surveillance. NTDS merged local data (ships' own radar detections) to form a large-scale picture. Local analysts in different commands were best placed to meet their own command's needs and had earlier knowledge of data collected locally. They were more aware of the local situation, and perhaps most important, the local commander knew them and thus could rely on them. This local knowledge had to be made available throughout an integrated system. As long as it was handled manually, it could not easily be transmitted. As in NTDS, the key information in the system should be the positions of ships, dead reckoned on the basis of known or estimated courses and speeds. A computer could easily tag each ship location with whatever additional information analysts collected. As in NTDS, an operator at a console could update the central picture periodically, its screen allowing the analyst to visualize the effects of various possible inputs. The key analytic functions would still reside in the people running the system. Each analyst would be able to call up programs as needed, contributing what he learned to the evolving overall picture.

CNA's key perception was that Moore's Law would soon make this sort of system possible. It would no longer be necessary to rely on batch processors to handle the flood of data. The future system would be built around a reduced number of centers linked by dedicated high-speed lines. Another key perception was that a single system needed access to all possible sources of information: SOSUS and HF/DF, for example, might both contribute to tracking a particular ship. Each regional center should have access both to local sensors and to wide-area sensors that might provide it with relevant information. Each would use all-source intelligence to form a surveillance picture in its area of responsibility. The analyst's graphic analysis and correlation terminal (GACT) would be the OSIS equivalent to the NTDS console at which an operator entered targets and monitored the system's projection of their positions. New software would make the analysts' workload bearable by analyzing and correlating data with the existing database. This was much what NTDS did when it continuously simplified its track data by attempting to correlate new reports with existing tracks.

CNA's vision was embodied in a proposed technical approach to meet the OSIS requirement issued in 1970. Revision 5 of GOR 35 (5 January 1970) envisaged creation of near-real-time databases that could be used tactically (although the more important role of the system would be strategic warning). A Specific Operational Requirement (SOR 35-15, derived from GOR 35) issued that fall (15 September 1970) directed the chief of naval matériel to develop a prototype ocean surveillance information center. By late 1970 a Technical Development Plan (TDP 35-15) was complete, ready for issue on 1 January 1971. The objective of ocean surveillance was changing to include provision of "dynamic situation displays to appropriate levels of command as an essential element of naval operations," a radically different position than that taken a few years earlier.[25]

Meanwhile ocean surveillance attracted high-level interest. In the summer of 1970 the Defense Science Board formed a task force on ocean surveillance, chaired by Dr. Charles Herzfeld, then chief scientist of ITT. Herzfeld became an important advocate for ocean surveillance, as well as a critic of what he considered unduly elaborate efforts. One of his ideas was that the existing *Soviet* ocean surveillance system could be exploited by U.S. ocean surveillance.[26] The U.S. Navy had long been able to reproduce the radar picture a Soviet system produced by detecting not only the main beam of the radar but also reflections off its targets, a concept called BRIGAND. Herzfeld suggested exploiting the downlinks of Soviet ocean reconnaissance satellites on the theory that they would detect, among other things, their own ships. Such intercepted data could be transmitted to U.S. ships in near real time. Soviet satellite downlinks were being intercepted and analyzed under a project called Cluster Buster. Precise knowledge of where U.S. ships were made it possible to calibrate the intercepted signals. Efforts were also made to improve reporting of U.S. merchant ships, even though they represented a declining percentage of world seaborne traffic.[27]

The OSIS centers were Navy headquarters (displaying but not inserting data), the Naval Ocean Surveillance Intelligence Center (NOSIC) at Suitland, Maryland; Fleet Ocean Surveillance Information Centers (FOSICs) for the Atlantic and Pacific fleets; and Fleet Ocean Surveillance Information Facilities (FOSIFs) for the Sixth and Seventh fleets, the forward-deployed ones. Because all the centers were on land, they could be connected by high-speed computer links, the system's much more capacious equivalent to Link 11. NOSIC became operational on 18 January 1971 and was formally opened at a ceremony attended by the vice chief of naval operations (VCNO) on 1 February 1971. It had a large-screen display connected to the existing computers, with a third-generation high-capacity data link (CDL) computer about to be installed. The hundred-words-per-minute teleprinter circuits between NOSIC Suitland and FOSIC Norfolk, FOSIC Hawaii, FOSIF Rota, and Current SIGINT Operations Center (CSOC) Fort Meade were all operational by late April. In the absence of dedicated communication lines, naval intelligence data were piggybacked on the circuits of the Naval Environmental Data Network, using modems, multiplexers, and crypto equipment. Guam was initially chosen for the Western Pacific FOSIF, but about April 1971 it was superseded by Kamiseya, Japan. Fleet Exercise ADMIXTURE (23 February–3 March 1971) used a temporary FOSIF at the headquarters of the Western Sea Frontier. Its experience suggested additional ways in which a FOSIF could be used. Probably as a result, by early 1972 the dynamic OSIS picture was seen as an essential element of naval operations.

In May 1971 the separate (duplicative) software development was approved at the fleet level to speed development. In October CinCLANTFLT was designated prototype site. Goals were automated communications by FY72, an interim system (online data exchange between all major centers) by FY74, and a complete system by FY76. NEL delivered a core Intelligence Support System (ISS) to CinCLANTFLT late in calendar year 1973, but its software failed test and evaluation. Attempts to solve problems by modifying the system were abandoned in September 1974, although CinCLANTFLT considered a further modified ISS partially operational in June 1975. This failure prompted Naval Electronics Systems Command (NAVELEX; successor to the Naval Electronics Command [NELC]) to begin yet another OSIS project in March 1974, making a new CinCLANTFLT system its prototype. Pacific elements of OSIS would be modified later to match the Atlantic, but there were enough differences that most communications software could not be reused. As of 1977, the Eastern Communications Net, which should have been operating in 1974, was not considered operational.

Plans required that all OSIS nodes reach initial operational capability (IOC) by June 1975. The following year, after seven years and $49 million of development, neither adequate hardware nor software existed, and it was estimated that another $37 million would be needed.

These problems explain why the Defense Science Board reported in 1973 that the proposed OSIS architecture was far too expensive and probably unrealizable. This report was cited as a reason to reject an ambitious OSIS upgrade proposed later in the 1970s. A naval audit blamed too many OpNav reorganizations, some of which reflected changing OSIS roles.[28] OSIS began as an intelligence system with functions like strategic warning, hence as an ONI (Op-92) project. It morphed into a program to support combat. Its intelligence side acted as a sensor. As a vital tactical command tool it was moved in 1971 to Op-094 (Director, Command Support Programs). Early in 1972 responsibility for requirements moved to Op-947 (C2 support), but Op-942 was responsible for implementation and would assume control when the system became fully operational. In an attempt to clear lines of responsibility, on 30 December 1974 Op-094 became resource and program sponsor. A new Op-0955 Ocean Surveillance Division was created within Op-095 (ASW and Ocean Surveillance), which became Mission Sponsor on 30 December 1975. Op-09B took over the program on 12 April 1976, raising the level of authority involved; it seemed that the program had finally been stabilized. Within NAVELEX, other projects enjoyed higher priorities, and OSIS moved from group to group. In August 1975 PME-108 was established as C3 program manager. By that time OSIS was envisaged as the sensor element of the Naval Command and Control System (NCCS). Another element of the system was the new ASW Command and Control System (ASWCCS) uniting SOSUS, the shore HF/DF net, and the P-3s. PME-108 was responsible for all of these elements, plus a new project to support a long-range antiship missile, over-the-horizon detection, classification, and targeting (OTH/DC&T).

The first SEAWATCH I software became operational at NOSIC in March 1973.[29] NOSIC used it to maintain the OSIS database.[30] By 1975 analysts at computer terminals updated the system by entering the observed courses and speeds of various ships. As had been imagined, the center looked like the CIC of an NTDS ship. OSIS could not process sensor reports quickly enough to maintain a dynamic picture, but the fleet increasingly saw surveillance as a vital long-range sensor. A 1976 report considered OSIS reasonably successful in the sea control role on a peacetime basis. In the aftermath of Vietnam, there was little interest in supporting power projection. Presumably that meant little attempt to track or analyze Soviet bloc coast defense forces, concentrating instead on blue-water warships. Presumably, too, the system was unable to track Soviet naval aircraft, which would have been the first line of defense against U.S. attacks, within a few hundred miles of the Soviet coast.

NOSIC was the contact point with the National Command Authority, providing data such as the locations of Soviet strategic submarines. (It was part of the DoD Indications and Warning Network.) The primary NOSIC product was the Daily Soviet Fleet Activities Summary, but the center produced seventy periodic reports plus special analyses as needed. To some extent manpower-intensive tracking made up for a lack of ship position data. Unfortunately, there was no direct computer-to-computer connection between NOSIC and the FOSICs, so they could not share the main OSIS database. Rapid secure analyst-to-analyst connections were limited.

The FOSICs were being automated, but much remained to be done. Most manpower was devoted to intelligence fusion for evaluation and analysis, but each FOSIC also produced flash (urgent) "heads up" or spot reports whenever threat platforms were detected. Typically, a FOSIC produced daily (twice daily in a crisis) briefings for fleet commanders in chief (CinCs) and their staffs, as well as a daily Naval Intelligence Summary covering Soviet maritime activities plus tailored reports for friendly navies. Limited automation made for limited exploitation of the mass of available information. FOSICs were particularly limited in their ability to track Free World shipping.

Similarly, the FOSIFs were still handling their data manually. They were managing to produce advisory messages within fifteen minutes of receiving information, but manual operation was manpower intensive, and it was impossible to exploit all the information being collected.

In 1976–77 interest shifted toward using OSIS to target cruise missiles, as the system became dynamic enough to provide tailored information timely enough for targeting. It also seemed possible that the National Command Authority would require OSIS information before allowing missiles to be fired. Thus the May 1977 Ocean Surveillance Master Plan mentioned OTH targeting as the planned operational use of the system. Tomahawk tactical targeting brought together the two parallel strands of ocean surveillance and tactical command and control because its range was such that it could not be fired on the basis of a ship's organic sensors, yet it was clearly a tactical weapon.

A new OSIS Master Plan for 1978–90 promulgated on 20 January 1978 was apparently even more expansive than the version killed by the Defense Science Board four years earlier; the earlier report was cited when this plan was killed. The only new sensor envisaged, the CLIPPER BOW active radar satellite, was considered the most important of all potential OSIS sensors because it would be least affected by any Soviet attempt to silence electronic emission.

What was left was an attempt to standardize OSIS in a baseline configuration. By 1983 OSIS was considered reliable (better in the Atlantic and Pacific than in London). It was primarily a Red force tracker, for both ships and submarines. The result was considered good enough at the theater level. Lower-level commands used OSIS and provided information for it; they provided some data to the FOSIF node at Rota. Uses included ASW mission planning and OTH targeting, but data were not good enough to be used by a ship firing a Tomahawk. Also, OSIS lacked automated air-track correlation—which was becoming more important in order to fight the outer air battle.

OSIS Baseline Upgrade

Given the many limitation of OSIS, TRW received a contract for an OSIS Baseline Upgrade (OBU) late in 1982, as a basis for further evolutionary upgrades. OBU envisaged buying new VAX processors to handle more track reports and adding an air tracking module and electronic intelligence (ELINT) capability. OBU was later officially described as intended to improve OSIS's timeliness to nearly real time (to 95 percent accuracy) without heavy investment in new sensors, by updating the OSIS database with each satellite pass and each new sensor reading. Most important, changes in the command systems made it possible for operational commanders to receive OSIS data in their command centers. A Navy Decision Coordinating Paper (NDCP) for OBU (presumably for further modifications) was issued in May 1987, an OSIS Decision Coordinating Paper in January 1990, and a Program Change Approval Document in January 1992. The dates suggest that the 1987 paper called for OBU development in accord with the new Evolutionary Acquisition (i.e., continuous computer upgrade) concept and that the later papers integrated new capabilities, such as the Relocatable Over-the-Horizon Radar (ROTHR). For example, under the FY90 program, a ROTHR Interface Module (RIM) was completed for the Pacific FOSIC. (The radar in question was later moved to the Caribbean.) There was also site consolidation; the FOSIC at Norfolk was closed down and its Atlantic support function amalgamated with that of the NOSIC at Suitland, Maryland.

OBU was exported to allied navies, presumably to form a network that could share operational intelligence.

Ocean Surveillance Sensors

Like the Soviets, the U.S. Navy initially relied heavily on HF/DF for surface ocean surveillance. It, too, developed a version of the late-war German Wullenweber (the Soviet version, described below, was Krug). At its peak the U.S. land-based Classic Bullseye system comprised thirty-two stations in three independent networks (Atlantic, Pacific, Mediterranean/North African—note the absence of Indian Ocean coverage). The Canadian, British, and Australian navies contributed the fruits of their own DF systems. The Classic Bulldog upgrade program automated the system.[31] About 1973 it was decided to link these systems with the shipboard Classic Outboard, partly because the United States lacked HF/DF stations in much of the world. Classic Outrigger was an associated system that provided command, control, and communications support, fingerprinted emitters, and semiautomated surveillance. The two test ships were USS *Josephus Daniels* and USS *Mitscher*. Plans called for installation on board nine cruisers and nine *Spruance*-class destroyers. The Royal

Navy bought Outboard for six frigates intended to work with its two operational short takeoff and vertical landing (STOVL) carriers. These systems were useful, because, at least through the 1970s, the Soviets relied heavily on HF radio. They were supplemented by SOSUS, which detected surface ships as well as submarines.

There were also the usual external sources, including merchant ship reports and Lloyd's List, plus material gathered from U.S. intelligence agencies. The absence of Lloyd's List in reports of the Cuban Missile Crisis, and its later presence in lists of OSIS sources, suggests that it was used as soon as it became available in computer-readable form.

The Navy became interested in radar satellites as early as 1964, and from time to time there may also have been interest in infrared (IR) ship detection from space. The U.S. Navy first publicly discussed ocean surveillance from space in the context of the abortive Manned Orbiting Laboratory of the mid-1960s.[32] The fourth flight was to have had an all-Navy crew, using radar and optics for ocean surveillance. By this time the Naval Research Laboratory (NRL) had built the Global Radiation and Background (GRAB), the first U.S. reconnaissance satellite. It intercepted signals from Soviet land-based radars and sent them to a ground station. Their positions could be deduced using its reception pattern.

By 1968 the Navy was considering NRL's ocean surveillance satellite system, soon designated Program 749 in the series of U.S. space systems. Phase 1 was a passive satellite that could measure the direction of signals it picked up, hence their location on the surface of the earth, where that line intersected the surface. Phase 2, an active radar satellite, was initially the public face of Program 749, Phase 1 (the one actually fielded) being secret. NRL was apparently capable of developing the Phase 1 satellite, but it could do only the initial analysis for the active radar satellite. Both versions avoided satellite-borne processing by sending raw data down continuously to ground stations rather than (as the Soviets did) processing it on board the satellite and periodically dumping it to earth. NRL thus offered the most sophisticated processing and also the greatest potential for upgrades after satellites were in place. For example, raw intercepts were a good basis for radar fingerprinting. Many other ocean surveillance sensors were then being considered.

The Clipper Bow radar satellite was attractive because the Soviets could not evade it by turning off their emitters, although they could detect its pulses and react accordingly. Zigzagging could ruin track prediction. The surveillance resolution cell was finite, so that no satellite could distinguish ships operating close enough together. Thus Soviet merchant ships already at sea on D-day might deliberately confuse surveillance to the point where it became impossible to distinguish Soviet warships. With the advent of Tomahawk, Clipper Bow became attractive as a way of detecting ships surrounding a target, so that the missile could be maneuvered to avoid locking onto them.

Work began formally in 1974. Each of a pair of satellites orbiting at 600 nautical mile altitude would look toward the horizon 1,800 nautical miles away, revisiting every point above 30 degrees north every 1.8 hours. Because Clipper Bow could not scan the entire ocean, it had to be cued, possibly by ELINT, via its control center. Ultimately, plans called for the satellite to be tasked from a ship or from a fleet area commander. Clipper Bow might be used mainly to detect all the ships in an area, its passive counterpart Classic Wizard picking out the most important. In August 1976 the Defense Directorate for Research and Engineering (DDR&E) urged the Navy to accelerate investment in radar satellites, so Clipper Bow was fully funded in the September 1976 Five-Year Defense Plan. An Operational Requirement was issued on 5 January 1977. A 1977 concept-verification study by the contractor confirmed a design-to-cost price of $296 million (FY76 dollars) for the two satellites. This did not include shipboard equipment. By 1978 plans called for launching the first satellite in FY83 and the second in FY84. A draft Navy Decision Coordinating Paper was circulated within OpNav in early 1978, and a Defense System Acquistion Review Committee (DSARC) II review approving full development was expected in the third quarter of FY79. Proponents pointed out that without Clipper Bow the United States lacked any equivalent to the Soviet radar ocean reconnaissance satellite (RORSAT).

However, Clipper Bow never materialized. In the summer of 1978 the U.S. Senate Armed Services Committee objected that Clipper Bow would duplicate other existing programs. The Navy assured the committee that its satellite was a unique specialized ship detector, but in mid-1979 it decided to reduce the program to study status.[33] Even this work stopped in mid-1980. The rationale was high cost and limited value. In theory the Clipper Bow program and an Army program conceived to track Warsaw Pact armored units were merged as the Integrated Tactical Surveillance System (ITSS).[34] Presumably, it was associated with the Lacrosse satellite, which uses a side-looking synthetic aperture radar. It is not clear whether the integrated program retained any naval element.

That left White Cloud or Classic Wizard, the passive part of the satellite program. The first experimental satellite was launched on board a Thor-Agena on 14 December 1971. Difference in the time a signal arrived at its three subsatellites indicated the direction of the emitter.[35] To make use of White Cloud output, the Navy mounted the hull-to-emitter correlation (HULTEC) radar fingerprinting project.[36] It became possible to confirm that the same ship was detected on two separate satellite passes. On that basis a track could be measured and ship position projected ahead. A track vector analysis capability (i.e., the ability to deduce the direction of a ship's course from a series of satellite sightings) was developed for OSIS specifically to exploit such data. Probably HULTEC accounts for the installation of precision signal analyzers aboard U.S. maritime patrol aircraft.

The ships White Cloud detected could never know they were being tracked. They were unlikely to maneuver evasively, so the system's projections were likely to be accurate. However, it could see only ships using the sensors to which it was tuned. It would miss ships using radars in which it was not interested. That did not seem terribly important in the 1970s, when attacks would be mounted by pilots capable of distinguishing important Soviet warships from the unimportant ones around them. It became much more important when OSIS was used to target Tomahawk missiles.

CHAPTER 16

Netting Tactical Intelligence: IOIC and Its Successors

F rom World War II on, a carrier's Intelligence Center was, in effect, the Combat Information Center (CIC) supporting her strike aircraft. As long as information arrived relatively slowly, there was little point in automating its operation. That changed when a new-generation carrier reconnaissance airplane produced a flood of data on each flight. In 1957 the requirement for a next-generation reconnaissance system was framed. Instead of cameras *or* electronic intelligence sensors, it would have both, plus side-looking (imaging) radar for night and bad-weather flights. Such an airplane would collect far more than its predecessors could.[1] Those who conceived the new sensor package seem not to have had automation in mind. However, as it moved closer to service, the reality of just how much it would produce must have become obvious. It would spew out data like one of the new electronically scanned or stacked-beam radars, far too much to sort or catalog quickly enough by hand. The airplane chosen to carry the new package was a reconnaissance version of the Vigilante bomber, the RA-5.[2]

The Office of Naval Intelligence (ONI) was responsible for handling the reconnaissance output. Its new Naval Intelligence Processing System (NIPS) was the obvious choice to handle the flood of information.[3] Beginning in 1962, ONI developed an Integrated Operational Intelligence System (IOIS): the new multisensor reconnaissance package plus the automated Integrated Operational Intelligence Center (IOIC) aboard the carrier operating it. Intelligence analysis was like tracking on a massively different scale. A target tracker compares each new data point with those in its memory to associate it with a particular earlier point and hence with a known track (or decides that it is a new object). The track makes it possible to predict what is about to happen and is the basis for action (e.g., engagement). Similarly, a photograph is a single data point, with only limited significance. Associated with others, it shows that something has or has not happened: the enemy has built new gun batteries, or has replaced the bridge recently knocked down, or has moved troops into position, or has built a missile base. Without an automated database, the system relies on the analyst's memory and on his ability to find past photography for comparison. Computerization made it possible for the IOIC to benefit from the increased mass of information per sortie. New techniques speeded extraction of data from the returned airplane; for example, the IOIC included a secret high-speed (one-hour) film lab. Like its contemporary, Naval Tactical Data System (NTDS), IOIC was built around a USQ-20 computer.

The IOIS was so important that ONI formed a special task force including representatives of ONI, the National Photographic Intelligence Center (NPIC), the Bureau of Naval Weapons (a combination of the Bureau of Aeronautics [BuAer] and Bureau of Ordnance [BuOrd]), and North American Aviation (the A-5 manufacturer). Priority may have been raised by the experience of the Cuban Missile Crisis (fall 1962), when Navy carrier reconnaissance aircraft provided vital intelligence. IOIS was first installed on board the carrier *Saratoga*, followed by *Ranger* (during her 7 August 1963–67 February 1964 overhaul), and then *America*. By 1967 it was on board all *Forrestal*-class carriers and the nuclear-powered *Enterprise*. It was planned for future carriers (older ships could not accommodate it). In theory, carriers with IOICs could now exchange data far more quickly and readily in the form of computer files. However, without any wideband communications channel between carrier and shore intelligence centers, or between the carriers themselves, massed data had to be transferred physically.

The IOIS proved strikingly successful in Vietnam.[4] According to a November 1967 Office of the Chief of Naval Operations (OpNav) memorandum (proposing that the concept be extended), automation alone made it possible to process up to a thousand records per day, to correlate new raw intelligence with existing information, and to maintain the operational database, in effect the tactical picture. Information collected on one RA-5C mission was routinely used to plan the next— a remarkable achievement, given how much the airplane could collect. Processing was so timely that strikes were sometimes diverted in flight, based on information just received. Not only local but also national information (i.e., information relevant to other forces or even other services) was updated on a massive scale. The dynamic tactical database was also used to continuously recalculate preplanned missions, which probably meant the planned nuclear strike missions to be executed in the event of a central war. The IOIS and NIPS also made it much easier for information about the rapidly evolving air war to get back to those who needed it in the United States.

Once the IOIS succeeded, it became necessary to automate shore intelligence centers that provided part of its database. Thus the three Fleet Intelligence Centers

(FICs) were automated to become compatible with the IOICs. An FIC provided a carrier with her initial database on deployment, and the carrier provided new data when she returned. Little could be done while the carrier was deployed because the data had to be handled physically.[5]

The IOIS paralleled other ONI automation initiatives. With data across ONI handled in standard machine-readable ("machineable," in the jargon of the times) or at least machine-cataloged (and retrievable) form, it became easier to transfer masses of information from one ONI activity to another, without having to manually file and catalog them. Such efforts went beyond the Navy. Navy VQ (ELINT) squadrons were part of a multiservice effort, and they provided their data in computer-usable form to special electronic reconnaissance centers (as well as to the fleet). Much of this data went into carrier intelligence centers. In the mid-1960s common machineable data standards were being widely adopted in the U.S. intelligence community. The Air Force was developing a transportable intelligence processing center (TIPI), broadly equivalent to the IOIC. Because the data standards were common, the TIPI could be used to support an amphibious operation by the Marines, who also used naval data.

The RA-5C was available for reconnaissance only because its original role of strategic air attack lapsed soon after it appeared. Its magnificent performance had been paid for with nonintelligence, or nonsurveillance, money. Given how tight money was after Vietnam, there could be no direct successor. As in other picture-centric systems, a solution was possible because the system was not inherently stovepiped. Data from the RA-5C was translated into a universal NIPS language so that it could be entered into the system. Other NIPS data could be handled the same way. Thus the post-Vigilante IOIC took its imagery from one source (the RF-8G fighter, later an F-14 with a Tactical Air Reconnaissance Pod System [TARPS] pod) and its electronic surveillance data from others. Until the late 1980s, it was still necessary to bring images aboard a carrier in physical form.

By the late 1980s there was a new possibility. Digital cameras could send their products down to the carrier via a high-capacity common data link (CDL, which is also used for unmanned aircraft [UAV] sensor data). The same processor that handled the images could also handle radar data. Because imagery could be linked down to the carrier while the airplane was in flight, the carrier could redirect reconnaissance as needed, or it could use the images to redirect strikes much more quickly. Because the images were digital, it became far easier to process them, for example, to correct them for the orientation of the airplane in flight or to turn them into images more like what a strike pilot might see. Images could now come from other sources, such as reconnaissance satellites, from archives in the United States via broadband satellite links. Digital images of a target area, moreover, could more easily be combined with nonimage data such as electronic intercepts, to gain a better idea of what was happening on the ground. Among other things, because the carrier's own aircraft were no longer her sole source of current imagery, an enemy could not rely on the appearance of those aircraft for warning. Also, an analyst on board the carrier might be able to make better sense out of what he saw if he could review a file of several years of photos of the same area. In effect the carrier strike capability turned from platform-centric to network- or picture-centric, with its characteristic support of surprise attacks.

RA-5C electronic intelligence in support of ground strikes became more and more important in Vietnam, as the North Vietnamese erected more and more elaborate defenses. The new mass of information was best exploited by an automated jamming airplane: Grumman's EA-6B Prowler. Like the A-6 Intruder, it was built around a computer. The initial approach, in which the computer automatically identified and tracked emitters and set jammers to attack them, was rejected. (The Marines bought this version of the airplane.) The Navy preferred a semiautomatic approach, in which the onboard computer helped the operator identify threats and select jamming modes. The EA-6B using this technique entered service in 1972. Operators used a preloaded threat map (in the central computer) to help identify emitters, based on aircraft position when a signal was intercepted. The computer triggered analog signal generators for jamming. By 1977, when the first upgraded version (ICAP I) appeared, operators were being overloaded by the increasingly dense pulse environment. This version offered better threat identification (better receivers and a better threat library). In ICAP II, first flown in 1980, the Navy reverted to automation, using more-powerful multiple computers. One computer carried the mission plan and kept track of the aircraft position, as well as the electronic emitter map. The map simplified automatic emitter identification, as the airplane knew where it was and from what direction pulses were coming. A second automatically identified emitters and generated digital waveforms to jam them. Later a third computer was added to control high-speed antiradar missiles (HARM). In this version, which is still being used, the operator usually monitors the system instead of initiating action. Much the same was happening with contemporary radars as automatic detection was introduced.

As in the RA-5C, the sheer volume of data involved was daunting. Somehow the limited relevant part of whatever was on board the carrier had to be fed into the Prowler at flight time. Even if the airplane operated continuously in one area, the enemy's electronic order of battle could change quickly as new radars were brought into service or existing ones reset. Moreover, mission planning was complicated, because how and where to jam depended in a detailed way on how terrain affected radar signals both from threats and from the jamming airplane. Mission planning for the jammer was far more laborious than for an attack airplane, so the jammer became an early candidate for computer help.[6]

The ICAP II project included the Tactical EA-6B Mission Support (TEAMS, TSQ-142) automated mission support system, which acted in part as a bridge between the intelligence database in IOIC and the airplane. In addition to mission planning, TEAMS recorded information the EA-6B collected as it flew over enemy territory for use in updating the database on the carrier. TEAMS communicated with the EA-6B via a data cartridge inserted at flight time. It programmed all three onboard computers. TEAMS also produced flight plans, kneeboard charts, and thirty-minute strip maps to illustrate the chosen route. Entering service in 1984, it seems to have been the first automated aircraft mission planner.

As with imagery, the electronic warfare data in an IOIC were held in universal form, so that whatever the RA-5C collected could be merged with data from other sources such as VQ squadrons and even ELINT satellites. Thus, the loss of RA-5C data was unfortunate but not crippling. The mass of data involved grew over time, so that carrier libraries typically held only the emitters in the areas in which they operated. A carrier shifting suddenly from one part of the world to another needed an entirely new database. For the U.S. Navy, this kind of requirement was one more reason to acquire communication satellites, with their relatively high data capacity and their ability to move data from sources in the United States to the deployed fleet. Particularly after the end of the Cold War, even the threat receivers on board tactical aircraft had to be made rapidly reprogrammable—assuming that the ship could receive enough data quickly enough. The British operation in the Falklands gave a first taste of the problem: new electronic warfare data had to be air-dropped to the task force on its way south, when it was near Gibraltar.

Extending the IC Concept

Once IOIS was well under way, a Specific Operational Requirement (SOR 36-06, 4 June 1964) was issued for other shipboard Tactical Intelligence Centers, which by 1967 meant AGC-IC (for an amphibious flagship, later redesignated LCC), NFC-IC (for a numbered fleet flagship), and CVS-IC (for the ASW aircraft carrier). Like the IOIC, all would support planning and hence did not have to operate in real time. Each type of ship had to handle increasing masses of data quickly enough to support something approaching real-time decision making. The success of IOIS showed that NIPS could do that, so it was natural to see it as the basis for systems for all three kinds of ship. OpNav pointed out that about 90 percent of NIPS used existing equipment, the rest entailing only low-risk reengineering. Surely it could easily be adapted to all three types of ship. In retrospect it seems remarkable that this 1967 proposal referred to the hardware but not to the software, which really might have differed from application to application. The FICs would provide intelligence support for all three types of ships; the amphibious flagship would also draw information from the shore-based TIPI. High-level systems on all three types would feed sanitized data into the ships' NTDS.

The AGC seemed analogous to the carrier. Its intelligence center produced amphibious plans much as a carrier's intelligence center produced strike plans. Instead of an RA-5C, it received data via helicopter from a shore processing center (a Marine TIPI). Because TIPI intelligence was machine coded, the AGC could easily request exactly what was needed. Turn-around between TIPI and an automated AGC could be much shorter than with existing manual systems. As in a carrier, manually supported planning was necessarily static: it took a long time to assemble a plan, and it was impossible to realign it in real time. The automated AGC system would still produce the earlier kinds of texts, photographs, and maps. However, it would maintain a more current picture of the situation. IOIC showed that if information could be handled quickly enough, plans really could be changed as they were executed. Outputs of the AGC system would include information in a form suitable for display and use by flag plot and by the Supporting Arms Coordination Center (SACC), the control center for close air support and for fire support.

The numbered fleet flagship had to maintain a reasonably current picture of activity throughout an area of interest extending well beyond the horizon of any force with which it operated. It had to fuse data from many sources, some outside the fleet. Plans called for a Flagship Data Display System (FDDS) as a basis of flag decision making, which in the 1960s might include planning for nuclear strikes (particularly if planning centers in the United States were destroyed). The picture could be less current than that of NTDS, because the flag system covered a wider area, but ideally it would involve more planning aids.

Antisubmarine (CVS) aircraft collected masses of acoustic data using their sonobuoys. Interpretation required reference to a massive graphic database of submarine signatures, to which the airplanes constantly contributed. Only an automated system could quickly and reliably classify submarines by comparing their detected signatures with the database. After classification, the intelligence center (IC) could correlate new data with all contacts and all-source information it held. It could also supply electronic countermeasures (ECM) "fingerprint" information for correlation with ECM contacts. The IC library of current environmental data would help interpret what the sensors picked up. As with the attack carrier, the ASW carrier IC would meld prior knowledge of local Soviet submarine activity with newly collected and interpreted data to create intelligence on the character, strength, and disposition of the enemy submarine force. The carrier would apply this data to the command of friendly ASW forces. Conversely, without the IC, carrier aircrew could still detect submarines, but they would have a much more difficult time using signature data to identify them. The signature library would give the IC an ability to analyze aircraft flight data to pick up submarines that aircrew did not realize their sonobuoys had detected. The machineable files produced by the IC could be transferred to any other ASW carrier that relieved it in a given area. IC functions would be carried out in the carrier's ASW Control and Analysis Center (ASCAC).

All of these systems would have appeared on board new ships, but by 1968 shipbuilding plans were collapsing. That February Secretary of the Navy Paul Nitze disapproved the IC proposal without prejudice to the attack carrier IOICs, pending modifications and better cost definition. He did approve one NFC-IC as part of a prototype integrated system. It became the basis for a new kind of naval command and control, described in the next chapter. Even so, the requirements were real, so equivalents to the AGC and CVS ICs appeared.

A kind of amphibious command IC predated the formal 1967 technical proposal. The two new amphibious flagships *Blue Ridge* and *Mount Whitney* had an Amphibious Flag Data System (AFDS), based on the same USQ-20 computer as IOIC and NTDS. Requirements were developed in 1964 by a study group convened for the purpose at San Diego. It combined an integrated automated operational intelligence center (equivalent to a carrier's IOIC) with an amphibious command-information system (ACIS). ACIS provided an amphibious commander with force-loading data (so that plans could be changed if, for example, a ship in the amphibious group were lost), with the landing plan, the shore-bombardment and air-support plans, a bomb-damage-assessment file, and intelligence data. It was not a real-time command system; it did not maintain a picture of the situation on the beach. Thus it could not command fire support or troops or boats. The associated NTDS was adapted to control aircraft over the amphibious objective area and to coordinate helicopter assault and resupply, close air support, and air defense. Presumably it employed Link 4 for strike control. Ultimately the ships were used as numbered fleet flagships, their command spaces filled with new-generation wide-area computer systems unrelated to ACIS and NTDS.

Given Moore's Law, the next large amphibious ships (*Tarawa* class) were effectively amphibious flagships (albeit on a smaller scale than the *Blue Ridge* class). Their new-generation (Phase 2) intelligence centers were connected directly to a new Integrated Tactical Amphibious Warfare Data System (ITAWDS) built around the next-generation UYK-7 computer. A Tactical Information Management (or Processing) System (TIPS) corresponded to ACIS. It incorporated the ship's intelligence center. Unlike ACIS, it had a dynamic database that could be used and queried during an assault. Given its picture of the current tactical situation, it could designate targets to weapons (including close support aircraft) via the combat direction element of the system. However, apparently it could not control boats and troop formations. Like ACIS, TIPS managed assault personnel, operational planning, and logistic coordination. "Integrated" meant that the ship's tactical data system and TIPS used a common executive/operating system. The follow-on *Wasp*-class LHDs had an updated version of ITAWDS.

The CVS disappeared altogether following the end of the Vietnam War. By that time it was mainly a means of defending strike carriers against the emerging Soviet nuclear attack submarines. The chief of naval operations (CNO), Adm. Elmo Zumwalt Jr., decided to move ASW aircraft onto the attack carriers, redefining them as multipurpose platforms. They needed something like the planned CVS-IC, compressed into even less space than there was on board a CVS. Moore's Law solved the problem.

The CVS-IC was a way to sort masses of paper Lofargrams collected by aircraft using sonobuoys. The new S-3 Viking had a digital sonobuoy processor and a digital mission computer, so what it fed into the carrier's system was already adapted to computer processing and storage. Sonobuoy data could even be fed back via data link while the airplane was in flight. The carrier had a Tactical Surveillance Center (TSC, later the ASW Carrier Module), which corresponded to the Antisubmarine Warfare Operations Center (ASWOC) that controlled and supported P-3s ashore. The TSC processed sonobuoy using a computerized signature library. Using that and other data it maintained a wide-area underwater picture. It used the picture in its computer planning element. The in-flight sonobuoy reporting connection made it useful to reroute aircraft in flight.

CHAPTER 17

A New Kind of Fleet Command: FCC and TFCC

T he intelligence-handling systems were really picture keepers for large masses of data. Just as the picture-keeping function in the Naval Tactical Data System (NTDS) was the core of a command system, a large-scale picture keeper could be the core of a larger-scale command system—a fleet command system. In effect this larger-scale system was a scaled-up equivalent of NTDS. It emerged in the 1980s as a paired shore and ship system—in effect an automated equivalent of what Admiral "Jacky" Fisher conceived eighty years earlier for the Royal Navy.

The Fleet Flagship System

In the mid-1960s the commanders of the two forward-deployed numbered fleets (the Sixth and Seventh) demanded a current picture of where their ships were and of what they had on board, largely as a basis for their central task of planning and carrying out nuclear strikes in the event of war. Once the Soviet surface fleet entered the Mediterranean in numbers after the 1967 Six Days' War, Sixth Fleet also wanted a picture of the surface situation, particularly the locations of Soviet surface ships and submarines within missile range of the carriers.[1] This information had to come at least partly from intelligence. The NTDS did not cover the area of responsibility of a numbered fleet commander. Its display could not easily be simplified as required. It could not show geography in detail. It offered no easy comparison with status board information on contacts. Nor did it provide any specific contact identification. It offered no track history, including the last known position of a contact, on which correlation with off-board data would be based. All-source information, such as special intelligence, was not readily adapted to computer input or display. The planned solution was the Naval Electronics Command's Flagship Data Display System (FDDS) connected to an automated

Numbered Flagship Center–Intelligence System (NFC-IC). Given U.S. ships' positions and courses, FDDS would dead reckon their positions. A separate flag plot system would show the surface situation. NFC-IC would also provide general intelligence summaries for display in the fleet commander's flag plot and machinable data for deployed tactical forces. The system sketched in 1967 resembled that on a carrier or an amphibious flagship, but without the graphic element. A prototype FDDS was ordered installed on board the Sixth Fleet flagship cruiser *Providence* when she was overhauled beginning in January 1970.

For a time it seemed that the display might not have to be automated at all because surface contacts moved relatively slowly. In the fall of 1970, Naval Air Refit Facility (NARF) Quonset Point made three multilayer plotting (MLP) boards for Sixth Fleet experiments. Layers were pulled out for plotting different kinds of pictures, then pushed back so that they could be viewed together as a kind of visual data fusion. The combination was side lit. The Extended Surface Plot (ESP) using these boards was considered a great improvement over the ordinary vertical plot or dead-reckoning tracer (DRT), the only available large-scale displays. Boards were installed on board the two Mediterranean attack carriers (*Independence* and *John F. Kennedy*) and on the Sixth Fleet flagship *Springfield*. *Springfield* had neither NTDS (which the carriers had) nor any digital link, so her ESP was kept up-to-date by message traffic, including Link 14. In tests, the Extended Surface Plot successfully tracked all surface ships (about twenty on average) in the area of interest. The fleet staff found it easy to correlate the flagship's all-source intelligence information with the ESP plot.

Intelligence information was not nearly current enough, so the fleet sought a more-or-less real-time sensor. It found the E-2 Hawkeye. Instead of concentrating on aircraft, an E-2 over a task force could use its radar mainly to detect surface ships. It could not identify them, so each time it detected one it vectored an A-6 or A-7 attack bomber for visual identification. The E-2 continued to track the target, the master plot on the flagship now knowing its identity. The E-2 could also detect snorkeling or surfaced submarines at ranges out to eighty-five nautical miles. Thus a typical plot included a Charlie-class missile submarine. Results of initial trials were so encouraging that in January 1971 Sixth Fleet ran a full-scale trial using the carrier *John F. Kennedy*, covering a 15,000 square mile area. ESP seemed to be so reliable that it was sometimes used to update NTDS, rather than the other way around. Sixth Fleet wanted it to become permanent. Although ESP proved awkward for Combat Information Center (CIC) installation, the important lesson was that Sixth Fleet wanted a wide-area plot.

If an E-2 had been effective in the ESP experiments, a higher-altitude airplane might be even better because it could cover a wider area. Longer sensing range was becoming more and more important as the Soviets deployed longer and lon-ger range missiles against the U.S. fleet. The larger the surveillance area, the more information the airplane would collect. As in the case of the RA-5C, a flood of information might require automatic handling. In 1972 a Very High Altitude Aircraft Sensor Platform (VHAASP) was proposed. It was envisaged as a modified U-2 controlled by (and feeding data to) a carrier or from the projected (but abor-tive) Sea Control Ship. It might be backed by electronic intelligence (ELINT) (VQ) aircraft. The Navy proposed modifying a U-2. Exercise HIGH BOY began in April 1973 using a U-2 carrying a converted weather radar, a tactical electronic warfare (EW) suite (ALQ-110), a radar beacon video processor, and an optical identifica-tion system. Aircraft sensors were downlinked to a surface terminal, which fused their information on a real-time basis for transmission to the carrier *Kitty Hawk* via a hundred-words-per-minute teletype link. The exercise report recommended that aircraft data be processed automatically rather than manually. In April–May 1974 the Operational Test and Evaluation Force (OpTEVFOR) showed that this could be done.[2]

Emergence of the FCC and TFCC

Meanwhile the Ocean Surveillance Information System (OSIS) was being assem-bled to use signals intelligence (SIGINT) (including high frequency direction finding [HF/DF]) as its primary source of information. The Vietnam experience suggested that correlating many SIGINT sources would provide useful informa-tion that no enemy could use to deduce what particular signals had given away his position. Such information could be used operationally. To test this idea, a Multi-Source Correlation Facility (MSCF) was built at the Sunnyvale Test and Evaluation Detachment. Tests showed that the correlated product could be handled outside the special intelligence community. The resulting OSIS picture could be used oper-ationally, just as Admiral Sir John Fisher had used his War Room pictures in Malta and London.

The U.S. Navy added a new twist. Instead of becoming the basis for commands from an ashore headquarters, the picture would be transmitted to a flagship afloat. Exercises already showed that enemy jamming could wipe out the tactical pic-ture used by an at-sea commander.[3] Without it, he might be unable to take effec-tive decisions. The picture assembled ashore might not be quite as good, but it would be a worthwhile backup. Fleet Command Support Centers (renamed Fleet Command Centers [FCCs] in June 1975) would combine own-fleet and merchant-ship information from the World-Wide Military Command and Control System (WWMCCS) with OSIS from collocated Fleet Ocean Surveillance Information

Centers (FOSICs) to create a timely, easily understood display of the sea situation.[4] It would be data-linked to Tactical Flag Command Centers (TFCCs) on board not only numbered fleet flagships but also task force and task group flagships. (For a time it was also proposed for large-deck amphibious ships, amphibious flagships, and even missile cruisers.) The TFCCs would correlate the wide-area information from the FCC with whatever local sensors picked up. They were envisaged as an extension of earlier work on the automated FDDS. The system would advise the local commander on the basis not only of the picture but also of capabilities and limitations of both Red and Blue forces, local threat intelligence (for the commander's geographical area of responsibility), and evaluated strategic and tactical intelligence information from both national and fleet-level sources. Given OSIS information, the tactical commander would focus his own ocean surveillance resources. That would help avoid duplicating intelligence resources. Work began in 1973.

The core of the evolving TFCC was a Flag Correlation Facility (FCF), which could correlate the SIGINT-based picture assembled ashore with the products of local fleet sensors. In 1974 an FCF on board the carrier *Kitty Hawk* was linked by a hundred-words-per-minute HF teletype (in effect Link 14) with the Sunnyvale MCSF. Special Outlaw Hawk software in the FCF correlated MCSF data with the ship's own sensor data, automatically comparing ships' attributes and their positions. All tracks were dead reckoned. As in NTDS, each time a new datum was received, the system provided the track manager (not automated in this case) with a list of candidates to which it might correspond. Generally, it proved possible to correlate a datum before the next arrived. Threat evaluation was simple, based entirely on effective range: distance of first detection by a remote sensor less the distance the target *could* have made good (steaming directly toward the ship) before it appeared on the plot. In tests, half of all potential threats were known to the flag before they came within 650 nautical miles, and 80 percent before they were within 200 nautical miles, even though some ships moved 100 miles before *Kitty Hawk* showed them on her plot. A Phase II test (20 February through 29 March 1975) added an experimental shore over-the-horizon (OTH) radar to pick up nonradiating targets beyond the carrier's horizon. This time FCF data were good enough to be used when NTDS was not working.

For simplicity, FCF and its display system were entirely separate from the ship's NTDS. The correlated picture was shown on a three-by-four-foot Large Group Display (LGD) in a special command center: the flag could view the tactical situation without leaving his command position. The LGD was used to brief the flag when he entered the command center and to brief the officer about to relieve the watch. Without it, plots would have been far less valuable—and they would not have been viewed nearly as often. The LGD system ran about forty-five minutes behind NTDS. The surface surveillance coordinator (SSC) updated it hourly with NTDS data. About two-thirds of the time the FCF display was used to view NTDS data. It was much clearer than that the usual NTDS picture because it showed scale factors and convenient geographical features (such as coastlines) directly.

In addition to the geographic display on the LGD, system output terminals in CIC showed call signs, threat characteristics, task force organization, fuel status, and task force readiness. However, many of the files normally maintained by grease pencil on status boards were not displayed. Examples of what flag could *not* see included the antisubmarine warfare (ASW) status board (units airborne, cooperating surface units, etc.) maintained by the ship's ASW Classification and Analysis Center (ASCAC), the reconnaissance mission list from the Integrated Operational Intelligence Center (IOIC), and even the usual Bogey Tote/Combat Air Patrol (CAP) status board for air defense. In one period of particularly hot action during an exercise, the displays answered only a third of the questions set by flag and senior watch officers. An attempt to solve the problem using closed-circuit television failed completely. Its information could not be digested or used easily enough. It was not enough to automate and link some of the information on the ship; virtually all of it had to feed into a single command system. Otherwise the flag could not make valid decisions. Conversely, FCF was hampered because it could not communicate automatically with the ship's communications intelligence (COMINT) and IOIC spaces, hence could not share data with them.

Meanwhile, a second U-2 experiment was conducted in the Mediterranean, using as its surface station either the multisource data processing center in Fleet Ocean Surveillance Information Facility (FOSIF) Rota or a similar center at the Naples, Italy, Maritime Surveillance Center (MSC). Either could be considered broadly equivalent to the FCF on board *Kitty Hawk*. Rota merged its own data with that from the airplane. Processed information went to a terminal at Sigonella, which transmitted it in Link 14 format. This time the U-2 had a more sophisticated radar, the APS-116 normally carried on board an S-3A Viking. Its EW sensor was cued to a limited extent, and it had an improved downlink. The airplane's sensors covered a 610-nautical-mile-diameter circle on the surface at any one time. Accuracy sufficed to target the new Tomahawk antiship missile.

Testing TFCC

In May 1975 the chief of naval operations (CNO) proposed a three-phase test of FCC-TFCC.[5] Phase I began with the 1975 RIMPAC exercise. It would merge the MCSF-FCF combination (representing FCC-TFCC) with the U-2 tested in the

Mediterranean. An interim FCC set up in Hawaii was built around a special display and computer in CinCPacFleet headquarters. This combination could analyze data to depict the interaction of Red and Blue forces. It was linked to the FCF on board *Kitty Hawk*. This experiment would further define what information and intelligence could be collected, synthesized, and passed to the forward commander in a more timely manner to help him use his own resources. Was the sort of automated data offered by FCC-TFCC what staffs needed? Was information being displayed as needed? How important were automated files of the Naval Intelligence Processing System (NIPS)?

The test went ahead even though the airplane was not available. The FCC, the connection, and the TFCC were separately tested. Surprisingly, without the airplane it was still possible to produce the sort of tracks needed for wide-area surveillance and missile targeting. Often the key seems to have been correlation of information from OSIS (via the FCC) with information collected by task force sensors. For Blue surface units, about two-thirds of correlations (which averaged one per day on 91 percent of Blue units) were between local and remote sources, but for Orange (simulated Soviet) surface units, most were between different local sources. During the final week of the exercise, when action was hottest, the system successfully correlated all simulated and actual Soviet contacts as well as all but two friendly contacts (Blue). It managed about four correlations per day for each simulated or actual Soviet ship. Simulated Soviet submarines were correlated about once each day. Overall, MCSF provided the most recent information on simulated Soviet intelligence-gatherers (AGIs) 45 percent of the time; and on all Soviet surface threats 25 percent of the time. Sometimes it was also the earliest warning of impending air attack. For example, its HF/DF gave the earliest warning of a simulated heavy bomber attack, triggering dispatch of CAP aircraft. This sort of remote support was particularly valuable when ships were operating in radar silence. The system had the potential to provide a seven hundred nautical-mile-radius picture for force self-defense and for OTH targeting. The exercise seems to have demonstrated that the LGD was a necessary part of any TFCC.

OSIS was tested as a strategic indications and warning system, as had long been envisaged. Also tested were the system's ability to combine partial data (e.g., an HF line of bearing) from different sensors, the reliability of computer-assisted surveillance data correlation, the timeliness of the Antisubmarine Warfare Command and Control System (ASWCCS) information, and the use of the Sound Surveillance System (SOSUS) to track surface targets. To see how much the FCC/TFCC combination was worth, Blue force organic information was compared with the joint products of the two centers. The ability of an FCC to support OTH targeting was demonstrated.

The experiment was intended to develop the requirements for a future satel-lite link, the Tactical Data Exchange System (TADIXS), between TFCC and FCC. In the first tests (26 August to 3 September 1975) the TFCC operated in radio silence two-thirds of the time, so that it could not report back to the FCC that it had received messages. Because HF radio performance was poor, the FCC routinely repeated each message three times. Most of them were twelve to twenty-four hours old. Once available, the Gapfiller naval communications satellite (a one-way fleet broadcast) was substituted for HF, linking FCC to TFCC and FOSIF/FOSIC to intelligence systems on a ship, in effect their outstation. The follow-on Fleet Satellite offered two-way links: TADIXS between FCC and TFCC, and tactical intelligence (TACINTEL) between FOSIC/FOSIF and shipboard intelligence centers. Using it, the fleet and the intelligence outstations could also update the files ashore, so that the picture could be created cooperatively.

Phase I was successful enough for Op-094 to order development of an inte-grated Naval Command and Control System (NCCS) embracing FCC, TFCC, and their chief sensors, particularly OSIS and ASWCCS.[6] NCCS was much affected by two new developments, the Harpoon and Tomahawk antiship missiles and direct submarine support of surface forces. Launching the missiles against targets beyond the shooter's horizon required the sort of wide-area picture TFCC was expected to provide. Direct support made it necessary to tie together air, surface, and subma-rine platforms more completely than before. A March 1976 review of Phase I led the Navy to create a five-year NCCS program, promulgated in May 1977. It called for baselining OSIS as a prelude to the OSIS Baseline Upgrade (OBU).[7]

Phase II tests introduced all-source data exchange between shore and ship, so that the amount and type of data the tactical commander needed could be esti-mated. FCC and TFCC would be linked by satellite. Limited online display capabil-ity was added to the FCC. Tests were expected to indicate software requirements. An interim TFCC was installed on board *Kennedy*, which would go first to the Pacific in January 1976, then to the Atlantic in April 1976, and then to European waters in September 1976. To some extent the European part of Phase II was analogous to Phase I in the Western Pacific. This phase included both open ocean (WestLant) and high-density (Mediterranean) cases. All of the usual Mediterranean basin restrictions were taken into account. Plans to link *Kennedy* to FOSIF Rota for exer-cises were dropped because FCC and TFCC were seen more and more as elements of a single common system.

Disaster

Martin-Marietta won the initial TFCC contract. Phase III (June 1977 through 1980) was to have been the FCC/TFCC operational evaluation and realization of full operational capability (FOC) of the FCC/TFCC combination. However, the contract was canceled in 1978 as too costly. Lockheed won a replacement contract using the new computer, USQ-81, which had just been demonstrated in Outlaw Shark (see chapter 18). The same computer would form the core of the Tomahawk antiship system, presenting its user with a picture of shipping activity including that of the target.

To make the system affordable, in August 1979 the CNO approved a new plan that spread out costs and also limited the time a carrier had to spend in shipyard. Increment 1 created the new TFCC space: a twenty-by-twenty-foot space suitable for handling special intelligence (SI) data with a central console, plots, and connections to the ship's combat system (i.e., to Link 11 data).

Increment 2 added the heart of the TFCC, now called the Flagship Data Display System. The ship gained the ability to receive, process, and display the ocean surveillance picture developed by OSIS. An Afloat Correlation System (ACS) fed by an ocean surveillance terminal (the initial version of which was POST, the Prototype OST) correlated off-board and battle-group data. It also sent battle-group track data back to OSIS to help ensure that the larger system carried the same tracks as the fleet at sea. A contemporary unclassified description of ACS showed it handling up to 4,000 tracks simultaneously, compared to 256 for the carrier's local combat direction system. Correlation was based on the same sort of statistical concepts that had been developed for OSIS itself: the computer could test whether a ship was likely to have moved from one reported position to another. Radar emissions (not fingerprinting) were used for identification. For example, the same type of radar detected thirty nautical miles and fifteen minutes apart would be taken as separate ships, whereas the system might conclude that two similar detections thirty nautical miles and seventy minutes apart came from the same ship. The carrier SUPPLOT, which collected and filtered at-sea (as opposed to land) intelligence, fed into TFCC, as did filtered data from the ship's NTDS. At this stage the TFCC did not yet read the local electronic warfare or ASW pictures. Typically, it displayed the situation within a 1,500-mile circle around the carrier. (It could zoom in to show the situation more clearly on a smaller scale.) Increment 3 would have been new software.

As a measure of its importance, in March 1980 TFCC development was ordered accelerated. By this time it was tied to the targeting needs of the new antiship Tomahawk missile. A cruiser version was designed. Once more there were interim installations: in the carriers *Midway* (June 1980) and *America* (January 1981) and in the cruiser *Josephus Daniels* (February 1981). All of these proto-TFCCs used commercial-grade equipment. They were soon removed pending development of a military-grade (mil-spec) equivalent. Fleet experience was so successful that in November 1981 the CNO ordered limited procurement. Two FDDS prototypes were bought (one for the carrier *America*, one for the Naval Ocean Systems Center [NOSC] test site). Six more were bought in advance of approval for full production and were quickly installed: on board *America* (completed 15 May 1983), *Constellation* (15 July 1983), *Nimitz* (15 September 1983), *Midway* (15 October 1983), *Ranger* (15 February 1984), and *John F. Kennedy* (1984). By about 1982 plans called for TFCCs aboard all fourteen carriers (the Reagan administration was enlarging the carrier force), the big nuclear-powered cruiser *Long Beach*, four *Belknap*-class cruisers, and, if possible, the two amphibious flagships (LCCs).

The other end of the system, the FCC, was not improving in parallel. In 1980 FCCs still combined data from their three main sources (OSIS, WWMCCS, and ASWCCS) manually because data were in incompatible forms. OSIS displayed a high-interest picture automatically. WWMCCS (with a six-year improved project under way) still used a 1960s batch-processing architecture feeding mostly alphanumeric cathode-ray tubes (CRTs). (It had a few black-and-white graphic terminals.) It was considered reliable but slow. ASWCCS was intended mainly to vector patrol aircraft out to handle a developing submarine situation. It generally reported via free-form RAINFORM messages and the UYK-7 computer, by this time obsolescent. Its limitations cost considerable time in correlating data. It communicated with Atlantic and Pacific FCCs via its Fleet High-Level Terminals (FHLTs), although CinCUSNAVEUR received this data via WWMCCS. Thus, FCC plots were updated only daily. In 1983 dual-screen black-and-white displays were being replaced with four-color displays bought in the late 1970s. Large-screen displays were being upgraded. A dedicated net was being installed to link system sites.

Throughout the system, communication was mainly via man-machine-readable message. Machine-produced in stereotyped form, as a high-level equivalent to Link 14, such messages were attractive because they could be used directly by a machine but also could still be read by a human recipient. In fact, making messages man-readable made them far bulkier. The necessary insertion of machine coding symbols in a man-readable format caused a high error rate requiring hand correction. CinCUSNAVEUR estimated that it had to correct 10 percent of RAINFORM messages and 50 percent of movement reports before inserting them into its database. It used a dozen men to make corrections. The Pacific Fleet needed sixteen.

In 1983 CinCPacFlt tested a prototype Integrated Information Display (IID), but there were no immediate plans to install it in other headquarters. IID maintained three permanent databases: positional, technical information (characteristics), and readiness. It used OSIS baseline software and four ASWCCS color direct view consoles (DVCs). An upgrade plan for other FCCS envisaged eventually making similar improvements. It did not help that FCCs differed. Norfolk relied on WWMCCS. With its less strategic role, NAVEUR (London) used Intelligence Support System (ISS).

The system was not organized for war fighting. It had no common navigational reference—key in any netted system. EW ("the bullet of tomorrow") was handled separately. There was a gap between the area in which a deployed force collected information and the area over which wide-area systems operated. There was only limited ability to exchange timely indications and warning (I&W) data, including sensor cues. In this forces afloat were worst. Data links were subject to jamming and to exploitation and lacked network management. Standardization was difficult because the role of the numbered fleet commander seemed to differ from theater to theater.

Thus, the fleet still did not see FCC and TFCC as an integrated whole. It could understand that TFCC made the fleet more effective, hence that it was worth improving. FCC was a headquarters system that, at first blush, had nothing to do with war fighting. Yet without something like an FCC, OSIS was worth far less, and without knowing where Blue forces were, long-range Red data could not be used effectively. Unfortunately, those responsible for long-haul communications and for the ashore parts of the system were unable to show how those elements contributed to overall U.S. seapower. Historically that has been the great problem of network-centric warfare. How many missiles is a bundle of fiber-optics cable worth? A few satellite channels? A more powerful picture keeper?

Moore's Law Strikes: JOTS and Its Successors

The TFCC offered something any naval officer badly wanted: the global shipping picture OSIS and WWMCCS jointly maintained. Was it really true, as it seemed, that that TFCC was so massive and so expensive that only capital ships could have it? TFCC contained one computer, which maintained the ocean surveillance picture on the basis of updates provided via satellite, much as an NTDS picture keeper did but on a grander scale. The rest of its computers applied that data to command problems. Almost at the outset of TFCC development, in 1976, there was an unfunded proposal to produce a stand-alone version of the Tactical Integrated Ocean Surveillance (TFCC TIOS) module called Ship Processing Module (SPM). It might offer a missile shooter the sort of ocean surveillance product demonstrated in Outlaw Hawk the previous year.

By this time the U.S. computer industry was booming, fully exploiting Moore's Law. Its new products outstripped military computers with lengthy development and testing cycles. They were acceptable in naval service as long as they did not control weapons. Naval ASW organizations found that they could write new software more quickly and more cheaply to run on the new commercial machines. In the mid-1970s, several of them—SUBDEVRON 12, Second Fleet (surface), ComPatWingsLant—produced computer Tactical Decision Aids (TDAs) that helped considerably in submarine search and localization. OpNav approved Fleet Mission Program Libraries (FMPLs) of these TDAs running on commercial computers. This was acceptable. The TDA did not affect the combat direction system that created the tactical picture it used. Since TDAs did not fire weapons, they were not subject to exhaustive testing and verification.

As commander, Carrier Group 1 (COMCARGRU I) in USS *Eisenhower* during the Northern Wedding 1981 exercise, Rear Adm. Jerry O. Tuttle had one of the principal TDA analysts on his staff. He had the analyst create a single package sharing a common geographic plot, an integrated database, and a common operator interface. All ran on a Navy-supplied commercial Hewlett Packard 9845B desktop computer. Admiral Tuttle wanted the picture TFCC provided, but his ship was not scheduled to receive it for some time. Tuttle also knew that his Hewlett Packard was more powerful than the USQ-81 at the heart of TFCC. Using TFCC-like software (rewritten in Rocky Mountain Basic to match his machine's operating system) and a satellite modem, his commercial computer could receive, display, and process the OTH picture normally handled by a TFCC. The local NTDS picture was entered manually because the commercial computer could not be allowed into a system capable of firing weapons. All of this was far easier and far less expensive than tearing a ship apart to install a TFCC.

Tuttle and his staff called this combination of TDAs and an externally supplied tactical picture a Tactical Search and Surveillance (TSS) system. It used all the computing power of the existing computer. Under commercial pressure, Hewlett Packard soon produced a far more powerful machine whose multiple central processing units (CPUs) could execute several programs simultaneously, with much more memory and color graphics. Tuttle got the first production machine from the manufacturer. With funds provided by the Atlantic naval air command, he ported the relevant programs from the earlier machine and demonstrated the result at a Naval War College game, all within thirty days. A very successful ocean test followed on board USS *America*.

This version, unofficially called Joint Operational Tactical System I (JOTS I), offered better TDAs for both antiair warfare (AAW) and ASW.[8] Because all the TDAs were in a single package, the system made multiwarfare planning easier and more effective. Tuttle claimed that the TDAs offered "historic forays into long range ASW prosecution and covert AAW interception." Long-range ASW meant using multiple sources of data to form a joint picture suited to action. Covert AAW interception meant using passive sensors on a joint basis. TDAs would determine whether proposed actions were feasible, and estimate their effects. Tuttle reported spectacular results: a complete sweep of deployed Soviet submarines to a thousand nautical miles, successful implementation of new automated surface surveillance techniques (i.e., those associated with OTH targeting), eight hundred nautical miles AAW intercepts, satellite vulnerability/deception exploitation.

COMNAVAIRLANT ordered JOTS I distributed to each carrier group commander in the Atlantic Fleet. The Navy selected its HP 9020 as its standard nontactical desktop computer (DTC I)—a normal supply item. Because software could be reproduced instantly, JOTS I could be deployed extremely quickly. Even so, for some time JOTS remained the preserve of the carriers. In JOTS II (1983, *Eisenhower* and *Independence*) available TDAs were further integrated. This version was given both to carrier group commanders and also to cruiser-destroyer group commanders in the Atlantic. CinCLANTFLT and COMNAVAIRLANT took over development. JOTS II+ (early 1984, *Coral Sea*) received data automatically from the ship's NTDS. (It was illegal only to enter data *into* NTDS from a commercial system.) JOTS III was a multicomputer network on a carrier to service tacticians in various warfare areas simultaneously. However, an attempt to make JOTS a standard Navy TDA failed.

Moore's Law had made powerful computing so affordable and compact that it could go on board any combatant ship. The March 1983 Surface Ship Combat System Master Plan showed a link it called Officer in Tactical Command Information Exchange System (OTCIXS) as an item under review for the FFG 1 (*Brooke*) class. As these ships had no combat system computers, the link must have been associated with JOTS.

In October 1985, in Carrier Group 6 (*Forrestal*), Rear Adm. "Duke" Hernandez sought to develop JOTS IV into a complete battle staff C3 system complete with a new command net Joint Operational Tactical System Information Exchange System (JOTSIXS) to pass tactical data between ships and between ships and shore. Admiral Tuttle described JOTS IV as the battle staff's answer to the Soviet Alfa-class submarine, which presumably meant particularly quick reactions and decision aids. This version became standard in both carriers and battleships. The mil-spec TFCC was abandoned in favor of JOTS IV (the name TFCC survived). An improved JOTSIXS was chosen as OTCIXS.[9]

The combination of JOTS and OTCIXS profoundly transformed the fleet. It was easy to install JOTS on a ship, even one without Link 11. Once every ship had JOTS, it could receive OTCIXS satellite messages, which became the basis of a fleet-wide command and control system. It was called the Navy Tactical Command

System–Afloat Element (NTCS-A). This was very much a development grown up from the fleet rather than down from high-level analysis.

Tuttle became savior of the high-level ashore system. In November 1985 he brought JOTS IV and his philosophy of commercial-off-the-shelf (COTS) computerization to CinCLANTFLT's FCC. The Navy procurement cycle could never compete with Moore's Law. It made much better sense to concentrate on software, preferably suited to translation from one generation of COTS machines to the next. At the Atlantic Fleet FCC, Tuttle replaced the mil-spec terminals with the standard off-the-shelf computers used in JOTS. Tuttle's view prevailed. Navy policy shifted to standardize on a chosen particular upgradeable commercial machine, then replace it wholesale with a new standard every four years or so. These ideas were adopted everywhere except in weapon systems and related systems such as NTDS.

Tuttle's FCC became a fusion center using data from over three hundred sources, broadcasting via satellites to all afloat subscribers, as well as to numerous land users. It carried, for example, data on Soviet satellites (to gauge vulnerability to detection), ocean meteorology, movement reports, sonobuoy fields, formations, and mission plans. To Admiral Tuttle, the key was to merge more and more kinds of data. In his view, systems had been separated (stovepiped) primarily because of computer limitations. It took energy to combine the products of different computers; better to use that energy for war fighting on the basis of a merged tactical picture. The Pacific Fleet established a similar net, albeit on a smaller scale.

Admiral Tuttle took these ideas with him when he moved on to command the U.S. Navy's Space and Electronic Warfare Command (SpaWar), formerly the Naval Electronic Systems Command—which had been responsible for TFCC. To him, JOTS was part of an evolution from communication systems limited to what central authorities in the United States decided to push out to the fleet. Instead, war-fighting commanders should demand what they needed. Push-out made sense when communications channels were limited. His demand-driven war-fighting system would inevitably need far more capacity. Tuttle often displayed a slide showing that the daily data needs of the Sixth Fleet far exceeded the capacity of any single channel. His powerful tactical computers offered a solution: the sort of packet-switching we now associate with the Internet. It exploited the often-idle capacity of the usual dedicated channels. Tuttle proposed that each message be broken down into packets, each packet being tagged with its addressee and with its serial number within a complete message. Thus tagged, the packets could be spread to fill all available space on all the channels. Receiving computers would recognize the packets addressed to them and store them until they could be reassembled into the original messages. This scheme depended on plentiful inexpensive computers to break down and reassemble all messages. It provided the badly needed capacity.

A few special channels, such as Link 11 for tactically urgent messages, were retained because the packet-switching scheme did delay reception. Tuttle's packet-switching concept made it possible to send the sort of unformatted messages now common.

The next version of JOTS (officially JOTS II) was powerful enough to join in the formation of the global picture rather than merely receive it. It was operationally evaluated on board the carrier *Independence* and the cruiser *Jouett* in June 1990.[10] Soon afterward, wide-area ship-tracking became crucial. After the Iraqis invaded Kuwait, the United States led a coalition embargo of Iraqi shipping. As in the Cuban quarantine, shipping had to be identified and tracked over a wide area. The tracking technique was roughly that used in the quarantine: sources such as Lloyd's List and weather reports indicated where ships were and made it possible to predict their tracks. However, the coalition had nothing remotely like the resources, either ship or aircraft, available in 1962, not least because the embargo was being enforced so far from home. Yet it was even more crucial to identify and track individual ships so that they could be intercepted and boarded.

With JOTS, the enforcers could receive the picture rather than simple vectoring instructions. That may have been particularly important when only one of several ships in proximity had to be intercepted. The Iraqis tried to break the embargo by enticing coalition forces into blunders. In one celebrated case, an Iraqi ship was loaded with baby food. Its crew, which included pregnant Iraqi women, was armed with camcorders with which to film the brutality of American Marines boarding their ship. The intelligence picture shared by the embargo enforcement ships included some additional information: below the layer of canned milk were other children's toys, such as 155-mm artillery shells for Saddam Hussein's army. The picture made it clear that the ship boarded was the right one, so the Marines felt comfortable looking below the layer of legitimate cargo. Saddam never got his shells, and the embargo was not undone.

The sheer speed with which JOTS was deployed was remarkable. Twenty systems were quickly produced for allied frigates (Australian, Canadian, and Dutch) helping to enforce the embargo. That was possible because the system was special software running on a computer available in large quantities in Navy warehouses. This was a spectacular success story.

What would have been JOTS III (1992–93) became the Joint Maritime Command Information System (JMCIS). The *S* was soon redefined as Strategy—development strategy. JMCIS was designed specifically to support further applications within a common operating environment (COE). Because the applications were all keyed to geographic position, their outputs could be fused. Within a few years, Admiral Tuttle's packet-switched approach to multimedia communications was selected for the WWMCCS replacement: the Global Command and Control

System (GCCS). The Navy element of GCCS was Afloat and Ashore segments (GCCS-M).

In the 1990s the U.S. submarine force adopted the JOTS computer upgrade idea on a very different scale as Acoustics-Rapid COTS Insertion (ARCI). The U.S. acoustic advantage had been bought expensively by a combination of large arrays and silencing. Now that advantage was declining, but there was no prospect of buying new submarines with new arrays. The ARCI alternative was more powerful computers accommodating new software to take better advantage of existing arrays, just as Tuttle's JOTS and GCCS-M had taken better advantage of existing communication systems. Submarine internal communication nets were redesigned to carry more acoustic and other data, using packet-switching. ARCI computers represented the "state of the (commercial) practice" rather than the more extreme "state of the art." The program produced successive versions of software operating on periodically replaced computers. The weapon-control issue was solved by separating the picture-keeping function (including sonar processing) running on commercial computers from fire-control functions, so that the latter could be tested thoroughly without slowing better picture keeping. This was a distinct departure from past practice, in which picture keeping and fire control had been integrated. ARCI was so successful that the surface fleet and, to a more limited extent, aircraft followed suit.

CHAPTER 18

Using Ocean Surveillance: OTH-T

Tomahawk

The U.S. Navy became interested in over-the-horizon (OTH) antiship missiles as the Soviets deployed missile-armed surface combatants into the Mediterranean after the 1967 Six Days' War. Devoting carrier aircraft to countering these ships would detract from the carriers' primary major-war mission, to slow or stop a Soviet ground advance toward the Mediterranean. The submariners suggested a submarine-launched antiship cruise missile. The evolving ocean surveillance picture was already circulated to the Submarine Operating Authority in each fleet, which fed targeting cues into the submarine broadcast. This method was already used to cue submarines to deal with targets detected by the Sound Surveillance System (SOSUS). In the late 1960s, the broadcast was expected to give way to the Satellite Submarine Data Exchange System (SSIXS). Periodically, submarines would come to periscope depth to receive it. This technique could be used by a submarine supporting a carrier group with antiship missiles.

SSIXS generally gave only an approximate target position. The sooner the missile arrived at the target, the less chance the target would have to move out of range. The submariners thus proposed a supersonic weapon, which the new chief of naval operations (CNO), Adm. Elmo Zumwalt Jr., supported when it was proposed in 1970. Unfortunately, it was associated with an extremely costly large new submarine, which Zumwalt soon decided was unaffordable. Yet, he agreed that submarines should help counter Soviet surface missile shooters. The U.S. Navy was developing the subsonic air-launched fire-and-forget Harpoon antiship missile. Zumwalt ordered it adapted to surface firing. Its range could be doubled to maximum submarine passive sonar range (140 nautical miles), but beyond that something new was needed. Zumwalt ordered the torpedo-size strategic cruise missile then under development adapted with as much Harpoon guidance as possible. To use this Tomahawk missile, the U.S. Navy had to turn its ocean surveillance system into a targeting system. The antiship Tomahawk operational requirement was released in November 1974.[1] Ideally, it would outrange Soviet antiship missiles. To achieve the desired hit probability (0.9), the missile would have to make multiple passes near the target, so that its effective range would be far less than the distance it could fly through the air. As built, the antiship Tomahawk flew at Mach 0.7. Operational range was 250 nautical miles, given its ability to fly 472 nautical miles in a straight line.

Multiple passes gave the target a better chance of detecting and killing Tomahawk before it hit. Ideally, the missile should be fired at the likely future target position rather than at its position at the time of launch (or, worse, at the time fire-control calculation began). The wide-area system cueing the submarine should track the target to predict its position at the moment the missile arrived. The incoming missile also had to be prevented from locking onto any nontarget near the target. By 1975 there was a formal requirement for an OTH Detection/Classification and Targeting System. About 1977 the target had to be located within one nautical mile, and the system as a whole needed data accurate to within four minutes. By this time plans called for arming surface ships as well as submarines with antiship Tomahawk.

In 1975 it seemed that individual ships would find even the much shorter-range Harpoon difficult to target. When he ordered an operational requirement for a Harpoon control system in August 1975, the CNO stated that without new capabilities ships could not engage targets more than five to eighteen nautical miles away.[2] In 1976 ships managed targeting at twenty-five to thirty nautical miles, but extended range (Harpoon range was about sixty nautical miles) required cooperation with aircraft. The OpNav report on "Over the Horizon Detection, Classification, and Targeting Current Capabilities" concluded that ships needed the ability to coordinate off-board sensors and to correlate multisource information, both onboard and off-board. Off-board information might come from sensors that could not report directly to the ship and hence had to be contacted through long-haul communications links. OpNav envisaged an automated system that would provide a ship with an over-the-horizon track picture of friendly, hostile, and unevaluated surface ships and submarines. Contacts would be reported via an OTH net and Link 14. This was the basis of the USQ-81 picture keeper eventually provided to support Tomahawk targeting. Meanwhile own-ship over-the-horizon sensors were developed that might be effective out to Harpoon range. They included a new shipboard high frequency direction finding (HF/DF) system (Outboard, operational in 1977), the use of the LAMPS III shipboard helicopter to extend a ship's horizon, and the innovative use of long-range sonar (SQS-26 and 53) as an under-the-horizon sensor capable of picking up the relatively loud signatures of Soviet surface combatants. These sensors did not approach the ranges Tomahawk needed. At about the same time, the Soviets were working on anomalous radar propagation, both ducting and troposcatter, specifically to target long-range missiles. Perhaps remarkably the U.S. Navy seems not to have considered either approach, and it does not seem to have been aware of the Soviet effort (which produced the series of "Band Stand" devices on many ships).

No single existing sensor could solve the OTH problem, but existing ones were ill-equipped either to exchange data or to pass it to likely shooters. Because systems were stovepiped, information often followed a tortuous route. In an anti-submarine warfare (ASW) exercise, it took six hours to pass tactical information from a P-3 to the carrier *John F. Kennedy*. The P-3 passed data to the shore Tactical Surveillance Center (TSC) via its HF radio teletype (75 bits/second). From there an Antisubmarine Warfare Command and Control System (ASWCCS) line took it to the Fleet High Level Terminal in Naples. Naples sent the data via land line to London. There CinCUSNAVEUR put it on the World-Wide Military Command and Control System (WWMCCS) net, which included the 75-bit/second radio teletype channel to the carrier. In another test, it took an average of seventy-six minutes to process each of 471 electronic support measures (ESM) contact reports for onward transmission to a ship. During a National Week exercise, HF/DF information took two to three hours to arrive. In May 1977 the CNO Net Assessment Panel (on Soviet antiair warfare at sea) concluded that problems of target identification at long range would limit the effectiveness of both Harpoon and Tomahawk.

The favored solution was the Clipper Bow radar satellite. The alternative was to rely mainly on the Ocean Surveillance Information System (OSIS) picture—to use a wholly network-centric solution.

Outlaw Shark and OTH-T

In 1976 the Advanced Studies Group of the Naval War College published a paper, later described as quite influential, rejecting the Soviet approach of developing dedicated target systems. The U.S. Navy was already collecting masses of information. Buried in that mass, perhaps not even recognized, was sufficient data for missile targeting. The solution was to find it—software rather than new hardware. Although the paper never mentioned Moore's Law, the key to success was clearly computer analysis of the data from existing systems. (The paper did strongly advocate the doomed Clipper Bow radar satellite.) In 1977 Pacific Fleet rated OSIS good enough for alerting but not for targeting. The afloat commander could not integrate organic, national, and OSIS information. Limited navigational precision compounded the problem.

Just as the satellite was canceled in 1979, the Tomahawk program office was trying to convince the Office of the Secretary of Defense (OSD) that the missile could be targeted effectively—which meant by OSIS. Data were often time-late (an hour or more from observation to receipt on board a launch platform) and inaccurate (typically sixty nautical miles off). However, the system often offered a history of ship positions, from which course and speed and thus future position could be deduced. The 1979 review led directly to a decision to develop a ship-tracking algorithm. The missile was given better search patterns. To discriminate targets, it received passive identification/direction equipment (PI/DE), a radar search receiver into which the waveform characteristics of the Soviet Head Net C radar, then on board missile destroyers and *Moskva*-class helicopter carriers, were hardwired.

The Outlaw Hawk experiments using *Kitty Hawk* (described in chapter 17) showed that OSIS itself might become a wide-area ship tracker suited to missile targeting. A new set of Outlaw Shark experiments tested this idea. (Outlaw became a code word for using OSIS data tactically.) Outlaw Shark referred both to the experiment and to the track-keeping computer at Commander, Task Force (CTF) 69 (Sixth Fleet Submarine Operating Authority) in Naples. The primary source of ship location data was the interim Fleet Command Center/Tactical Flag Command Center (FCC/TFCC) system, connecting Fleet Ocean Surveillance Information Facility (FOSIF) Rota, USS *John F. Kennedy*, and CinCUSNAVEUR by ultrahigh frequency (UHF) satellite channels. The computer at CTF 69 correlated new data with its database to create tracks. It projected them forward and backward in time (by dead reckoning), storing track histories for display. It performed various geo-position calculations and generated graphic and alphanumeric displays. It could search numerous data parameters to clarify the situation. Each track file could be provided with target characteristics (e.g., emitter and acoustic data). The database could be searched on particular parameters of interest so that newly detected targets could be correlated with those already in the base. Finally, the computer generated paper tapes used to transmit data to the submarine via the SSIXS satellite link. The submarine's USQ-81 computer, installed for the test, handled the stream of incoming data.

Testing began in January 1977. In the first phase a submarine made dummy shots against both simulated targets and real targets of opportunity, as well as against targets selected by CTF 69. In a second phase the destroyer *Richard B. Russell* acted as Outlaw Shark, using a submarine-type BRD-7 DF set. The frigate *Julius A. Furer* simulated a Soviet Kresta II–class cruiser maintaining a predetermined HF transmitting schedule. The main sensors were the Mediterranean

HF/DF net and the Outboard (shipboard HF/DF) system aboard USS *Mitscher*. She located targets by crossing the HF lines of bearing she measured with those from the shore Bullseye system. Twenty simulated shots were tried. The Outlaw Shark shore computer greatly simplified selecting and routing national-sensor data (e.g., signals intelligence [SIGINT] from satellites and from shore HF/DF) for the submarine. The submarine computer eliminated what would have been crippling time delays while such data was routed within the submarine and plotted. Its built-in search function was expected to cut data correlation time, and it could show which targets the submarine could engage.

Additional trials were conducted in the Tyrrhenian Sea between 12 and 16 May and between 19 and 23 June, again in two phases. In one an attack submarine supported a carrier battle group. In a second, USS *Blakely* (FF 1072) simulated a Soviet Kresta II–class cruiser. The main sensors were an EP-3E electronic intelligence (ELINT) airplane and the Classic Wizard satellite. Others included the submarine's own BRD-7 radar direction finder, which could exploit ducting. On forty-five runs, only in six was the target well enough located for a Tomahawk sensor to have better than a 50 percent chance of acquiring it when the missile arrived. The problem was a combination of time-lateness in reporting (almost always more than an hour late) and location errors by the sensors (HF/DF was worst). Ranges at time of launch varied from visual to about 290 nautical miles. This series demonstrated the problem of nontargets in the target area: thirty-two in one case, eight of them in the swath the missile seeker would have searched trying to acquire the target. On another run, although there were fewer nontargets in the target area (seventeen), the missile would have acquired eleven of them. A Tomahawk shooter needed far more information about nontargets in the target area.

These trials were among the first to emphasize data fusion from numerous sources: data were taken directly from P-3s (via Link 11), Classic Wizard, the fleet ESM contacts broadcast, and Outboard. P-3s passed data via Link 11 to their ASW Operations Center (ASWOC) at Sigonella, which passed it on to CTF 69 via a Fleet High Level Terminal, whence it was manually inserted into the Outlaw Shark computer. Even so, average time late from aircraft sensor to Outlaw Shark correlation facility was twelve minutes. Unfortunately, no computer-to-computer link could be established between the TFCC on the carrier and Outlaw Shark on the firing ship. Rota entered SSIXS data manually because it did not have the planned submarine operating center computer. Sixth Fleet considered Outlaw Shark outstandingly successful. It proved that a shore correlation center could create a viable targeting picture by combining remote sensor data with task force data and then transmit it to the shooter on a computer-to-computer basis.

Within a few months the Sixth Fleet Submarine Operational Command Center (SOCC) had a new Tactical Data Correlation System (TDCS) and an associated Tactical Data Display System (TDDS). The system was computer driven but manually controlled, offering near real-time data. TDCS sanitized special intelligence data for transmission as track files via UHF satellite and HF radio. TDDS maintained the system track files. Each file included both acoustic and electronic emitter attributes. As in the Naval Tactical Data System (NTDS), operators sought to correlate each new bit of data with an existing track file, using a technical database to match attributes. Positions were automatically dead reckoned. An ambiguity file contained records that had not been correlated with existing tracks. The computer screened and logged messages as they arrived to eliminate redundancy. Thus, TDDS maintained a current ocean surveillance picture mainly using time-late information.

These new command systems were tested in a further series of exercises (November 1977–September 1978).[3] The notional missile was programmed on the basis of the TDDS picture.[4] Participating units were Submarine Shark (*Archerfish*), Ship Shark (*Josephus Daniels*), Air Shark (an EP-3E), and Target Shark (*Blandy*). *Archerfish* automatically received Outlaw Shark data via the SSIXS satellite, handling her own sensor data manually. The airplane's Airborne Information Correlation System (AIC), equivalent to a TDDS, correlated own-sensor and track data and also speeded analysis and processing of onboard data. It often provided final prelaunch location at about 180 nautical mines. In this network-centric operation, navigational capability was important. The submarine had the Ship Inertial Navigation System (SINS), *Daniels* had Loran C, and the EP-3E had both Loran C and an inertial system (LTN-51).

CinCUSNAVEUR found Outlaw Shark the best effort to date to provide the capability to transmit, correlate, and evaluate sensor data quickly enough to provide the complete surface picture operators needed to make over-the-horizon targeting (OTH-T) decisions. It became a basis for further development. The Pacific Fleet test system linked a Shore Targeting Terminal (STT) in a submarine headquarters and the equivalent TDCS at a fleet headquarters with a Submarine Tactical Data Display System (STDDS) equivalent to TDDS on board a submarine, an AIC on board an EP-3E, or a TDDS on board a surface ship.[5] At this stage special intelligence data were sanitized manually, but that would not be fast enough in a complex situation.

The Johns Hopkins University Applied Physics Laboratory was largely responsible for Tomahawk targeting. With Clipper Bow dead, it saw Outlaw Shark—the use of OSIS for targeting—the only real option. Many were unhappy. The commander of the Operational Test and Evaluation Force pointed out that everything depended on whether the prospective target emitted signals detectable by Navy and national sensors. The technique was usable only if the target ship was in an area empty of nontargets, subject to continuous surface surveillance.

Tomahawk OTH-T engendered the slogan of ensuring "sensor to shooter connectivity." That decidedly did *not* mean sending raw sensor data to the shooters, although in some cases shooters wanted such data so that they could better correlate organic and nonorganic information. It meant pouring multisource intelligence into a fusion center that could turn that information into a usable tactical picture that went to the shooter. Sensor fusion is a demanding task, often involving large numbers of specialists. That is the moral of the Combat Information Center (CIC) story. Remember the British term for an air defense fusion center: the filter room.

Exercises in the 1980s were depressing. In one series, 139 Tomahawks were notionally fired. Only seventeen (12.2 percent) hit their intended targets. Another fifty-three (38 percent) hit other enemy ships. Another eight (6 percent) hit neutral ships. As might have been expected, the shorter-range Harpoon did better—23 percent hit their intended targets. The Operational Test and Evaluation Force (OpTEVFOR) concluded that Tomahawk was unusable. Data were not nearly good enough. For example, data time-late by ten minutes, rather than the maximum of four, would preclude hitting—and likely time delays were more like sixty to ninety minutes. To the Operational Test and Evaluation Force, the worst thing was that there was no single point of operational fleet responsibility for OTH targeting and for antiship Tomahawk firing. What we might now call a network-centric concept was rejected outright. The Tomahawk glass seemed at least half empty.

There was another point of view. No enemy could know that he was being tracked and targeted. All attacks would have been surprises. The Soviets had developed an elaborate targeting system that required repeated confirmation of target position. They accepted that it would provide the U.S. Navy with tactical warning. The shock of being targeted without warning might well upset whatever tactical plans the Soviets had in mind, even if relatively few of their surface ships were sunk. U.S. tests captured none of this, yet psychological effects are often decisive in war. The goal was not so much to destroy the Soviet surface fleet as to upset Soviet operations so that the U.S. naval striking force (hitting land targets) could survive. Moreover, the system could achieve this without diluting valuable carrier air resources.

Many officers refused to fire missiles in exercises because they did not trust the OSIS picture and also because they disliked betting on probabilistic estimates of future target motion. I once stressed this problem during a talk on network-centric warfare at Point Mugu. A participant recalled that his commanding officer had been willing to fire. He bagged a carrier. Perhaps he considered requirements (such as 90 percent probability that a missile would lock on given initial information) unrealistic.

Another View of OTH-T

Far more than the U.S. Navy of the 1960s and 1970s, the Royal Navy was interested in antiship warfare. Its favored weapon, the Buccaneer bomber, was viewed almost as an antiship missile. It had to be directed almost to the target because it would probably be shot down if it spent time searching. According to a British tactical analysis (1969), the airplane would be sent out on the basis of "intelligence, such as a shore HF/DF net," that is, on a British equivalent to OSIS. That system, presumably reporting to the Admiralty (as in the past), was expected to place the bomber within thirty nautical miles of its target. The Buccaneer would cruise toward the target at high altitude for fuel economy (35,000 feet at Mach 0.8, about 480 knots), confirming target position using its ESM and perhaps its radar. The Buccaneer's active radar was expected to enjoy a range advantage over the enemy's, but using it would reveal the airplane's identity. Once the position of the target was known, the Buccaneer no longer had to keep it in sight, so it could descend to remain just beyond the target's radar horizon. During the descent, the airplane's computer memorized target position, as indicated by ESM. When seventy-five nautical miles from the target, the Buccaneer would begin a run-in at fifty-foot altitude, in hopes that the enemy could not engage anything flying so low. Only after the Buccaneer crossed the enemy's radar horizon, at a range of about twenty nautical miles, and thus could be detected, did it turn on its own radar for the attack phase. It reacquired the target, locked on, and began a fully automatic attack using the onboard computer.

This is much the pattern the Soviets adopted for their SS-N-12 Mod 1 (P-500 Bazalt). After initially acquiring the target, it shut down its radar, flying on the basis of the memorized target position, course, and speed. The radar was switched back on when the missile crossed the target's horizon.

In either case, the success of the attack depended crucially on the ocean surveillance system supporting it. In the late 1960s, the British used the same manual plotting methods that had served in World War II and, for that matter, in World War I. They became interested in automation, apparently quite independently of the U.S. Navy. At the same time, as part of an effort to cut defense costs, they decided to combine navy and Coastal Command (Royal Air Force–controlled land-based maritime aircraft) commands in a single maritime headquarters (MHQ), Northwood. About 1970 the project changed to incorporate an automated command information (i.e., tactical picture) system, which would also handle the rising message load.[6] The project was complex, and it suffered serious delays. When conceived in 1967, it was expected to be complete in 1972. By 1970 the date for completion of the computer system had been set back to 1981, and a preliminary Pilot Stage introduced to provide some capability before that. The computer Operational Control (OPCON) system became fully operational in 1984.

Northwood was conceived as a North Atlantic Treaty Organization (NATO) command center, in which the new NATO system would connect with the new British national system. The two could not be integrated because, like every other national military, the British limited the information they would share with others. That kind of limitation caused particular problems within NATO because different countries had different levels of access. This is a more general network-centric issue. The shared tactical picture is the basis for decisions with life-or-death consequences. The picture itself is likely to be shared because without it operations may fail. However, the basis for the picture is likely to include intelligence sources and methods that absolutely cannot be shared. Different alliance partners may have very different views of the validity of intelligence conclusions and reasoning, and it may be difficult to convince them to risk their forces on the basis of what they may not entirely trust. It is not clear how this problem can be overcome. About 2005 the U.S. position was that to further coalition cohesiveness, all allies and coalition partners (they are not the same thing) would have full access to the classified U.S. military Internet (SIPRNET), the system that carries much of the information on which tactical planning is based. That was not the same thing as providing full intelligence access, but even so it raised serious questions of overall security. Thus access was later somewhat restricted by firewalls. It might be argued that tactical intelligence can and should be shared because it has only transitory value, but SIPRNET also carries a mass of technical data, the compromise of which would surely be embarrassing.

Northwood became more or less equivalent to a U.S. FCC. OPCON maintained a plot of past, present, and predicted positions (and tracks) of all British naval vessels, together with maritime air patrols and reported contacts. It is not clear to what extent information on foreign ships was overlaid on this plot. Coastlines and depth contours were also shown. As a measure of its size, OPCON had 150 workstation/terminals at Northwood. British ships used a dedicated satellite Link R to receive OPCON data, which was in message rather than graphic form. A second OPCON, linked to the first, was bought by the Royal Netherlands Navy in September 1988 for commander, Benelux Channel Command. Once the Dutch bought their system, a Dutch ship could contact the Dutch OPCON at den Helder, which could link to Northwood, and thence to a Royal Navy ship via Link R. As of early 1989 OPCON workstations or terminals were planned for NATO Supreme Allied Commander Atlantic (SACLANT), for the German naval headquarters at Glucksburg, for the Allied Forces Northern Europe headquarters at Kolsas near Oslo, and for NATO Supreme Allied Commander Europe (SACEUR) headquarters at Brussels. An

OPCON terminal was installed on board the U.S. flagship *Mount Whitney* for North Atlantic exercises.

Given rapid computer development, the British bought a Fleet Operational Command System Life Extension (FOCSLE) replacement equivalent to a U.S. FCC. Like an FCC, FOCSLE managed the Recognized Maritime Picture (RMP) as well as databases used by deployed forces, and it incorporated tactical decision aids. It also transmitted commands to forces afloat, and it was connected with Royal Air Force (RAF) command systems; the RAF is responsible for British maritime patrol aircraft. FOCSLE received the U.S. Navy element of Global Command and Control System (GCCS-M) broadcast of the world shipping picture and added its own information. FOCSLE presumably used mil-spec computers. If the message structure of OPCON could be likened to Link 14, that of FOCSLE was more like Link 11. The FOCSLE development contract was awarded to Siemens Plessey (now BAE Systems) early in April 1995. The key element of FOCSLE was delivered in September 1998. Initial operational capability (IOC) had been expected in 1995, but the system was fully accepted only in 2001. BAE Systems claimed that it was the first operational multilevel secure (MLS) command system. Note the importance of multiple security levels in OTH-T.

Moore's Law had much the same effect on the British as on the U.S. Navy. Their equivalent to Joint Maritime Command Information System (JMCIS) and GCCS-M was the Command Support System (CSS), which exists in both ashore and afloat versions.

The Outer Air Battle

OTH-T became the basis for U.S. attempts to fight an outer air battle against Soviet missile-bearing bombers designed to destroy U.S. carriers. The U.S. maritime strategy of the 1980s envisaged decisive battles to destroy the Soviet fleet. Once that threat was gone, the U.S. fleet could affect the ongoing battle ashore without fearing the naval consequences of losses in so risky an endeavor. Soviet missile-carrying bombers were a major part of the Soviet fleet, and incidentally, the part that other NATO navies were least well equipped to counter. Thus they were a devastating threat against NATO shipping in the North Atlantic. The only land-based fighters that might engage them at all, the few in Iceland, probably would be unable to deal with a stream of bombers rushing past (in effect, crossing targets, the most difficult kind).

If the bombers sought to attack a carrier, her fighters could fight an equivalent of the Battle of the Philippine Sea, seizing maritime air superiority. As in 1944, crews shot down could not easily be replaced. The carriers became combination bait and trap. The new concept was an antibomber equivalent of the way convoys were expected to destroy enemy submarines: by concentrating submarine-killers at the submarines' targets. The new concept was to "shoot the archer rather than the arrow": the carrier fighters should concentrate on the Soviet bombers rather than on any missiles they fired.

In theory the fighters could engage either bombers or missiles. With the advent of Aegis and New Threat Upgrade, the missiles could be left to the surface ships. The fighters could concentrate on the bombers in what the U.S. Navy called the outer air battle (the inner battle was the fight against the missiles). It would be fought largely beyond the battle group's horizon, which might be defined by the radar range of an E-2C orbiting above battle group center (so as to detect threats approaching from any direction): 250 nautical miles. The attacking force of one or more regiments (eighteen to twenty-four bombers each) supported by reconnaissance and jamming aircraft would probably begin to launch missiles from about two hundred nautical miles. In 1982 it was estimated that an F-14 could deal with two or three bombers. It would take a full fourteen-airplane fighter squadron to handle a full regiment. The squadron could sustain its defensive posture for about six hours, so the carrier needed enough warning to estimate the attack window within four to six hours. The Soviet Tu-22M (NATO Backfire) complicated the situation. Supersonic rather than subsonic, it had twice the range of the earlier Tu-16 Badger, so it could fly a much more circuitous path from bases in the Northern Soviet Union. The bomber's supersonic AS-4 (Kh-22) missile could be fired from beyond the range at which fighters normally orbited their carrier, 150 nautical miles (however, E-2C radar range was 250 nautical miles).

One carrier could not possibly project enough F-14s far enough out to fight an outer air battle in all directions. Conversely, if the direction of the raid could be predicted, the F-14s could concentrate on a narrow sector hundreds of miles deep. Their controlling E-2C could loiter well out on the threat axis. Ships might even be stationed below the predicted line of bomber approach, waiting silently to surprise the enemy aircraft when cued by an E-2C. This would have been a network-centric surprise, as the ships would fire on the basis of a tactical picture supplied by other assets (mainly the E-2C).

No carrier-based sensor was effective far enough out. S-3As were outfitted to pick up signals the bombers emitted, not least to coordinate their own action (and to coordinate with the cooperating jammers and chaff layers). The supersonic Backfire made such measures particularly inadequate. Carriers were already being linked to OSIS. A Backfire could be visualized as an ultrafast ship, subject to the same sort of tracking and dead reckoning that OSIS already applied to Soviet surface warships. Existing OSIS sensors were not enough, but there were other possibilities. Space-based radar was considered but rejected as too expensive.

It took too many satellites to cover potential bomber routes thoroughly enough. Instead of satellites, Secretary of the Navy John Lehman chose the earth-based Relocatable Over-the-Horizon Radar (ROTHR). A ROTHR in Scotland could cover the North Atlantic, and one in the Aleutians could cover Soviet Pacific Fleet bomber routes. ROTHR could be moved (in theory in about two weeks) to meet changing requirements. It had the added advantage that its low frequency signals would not be much affected if the Soviets managed to build stealthy aircraft. The prototype became operational at Amchitka in the Aleutians in 1985.

A network-centric system uses whatever is available. The United States operated geostationary Defense Support Program (DSP) satellites to detect Soviet missile firings, using arrays of infrared detectors to see the hot exhaust of a rising rocket against the cool earth. It turned out that they could detect the afterburners of jets—such as Backfires—flying at high altitude. After eight years of fruitless attempts to interest the Air Force in this capability, Aerojet-General (which built the satellites) turned to the Navy about 1982. Almost at once the Navy sent a contingent to the Nurrungar (Australia) DSP ground station. Jets were called Slow Walkers because they seemed to crawl across the vast area monitored by each satellite. (Satellites, visible by the glint of sunlight they reflected, were Fast Walkers.) The Navy briefed the commander of the Air Force Space Command on its bomber-tracking Project Slow Walker on 3 May 1983. The first formal U.S. Navy Operational Requirement was drafted in 1984. This Slow Walker Reporting System (SWRS) used the techniques already developed for reporting ship movements for OTH Targeting. When Slow Walker was demonstrated in the Ocean Venture fleet exercise, the fleet commander commented that he had never before received such timely data.

Probably the earliest warning would come from the radio chatter of bomber pilots preparing for takeoff. According to Russian accounts, National Security Agency (NSA) satellites detected exactly such chatter during the Soviet buildup in East Asia. Given a takeoff warning, the arrival of the bombers near the fleet could be predicted to within a few hours. Badgers would probably have to fly straight toward the carrier, but Backfires had the range to turn so as to approach from the flanks. Slow Walker and ROTHR would track them. Combining such data, OSIS could create tracks for what amounted to extremely fast ships. Off Southern California in the 1980s it demonstrated that F-14s could indeed intercept them: the outer air battle could be fought.

As with OTH-T, the outer air battle had a 1991 Gulf War echo. Slow Walker opened up the possibility of using DSP data tactically. DSP satellites detected Scuds being launched. Their stereo data was precise enough to predict roughly where missiles were aimed (at Saudi Arabia or Israel). Timely warnings could be issued, and Patriot batteries alerted. Without cueing Patriot probably would not have been able to hit any of the incoming Scuds. In effect the satellites were supporting the Patriots' over-the-horizon battle.

CHAPTER 19

The Other Side of the Hill

T he U.S. Navy learned in 1964 that the Soviets were basing their operations on some sort of surveillance system.[1] For the first time, Soviet reconnaissance aircraft flew directly to intercept U.S. carrier task forces well out to sea, rather than conducting searches for them. The airplanes flew far enough and for long enough that they could not simply be heading to where the carrier had been when they took off; it would have moved too far while they were in flight. Instead, they were heading to a predicted position. The flights could not have been mounted unless some external system had cued the aircraft. The experience was sobering because at the time it seemed that Soviet land-based missile bombers were the main threat to U.S. strike carriers operating outside Soviet coastal waters. The single reconnaissance aircraft could as easily have been regiments of Badgers. Much the same might be said of the 2006 interception of the *Kitty Hawk* battle group by a Chinese diesel submarine, which surely could not have moved fast enough to do so without cueing.

The U.S. Navy called the supporting system the Soviet Ocean Surveillance System (SOSS). To the extent that other navies, particularly the Chinese, learned how to operate from the Soviets, an understanding of the Cold War Soviet system may be of much more than academic interest. The U.S. response to the SOSS gives some idea of how an enemy network- or picture-centric system may be discovered and then evaluated. Since much of what the U.S. Navy learned about Soviet systems and tactics was highly classified, the current account should be considered suggestive rather than complete.

Initially, the only long-range sensor available to the Soviets was high frequency direction finding (HF/DF), exploiting the HF radio the U.S. Navy, like others, relied on for long-haul communications. Like Western countries, at the end of World War II the Soviets captured German Wullenweber array DF technology, which could capture and exploit even short signals. The U.S. Navy called the Soviet system Krug. It was apparently a Soviet national system that passed relevant information to the Soviet Navy (HF was also a way of tracking aircraft, as they used HF radio for long-haul communication). U.S. naval intelligence dated the origins of Krug to 1951, and probably to a decision that the Soviet Union needed to be able to detect carrier forces within two thousand kilometers (carrier strike range) of its coast.[2] The Soviet navy had its own mobile truck-mounted HF/DF sets, and it may also have had its own fixed systems.

Although not formally part of the SOSS, submarines and surface combatants off the Soviet coast were considered pickets helping to detect and track inbound enemy ships. For example, the Soviets apparently saw the numerous Whiskey-class submarines they built after World War II mainly as extended coast defense assets; only the many fewer Zulus and their Foxtrot-class successors were considered useful for deep-ocean operation.[3] Soviet frigates of the initial post–World War II program, like the Rigas (Project 50), were designated guardships (SKRs), which suggests that they were intended as coastal pickets (and as a peacetime means of preventing Soviet citizens from fleeing by sea).

In 1956 the Soviets began to deploy intelligence-gathering ships (AGIs), which were often erroneously called spy trawlers. (Early ones were modified from fishing hulls, but later ones were specially built.)[4] By 1966 U.S. naval officers associated the AGIs with the SOSS.[5] They were not mobile enough to trail carrier groups, but they were stationed off naval bases and near choke points, where they could register the presence of a formation of interest. Having registered the departure of a carrier group from its base, SOSS would dead reckon it across the ocean toward the Soviet Union, alerting other systems, such as Krug and reconnaissance bombers, when it was expected to arrive in more sensitive areas. Some U.S. officers wanted counter-AGIs.[6] When the Soviet fleet entered the Mediterranean on a sustained basis after the 1967 Six Days' War, an AGI provided it with signals intelligence (SIGINT) support. Another AGI was already observing U.S. operations in the Tonkin Gulf , presumably providing early warning to the North Vietnamese and also collecting SIGINT indicators for use in the event U.S. carrier groups approached the Soviet Union. At the end of the Soviet period, a fast AGI was designed to work as a picket with fleet units, but it was never built.

Apparently, much unlike the West, the Soviets were perfectly willing to use sensitive intelligence information operationally. Russian military intelligence is described by the same word the Russians use for reconnaissance, whereas in the West the two are clearly separate. Experience suggests that the Russians were right. American analysts always assumed that the Soviets exploited human intelligence, such as that which might be collected in bars near a base, before a ship or a formation put to sea.[7]

Once ships entered an area of interest, radar-equipped bombers, like those seen in 1964, were vectored out to confirm their identities, courses, and speeds. They could refine Krug data, and they could collect further signature data, for example, for further expansion of passive ship tracking. The Soviets also used electronic intelligence (ELINT) aircraft to detect and track ships. In 1962 they launched their first ELINT satellites, though it is not clear that they were intended specifically to detect surface ships. By 1970 the SOSS was using ELINT satellites, and a radar ocean surveillance satellite was well along in development.

After a time the SOSS could track U.S. carriers transiting toward areas of interest. Perhaps the most dramatic case in point was the 1968 interception of the carrier *Enterprise*, en route to Vietnamese waters, by a November-class nuclear attack submarine.[8] The U.S. Sound Surveillance System (SOSUS) tracked the submarine's high-speed run down the Kuriles toward the carrier. She never searched for the carrier. Clearly the SOSS had tracked the carrier and vectored the submarine into a potential attack position. This interception occurred much further out to sea than the bomber interceptions previously seen, implying that SOSS had a much wider-area capability than had been suspected. Another unpleasant surprise was that the submarine was fast enough to exploit SOSS information; it had been assumed that Soviet submarines were substantially slower. The interception increased support for the construction of U.S. nuclear submarines fast enough to work with nuclear carriers, the *Los Angeles* class. If the Soviets could intercept a fast carrier in the vastness of the Western Pacific, how much more easily could they find and destroy the Sixth Fleet in the much narrower Mediterranean?

Once the Soviets began conducting surface operations in the Mediterranean after 1967, it became clear that their fleet was centrally controlled on a netted basis. The ranges of their ship-launched anticarrier missiles far exceeded ships' sensor ranges. They needed an external means of finding their targets: the SOSS. The Soviets could disperse their missile shooters, making it difficult for the U.S. Navy to deal with them quickly enough to abort attacks. Central control and dispersed formations would offer the least warning to the target. Central control also made it possible to coordinate ships with submarine and air attackers; one classified Soviet article explained that bomber missiles had to be air burst so as not to endanger submarines simultaneously attacking with torpedoes.

By 1970 authoritative Soviet naval writers were describing a "battle for the first salvo." Modern weapons, particularly missiles, were so devastating that surely victory would go to whoever managed to shoot (and hit) first. U.S. Navy rules of engagement prohibited a preemptive strike against the Soviet fleet. The

U.S. fleet was dispersed around the world, with major striking forces in both the Mediterranean and the Pacific at any given time. If the Soviets hit only one such concentration first, the others would be justified in striking before being struck. Thus, Soviet doctrine demanded a global command system to set up nearly simultaneous strikes against all U.S. and other NATO forward-deployed forces. It was demonstrated in the Okean 70 exercise, conducted simultaneously in the different Soviet fleets, meaning in different oceans.[9] It was the first time such interfleet coordination had been observed, and it was massive, with 306 ships, naval aircraft, and aircraft from the separate long-range aviation and fighter defense forces participating. ASW, anticarrier, and amphibious warfare were all demonstrated. American observers were struck by the Soviets' ability to mount attacks simultaneously in all areas. They saw Okean 70 as proof that the SOSS had become a unified system controlled from Moscow rather than from the individual fleet headquarters. It now employed global resources such as ELINT satellites (a second-generation ELINT satellite was launched at the outset of the exercise to supplement the one already in orbit). AGIs were assigned to forward areas, presumably on a centrally controlled basis. Fleet reconnaissance aircraft now used airfields in Soviet client states, such as Cuba, to extend their effective range.

In 1970 the Soviets began to deploy a space-based naval surveillance system that could provide something close to targeting data. It resulted from a 1961 proposal to Soviet leader Nikita Khrushchev by an ambitious Soviet missile designer, V. M. Chelomey, that the entire naval mission be moved into space. A ship-detecting satellite could cue land- or sea-based missiles. As Khrushchev's favorite (he employed Khrushchev's son as an engineer), Chelomey received permission to go ahead with the satellite system, comprising a passive (ELINT) satellite and an active-radar one. When Khrushchev fell, the satellite project survived.[10] Like the U.S. White Cloud, the first dedicated naval passive satellite, orbited late in 1970, could locate a ship on the earth's surface. An operational three-satellite net was in place by 1975. A further improved ELINT ocean surveillance satellite (EORSAT) was introduced in 1974. ELINT satellites were first maneuvered in orbit to observe U.S. carrier transits in 1971 and 1972. For the 1973 October War in the Middle East the Soviets changed ground programming and downlinks so as to provide more timely intelligence.[11] The first active radar satellite (RORSAT) became operational in 1972. Although RORSAT attracted much Western attention, its problems killed it in 1988.

Both satellites stored data and dumped it to ground stations on Soviet territory. Bandwidth and time over the station limited what they could dump. Probably satellites were commanded to concentrate on a limited patch of ocean, having been cued by a wider-area wide-open system like Krug. Thus they were not equivalent to the inherently wide-open U.S. White Cloud system. Support to deployed ships was awkward because data dumps were made only on command from the single control station in Moscow (which could exercise command only when the satellite was overhead). Ships and submarines had receivers but no control equipment. The Soviet naval command system had to cue a missile-firing ship or submarine into a preplanned position, to receive a planned data dump. To make the most of available time and onboard storage, the passive satellite was limited to recognizing a few radars and transmitting their coordinates. Probably it could not measure radar parameters for fingerprinting. The radar satellite transmitted only target coordinates (it seems to have had the first Russian autodetection radar).[12]

Okean 70 may have demonstrated to the Soviets that full centralization was impractical. They conducted another large-scale exercise five years later (Okean 75). At least to U.S. observers, this exercise differed radically from its predecessors. Instead of the usual defense of contiguous sea areas against U.S. carriers, it envisaged a multiforce graduated-response war not too different from that imagined in the West. This time satellites were rapidly reprogrammed to meet task force or even individual strike unit requirements. Given a picture of where satellites were and also of where surface units were, Moscow ordered satellites to dump their data as required to support local operations.[13] This more tactical emphasis may explain efforts late in the Soviet period to build an AGI capable of operating with Soviet task groups.

Given their predisposition toward tight central control, the Soviets preferred to coordinate all-arms forces from above rather than by allowing them to communicate with each other. In the 1960s, that is, before Okean 70, they began to deploy flagships. They could be distinguished by their long-range HF antennas (NATO Vee Cone), presumably intended to support communication with shore headquarters. (These antennas were later replaced by Low Ball satellite antennas.) The first-generation flagships were submarine tenders, *Moskva*-class helicopter carriers, and two converted *Sverdlov*-class cruisers, in which extra superstructure replaced one six-inch turret. It appears that the successors were the *Kiev*-class carriers and the *Kirov*-class cruisers. These ships seem to have been envisaged as the cores of tactical groups, the carriers for pro-strategic ballistic missile submarine (SSBN) ASW and the cruisers for surface action, although that may be an oversimplification. As noted, task groups appeared in the Okean 75 exercise, though not in Okean 70. It appears that later flagships had special data links connecting them to subordinate units.

By 1974 U.S. analysts divided the SOSS into two layers. One provided wide-area information on U.S. (and allied) naval activities, but it was not precise enough for targeting. It cued the more precise assets used for targeting (tattletales). At this stage it seems not to have been understood that the Soviets considered a third level, which confirmed the position of the target within the formation, essential.[14] The main wide-area sensors were HF/DF and ELINT satellites. They cued manned plat-forms (e.g., aircraft such as Bear Ds) and radar ocean surveillance satellites. It was assumed that the SOSS also benefitted from whatever submarines or surface ships happened to detect U.S. or allied warships, as well as from patrolling aircraft.[15] It was not clear whether the SOSS generally vectored such assets into place to pick up warships or formations of interest. How well they could detect targets helped determine how precisely the SOSS had to vector them.

Tattletales

Soviet tactics became clearer once their surface forces operated in numbers in the Mediterranean after the 1967 Six Days' War. Once the carrier or other formation of interest arrived, the Soviets often tried to attach a surface "tattletale," generally a modified destroyer, to it. These fast surface warships tried to maintain station on likely missile targets. U.S. officers became interested in operating tattletales of their own, largely to gain the earliest possible warning of an impending Soviet missile attack.

Gradually it became clear that the SOSS cued the tattletales. They were part of the fire-control process. It was not enough to target a U.S. formation because missiles might lock onto the wrong ships, particularly after the U.S. Navy installed blip enhancers on many of its destroyers (which would then seem, on radar, to be aircraft carriers). The solution was for a Soviet ship or airplane to get so close that she could positively identify the high-value unit within the formation. Given this information, missiles could be locked onto the right targets. Airplanes locked on their missiles at launch time (only in the 1980s did they get data links). The P-35 antiship version of the long-range SS-N-3 "Shaddock" had a video data link back to the launching ship. An operator on the ship matched the missile's radar picture with a picture received from a radar-equipped Bear D (Tu-95RTs) bomber. The appearance of a Bear D became a useful warning of impending attack: a Sixth Fleet saying was "Bears in the morning, missiles in the afternoon."

One mark of the tattletale role was the unusual backward-facing missile battery installed on ships, such as Kildins and Kashin-class destroyers, modified for this role. As the attack neared, the ship had to leave the formation so as not to attract (and waste) any incoming missiles. She would make a 180-degree turn—pointing her own missiles at the target formation. After the Cold War, it became clear that missile bombers also relied on air tattletales. Thus a bomber regiment in the Black Sea Fleet included reconnaissance aircraft that would fly into the target formation to confirm visually which ship was the target, radioing back (presumably just before being shot down) via high-altitude relay aircraft. The targeting radars on board the attacking bombers provided the overall picture a Bear D supplied to a surface shooter. When a Badger cartwheeled into the sea in 1968 after making low passes over the U.S. carrier *Essex*, it had probably been practicing this mission, though this was not understood at the time. Indeed, the tattletales' role apparently was not understood for many years. The Soviets had plenty of other ways of detecting and tracking any U.S. formation, like a battle group, which had no alternative but to radiate. The typical explanation, at least through the mid-1970s, was that they were insurance against last-minute errors. Whatever the explanation, the presence of a tattletale was evidence that the SOSS was tracking a formation.

Expansion to ASW

Once the U.S. Navy deployed missile submarines, the SOSS expanded to track them. AGIs were assigned to lie off their bases to detect their sorties.[16] An effort was mounted to develop an underwater equivalent to Krug. After the Cold War, it became clear that this project had been protracted and largely fruitless. Geography was largely unfavorable, and technology was not up to the job. Thus, Westerners did not realize that the Soviets had tried to develop an equivalent to SOSUS.[17] The Soviets also became interested in placing long-range sonar pingers in the open ocean aboard specialized ships, but only one was built.[18] Only after the end of the Cold War did the Russians bring a long-range active acoustic surveillance system into service, and it had nothing like the requisite range. The Soviets may also have assumed that their HF/DF net would pick up transmissions from the submarines, much as the U.S. HF/DF net was part of the U.S. ASW ocean surveillance system. The U.S. strategic submarine force never transmitted enough messages to make HF/DF an effective ASW sensor. Choke point sensing in general bought little once the initial 1,200-nautical mile Polaris missile had been superseded. It was still possible to imagine trailing the submarines, beginning near their bases, but that would have been difficult in the face of SOSUS (which would probably pick up the prospective trailers) and U.S. acoustic advantages. Assuming that their system would eventually succeed, the Soviets developed the interceptors their picture-centric system would have wielded, had it ever become fully operational: the Il-38 May maritime patrol aircraft (equivalent in concept if hardly in capability to a P-3C). It is not clear to what extent submarines had a parallel role. The big sonar in the "Alfa" (Project 705) fast submarine had dramatically improved ASW capability, and this submarine was sometimes described as an interceptor (possibly, however, of fast carriers rather than of submarines).

Weaknesses

U.S. exercises showed that the SOSS could be fooled: according to a 1974 paper, "analysis indicates that combinations of counters to SOSS can introduce a transient into SOSS operations and increase the time required for attack platforms to move into the targeting mode. This time delay can permit U.S. carriers to transit to and arrive at a desired area. In addition, such counters will force the SOSS to commit resources overtly to obtain additional search capability, thus providing information to the U.S. on intent and possibly allowing dilution or destruction of the Soviet attack."[19] The reference was to a combination of HF silence (relying on less-detectable communications) and decoying. The radars on board Bear Ds and Badgers could be countered by shipboard versions of the jammers normally carried by EA-6B Prowler electronic countermeasures (ECM) aircraft.

Because the SOSS was not good enough to provide fire-control quality information in its usual tracking mode, it had to intensify operations to prepare for an attack: it warned its victim. That was obvious in the form of Bear D radar reconnaissance aircraft and also of tattletales. Conversely, if such operations could be frustrated, attacks might become quite difficult. A more basic weakness was the rigidity of the system. It was conceived for use at the outbreak of war, but throughout the Cold War, it was far likelier that events would slip into war than that either side would suddenly decide to destroy the other. For example, SOSS satellites could dump their data only as programmed from Moscow, and the data would rain down whether or not the desired recipient was in place as planned. If war began at a low level of violence, without mass strikes on carrier and other deployed NATO forces, there was every chance that they would kill AGIs and tattletales at the outset.[20]

The Soviet navy was not well structured for the surprise initial attack for which the SOSS seemed to be designed. The bases of its powerful air striking force were poorly situated. NATO forces would almost certainly have considerable advance warning that the big missile bombers were on the way. Thus, surprise would depend on ship- and submarine-launched missiles, but even they required visible support (entailing warning). By about 1981 it was known that particular operating modes of the Big Bulge radar on a Bear D indicated that it was targeting, rather than searching the sea.[21] Satellites could reduce this problem (although their downlinks were certainly detectable). Tattletales could radio back key information, such as where the high-value unit was in the formation, but they were never credited with the ability to control incoming missiles. That resided on the missile-firing platforms, so the platforms needed a tactical picture on the basis of which to program their weapons.

There was a further potential weakness. How many ships could the SOSS handle at any one time? Western experience with manual Combat Information Center (CICs) suggested that the number might be surprisingly small. The Soviets apparently agreed because about 1981 they opened a computer ship-tracking center in Moscow.[22]

Origins

The Soviet approach to naval warfare seems to have been a greatly scaled-up coast defense evolved from the German World War I all-arms defense of the Belgian coast. The predecessor tsarist navy established a coastal observation system in 1909, but the Communist-era idea of using it to direct offshore operations seems to have been new.[23] German collaboration with the Soviets in the 1920s and early 1930s probably exposed the new Soviet navy to German wartime experience. Soviet writers of the time emphasized that a new kind of warfare was being developed, as an alternative to classical ("bourgeois") large-fleet concepts. It made a virtue of Soviet poverty. There is a hint of the need for surveillance in the designation applied to small ocean-going combatants: SKR, guardship. In peacetime, SKRs would maintain sea frontier security, which often meant keeping Soviet citizens from escaping. In wartime they were pickets intended to detect enemy formations while they were still well offshore. Presumably the offshore elements of the system were backed by a radio direction-finding network. Unfortunately, no history of prewar Soviet ocean surveillance has appeared. The central control feature of a German-style coastal system fit the new Soviet-era demand that a commissar countersign all orders.

The coastal force survived Stalin's attempts to build a blue-water navy both before and after World War II. After 1945 the Soviet navy was probably unique in pursuing the mass production of coastal torpedo craft. To some extent the postwar Soviet submarine program extended this force further out to sea (in effect Whiskeys superseded the small coastal M class of the past). The massive Soviet land-based naval air arm needed ocean surveillance in order to be fully effective. None of this was obvious in the West.

The post–World War II Soviet coastal system was built around central stations in what amounted to naval districts. They coordinated the boats' activities and may even have controlled when they fired. The main sensors feeding the central station were HF/DF, coastal radars, coastal pickets, and coastal sonar. ASW practice was probably typical. The central station vectored subchasers out to an offshore contact. (The Soviets emphasized underwater communications so that the central station would not attack friendly submarines operating as part of the coast defense system.) As in many other ASW systems, the subchasers reacquired the target and attacked. By the 1960s the central stations had simple computers that monitored sonars on board the group of subchasers to decide when to fire their RBU-6000 rocket launchers together to saturate an area likely to contain the submarine. During the 1960s the Soviets moved their coastal ASW system to sea by putting the shore computer aboard a destroyer, which could now control subchasers. Torpedo boats and then missile boats were probably similarly controlled. Soviet-era literature often showed crews scrambling onto their missile boats. Since missile boats fired at targets beyond their own horizons, some form of external control was necessary. This sort of operation seemed evident when the U.S. Navy examined a former East German Tarantul-type missile boat after the end of the Cold War. Presumably the Soviet technique of coastal forces command and control was exported to friendly navies during the Cold War.

The localized naval defense sufficed against threats at or near the coastline. U.S. World War II carrier operations apparently made it clear that something further offshore was needed. Hence the SOSS and its big HF/DF arrays. As in the United States, initially digital computers were too massive (and too scarce) to be used in anything short of a fleet command or tracking center. According to a recent Russian book on naval electronics, the Soviet navy established a fleet computer development center in 1954. Probably in the early 1960s computer centers were created at the fleet and main naval headquarters level. Like their U.S. counterparts they depended on batch processing. Russian accounts suggest that initially computer development was rapid, leading to time-shared systems with computer terminals (APMs, BESM-6 computer) in the 1960s, but then it faltered partly because of a decision to stop domestic development (which was producing machines suited to networking) in favor of copying the U.S. IBM-360 and its batch-processing software. In theory fleet-level computers were accepted as the basis of an automated command information system, but officers persisted in displaying information on cards (presumably status boards) and plotting tables, using manual calculations. The computers handled slowly varying data such as structure and location of own-forces and levels of equipment stocks, whereas rapidly changing tactical data were handled manually. Computer workstations supported logistical rather than combat functions. Even once psychological barriers had been overcome, systems suffered because they lacked any automated messaging system. (Development of such a system was under way as the Soviet Union began to collapse).

CIC Systems

The Soviets seem to have learned from their World War II allies to create combat information centers, which they called battle information posts (BIPs). The idea was initially adopted by the Soviet air defense service (PVO). In 1946 S. P. Chernakov of the naval radar institute showed the need for a shipboard BIP and wrote a tactical-technical requirement. The first BIP, tested on board the cruiser *Molotov* in the Black Sea, had separate plots for air, surface, and underwater pictures (scales were, respectively, 100–150, 20–25, and 1.5–2.0 nautical miles). Functions matched those of Western CICs. An analogous system for ships of medium displacement, such as destroyers, accommodated only a single vertical plot, which could handle only one picture at a time. The *Molotov* installation was formalized as the Zveno system (1949). It could handle four to five surface and seven to nine air targets. Despite its low throughput and its considerable track error (6 to 8 degrees, 5 to 7 percent in speed), Zveno was an enormous improvement over non-BIP practice. It was installed on board cruisers, destroyers, and patrol ships. For example, Zveno-42 equipped "Kola"-class frigates (Project 42). The successor Tsel' system entered service in 1950.

Like their Western counterparts, Soviet BIPs suffered from too many delays between a radar operator's detection and plotting. In the late 1940s the U.S. and Royal Netherlands navies tried a solution. The radar scope operator marked targets using a special grease pencil. A television camera in the base of his console picked up the mark but ignored the radar blips projected on the operator's scope. The images of the plots from various consoles were mixed and the result projected as a combined or summary plot. This method drastically reduced latency time and plotting errors. It seems to have been the basis for the next Soviet BIP system, Planshet (tablet, i.e., plotting board). Throughput increased by a factor of tens and accuracy improved (errors of 2 to 4 degrees, 4–6 percent of speed). Because the system was analog, it could control only one or two pairs of fighters. Attempts to transfer data from ship to ship were frustrated because images of the operators' marks were not bright enough to overcome noise. Planshet was tested in the Pacific and in the Black Sea in 1953–54. There were many versions: Planshet-30bis for the *Skoriy*-class destroyer; Planshet-35 for the Krivak class (Project 1135); Planshet-50 for the Riga class; Planshet-56, 56M, and 56U for Kotlin and variants; Planshet-57 for Kildin; Planshet-58 for Kynda-class missile cruisers; Planshet-59 for the Petya class (Project 159); Planshet-61 for the Kashin class; Planshet-1134 for the Kresta I class; Planshet was installed in the two *Sverdlov*-class cruisers converted to command ships.

Work on surface ship computer combat direction systems began in 1958 but was badly protracted. It apparently began with an attempt to process radar information automatically. Radar plots were probably entered by an operator using a foot pedal (equivalent to the ball-tab of the U.S. Naval Tactical Data System [NTDS]). The first such system, MRO-315, appeared in 1966. It could handle up to fifteen air tracks. It was a short-range track keeper intended to feed a target designator. The next step (1967–68) was the Koren' (Root) command information system for the large ASW ships (BPKs [large, antisubmarine warfare ships]: "Kara" and "Kresta II" classes) and for *Moskva*-class helicopter carriers. A version may also have been installed on board the submarine tender *Volga*. As in NTDS, command management (combat information) was separate from weapon control. Unlike the U.S. Navy, the Soviet navy physically separated its radar consoles, from which information was entered, from the command information element (summary consoles) and the weapon control element. The commanding officer (CO) had the summary display.

Another difference from U.S. practice was a much greater emphasis on command advice, based on rules applied to the tactical picture. Thus *Moskva* had the first "Second Captain," which seems to have provided advice based on both external and internal information. When it was installed, the ship's commander told his officers that they would no longer have to bother thinking for themselves. Koren' was built around a single computer operating at 250–300,000 operations per second (KOPS; the somewhat earlier U.S. CP-642B operated at a similar speed, and the somewhat later UYK-7 at about 670 KOPS).[24] From the console an operator could set either combat or system management mode, select a particular sensor picture for display on a separate indicator, or change display scale or the structure of the alphanumeric displays. Koren' could automatically control weapons and electronic equipment, and it could guide a helicopter and ASW cruise missiles. The *Moskva* version (and probably the *Volga* version) initially passed information to other ships via a burst transmitter, Akula, sending data from a tape punched by the computer.

The Russians considered Koren' inadequate. The main screens showed tracks, but separate alphanumeric boards showed target designations and track data (e.g, speed, height) and sometimes even coordinates (bearing and range). Manual vertical plots were still essential. Later versions of Koren' had more complete electronic plots, whose operators could order tactical actions and could also structure status boards. Such systems could handle tens of targets.

For Kashin-class missile destroyers (Project 61) the Soviets developed a smaller-ship Morye (Sea) system, with its own automatic line of sight (centimetric frequency) digital link to distribute target designation and to exchange command information on a limited scale. This was nothing like the computer-to-computer Link 11. It was simply a radio signal digitized to overcome noise. Morye did not control shipboard weapons. Introduced in 1969 on board two ships, it was apparently unsuccessful, as all other Kashins had the earlier analog Planshet.

Work on computer command systems for submarines apparently began in the 1960s. An unclassified Russian article of the mid-1970s described how a computer specialist on board a missile submarine fed data into the ship's computer, which the CO used to communicate with the ship's weapon system. Work on the first such system, Tucha (Cloud), was apparently inspired by the development of the Yankee (Project 667A) class, the first to carry sixteen missiles. The submarine had to be able to fire all in a rapid salvo, to avoid losing them if an enemy submarine began attacking when the first was fired (just such attacks were a goal of the Soviet anti-Polaris project). Missile aiming therefore had to be automated. The missile fire-control digital computer could also be used for combat direction. This story is broadly similar to that of the U.S. Mk 113 Mod 9 submarine fire-control system. The Russian system was connected to the sonar, radar, navigational, and missile/fire-control systems. It displayed information about conditions (ship, opponent, weapon), about tactical maneuvers, and about whether missiles and torpedoes could be fired. Thus, it broadly resembled the abortive U.S. submarine systems conceived about 1965. Tucha was also installed in Delta I (Project 667B)–class submarines. These ships had a different missile, and they apparently had a separate missile control system, Al'fa (1972). Later submarine computer systems were also connected to power plants and to life-support systems.[25]

A parallel Akkord project automated Alfa-class (Project 705) ASW submarines, which could not accommodate large crews.[26] Begun in 1960, it was completed in 1972. In an Alfa, Akkord was associated with the MGK-1000 Okean integrated sonar. The system included underwater communications, which the designers saw as a link between the combat system computers of two submarines operating together. Additional evidence of the networked character of the "Alfa" submarine was the integrated navigational system, which used Doppler sonar to measure the submarine's speed over the bottom. Note, however, that recent Russian accounts of "Alfa" do not make this point. For the designers the submarine's high speed and deep diving capabilities apparently came first, before its possible mission. Although sometimes described in the West as an interceptor of submarines, "Alfa" was not usually included in lists of anti-Polaris systems, and it was more probably a carrier interceptor. Akkord was also installed in Victor II (Project 671RT) class. It became the basis for next-generation systems.

Apparently an effort to automate diesel submarines was completely separate, an offshoot of a project to develop a Soviet minicomputer. Development of this Uzel (MVU-110) system was completed in 1973, and it equipped the Project 641B (Tango) class and the Project 877/636 (Kilo), which was widely exported.[27] Unlike the combat information and control automated naval command system (BIUS) on nuclear submarines, Uzel has only one single-operator console, providing a plan position indicator (PPI)–like display and torpedo presets (it is separate from the

Rubikon sonar system). The system is run by three digital computers, each operating at 100 KOPS.[28]

Probably generations of computer submarine combat systems were associated with generations of integrated sonars incorporating underwater data links (before integration, the underwater links were stand-alone devices). Presumably such linking was possible in the face of severe distortion because the Soviet systems used very limited vocabularies. To avoid revealing the submarine's presence, the Soviets used a spread-spectrum (direct-sequencing) technique. It is not clear just how effective it was because throughout the later Cold War NATO detected and named different Soviet underwater communications devices.

Roughly parallel to these submarine systems the Soviets produced a new generation surface ship Alleya-1 (Avenue) system (1972). The corresponding data link, Bell Crown (there seems not to have been any specific Russian designation) was first tested in 1973–74. That it uses a small radome implies that it is a directional system working at microwave frequency. It is a three-part link: operation presumably begins with interrogation by the master ship, followed by a directional reply. Presumably the master ship samples the slaves in roll-call fashion and then broadcasts a summary of what they have sent. It is not clear whether this was a computer-to-computer system capable of conveying commands. Apparently Bell Crown is an antiair warfare (AAW) system. *Kiev*-class aircraft carriers had Alleya-2, and *Kirov*-class missile cruisers had the improved Alleya-2M.

Probably the advent of newer-generation computers made it possible to develop a further generation of submarine and surface-ship systems. Versions of the Omnibus (MVU-132) submarine system were expected to equip all the different nuclear submarines: strategic, cruise missile, and attack. It introduced color displays (two of them in this system), which for the first time in Russian practice could display results of calculations in graphic form on their circular PPI-like displays. According to a Russian account, the first versions of Omnibus could perform over fifty tasks, some of them simultaneously. Omnibus was introduced in the Victor III (Project 671RTM) class and equips other attack submarines (Sierra and Akula), Oscar II–class missile submarines, and the later strategic submarines (Delta IV and Typhoon). All of these classes (plus Oscar I) have versions of the Skat integrated digital sonar. Skat was conceived in 1964 as an analog sonar with long-range passive capability and automated secondary data processing (e.g., for Target Motion Analysis [TMA]). Thus, some of its functions would be parts of a U.S. submarine combat direction system.

The corresponding third-generation large-ship system was Lesorub (Woodcutter). It controls the air and missile assets of an entire formation for both air and ASW defense, and at the least it offers tactical advice for formation maneuvers.

As observed on board a *Slava* and on board an *Udaloy* in the mid-1990s, Lesorub employs a pair of workstations on the bridge, with a comparable pair in a separate below-decks battle information post, and other workstations in the AAW weapon control space. Presumably it employs a computer-to-computer data link, probably for the first time in Soviet practice. Thus subordinate ships in the formation needed compatible combat systems. Thus Lesorub-44 equipped the cruiser *Admiral Lazarev*, while Lesorub-1164 equipped *Slava*-class cruisers apparently intended to work with her. Lesorub equipped the carriers *Admiral Gorshkov* and *Kuznetzov*. Lesorub-1155, probably a flagship version, equips *Udaloy*-class destroyers. A Russian account suggests that such systems had to solve novel problems, including accepting off-board radar and sonar data and controlling formation radar countermeasures. In Western systems, at least until the end of the Cold War, electronic warfare was handled mainly on a single-ship basis. Against such sophistication, the Soviets had to cope with the limitations of a conscript navy. They therefore tended to provide systems with limited numbers of precut actions, rather than, as in the West, trusting system operators to make sense of a tactical picture and to react on that basis.

The Lesorub workstations (S-170-M) on board a *Slava*-class cruiser are probably primarily or entirely for AAW. Near the bridge workstation is a separate console to designate targets to the ship's SS-N-12 (Bazalt) antiship missiles. A similar console, with further SS-N-12 consoles, is in the BIP. A separate weapon direction space contains launching consoles for the ship's SAN-6 defensive missile system. It maintains a close-in picture (for engagement) using a secondary radar (Top Steer), in effect a higher-frequency equivalent to the main radar (Top Pair) feeding Lesorub. The ship's below-decks BIP contains another pair of Lesorub consoles and a manual vertical plot. Adjacent to the BIP is a weapons-control space, containing a Lesorub console that designates air targets. Neither on the bridge nor in the BIP were any ASW displays; apparently the ship's sonar and ASW weapons were intended as a self-contained self-defense system.

In an *Udaloy*, Lesorub (MVU-211) is built around a computer running at one MOPS (millions of operations per second). As in other Soviet systems, this command information system is separate from both AAW and ASW weapon controls. Computer and consoles are on a digital bus that can carry up to a hundred devices. A published diagram shows a workstation with a trackball, a text display station with keyboard, and an electronic plotting table. Because the ship is primarily an ASW unit, a large sonar display is located between the two Lesorub consoles on the bridge.

Presumably the Sapfir system in *Sovremennyy*-class destroyers was developed at the same time using the same command data link because *Sovremennyy*s and

*Udaloy*s were intended to work together. *Sovremennyy* also has a Mineral over-the-horizon targeting system using both the antennas inside the "Band Stand" radome and dedicated ship-to-ship and air-to-ship data links. This system is apparently separate from the Lesorub dedicated largely to AAW. Unlike an *Udaloy*, a *Sovremennyy* has only one air defense radar, which suggests that there is no separate longer-range track keeper. That makes sense because although the ship's SAN-7 missile is physically similar to the U.S. Standard, its effective performance is closer to that of the Sea Sparrow point-defense weapon. *Sovremennyy* is much more a surface missile shooter, a modern equivalent of the classical destroyer armed primarily with torpedoes. Thus her AAW system is probably built up from her weapons control system rather than separate from it. That may explain why the ship seems to have her BIP (command system consoles) and weapon control amalgamated below decks. As in the *Slava* BIP, there is a vertical plot. (In this case, a pair of perspex boards in the center of the space.)

When in the BIP, the ship's commanding officer used a standard Lesorub console (S170-M). The BIP contained a second S170-M and a circular horizontal console (S-170AM), perhaps equivalent to the conference consoles used in Western systems. The separate missile control section had its own situation display and a target-engagement console. The ASW module of the system consisted of a single passive/active sonar display connected to the separate sonar room. There were separate BIP consoles for navigational radar, electronic warfare (EW) and, apparently, chemical warfare. Guns were apparently locally controlled, their targets designated from the BIP.[29]

Unfortunately for the Soviet navy, the Soviet economic system dictated that projects, such as generations of combat direction systems, be developed as integrated projects. Each new system had its own entirely new computer, data links, and displays. Links developed for one generation of systems were not interoperable with other generations, but formations necessarily mixed generations. Thus, hopes that automation would make for mutually supporting formations could never be realized. Ships extracted information from their own sensors, although they did report air and submarine contacts to flagships. Because data links were not used, and because reporting was not automatic, as a rule the flag BIP did not receive the necessary information on a timely basis. According to a recent Russian account, progress was badly slowed by the rigid and exclusive division of functions among scientific institutes and the various ministries, who had sufficient political power to block any attempt to develop a uniform automation strategy. For example, different ministries created their own computers. There was no staff capable of developing uniform technical standards and algorithms.

CHAPTER 20

Net versus Net:
U.S. Ocean Surveillance versus the SOSS

How do you evaluate—and counter—a network system like the Soviet Ocean Surveillance System (SOSS)? Its most basic parameter is the sheer number of objects it can handle—its saturation level. A related question is how current the track data are: how close is the picture on the screen to reality? Close enough for ships or aircraft to be vectored? For weapons to be fired? Once the U.S. Navy realized that there was an SOSS, it sought to measure the system's characteristics. As understanding deepened, the U.S. Navy began to develop information-destruction techniques—deception. The alternative, physical destruction, would have been difficult or impossible early in a war.

At the outset the main SOSS sensor was obviously high frequency direction finding (HF/DF). Beginning at least as early as 1963, U.S. carrier groups experimented to see how long they could operate within striking range of the Soviet coast undetected.[1] One of the first experiments was Operation *Kitty Hawk* Express (January and February 1963) east of Japan, which elicited the highest levels of Soviet activity yet detected in that area. *Kitty Hawk* and her four escorting destroyers used complete HF silence for periods of ten and twenty-one hours. No Soviet aircraft or ships approached them—but that was not conclusive because sometimes the ship was not approached when she did communicate. Moreover, it appeared that Soviet reconnaissance aircraft operated only in daylight. All of one and part of the other emission control (EMCON) period were conducted in darkness, on the reasonable theory that the ship might be spotted anyway in daylight. The Soviets apparently used the operation to conduct simulated missile strikes by Badger bombers. That they were centrally directed was indicated by the fact that the bombers flew directly to the task group without making extensive area searches.

A more sophisticated experiment with the *Shangri-La* battle group, transiting from the Mediterranean to Mayport, Florida, was conducted in May 1964. Having been spotted by an AGI at the Straits of Gibraltar, the group split into a deception group and a smaller group built around the carrier. The smaller group went into HF silence, but the deception group radiated freely. A Bear reconnaissance bomber overflew the deception group but did not approach the carrier, even though its crew could see that no carrier was present in that group. After the carrier made a fourteen-minute transmission, a second Bear overflew the deception group and then went on to overfly the carrier. It was clearly vectored to the carrier. Conversely, HF silence did not keep the Soviets from maintaining almost constant contact with the carrier *Independence* during a two-week North Atlantic and Norwegian Sea exercise in September 1964. The Soviets had so many surface ships in the area that the ship could not shake contact. There were at least twenty-five aircraft incidents, including eighteen raids approaching the carrier directly, some of them simulated attacks. Numerous submarines were involved.

In a 1968 exercise, USS *Essex* used HF silence to enter the Mediterranean unobserved. As she transmitted for one to two hours at night, a nearby Soviet missile destroyer (tattletale) made for her estimated position. She closed down her HF transmitter, set up merchant-ship style lighting, and left the area at high speed. The destroyer did not make contact. She was not detected again for the next five weeks, until a tattletale trailing another carrier (*Shangri-La*) happened upon her while the two carriers were working together. Because the tattletale had been assigned to the other carrier, it did not stay with *Essex*, which escaped. After the carrier made another HF transmission off Sicily, a Soviet intelligence gatherer (AGI) turned toward the position thus indicated. Having set total EMCON, *Essex* left at high speed. The slow AGI could not follow. U.S. analysts were impressed by how quickly the Soviets responded to HF transmissions, but it is also clear that they lacked the means to handle high-speed targets. Later *Essex* managed to leave Portsmouth, England, unobserved despite the presence of an AGI near the harbor entrance. The keys were high speed, darkness, and HF silence. The carrier reached the Norwegian Sea undetected, but despite her HF silence, she was picked up by two Bears. Their "Puff Ball" sea search radars had already been detected, suggesting that they were searching rather than simply following a vector to the carrier. Once detected, the carrier lifted her HF restriction. Soon a Badger appeared overhead without having used its radar, that is, vectored out on the basis of HF/DF.

In March 1969 *Ranger* conducted strike operations for three days in the Yellow Sea and in the Sea of Japan without any contact with Soviet forces, thanks to HF silence. (She was eventually detected by searching Bears, using their radars.) This was a striking success: the carrier was doing exactly what the Soviet fleet was intended to prevent. Similarly, in June 1970 the carrier *Wasp* eluded detection and contact for three and possibly four days in another sensitive area, the North Sea and the Norwegian Sea. Keys were HF silence, deceptive tactics, a dispersed formation, and exploitation of a lapse in tattletale trailing. The Soviets were relying on slow AGIs in choke areas and on Riga-class frigates, which apparently lacked the endurance to keep up with the carrier. Eventually *Wasp* was located by air searches. In August 1971 the carrier *Intrepid* avoided detection for about forty hours during a sortie from Scotland into the Norwegian Sea, despite what appeared to be active Soviet interest in her movements. Keys included the use of a deception group (four destroyers), HF silence, and further deception in the form a destroyer that remained in port radiating carrier-like communication signals after the carrier group had left. Perhaps most spectacularly, between her departure from Mayport on 11 April 1972 until her arrival in the Indian Ocean on 29 April, the carrier *Saratoga* seems to have been lost to Soviet surveillance. At that point she resumed normal communications and radar usage and was picked up. Among the measures taken by the ship, her computers were programmed to identify periods when she was subject to Soviet satellite cover; she turned her air search radars off during those times.

U.S. analysts concluded that the Soviet system was based on HF/DF. Other sensors, such as electronic intelligence (ELINT) satellites, were typically cued by HF/DF data, being redirected in orbit as required.

At least in the Mediterranean, tattletales were an even better measure of SOSS capacity.[2] If a carrier group evaded its tattletale, then the SOSS would try to vector another into position. Often the tattletale searched frantically but unsuccessfully. It seemed to follow that the SOSS had been unable to track the carrier. Through the 1970s the U.S. Navy built up an understanding of SOSS capability and limitation in this way. It became clear that the SOSS could be saturated. It could probably handle the five forward-deployed carrier groups at any one time, but not too much more, and perhaps not even that

A June 1973 exercise involving the U.S. carrier *Franklin D. Roosevelt* and the British *Ark Royal* gives some idea of what was involved.[3] USS *Leary* was assigned to play a Kotlin-class tattletale trailing the U.S. carrier. The carrier never managed to evade her. The submarine *Spadefish* played a Charlie-class missile shooter. She was intended to join with *Leary* and covertly trail the carrier, but she never managed the planned rendezvous—like a real-life Charlie, she was too slow. The destroyer *New* simulated a Kresta I working with the simulated Echo II–class submarine USS *Shark* to simulate Soviet standoff missile capability (SS-N-3 missiles). They were intended to provide mutual support for each other. The destroyers *Sarsfield* and *Cone* simulated a Kresta I (long-range missile shooter) and a Krivak (thought at the time to have a shorter-range antiship missile, which turned out to be an antisubmarine warfare [ASW] weapon). They were expected to provide both antiship missile fire and antiaircraft fire against any maritime patrol aircraft supporting the high-value units.

The exercise showed that a tattletale could pick up one unit in the kind of spread formation the U.S. Navy was then adopting, then close in on the high-value unit at its core. The formation was intended to fool reconnaissance, but it was not spread out enough. Even so, the two carriers were too far apart for mutual antiair warfare (AAW) support (Aegis would change that). The exercise report showed how important electronic silence could be. With their almost obsessive electronic discipline, the British were far more successful. *Ark Royal* maintained total electronic silence, including "zip lip" air operations. She used her own electronic support measures (ESM) system as her primary sensor and was able to control her integrated task force without revealing it to enemy ESM, presumably using short-range radio and visual signals. She also exploited weather because without electronic tips, a searcher had to be visual. She remained undetected for two days. "The interception of the recce aircraft that finally detected her was a classic; his HF frequency contact report was jammed and he was shot down by an aggressive Combat Air Patrol (CAP) before it could be retransmitted." U.S. units within the *Ark Royal* group used their radars and HF radio and so were detected even though the group was supposed to be practicing total electronic (including sonar) silence.

The U.S. carrier was located by "luck of the reconnaissance," ESM contacts, and confirmation by tattletale.

Overall, tactical HF radio nets were easily detected and jammed, as in previous exercises. As tattletale, *Leary* completely blocked the nets—surely including Link 11—being used by the target formation. Command and control collapsed; "trigger happy" U.S. units fired on the Orange (simulated enemy) units without authorization. U.S. attempts at communications deception failed entirely. Ominously, "Link 11 appeared to be a failure from view point of reliable data exchange with P-3/ATDS/NTDS ships. Link 14 generally unreliable."

Perhaps the most depressing feature of the exercise was poor radar and, by extension, combat system performance. During the air raid phase, of thirty-seven missiles fired by simulated bombers (forty-two scheduled), only twenty-two (68 percent) were detected and weapon systems locked onto only twelve. That compared to 57 percent of the fourteen surface-launched missiles (from a fixed ground position), and 28 percent of the thirteen bombers (three lock ons).[4] Combat Air Patrols assigned to deal with Orange bomber strikes were poorly coordinated with the ships' own antiaircraft missile batteries. Aircraft orbited too close to the likely line at which the incoming bombers would launch. They concentrated on the incoming missiles. Few initial head-on interceptions worked, so the fighters often found themselves pursuing the missiles into the U.S. ships' missile fire.

The group defense orbited a Surface Combat Air Patrol (SUCAP) above the enemy surface shooters to sink them before they could do any damage. Unfortunately, carrier capacity was limited, with only one or two aircraft attacking each Kresta or Krivak. The simulated Soviet missile submarines were credited with a total of five hits: two on visual bearing, two based on tattletale data, and one on radar. The report of the exercise observed that this probably approximated reality. Six of the nine times *Spadefish* was detected were by spotting her periscope. (Five detections were by patrol aircraft.)

The exercise report added that enemy operations were hampered by the same problems that had surfaced in earlier exercises: poor communications facilities, an inability of surface units to recognize attacks, and submarine problems. Presumably, at least some of these comments mirrored experience with Soviet formations.

When he became chief of naval operations (CNO) in 1970, Adm. Elmo Zumwalt Jr. included antitattletale measures in the initial program he called Project SIXTY. U.S. countertattletales (modified missile motor gunboats [PGMs]), armed with new antiship missiles, would be deployed against Soviet surface action groups, to shoot as soon as the Soviets displayed evidence of hostile intent, such as opening missile tube doors. A complementary program developed deception devices, such as acoustic simulators and false-target generators.[5] Procurement began under the FY75 program. About 1973 the U.S. Navy became interested in systematic emission control as a means of defeating the SOSS.[6] For example, it deployed centralized emission control units (Multiple Unit Transmission Elimination [MUTE] and its successors).

Replacing HF radio with satellite links neutralized the main SOSS sensor, although the U.S. Navy's Fleet Satellite program was not described as an anti-SOSS measure. Satellite uplink beams were clearly too narrow to intercept, except by spacecraft very close to U.S. satellites. (The broad downlinks were another story, whose significance was not yet appreciated.) In U.S. eyes, the combination of active and passive ocean surveillance satellites could make up for the loss of the HF/DF net. The passive satellite threat may explain a dramatic change in U.S. naval radar policy. In the 1960s, the U.S. Navy deliberately developed multiple air search radars operating at different frequencies, on the theory that the Soviets could not field enough jammers to handle all of them at the same time. In the 1970s it standardized on the SPS-49 air search radar. Although this policy simplified logistics, almost certainly it was intended to confuse Soviet electronic intelligence. Both carriers and frigates used the same main air search set. The Soviets could not tell which was which unless they also sought other radar signatures, such as those involved in carrier air traffic control. (At least as of the mid-1970s, the Soviets were not fingerprinting radars.) The U.S. Navy discovered that it could control a carrier's aircraft largely remotely, using an E-2C. The U.S. Navy also warned ships when Soviet satellites were in range, based on its satellite tracking system. Insights into details of the active radar satellite made countermeasures, both tactical and electronic, possible.

The experience of the 1970s convinced the U.S. Navy that the SOSS could be saturated. The Soviets were known to track all potential nuclear attack platforms (carriers) and all amphibious groups. They might total no more than ten or fifteen formations at sea at any one time. By Soviet standards, a surface ship equipped with nuclear Tomahawks was virtually as important a target as a carrier, hence as important to track.[7] The Soviets could not, moreover, tell whether a given ship was carrying the nuclear or the antiship version. Once vertical launchers had entered service, it was not even possible to be sure whether a given surface combatant was armed with Tomahawks or with antiaircraft missiles. Once Tomahawk was deployed aboard U.S. surface warships, the SOSS suddenly had to track many times as many ships. Whether or not the nuclear version was worthwhile in a strategic sense, its mere existence paid immense dividends. The SOSS might cope, but only by stretching its resources, laying itself open to other attacks.

By the late 1970s, U.S. officers thought of the SOSS as an integrated information system. Systematic deception could degrade its information. New deception devices were publicized (to help unnerve SOSS operators), but they were never displayed or described in detail. They included deception transmitters and devices that could simulate a carrier's acoustic signature. Against the threat of active radar satellites, the U.S. Navy (and probably the Royal Navy) deployed powerful blip generators as well as air-delivered chaff bombs. Using combined devices, it seemed that a destroyer could simulate a carrier battle group. With the advent of longer-range antiaircraft weapons such as Aegis and the F-14/Phoenix combination, plus satellite communication, much wider forms of dispersal became practicable. The fleet adopted an extremely dispersed, hence unrecognizable (from space), formation, the 4-W Grid.

There was also interest in destroying the satellites feeding the SOSS. For example, an antisatellite (ASAT) missile (which would have been fighter launched) was developed. By 1978 Soviet naval satellites were its primary planned targets. This idea was dropped because it appeared that the Soviets had numerous spare satellites and launchers. A U.S. ASAT campaign would have to include the destruction of the launch facility—which would be impossible to justify early in a war.

Without the SOSS the Soviets could not have waged maritime war. In 1981 they opened a computer ocean surveillance center, which should have made the system less vulnerable to saturation. They found an alternative to HF/DF. Probably in the 1980s they discovered that the downlinks from U.S. satellites carried useful information. In effect they retransmitted whatever a ship sent up. Because the satellite moves slightly, despite its nominally fixed position, it receives the uplink with some Doppler, the amount of which depends on where the transmitting ship is. The transmitting ship can be identified by fingerprinting, which will survive in the retransmitted signal. The U.S. Fleet Satellite used broad ultrahigh-frequency (UHF) beams that could be detected almost throughout a hemisphere. This kind of satellite tracking was used by the Argentines in 1982 to track the British fleet approaching the Falklands but was little publicized at the time and seems not to have shaken U.S. confidence that satellite links were safe. The Russians announced their new technique after the 1991 Gulf War, having used it to track the buildup of forces in the Gulf. Soviet use of satellite downlinks was equivalent to Krug; it did not provide sufficient precision for missile targeting. This time the U.S. Navy noticed. It adopted practices that overcame the problem.

The Soviets were aware of their own vulnerabilities. They took basic precautions, like substituting shorter-range medium frequency (MF) for HF and using burst transmissions when they had to use HF. However, there is no evidence of any concerted tactical deception campaign on the scale the U.S. Navy mounted against the SOSS. Knowing that their own offensive power was concentrated in submarines and in bombers, the Soviets could not understand the surface ship-oriented U.S. OSIS. They seem to have concluded that it was a deceptive cover for a "black" nonacoustic antisubmarine program.[8]

We don't know how well the U.S. Navy did against the SOSS. In the face of the U.S. maritime strategy of the 1980s, the Soviets retreated from the open sea to concentrate on protecting the bastions where their main assets, ballistic missile submarines, were expected to operate in wartime. The Soviets seem to have gone out of their way to deny the U.S. Navy information on the modernized SOSS, deliberately not reacting to U.S. exercises such as a three-carrier operation in the Northern Pacific. They did continue to mount operations intended to deter the U.S. Navy, such as the interception of carrier battle groups by Victor-class submarines presumably cued by the SOSS. The former chief of Soviet naval intelligence later claimed that he always had a submarine trailing any U.S. carrier group, that he could always know within half an hour where the carriers were. He would say that, wouldn't he?

CHAPTER 21

What Does It All Mean?

A bove all, *the picture is what matters.* Creating effective tactical pictures makes systems work, and it supports a new kind of warfare. The better the picture, the more efficient the operation. That does not mean that more is better. A picture that is incomprehensible is useless. After the first Gulf War, a U.S. commander remarked that his system undoubtedly contained far more information than he could use, but it did not present him with the actionable information he needed. Some commanders complained that their screens were filled with so many symbols that they seemed whited out. More information was not always better. Some writers express this as the need for knowledge rather than information, but probably well-presented and reliable information is enough. Commanders and their staffs have long experience converting it into the knowledge they need. Given the picture, it is worthwhile asking how it can be spread around by a communication net and used as the basis for collaborative planning.

The combination of a useful picture and effective command and control links makes it possible to fight in a new way. The examples in this book suggest what such an approach means. If one side uses a networked approach, it gains enormous *potential* advantages. For example, a picture-centric approach offers the potential for surprise attacks. Targets no longer gain warning from reconnaissance. The sustained threat of surprise may be the most valuable effect on the enemy, wearing him down psychologically. The enemy may be unnerved by the sheer speed with which attacks are mounted. The advantage can be thrown away. In the Millennium Challenge exercise of 2000, retired Marine Corps Lt. Gen. Paul K. van Riper relied on slow communication by motorcycle messenger to frustrate his enemies' surveillance system. Had they exploited the sheer speed of which they were capable, he could not possibly have kept up. Instead, they concentrated on the absence of the electronic intercepts they expected. They lost.

The North Atlantic Treaty Organization (NATO) air war against Serbia may be another case in point. Decisions on targeting were slow because targets had to be approved by all participants. Often it seemed that the results were more like pin-pricks than the sudden unpredictable thrusts envisioned in loop or cycle of military operations (OODA) warfare. Mobile and relocatable targets generally were not hit. When the Serbs withdrew from Kosovo, it was never clear whether that represented a NATO victory. It may have been that Serbian dictator Slobodan Milosevic saw that he could best maintain his power by seeming to yield to overwhelming force—in some ways a positive move in the Serbian culture of victimization. He had always seen occupation of Kosovo not as an end in itself but rather as a means of enhancing his Serb nationalist image. His own statements that surrender saved Serbia from carpet bombing (which was never remotely within NATO capability) was less than convincing. Possibly he decided to withdraw when he realized that the Russians were not going to force NATO to abandon the war. Possibly also, he pulled out when NATO finally realized that it could use the Kosovo Liberation Army to draw his paramilitaries out so that they could be attacked from the air. The same paramilitaries guaranteed his rule in Serbia itself. So, was precision decisive?

Picture-centric approaches are attractive because they justify reducing the number of ships or airplanes or troops or weapons. However, the picture is rarely complete. How much backup is needed? For example, a ground force with perfect information would need no armored vehicles because it could wipe out enemy forces before they could strike. If the force had almost no information, however, its survival would depend entirely on its armor. Reality is somewhere in between. Because it is so difficult to create a good tactical picture, much effort has been concentrated instead on reliably tracking friendly (Blue) forces, so that at least whatever is fired at beyond the horizon is not friendly. Speed and networking go together (to reach distant targets before they vanish), though in subtle ways. Networking favors a dispersed force, as it can both exploit long-range weapons the picture makes usable and reduce the threat of fratricide resulting from errors in the tactical picture. Overall, networking can make individual units more lethal, if they are equipped to take advantage of it.

It may seem that sensors and computers and links are inexpensive compared to ships and airplanes and vehicles. Somehow a networked force is lighter and more supple. It is by no means clear that moving investment from platforms and weapons toward surveillance and communications saves much money. The question of how to balance the two kinds of investment has not yet been answered, partly because the new kind of warfare has been misnamed. If we call it network-centric, then investment will go to produce a better or more reliable network. If instead we call it picture-centric, then at the least we can trade off picture quality against weapon requirements. How many weapons or platforms would be needed if the picture were slightly less precise, or slightly better? The link aspect can be taken into account by calculating probability that a platform that has the picture can use it to hit a particular target. Unfortunately, these measures of effectiveness capture only a small part of the situation. They do not touch on the psychological effect of the sort of operations networking makes possible. That is probably best assessed by two-sided gaming and by field exercises. Even then, real questions remain about mass versus precision. They are likely to be particularly important for land warfare.

Networking—actually, picture making and picture exploitation—depends on a combination of data fusion and precise navigation. Fusion is impossible unless data from different sensors can be matched up in terms of position (and, often, time). The picture cannot be exploited unless the places on it mean the same thing to all involved. All participants in a network use the same set of coordinates, either rooted in the earth or created by the network. This combination makes navigationally guided weapons, like Global Position Systems (GPS)–guided bombs, the natural weapons of network-centric warfare. Conversely, attacking our navigational systems becomes a natural counter to the new kind of warfare. Hence recent attempts to find alternatives to GPS.

By widely distributing the tactical picture, networking can give individual lower-level commanders more autonomy and can thus make for more flexible and effective—and rapid—operations. However, networking is double-edged. A higher-level commander can use the dynamic picture of his subordinates' situation to attempt to control them in greater detail. How much is his greater experience and access to some additional information worth? Remember the disaster to Convoy PQ-17 in June 1942 (see chapter 2).

Just as networking demands that all available information be fused to form a useful tactical picture, a picture justified for one type of operation often proves valuable for another. The existence of a usable picture often inspires further operations not envisaged when the system is invented. This book is full of examples.

Conversely, operators often resist network- or picture-centric forms of warfare because they seem unnatural. In some cases modern netted systems were acceptable because they directly replaced earlier manual netted ones. Large-area netting has been the least acceptable because the sensors involved are the least familiar and the functions involved are not readily apparent.

Finally, two notes of caution: First, however precise, a picture of enemy dispositions is not a picture of the enemy's intent or policy. Interpretation can be tricky. In the spring of 1944, it became evident that the Japanese fleet was moving from its forward base at Truk to what is now Indonesia, at the entrance to the Indian Ocean. The British, who had suffered from a 1942 Japanese sortie into the Indian

Ocean, wondered whether they should guard against another. We now know that the Japanese moved to Indonesia because they could no longer rely on tanker traffic within their empire. Their fleet was falling back on its best source of fuel. That this indicated weakness, not strength, was by no means obvious.

Second, note the potential for self-damage. Much effort has been concentrated on protecting networks against enemy penetration. However, errors by those running the network can also be devastating. On board a ship, the captain knows which sensor operators are best, so he can weigh their conclusions against those he may consider less reliable. That is why the submarine captain in Tom Clancy's *Hunt for Red October* asks Jonesy, his best sonar man, to take over when the situation becomes serious. In a networked situation, the captain of a ship has no idea who inserted various bits of information into the netted system. He may well have some means of drilling down into data to find out, but that takes time, and the whole point of netting is to compress time. Even if the captain wants to drill down, the pace of warfare may well make that impossible.

If this seems theoretical, think about the 1999 attack by a U.S. B-2 bomber against the Chinese embassy in Belgrade. The B-2 dropped a GPS-guided bomb; the attack was network-centric, in that the bomb was dropped to hit a preset geographical spot. The pilot never saw the embassy at all; in effect he was nothing more than a chauffeur for the bomb. Who was responsible for that error? Was it the officer who approved the attack on a target in Belgrade? The source of the wrong coordinates? Probably the error can be traced back to whoever associated the wrong coordinates with the stated target, the Yugoslav arms export agency. No specific individual was ever identified. Networking in effect wiped out a key military virtue, the direct connection between an individual and a deadly attack. Because intelligence is the source of much of the tactical picture, intelligence agencies may now in effect have military responsibilities—for which they are not yet equipped. Their historic role is to sift the vaguest kind of evidence for conclusions, which they usually present more as solid fact than as the wisp they are. That is inescapable, but it may be a real problem for the future of networked warfare, particularly on land.

Acronyms

AAW	antiair warfare
ACDS	Advanced Combat Display System
ACIS	Amphibious Command-Information System
ACS	Afloat Correlation System
ACSC	Aegis Combat Systems Center
ACTD	Advanced Concept Technology Demonstration
ADA	Action Data Automation
ADAC	All-Digital Attack Center
ADAWS	Action Data Automation Weapon System
ADLIPS	Advanced Data Link Information Processing System
ADR	Aircraft Direction Room; British
ADT	automatic detection and tracking
AEW	airborne early warning
AFDS	Amphibious Flag Data System
AGIs	Soviet intelligence-gatherers
AIC	Action Information Centre (British)
AIC	Airborne Information Correlation System
AIO	Action Information Organization
AIP	ASUW Improvement Program
AMRAAM	Advanced Medium-Range Air-to-Air Missile
AMVER	American vessel reports
AMW	antimissile warfare
A-NEW	new antisubmarine warfare weapon system
APL	Applied Physics Laboratory

ARCI	Acoustics-Rapid COTS Insertion
ARL	Admiralty Research Lab
A/S	antisubmarine
ASAT	antisatellite
ASCAC	ASW Classification and Analysis Center
ASCIET	All Services Combat Identification Evaluation Team
ASDEC	Anti-Submarine Development and Experimental Center
ASDEVEX	Antisubmarine Development Exercise
ASMD	antiship missile defense
ASMS	Advanced Surface Ship Missile System
ASP	automatic surface plot
ASPECT	acoustic short-pulse echo classification technique
ASTDA	Air Strike Timing Decision Aid
ASUW	anti-surface ship warfare
ASW	antisubmarine warfare
ASWCCS	Antisubmarine Warfare Command and Control System
ASWCS	Antisubmarine Warfare Control System
ASWOC	ASW Operations Center
ASWSCCS	ASW Ship Command and Control System
ATC	Automatic Tracking Computer
ATDS	Airborne Tactical Data System
ATES	Aegis Tactical Executive System
AVAP	audio-visual alarm panel
AWACS	Airborne Warning and Control System
BGAAWC	Battle Group AAW Coordination
BGIXS	Battle Group Information Exchange System
BIP	battle information post
BIUS	Russian automated naval command system
BLOS	beyond-line-of-sight
BPDMS	short-range defensive missiles
BuAer	U.S. Navy Bureau of Aeronautics
BuOrd	U.S. Navy Bureau of Ordnance
BuShips	U.S. Navy Bureau of Ships
BVP	beacon video processing
C2P	command and control processing
C&D	Command and Decision

CAAIS	Computer-Assisted Action Information System
CACS	Computer-Assisted Command System
CAFO	confidential fleet order
CAL	Cornell Aeronautical Laboratory
CANUS	Canadian-U.S.
CAP	Combat Air Patrol
CAPTAS	Combined Active-Passive Towed Array System (French)
CATCC	Carrier Air Traffic Control Center
CATE	Computer-Assisted Target Evaluation
CBT	continuous boat tracking
CCIS	Computer Command Information System
CCS	Combat Control System
CDL	common data link
CDS	Comprehensive Display System
CEC	Cooperative Engagement Capability
CEP	circular error probable
CEPLO	Command Electronic Plotting System
CHESS	Carrier Horizon Extension Surveillance System
CHURN	technique for automatic submarine tactical data calculation
CIA	Central Intelligence Agency
CIC	Combat Information Center
CIDS	Coordination in Direct Support
CinC	commander in chief
CNA	Center for Naval Analyses
CNI	communication, navigation, and identification
CNO	chief of naval operations
CO	commanding officer
COC	Combat Operations Center
CODAER	Combat Data Exchange Relay
COE	common operating environment
COMCARGRU I	Commander, Carrier Group 1
COMFEWSG	naval EW training group
COMINCH	commander in chief
COMINT	communications intelligence
CONFORM	concept formulation
COP	common operating picture

COTS	commercial-off-the-shelf
CPA	closest point of approach
CPU	central processing unit
CRT	cathode-ray tube
CSED	Combined System Electronic Design
CSGN	strike cruiser
CSOC	Current SIGINT Operations Center
CSS	Command Support System
CTF	commander, task force
CVA	attack carriers
CVS	antisubmarine (S) aircraft carrier
CW	continuous wave
CWAT	CW acquisition tracking
CWCS	Common Weapon Control System
DARPA	U.S. Defense Advanced Research Projects Agency
DATACORTS	Digital Data Correlation and Transfer System
DATAR	Digital Automatic Tracking and Remoting
DC&T	detection, classification, and targeting
DCNS	deputy chief of the naval staff
DD	destroyer
DDG	missile destroyer
DDR&E	U.S. Defense Directorate for Research and Engineering
DF	direction finding
DIA	Defense Intelligence Agency
DICASS	Directional Command (-Controlled) Active Sonobuoy System
DIFAR	Directional LOFAR Sonobuoy System
DIMUS	Digital Multibeam (Sonar) System
DLG	missile "frigate"
DLGN	nuclear frigate
DMR	Dynamic Modular Replacement
DPT	digital plot transmission
DRT	dead-reckoning tracer
DSARC	U.S. Defense System Acquisition Review Committee
DSM	Distinguished Service Medal
DSP	Defense Support Program

DSU	digital storage unit
DTC	desktop computer
DTD	data transfer device
DTMA	distributed time multiple access
DVC	direct view console
EBO	effects-based operations
ECCM	electronic counter-countermeasures
ECM	Electric Cypher Machine
ECM	electronic countermeasures
EDS	Electronic Display System
ELF	extremely low frequency
ELINT	electronic intelligence
EMCON	emission control
EMCU	extended memory control unit
EOC	Engage on Composite
EOR	Aegis Engage on Remote
EORSAT	ELINT ocean surveillance satellite
EPLO	Electronic Plotting System
ESM	electronic support measures
ESP	Extended Surface Plot
EW	electronic warfare
FCC	Fleet Command Center
FCDISSA	Fleet Combat Direction Systems Support Activity
FCF	Flag Correlation Facility
FD	fully distributed
FDDS	Flagship Data Display System
FDS	Fixed Distributed System
FHLT	Fleet High-Level Terminal
FIC	Fleet Intelligence Center
FLIR	forward-looking infrared
FLIT	frequency line integration tracking
FMPL	Fleet Mission Program Library
FOC	full operational capability
FOCSLE	Fleet Operational Command System Life Extension
FOSIC	Fleet Ocean Surveillance Information Center
FOSIF	Fleet Ocean Surveillance Information Facility

FRAM	Fleet Rehabilitation and Modernisation Program
FRISCO	Fast-Reaction Submarine Control
GACT	graphic analysis and correlation terminal
GCCS	Global Command and Control System
GCCS-M	Navy element of Global Command and Control System
GOR	General Operational Requirement
GPS	Global Position System
GRAB	Global Radiation and Background
HARM	high-speed antiradar missile
HF	high frequency
HILAST	high-altitude large-area
HITS	high-interest target
HS	horizon search
HUD	heads-up display
HUK	hunter-killer
HULTEC	hull-to-emitter correlation
I&W	indications and warning
IACS	Integrated Acoustic Communications System
IC	intelligence center
ICAD	Integrated Cover and Deception System
IFF	"identification of friend or foe"
IID	Integrated Information Display
ILAAS	Integrated Light Attack Avionics System
IOC	initial operational capability
IOIC	Integrated Operational Intelligence Center
IOIS	Integrated Operational Intelligence System
IR	infrared
ISS	Intelligence Support System
ITACS	Integrated Tactical Air Control System
ITAWDS	Integrated Tactical Amphibious Warfare Data System
ITNS	Integrated Tactical Navigation System
ITSS	Integrated Tactical Surveillance System
JCS	Joint Chiefs of Staff
JMCIS	Joint Maritime Command Information System/Strategy
JMPS	Joint Mission Planning System
JOR	Joint Operational Requirement

JOTS	Joint Operational Tactical System
JOTSIXS	Joint Operational Tactical System Information Exchange System
JPTDS	Junior Participating Tactical Data System
JTDS	"Jeep" or "Junior" Tactical Data System
JTIDS	Joint Tactical Information Distribution System
KAST	Kalman Assisted Tracking
KOPS	thousands of operations per second
LADA	London Air Defence Area
LAN	local area network
LCC	amphibious flagship
LF	low frequency
LGD	Large Group Display
LO	low end; also low observable
LOCAP	Low-Altitude Combat Air Patrol
LOFAR	narrow-band analysis technique
LOP	local-area operational plot
MARIL	Swedish tactical command system
MARTADS	Marine Tactical Data System
MATCH	British shipboard helicopter-control system
MATE	manually aided target evaluation
MC	Military Characteristics
MCS	Modular Combat System
MEW	Microwave Early Warning
MF	medium frequency
MHQ	Maritime Headquarters
MIDS	Miniature Information Distribution System
MIRV	multiple independently targetable reentry vehicle
MLP	multilayer plotting
MLS	multilevel secure
MNS	mission need statement
MOL	Manned Orbiting Laboratory
MOPS	millions of operations per second (measure of computer speed)
MOSC	Modified OSC
MOVREPS	movement reports

MRC	Movement Reporting Center
MRCC	Movement Reports Control Center
MSC	Maritime Surveillance Center
MSCF	Multi-Source Correlation Facility
MSS	Moored Surveillance System
MUTE	Multiple Unit Transmission Elimination
MZRK	small intelligence-gathering ship (Russian)
NAAWS	NATO AAW System
NADC	Naval Air Development Center
NARA	U.S. National Archives and Records Administration
NARF	Naval Air Refit Facility
NATO	North Atlantic Treaty Organization
NAUTIS	Naval Autonomous Information System (British)
NAVAIR	Naval Air Systems Command
NavAirPac	Pacific naval air force
NAVELEX	Naval Electronics Systems Command
NAVFAC	Naval Facility
NAVIC	Navy Information Center
NAVSEA	Naval Sea Systems Command
NCB	Navy Cipher Box
NCCS	Naval Command and Control System
NDCP	Navy Decision Coordinating Paper
NDRC	U.S. National Defense Research Committee
NEL	Naval Electronics Laboratory
NELC	Naval Electronics Command
NFC-IC	Numbered Flagship Center–Intelligence System
NFOIO	Naval Field Operational Intelligence Office
NGS	naval gunfire support
NHB	Naval Historical Branch (British)
NICS	NATO Integrated Communications System
NILE	NATO Improved Link Eleven
NIPS	Naval Intelligence Processing System
NIPSSA	Naval Intelligence Processing Support Center
NMCC	national military command center
NOIC	U.S. Naval Operational Intelligence Center
NOSC	U.S. Naval Ocean Systems Center

NOSIC	Naval Ocean Surveillance Intelligence Center
NOTS	Naval Ordnance Test Station
NPIC	National Photographic Intelligence Center
NRL	Naval Research Laboratory
NSA	National Security Agency
NSG	Naval Security Group
NSIA	National Security Industrial Association
NSWC	Naval Surface Weapons Center
NTCCS	Naval Tactical Command and Control System
NTDS	Naval Tactical Data System
NTU	new threat upgrade
NUSC	Naval Underwater Systems Center
NUWC	U.S. Naval Underwater Center, New London
NWC	Naval War College
OBU	OSIS Baseline Upgrade
OEG	Operational Evaluation Group
OFP	Operational Flight Program
OIC	Operational Intelligence Centre (British)
ONI	Office of Naval Intelligence
ONR	Office of Naval Research
OODA	observation orientation decision action loop or cycle of military operations
OPCON	Operational Control (British)
OPEVAL	operational evaluation
OPFAD	Outer Perimeter Fleet Air Defense
OPINTEL	operational intelligence
OpNav	Office of the Chief of Naval Operations
OPO	underwater situation illumination ships
OpTEVFOR	U.S. Operational Test and Evaluation Force
OSC	Operations Summary Console
OSD	Office of the Secretary of Defense
OSIS	Ocean Surveillance Information System
OTCIXS	Officer in Tactical Command Information Exchange System
OTH	over-the-horizon
OTH-T	over-the-horizon targeting

PAIR	performance and integration refit
PALIS	Passiv-Aktiv-Link-Lage-Informationssystem
PCR	Program Change Recommendation
PECM	passive ECM
PEP	Parameter Evaluation Plot
PF	patrol frigate
PGM	missile motor gunboat
PHM	missile hydrofoil
PI/DE	passive identification/direction equipment
PIRAZ	Positive Identification Radar Advisory Zone
PPI	plan position indicator
PRC	Planning Research Corporation
PSL	Predicted Ship Listing
PUFFS	passive ranging sonar
PVO	Soviet air defense service
QR	quick reaction
RADDS	Radar Data Distribution System
RAF	Royal Air Force
RAFAD	Research Analysis of Fleet Air Defense
RAIDS	Rapid Anti-Ship Missile Integrated Defense System
RAM	Rolling Airframe Missile
RAN	Royal Australian Navy
RDR	Radar Display Room (British)
RDT&E	Research, Development, Testing, and Evaluation
R/E	range estimation
RFP	radio fingerprinting
RIM	ROTHR Interface Module
RMP	Recognized Maritime Picture
RNLN	Royal Netherlands Navy
RNTDS	Restructured Naval Tactical Data System
ROH	regular overhaul
ROLE	Receive-Only Link Eleven
RORSAT	radar ocean reconnaissance satellite
ROTHR	Relocatable Over-the-Horizon Radar
rpm	revolutions per minute
RTIC	Retargeting in the Cockpit or Real Time in the Cockpit

RVP	radar video processing
SAAICS	Semi-Automatic Air Intercept Control System
SACC	Supporting Arms Coordination Center
SACEUR	NATO Supreme Allied Commander Europe
SACLANT	NATO Supreme Allied Commander Atlantic
SACU	separate data link unit
SADOC	Systema Dirizione della Operazioni di Combattimento (Italian)
SADZAC	Semi-Automatic Digital Analyzer and Computer
SAGE	Semi-Automatic Ground Environment
SAMID	Ships Anti-Missile Integrated Defense
SAR	search and rescue
SASS	Suspended Array Surveillance System
SATIR	System zur Auswertung Taktischer Informationen auf Raketenzerstoren (German)
SCS	sea control ship
SEATDS	Southeast Asia Tactical Data System
SEAWATCH	Ocean Surveillance Information Handling System
SENIT 1	Systeme d'Exploitation Navale des Informations Tactiques (French)
SESCO	Secure Submarine Communications
SEWACO	Sensor, Weapon, Control
SHINPADS	Shipboard Integrated Processing and Display System
SHM	Service Historique de la Marine (French)
SI	special intelligence
SIGINT	signal intelligence
SINS	Ships Inertial Navigation System
SIPRNET	secret-level (U.S.military) Internet
SIT	situation display
SKR	frigate intended mainly for coast defense (Russian)
SLAR	side-looking radar
SM	U.S. Standard Missile
SNIP	Single Net Information and Position
SOCC	Sixth Fleet Submarine Operational Command Center
SODS	Subordinate Operations Control Center Data Systems
SOR	Specific Operational Requirement

SOSS	Soviet Ocean Surveillance System
SOSUS	Sound Surveillance System
SPADE	Signal Processor and Display Equipment
SpaWar	Space and Electronic Warfare Command
SPM	Ship Processing Module
SPUME	Short Pulse Message
SQUIRE	submarine quickened response
SS	sector search
SSBN	hull designation for a nuclear-powered strategic ballistic missile submarine
SSC	surface surveillance coordinator
SSCDS	Small Ship Combat Direction System
SSCS	Surface Ship Command System
SSDS	Surface Ship Self-Defense
SSE	sector scan engage
SSES	Ship Signals Exploitation Space
SSIXS	Submarine Data Exchange System
SSK	antisubmarine submarines
SSMS	Submarine Safety Monitoring System
SSPA	SOSUS Probability Area
SSS	strike support ship
SSV	Soviet auxiliary ships designation
STACOS	Signaal Tactical Command and Control System
STDDS	Submarine Tactical Data Display System
STOVL	short takeoff and vertical landing
STRIKA	Swedish coast defense command system
STRIL	Swedish national air defense system
STT	Shore Targeting Terminal
STTDS	Shore Targeting Terminal Display System
SUBIC	submarine integrated control
SUBROC	submarine rocket
SUCAP	Surface Combat Air Patrol
SWC	ship weapons control, part of SAMID
SWRS	Slow Walker Reporting System
SZRK	medium intelligence-gathering ship (Russian)
TACAN	tactical air navigation

TACCO	tactical coordinator
TACINTEL	tactical intelligence
TACTICOS	Tactical Information and Command System (Dutch)
TADIXS	Tactical Data Exchange System
TAMPS	Tactical Automated Mission Planning System
TAPS	Tactical Aircraft Planning System
TARPS	Tactical Air Reconnaissance Pod System
TAS	Torpedo and Anti-Submarine
TASES	Tactical Airborne Signal Exploitation System
TASS	towed surface ship surveillance arrays
TAVITAC	Traitement Automatique et Visualisation Tactique (French)
TBP	time-bearing plot
TBS	talk between ships
TCN	Tactical Component Network
TDA	Tactical Decision Aid
TDC	Torpedo Direction Computer
TDCS	Tactical Data Correlation System
TDDS	Tactical Data Display System
TDMA	time-division multiplexed access
TDP	Technical Development Plan
TDPS	tactical data processing system
TDT	target designation transmitter
TEAMS	Tactical EA-6B Mission Support
TENCAP	Tactical Exploitation of National Capabilities
TEWA	target evaluation and weapon assignment
TFCC	Tactical Flag Command Center
TFDS	Tactical Flag Data System
TIDE	Tactical Information Distribution Equipment
TIDY	Teletype Integrated Display System
TIOS	Tactical Integrated Ocean Surveillance
TIPI	transportable intelligence processing center
TIPS	Tactical Information Management or Processing System
TIR	Target Indication Room (British)
TLR	Top Level Requirement
TMA	Target Motion Analysis
TMPC	Tomahawk Missile Programming Center

TN	track number
TOPS	Teletype Optical Projection System
TOR	Tentative Operational Requirement
TRAM	target recognition and attack multisensor
TRIP	Tactical Response Planner
TSC	Tactical Surveillance Center
TSOR	Tentative Specific Operational Requirement
TSS	Tactical Search and Surveillance
UAV	unmanned aircraft
UUV	unmanned underwater vehicle
VCNO	vice chief of naval operations
VHAASP	Very High Altitude Aircraft Sensor Platform
VHF	very high frequency
VLS	vertical [missile] launching system
VQ	electronic reconnaissance squadrons
VTOL	vertical takeoff or landing
WAA	Wide Aperture Array
WCS	Weapon Control System
WDE	Weapon Designation Equipment
WDS	Weapon Designation Systems
WSA	Weapon System Automation
WSEG	Weapon Systems Evaluation Group
WSP	weapon support processor
WWMCCS	World-Wide Military Command and Control System

Notes

Note on sources: ADM and DEFE are record groups in the British National Archives at Kew; NARA is the U.S. National Archives and Records Administration (College Park branch); NHB is the British Naval Historical Branch at Portsmouth; NWC is the U.S. Naval War College; OA is the U.S. Navy Operational Archive at the Washington Navy Yard; RANHB is the Royal Australian Navy Historical Branch; SHM is the French Service Historique de la Marine (now merged into the Defense Historical Service).

Introduction

1. Adm. Arthur K. Cebrowski often used the "dot coms" to exemplify self-synchronized enterprises. They crashed largely because central financial control—discipline in using common resources—was not imposed on the separate units within companies and commander's intent was poorly understood. Self-synchronization probably works best when units are far enough apart that they do not interfere with each other.

2. I am indebted to Chris Carlson for this formulation. Concentrating on the picture makes it possible to be explicit about what is needed. One measure of information load would be the number of bits needed to describe a tactical situation over a set length of time adequately. Each object (including nontargets) is represented by a track (a series of points) in a three-dimensional space (four if time is included). The number of such points is set by how precisely the track must be described (i.e., by how frequently the target must be located). The number of bits per point measures both how precisely the target must be described (how many categories there are, for example, which also indicates how well damage can be assessed) and how accurately it must be localized within the volume involved. (Volume size can be traded off against precision.) The system could trade off a greater number of less-precise tracks against a smaller number of better or more frequently reported ones. This trade-off is evident in some Swedish combat direction systems. All of this is aside from more or less static background detail, as in land warfare.

Chapter 1. Ocean Surveillance: World War I

1. Much of the discussion of Fisher's command and control revolution is based on Nicholas Lambert, "Strategic Command and Control for Maneuver Warfare: Creation of the Royal Navy's 'War Room' System, 1905–1915," *Journal of Military History* 69 (April

2005). I have also benefited heavily from discussions with Dr. Lambert. I am responsible for identifying the battle cruiser with Fisher's style of operation, based on my own experience with network-centric concepts.

2. In his 1901 "Mediterranean Lectures," Fisher commented that the French could do any of five things in the Mediterranean, but only one in the Channel. It became vital to know what the French and their Russian allies were doing. ("Mediterranean Lectures," 23). Lectures courtesy of Dr. Nicholas Lambert. Fisher's biographer, Admiral Sir Reginald Bacon, points out that Fisher worried that the British Channel Fleet could not have reinforced him in time. He was particularly exercised over his lack of cruisers and destroyers—the ships that would watch enemy bases in wartime. *The Life of Lord Fisher of Kilverstone* (London: Hodder and Stoughton, 1919), I: 137.

3. NID 706 in ADM 231/38.

4. J. W. M. Chapman, "British Use of 'Dirty Tricks' in External Policy Prior to 1914," *War in History*, no. 9 (2002). The reference is to communication intercepts and code breaking, not black operations. According to Chapman, Fisher used the fact that Britain was at war (with the Boers, in South Africa) to issue orders to British cable companies to censor cables passing through Malta. W. H. Cottrell, manager of the Eastern (Cable) Extension Office at Syra, provided copies of cables that seemed interesting. He was paid annually between 1902 and 1907 and appointed British Consul at Syra on Fisher's recommendation.

5. Lambert, "Strategic Command and Control," 367.

6. Bacon, *Life of Lord Fisher*, I: 150–51. Fisher was also concerned with an announced French shift to a doctrine of attack at the beginning of the war, and he needed some way of avoiding a bolt from the blue. See, for example, his 5 January 1901 letter to Lord Selbourne (First Lord) in Arthur J. Marder, ed., *Fear God and Dread Nought* (London: Jonathan Cape, 1952), I: 174–76. French development of the base at Bizerte brought their battle fleet within a few hours of his own base at Malta; Fisher wanted another base further away, at Alexandria.

7. Nicholas Lambert, *Sir John Fisher's Naval Revolution* (Columbia: University of South Carolina Press, 1999), 22.

8. Lambert, "Strategic Command and Control," 381, describes how the trade and intelligence sections pooled their data to track rather than merely locate ships. Sources included sighting reports from regional intelligence officers, consular and diplomatic sources, and Lloyds, as well as data on the traffic in steaming coal, most of which came from Wales.

9. Lambert, "Strategic Command and Control," 384, quoting letters to, respectively, Garvin and King Edward VII. The third quote, dated August 1904, is from Peter Kemp, ed., *The Fisher Papers* (London: Naval Records Society, 1960), 161, as quoted by Lambert, 378. The 1904 passage can be found in Fisher's *Naval Necessities*, in effect the manifesto he sent to the First Lord on accepting office (the copy in NHB is dated 21 October 1904, i.e., Trafalgar Day). Lambert notes that a September 1902 draft of this paper omits Admiralty control of far-flung forces. About 1912 the single war room was replaced by separate ones for home and more distant waters. Lambert, "Strategic

Command and Control," 392. "The First Sea Lord and the Chief Admiral afloat have got to be Siamese twins. And when the war comes, the Naval War Staff at the Admiralty, listening every moment to the enemy's wireless messages (if he dare use it) enables the First Sea Lord to let his twin at sea know exactly what is going on. He takes in the wireless, and not necessarily the Admiral afloat, on account of the far greater power of reception in a land installation. . . . When you see that spider's web of lines of wire on top of the Admiralty, then thank God." Admiral Fisher, *Memories* (London: Hodder and Stoughton, 1919), 108–9. Fisher mentions British code-breaking as "one of the crowning glories of the Admiralty work in the late war." On 26 January 1909, he wrote Lord Esher, "The Admiralty hear (by wireless every moment) what all the Admirals and Captains are saying to each other anywhere in Europe and even over to the coasts of America." Immediately above is a reference to wireless cruisers that should be stationed along the German coast so that "not a dog will wag its tail without being reported" (188). They would make invasion of England impossible.

10. Lambert, "Strategic Command and Control," 390, quoting "Wireless Telegraphy in War" in PRO ADM 116/1043B1, a collection of war planning documents. This secret paper is marked "printed at the Foreign Office by J. W. Harrison—4/8/1908."

11. Vice Admiral Sir Arthur Hezlet, *Electronics and Sea Power* (New York: Stein and Day, 1975), esp. 61, 69–70. The Royal Navy seems to have wanted ships with long-range receiving and transmitting sets as links between shore stations and formations at sea with shorter-range sets. Such ships figured in fleet exercises. The armored cruiser *Defence* was converted into a command ship with special spaces to accommodate intelligence personnel (presumably maintaining a mobile war room). The converted cruisers *Europa* and *Vindictive* may have figured in plans to control flotillas from shore. In November 1914 *Europa* was ordered fitted with a new Poulsen arc radio transmitter so that she could act as link ship, working with *Vindictive*, which was already so fitted. (*Defence* could receive but not send on this frequency.) *Vindictive* was considered a great asset because she could communicate with Horsea or with *Defence* at a range of 1,200 nautical miles in daytime. An Admiralty Minute proposed that *Europa, Arrogant*, or *Amphitrite* immediately be fitted to work with *Vindicative*. She would retain her guns because so valuable a ship might be attacked. A high-power ship station near Fayal could communicate easily with Horsea and Gibraltar and with ships half way or more to America. Similarly for St. Vincent. A ship to the Southeast could assure communication between Ascension Island and Cape Horn. ADM 1/8403/430.

12. Nicholas Lambert, "Admiral Sir John Fisher and the Concept of Flotilla Defence, 1914–1909," *Journal of Military History* (October 1995): 59. Lambert later associated the flotilla concept with the new style of command developed by Fisher.

13. Lambert, *Fisher's Naval Revolution*, 195.

14. Early in 1907, Captain G. A. Ballard was ordered to write a new formal war plan. Many years later he wrote that he had developed an idea dating from 1902, inspired by British strategy in the Dutch wars. To Ballard the problem was to force the Germans to come out to fight on British terms. He planned to deploy cruisers to bottle up the exits of the North Sea and thus cut off German seaborne commerce. The Germans would surely react. Flotillas cruising in the North Sea would spot any German sortie in time to

vector the British fleet into position to intercept it. This was radically different from conventional plans in which the German fleet was blockaded. If radio reconnaissance is substituted for scouting flotillas, Ballard's was the British World War I war plan. ADM 1/8997.

15. Given Fisher's view of intelligence, the division's mass of information became the basis for predictive shipping surveillance. The likely current position of any given merchant ship could be estimated on the basis of an assumed great-circle route. Without a computer, calculation of the current position of any particular ship was laborious: no global plot of merchant ship positions could be maintained. However, ships of particular interest could be tracked, for example, those carrying subversives to or from colonies such as India. British consuls in the major ports reported ship departures and expected destinations. Lloyd's was another source. The British became worried about trade warfare when the Germans supported the Boers during the Boer War (1899–1902). In September 1901 Captain Edward Inglefield formed the trade division to develop detailed trade protection plans. The Naval Intelligence Department had been formed on 1 February 1887 out of the earlier Foreign Intelligence Committee (formed in 1883), the latter having been created largely for trade defense (it was also responsible for planning during the 1885 Russian war scare). Lambert, "Strategic Command and Control," 369.

16. NID began collecting information to protect British shipping in October 1893, an officer being appointed to the staff of the Mediterranean Fleet. A second, for the China Station, followed in November 1900. Permanent intelligence centers were needed because officers afloat had no fixed addresses and lacked office facilities. "It was soon proved that the establishment of a clearing house (i.e., Intelligence centre) through which reports from every source could pass was of inestimable value to HM Fleets and Squadrons." The first permanent NID centers were set up in Malta and in Gibraltar, supporting the War Room in Malta, in March 1903. Further centers were established at Colombo, Singapore, and Hong Kong in December 1904; at St. Vincent, Pernambuco, and Montevideo in June 1911; at Capetown, Freemantle, and Sydney in September 1911; at Shanghai in December 1913; and at Jamaica in February 1914. Note the shift from concentration on the Mediterranean to East Asia and then, as the German raider threat emerged, to areas further afield. PRO ADM 116/1842, "Naval Intelligence Organisation 1918–26," responding to Treasury pressure to shrink the NID organization after 1918. This paper ascribed the disaster of the Battle of Coronel, in which von Spee sank most of a British squadron, to the failure to set up a regional center south of the River Plate, or in Chile. Admiral Fisher ascribed the survival of the German cruiser *Dresden* after the Falklands battle to Admiral Sturdee's failure to send a ship to contact the nearby intelligence center, which knew where she was coaling.

17. See Nicholas Lambert, "Sir John Fisher, the Fleet Unit Concept, and the Creation of the Royal Australian Navy," in D. Stevens and J. Reeve, eds., *Southern Trident: Strategy, History, and the Rise of Australian Naval Forces* (Canberra, Australia: Allen and Unwin, 2001).

18. This idea is illustrated by the U.S. report on the Japanese Grand Fleet exercise of June–August 1933, conceived as a feasibility test of using traffic analysis rather than the code-

breaking used for the Japanese 1930 maneuvers. The Japanese had changed codes in 1930, and they might well do so upon the outbreak of war (as they did in 1941). Traffic analysis rendered such security measures nearly pointless. "Codes and ciphers may be changed readily upon the outbreak of war. However, the *communication system*, or method of handling traffic, which has taken years to evolve and perfect cannot be so easily superseded . . . the *communication system* alone can be the source of valuable intelligence. . . . Provided the enemy employs radio to a reasonable extent, and uses no further precautions for security . . . sufficient trained personnel and suitable equipment [can] obtain by a mere analysis of traffic *without reference to the subject matter of such traffic* . . . strategical intelligence of great importance." NARA RG 457, SRH-223. The U.S. Navy had already achieved a remarkable success by following the 1930 Japanese maneuvers using code-breaking. These maneuvers simulated defense against the U.S. fleet. The great surprise was how accurately the Japanese understood the U.S. war plan then in effect and how effective their attrition tactics (using light forces based in the Japanese-controlled Mandated Islands) would have been during the planned direct U.S. advance to the Philippines. The U.S. Orange war plan was changed accordingly. Analysis revealed the composition and location of the two opposing fleets (Blue and Red), the nature of forces in the Mandates, and the names and locations of all island bases used (which would presumably be used in war). It revealed that main defenses were concentrated near Tokyo and along the chain of Mandated Islands between the Bonins and Saipan. In this exercise the Blue fleet (representing the U.S. Navy) "advanced towards the Philippines via Formosa, then moved eastward toward the Marianas via Palau, later moving northward from Saipan." The intercept team's list of Japanese ships and units involved tallied almost exactly with that published after the maneuvers. The team determined the complete organization of Japanese forces (detecting major reorganizations and renamings of units just before the maneuvers).

A report quoted in the later Naval Security Group (NSG) History (SRH-355) adds that the maneuvers included a concentration off the Chinese coast, interpreted then as a blockade but later seen as presaging Japanese landings, and also a simulated landing on Luzon in the Philippines. In the tactical phase of the exercise, the Japanese First and Second Fleets simulated the U.S. Battle and Scouting fleets, assumed to have held or recaptured Guam and to have seized the Marianas. The Japanese mounted their defense from the Bonins, the decisive battle being fought about four hundred miles southeast of those islands. The commander of the Japanese fleet commanded the simulated U.S. fleet, the Japanese emperor the simulated Japanese fleet (Red). The Japanese fleet train (Base Force) set up six temporary air bases at Chichi Jima, Iwo Jima, Pagan, and Saipan. Seaplanes were flown from Yokosuka to Saipan "a long hop for those days and much better than anything the U.S. Navy had credited the Japanese Navy with being able to do." According to the NSG history, details of Japanese war plans revealed by the code-breakers 1930 maneuver convinced the chief of naval operations (CNO) that the U.S. Navy could not intervene. Even details of the code book used by the U.S. codebreakers were important. That it listed even the smallest towns in China, and that it totally ignored Africa, Europe, and the Americas was seen a forecast of Japanese intentions against China, Manchuria, and the East Indies. Other information gained using this code included various incidents and casualties; "general knowledge that Japanese naval

maneuvers were much more realistic than ours, particularly in night torpedo attacks";
"early knowledge of Japanese advances in naval aviation"; and knowledge of Japanese
fuel supplies.

U.S. efforts to track the 1933 maneuvers began with a prediction of their timing, before
any official announcement. The transport *Gold Star*, "due to make a health trip to
Japan at that time," was fitted out as an intercept ship with an additional radio direction finder; her three radio operators were replaced by four intercept operators. She
supplemented the three Asiatic Fleet intercept stations (Guam, Olongapo, and Beijing,
all of which lacked radio direction finder). Analysis was badly hampered by one to three
month delays in collecting material from the different stations. It became clear that the
Navy needed a secure means of communicating with its remote intercept stations (i.e., a
code machine). According to the NSG History (SRH-355), success in the 1933 maneuvers sold radio intelligence to the Asiatic Fleet commander, who agreed to move the
Philippines intercept station to a position within the Ultimate Defense Area (of Manila
Bay), so that it could continue to function once war began. It also led to a decision
to furnish all the intercept stations with HF/DF (completed by December 1938), and
to other improvements. For the 1935 maneuvers, the three shore stations (Shanghai
replacing Beijing) and *Gold Star* were supplemented by an intercept unit on board the
fleet flagship.

Observation of exercises was worthwhile because the Japanese tended to evolve and
then exercise in detail their wartime plans. For example, exercises might reveal changes
in normal operation practices indicating that war was imminent. History (the Russo-
Japanese War) suggested that although Japan would attack by surprise, she would be
unable to conceal some preparations. Observation of Japanese maneuvers made it
obvious that the Japanese were aware of the potential of signals intelligence. According
to the U.S. NSG history (SRH-355), 225, about July 1937 the U.S. Navy deciphered
Japanese messages indicating that they had obtained information about Fleet Problem
XVIII by breaking U.S. messages intercepted by their tankers. More important, the
messages showed that the Japanese understood and appreciated the possibilities of traffic analysis. Radio security became vital. U.S. intercept officers observing the fleet problem blamed the large number of acknowledgements preceding the exercise; the use of
peacetime call signs for umpire traffic; the use of peacetime calls and plain language
by ships not involved in the exercise; careless use of plain language; an inflexible frequency plan; insecurity of the methods of reporting weather; and insecurity of radio
call signs. Initial countermeasures were to introduce varying call signs and to encipher
certain operators' signals, such as those involving frequencies. Given this understanding, the Japanese adopted security measures including adoption of a fleet broadcast
(specifically aimed at traffic analysis, for the first time in this exercise, and not yet fully
used) and limiting the range of their tactical radio by using lower frequencies and lower
power (as observed by USS *Augusta* when operating near Japanese ships). The poverty
of U.S. sources is shown by the fact that the U.S. report quoted a Jesuit priest, who said
that while trying to receive weather broadcasts in the spring of 1935, he had "heard the
'whole' fleet communicating on 2.5 m (120 MHz)." His report seemed plausible in view
of U.S. experiments with VHF as a way of maintaining tactical communications without risking interception. NARA RG 457, SRH-225. After World War II, it became clear

that although the Japanese had VHF radiotelephones (30–50 MHz), most communication was at HF and lower frequencies.

19. ADM 116/1109, "Case 113, Vol. 1, Maneuvers 1909 and Tactical Exercises," PRO.

20. Code breaking was revealed as early as 1919, for example, in Fisher's memoirs, and then in Winston Churchill's 1923 *The World Crisis*. Many writers have pointed to Churchill as the reason the Germans began buying the coding machines that evolved into the World War II Enigmas. Hezlet considered DF not considered particularly secret, but that may reflect World War II practice.

21. ADM 116/866B, "Naval Staff Memoranda, 1896 to 1912" (actually 1896 plus 1905–12), PRO.

22. The 1913 maneuvers simulated war against an Austro-German alliance, in which the Austrians sent their fleet to the approaches to the Channel at the outset. This scenario tested British ability to deal with a raid while the intact main enemy fleet tied down most British forces. It stressed the ability to gain what would now be called wide-area situational awareness. ADM 116/1214, "Maneuvers for 1913" (29 January 1913), PRO.

23. ADM 116/1169 (1913 maneuvers) includes a 3 June 1912 exchange between the First Sea Lord and First Lord Winston Churchill: until the war warning telegram, the Admiralty would maneuver the Blue Fleet. "Thereafter full discretion will rest with the CinC, but Admiralty will assist him with all their W/T [radio] information, and the situation may arise which will entail a direct order." Army officers observing the exercises remarked on what they considered extreme centralization. Orders did not give the commander in chief's intentions, seemed to mix administrative and operational aspects, and laid out the dispositions of subordinate commanders' squadrons. Detailed orders led to considerable confusion. Orders sometimes seemed to take no account of possible enemy action. That is, the Admiralty acted as though it had a much better picture of what was happening at sea than did those on the spot. Brigadier David Henderson, 29 August 1913, ADM 116/1214.

24. For the messages, see E. W. R. Lumby, ed., *Policy and Operations in the Mediterranean, 1912–1914* (London: Navy Records Society, 1970).

25. On 12 April 1916, shortly before Jutland, the Germans decided that defense of their North Sea coast required a new unified command, as in Flanders, which received resources that might otherwise have gone into the land war. The German high command thought the British planned to debark in Jutland, violating Danish neutrality, to attack Kiel and even the heart of Germany. French report, dated 3 February 1920, in 1BB2, 71 of SHM, translation of an interview with the former chief of staff of the Oberkommando der Kuesterverteidigung o.d.k. (High Command for Coast Defense).

26. The Germans began to appreciate how much they were giving away after they set up their own intercept station at Neumunster in the summer of 1915. The resulting radio discipline kept the British from learning of a 5–6 March 1916 sortie until the flagship broke radio silence. The sortie was canceled when Neumunster intercepted a British order withdrawing patrols; the Germans probably did not decode a simultaneous British signal sending the Harwich strike force out to intercept them. In April the

High Seas Fleet sortied on the basis of radio intelligence (indicating the British battle cruisers were at sea), but the British intercepted indications of the German sortie, and recalled the battle cruisers in time. Despite warnings by Neumunster, the British picked up indications of other German sorties before they got very far, for example, when the Germans shelled Lowestoft in April 1916. Several times British radio intelligence indicated a German sortie, and it exploited German signals produced when a British submarine torpedoed a German fleet unit. Vice Admiral Sir Arthur Hezlet, *Electronics and Sea Power*, 110ff. Hezlet, 136–37, notes that the Germans managed to conceal destroyer raids on the Dover Barrage and the Downs (26–27 October and 23 November 1916) and the departure of commerce raiders during the fall of 1916. Destroyer raids in 1917–18 were also often undetected. The Germans concealed the April 1918 sortie by their entire fleet. Conscious German counters to code breaking and traffic analysis included the usual code changes and also changing radio operators (hence "fists") and call signs when ships went to sea. By 1917 surface ships, but apparently not the U-boats, were practicing a useful degree of radio silence.

27. As pointed out by a U.S. officer on a British E-class submarine on patrol in 1918. Office of the Chief of Naval Operations (OpNav) Underwater Warfare branch records, OA.

28. Apparently the envisaged anti-U-boat weapon was an explosive sweep trailed by a destroyer, which could keep a narrow path clear of submarines. To attack a convoy, a U-boat had to lie in its path, within what were later called "lines of approach." Thus destroyer screening of a moving force seemed to require large numbers of ships arrayed ahead of the moving unit (much the same logic was applied to destroyers screening the Grand Fleet and other naval formations). Convoying became practical partly because it was realized that by attacking, a submarine revealed herself, and a destroyer or other antisubmarine craft could counterattack using depth charges. The U-boat might well sink one or two merchant ships, but at the cost of her own existence.

29. ADM 186/380, pamphlet *Submarine Warfare* (CB 0259, 1917).

30. This section is based largely on Capt. L. C. Howeth, USN (Ret.), *History of Communications-Electronics in the U.S. Navy* (Washington: GPO [Office of Naval History], 1963).

31. Jonathan Steinberg, *Yesterday's Deterrent: Tirpitz and the Birth of the German Battle Fleet* (New York: Macmillan, 1965) quotes a June 1897 Tirpitz memorandum on ship design. In January 1896 Tirpitz, who was already the kaiser's favorite naval adviser, said that England should be the main future naval enemy. Carl-Axel Gemzell, *Organization, Conflict, and Innovation: A Study of German Naval Strategic Planning, 1888–1940* (Lund: Esselte Studium, 1973).

32. In January 1912 the Germans received "positive information" (which was reasonably accurate) that on the outbreak of war, the British would maintain a watching line of destroyers off the German coast. Gemzell, *Organization*, 83.

33. I am indebted to David C. Isby for this idea. Robert W. Herrick, *Soviet Naval Strategy: Fifty Years of Theory and Practice* (Annapolis: Naval Institute Press, 1968), 13–14, quotes early Soviet experts on the needs of a small navy. In *Morskoi Sbornik* in September 1923, for example, Professor M. Petrov argued that the two greatest requirements were

an offensive concept and exceptionally complete intelligence—which amounts to local ocean surveillance. In the August 1925 issue, Iu. Rall argued for exploitation of World War I experience—"tactics of limited engagement, active defense, resolution of a series of specific tasks stemming from conditions of a given theatre." Only the German operations in Flanders seem to fit all of these terms. On 31 October 1926, the U.S. attaché at Riga (there was as yet no Moscow embassy) reported that the 1926 Soviet war plan called for the two Baltic battleships to form a strong point at Kronstadt from which submarines, torpedo boats, and destroyers would sortie to the mouth of the Gulf of Finland to engage invaders. Such operations required sea surveillance. Much the same tactics were practiced in the 1927 maneuvers, which also envisaged coastal minefields covered by the battleships or by shore batteries. Again, this was much what had been done in Flanders.

34. For a recent detailed account, see Mark D. Karau, "Wielding the Dagger: The MarineKorps Flandern and the German War Effort, 1914–1918 (Westport, Conn.: Praeger, 2003).

35. The two-volume report is PRO ADM 239/27. The British made no such studies of any other German coast defense systems.

36. Private communication from Alexandre Sheldon-Dupleix, SHM, engaged in a history of French naval intelligence through the 1930s.

37. EMG 1 (first section of naval general staff) Archive, paper from 3rd Bureau (construction) on the armament of the first contre-torpilleurs, 20 June 1921, SHM. The last of the contre-torpilleurs, the Mogadors, were apparently conceived for the very different role of working with the new fast French battleships.

38. Marc' Antonio Bragadin, The Italian Navy in World War II (Annapolis: Naval Institute Press, 1957) begins with a discussion of Supermarina, 11–14: "Modern means of communication and warfare have made it indispensable to concentrate in one organization, land-based in a protected headquarters, all the duties of collecting and coordinating every bit of information on naval operations. This . . . applies especially to operations . . . in a relatively narrow basin, such as the Mediterranean." Supermarina operated in the Navy Ministry in Rome until that city was declared open, after which it transferred to the Navy Underground Radio Communications Center at Santa Rosa. Bragadin's description of how Supermarina ran the Italian navy (whose groups at sea were "only the pawns") correspond exactly to the way the Admiralty ran the Royal Navy, except that commanders at sea apparently had less independence, "always feeling the invisible presence of the Supermarina at their backs [and thus] sometimes preferred to wait for orders or to request them from Supermarina, even though they could have acted or should have acted on their own initiative. However, in so far as the writer was able to observe personally, he feels that Supermarina committed more errors of omission than of commission" as it tried to refrain from interfering with freedom of action of the higher commanders at sea during pretactical or tactical phases. The core of Supermarina was an operations room with wall maps (plots) showing the locations of all units, friendly and enemy, at sea. It functioned without interruption from 1 June 1940 to 12 September 1943, when the chief of staff moved command to Brindisi.

Chapter 2. Ocean Surveillance after 1918

1. In 1920 an FBI-Office of Naval Intelligence (ONI) team broke into the Japanese Consulate in New York and stole the Imperial Japanese Navy Secret Operations Code 1918, which was photographed and returned. This code (which Op-20G called "Red" for the color of the binder in which the photographs were kept) was used until 1 December 1930. Experience with Red taught U.S. code breakers what they had to do and to know, which extended far beyond the code itself, to the changing encipherment tables (recovered by analysis) and to translation, interpretation of messages, and analysis. Unfortunately, none of the analysis seems to have survived. The next Japanese code (Blue), in force until 31 October 1938, was broken rather than stolen (the NSG history describes this as the most brilliant cryptologic success to date because there were no cribs or translations of the kind used later to solve the Purple diplomatic machine). The problem was that messages were encoded and then enciphered; the U.S. analysts had to solve both code and cipher simultaneously. That was apparently unprecedented. During World War I, for example, the British started with a German code book and then solved its encipherment. IBM tabulating machines were used in this project. Even recognizing that a new code had been introduced was a major achievement. Safford's 1943 history of U.S. naval code breaking, which gave the details above showing how valuable Red had been, gives only one fruit of the Blue solution, the revelation that the rebuilt Japanese battleship Nagato, and by inference the Japanese battle line, had a speed of 26.5 rather than 23.5 knots, with dramatic consequences for the design of the new U.S. battleships. Apparently no other major technical intelligence was recovered.

On 1 June 1939 the Japanese introduced a new type of code (Operations Code), which was reconstructed, but with difficulty because of its complexity. This code became unreadable (because of a key change) on 1 December 1941, presumably as part of Japanese war preparations. Unfortunately, the change was not an unambiguous war warning because it could also have been a routine change after the existing code had been in use for two and a half years. The decrypt station at Corregidor discovered about 15 December that this was the existing code with new keys, and it became more or less readable until 1 June 1942. (The NSG History points out that had this been a new code, the U.S. Navy would have been unable to ambush the Japanese at Midway.) Apart from an attaché code used in 1931–38 (which the U.S. Navy broke using a machine it built), the Japanese navy, unlike the German, used only book codes. In 1935 U.S. Navy cryptanalyst Lt. K. S. Goodwin suggested why. A machine code would transmit the sounds of Japanese, but many characters sound identical (in conversation the solution is often to sketch the character intended in the air). Thus, "Japanese communicators tended to use their code books much as dictionaries to convey their exact and unequivocal meanings, as they did for concealment of the information." (SRH-355, 249) The "Purple" machine devised for high-level diplomatic traffic was the exception, not the rule. These notes are based on the NSG History, on SRH-355, and on Laurence F. Safford, "A Brief History of Communications Intelligence in the United States" (SRH-149), prepared March 1952 and declassified March 1982, in *U.S. Naval Communications Intelligence Activities* (Laguna Hills, CA: Aegean Park Press, 1994).

2. John Prados, *Combined Fleet Decoded: The Secret History of American Intelligence and the Japanese Navy in World War II* (Annapolis: Naval Institute Press, 2001 [reprint of 1995 edition]), recounts instances in which U.S. attachés in Japan became aware of developments like the oxygen-fueled 24-inch torpedo (31–32). Their reports were dismissed by the technical bureaus at home whose own efforts in such directions had failed. Decoded messages would have been impossible to dismiss so lightly. Much the same applied to the Royal Navy. The big Japanese torpedoes were particularly important because they did so much damage in the South Pacific. Their existence was not officially acknowledged until 1944 (Prados cites a 1943 ONI report of a Japanese 24-inch torpedo, but the file of reports at NARA suggests that the combination of size and long range was reported only the following year).

3. In a history he wrote in 1943, Captain Safford wrote that the U.S. inability to track the Japanese fleet "demonstrated the necessity of establishing a strategic DF network as part of the Radio Intelligence organization . . . the urgency of obtaining some sort of HF/DF (regardless of how crude), and the desirability of prosecuting the development of both HF and IF [intermediate frequency] DF." The U.S. Naval Research Laboratory, responsible for developing U.S. naval electronics at this time, doubted that an effective HF/DF could be built. Crucially, the code breakers were able to show that the Japanese had already solved the problem. In the 1933 maneuvers, the Japanese Base Force set up an HF/DF net comprising four temporary island stations to supplement the one at Yokosuka (stations at Sasebo and Hozan apparently did not participate). This net was calibrated with the assistance of Japanese minesweepers, and it tracked Japanese aircraft for practice (presumably inspiring the Air Net the U.S. Navy tried in its 1938 maneuvers). The net took bearings on USS *Houston*, anchored at Tsingtao, at 12.8 MHz, and on USS *Monocacy*, at Shanghai, at 335 kHz, demonstrating Japanese capability. The bearings were not very accurate, but they were comparable to what the U.S. Navy achieved in its first HF/DF sets. By 1934 Japanese radio DF was considered fairly accurate and reliable. According to a November 1935 report to CinC U.S. Fleet, it operated at 4 to 13 MHz. Messages intercepted in February 1938 (concerning tracking of U.S. and Australian cruisers visiting Singapore for the opening of the new dockyard) revealed that the Japanese DF net was operational and effective (SRH-355, 284–85). Later, the U.S. Navy learned from intercepted messages that in 1940 the Japanese successfully tracked three U.S. cruisers on a secret mission, all the way from Pearl Harbor to Singapore, predicting their destination twenty-four hours in advance of arrival.

The 1933 intercepts justified redoubled pressure on the Naval Research Laboratory (NRL) Radio Division. According to SRH-355, HF radio communications in the United States began in 1924, but the DF loops then in use were useless above 1.5 MHz. In May 1927 NRL was assigned to develop a DF useful at 1–4 MHz, but it did not succeed until 1930, when it tested a "rotating Adcock." The prototype (XAB-RAB) appeared in January 1931, and the preproduction version (CXK) emerged only about 1935 and proved unsuccessful. XAB-RABs set up at Cavite and at Guam formed the Navy's first HF/DF net when they were commissioned in May and July 1937, but they were unsuccessful and were replaced that December by an alternative type, DT. Even so, the Cavite unit tracked Japanese ships on maneuvers between 1 and 16 August 1937. Presumably on NRL advice, the Bureau of Engineering (responsible for buying Navy radios) insisted on pressing ahead with development of the CXK rather than investigate alternatives.

By this time Pan American Airways had a viable alternative, a fixed Adcock, because it needed an HF/DF to home its transpacific airliners into landings on small islands for refueling (SRH-355, 169). In 1940 Pan American agreed to place its net at Navy disposal in an emergency. Meanwhile Ray Gordon of NRL invented a much better rotating Adcock (patented 1933); a prototype (XAB-HRO) tested in 1936–37 was found much superior for intelligence work. It was somewhat unwieldy, as its rotating arms were twenty-eight feet across. In February 1937 CNO decided to assign one each to USS *Saratoga* and to the fleet flagship for the coming Fleet Problem; another four (plus a CXK) ashore would form a DF net. The first production version was designated DT (twenty-five were made by Washington Navy Yard). DY (1939; originally DT-2) was an improved model (fifty-nine built by Washington Navy Yard 1939–42) (SRH-355, 185, 335).

Alternatives were sought. In 1936 Cavite and Guam tested loop type HF/DFs, which had been used by the Coast Guard (e.g., to run down smugglers) since 1929 (CXM and CXN), both apparently unsuccessful because they lacked sensitivity and were designed for higher frequencies (12–16 MHz). In 1938 Bell Labs demonstrated a fixed Adcock using a CRT indicator and remote controls (the description in SRH-355 suggests something like the wartime British HF/DF). The fixed Adcock offered instantaneous bearings. In March 1940 CNO officially asked BuEng to investigate fixed Adcocks. A May 1940 reference to a Collins DF (to be purchased in FY41, with ten to follow in FY42) seems to refer to a fixed Adcock (but the Collins DF standardized by the Navy was a rotating type).

By October 1941 a British Marconi Adcock HF/DF, their standard type, was operating at Cheltenham, and another was en route to a new DF site in Greenland. It was considered far superior to DT and DY, "though not the last word in direction finders." A single Collins HF/DF was being tested at Cedar Rapids but had not yet been delivered. The prototype IT&T (Busignies) shipboard HF/DF, the principle of which would be adopted for tactical HF/DF on board U.S. Navy warships, was under test, but not yet delivered. Examined on Long Island on 4 October, it was rated "superior in sensitivity, accuracy, and speed of operation" to any existing HF/DF, including the British Marconi, the best yet available. Four might be ready for quick delivery. NRL had a new Adcock. Collins used a single antenna for 2 to 18 MHz, sacrificing some sensitivity, and it had a rotating receiver element. The Busignies maintained sensitivity by using four separate antennas to cover the full desired range (1.5 to 30 MHz) and hence required four times as much land. However, it was preferable because it was instantaneous and automatic. Fifteen Collins sets were on order, and fifteen Busignies were being requested.

By December 1941 the U.S. Navy had 20 HF/DF stations, 3 net control stations, and 175 operators. SRH-355, quoting Safford's 1943 radio intelligence history. The much later SRG history includes photographs of a CXK-1 and of a wartime DAJ (6). CXK-1 used a central hut with a big pole at either end of a twenty-eight-foot arm, the entire structure rotating to take a bearing. The Busignies-type DAJ, the standard wartime shore HF/DF, used four sets, at least 100 yards apart, each composed of two pairs of masts at right angles plus a fifth (at the center) for sensing, each with its own receiver. This device was produced by Federal Telegraph and Radio. Louis A. Gebhard, "Evolution of Naval Radio Electronics and Contributions of the Naval Research Laboratory" (Washington, D.C.: Naval Research Laboratory, 1979; NRL Report 8300), 307, dates the successful HF direction finder to 1936. Techniques that worked at lower frequencies gave unacceptable bearing errors.

4. This system seems to have originated in the Naval Communications War Plan dated 18 March 1936 (SRH-355,174–75), which called for establishment of seven long-range radio tracking stations on the West Coast and in the Pacific Islands, plus stations for local tracking on the coasts and in the islands, plus five intercept stations and two crypt analysis units. SRH-355,184–85 describes the problem: engineers had to be convinced to see DF as a long-range intelligence sensor rather than as an aid to navigation (as reflected in a May 1936 letter forwarding engineering recommendations to CNO). The May 1937 version of the Orange (Japan) War Plan listed wartime communications intelligence nets: Asiatic (Fleet) net (for the area west of 180 degrees), U.S. Fleet net (fleet based at San Diego), Mid-Pacific net (controlled from Hawaii), West Coast net, East Coast net, Caribbean net, and Gulf Coast net.

The U.S. Fleet net would include advanced bases, moving with the fleet as it approached Japanese waters. It was assumed that the Japanese would overrun the Asiatic net early in a war, so the Mid-Pacific net was intended as a standby. The U.S. Fleet net overlapped the Asiatic and would absorb surviving Asiatic Net elements as the fleet moved West. As an indication of how understaffed U.S. COMINT was at the time, it was still working on material gathered during the 1933 Japanese maneuvers (partly because the codes involved were still being solved). That was acceptable because analysis of the maneuver provided strategic rather than tactical intelligence.

The Mid-Pacific strategic net was formally outlined by CNO in July 1939, and ordered placed in operation as soon as possible. Its Dutch Harbor station was activated in May 1940, and its Samoa station in June. Lualualei was already operating at this time. When war broke out in Europe, priorities reversed; for a time it was suggested that Japan might be a U.S. ally in a future war because of her former alliance with the British. The COMINT organization was told to maintain the Pacific stations but to shift emphasis to the Atlantic, previously largely neglected (it narrowly avoided the loss of the Pacific operators, with their special Japanese Morse and language skills).

5. Timothy Scott Wolters, "Managing a Sea of Information: Shipboard Command and Control in the United States Navy, 1899–1945" (MIT Ph.D. thesis, 2003), 181–82. Each of the opposing fleets had an HF/DF net, Black centered on San Francisco and White on Pearl Harbor. Black had an additional "Air Net" to track its own patrol aircraft, to corroborate their positions when they sent sighting reports, and to help find downed aircraft. None of the nets succeeded. When they were again set up for Fleet Problem Twenty (1939), Black Fleet had a DF control and tracking center on his flagship. He wanted his DF analyst right at hand. As in 1938, success was limited, although Black found it valuable to exchange DF information over its long- and short-haul HF circuits. According to the Cryptologic Veterans history (based on SRH histories), in 1939 the net comprised stations at Manila, Guam, Midway, Oahu, Dutch Harbor (Alaska),

Samoa, and the Canal Zone, and at selected U.S. coastal stations; later one was added in Greenland. By 1940 the East Coast net was successfully tracking U-boats (DF bearings were exchanged with the British from 1941 on).

6. SRH-355, 351, quoting personnel records.

7. SRH-355, quoting Safford's 1943 radio intelligence history.

8. A November 1935 message quoted in SRH-355 mentions extensive Japanese experiments to measure the ability to intercept messages in various places at various frequencies, leading to changes in radio procedures and thus to a marked reduction in U.S. intercepts; the reported adoption of ultrahigh frequency, that is, limited to line of sight, for intership communication; and the adoption of different codes for different purposes (operations, material, administration, liaison, etc.). The latter was a particular blow because Op-20G had so few personnel. Although it had broken important Japanese systems, it was often reading messages (from maneuvers) as much as two years after they were received. This split in Japanese codes probably badly limited U.S. technical intelligence, for example, about new developments such as the "Long Lance" torpedo.

9. ONI may have had a small code-breaking operation in 1917–18. Op-20G began in January 1924 as the Research Desk of the Code and Signal section of the Office of Naval Communication, with one officer, four civilians, and some radiomen. In June 1940 the system employed 12 officers, 121 enlisted, and 15 civilians, which by January 1941 had grown to 44 officers, 489 enlisted, and 10 civilians, and by December 1941 to 75 officers, 645 enlisted, and 10 civilians. Intercept stations were established in approximately the following order: Shanghai (1922), Oahu (1922), Beijing (by 1927), Guam (by 1930), Manila, Bar Harbor (Maine, by 1931), Astoria (Oregon, 1932), and Washington. There were also stations at Amagansett and Cheltenham, among others. Asiatic Fleet began operating a mobile unit on board its flagship about mid-1929. Advanced decryption units were set up in 1932 and 1936, respectively, in Manila and in Pearl Harbor to support the Asiatic and U.S. (later Pacific) Fleets. NARA SRH 355, *Naval Security Group History to World War II*, supplemented by the NSG History.

10. At British suggestion, the U.S. Navy created an all-source operational intelligence center, Op-38W. Christopher Ford and David Rosenberg, *The Admirals' Advantage: U.S. Navy Operational Intelligence in World War II and the Cold War* (Annapolis: Naval Institute Press, 2005), 9. It failed because OpNav was not an operational command center like the Admiralty. After war broke out, Op-38W shifted to the new COMINCH operational command structure, ultimately supporting U.S. antisubmarine warfare (ASW) in the Atlantic—which was controlled out of COMINCH (Tenth Fleet). Accounts of Pacific Fleet intelligence omit whatever existed in San Diego when that was fleet headquarters, and the establishment of the combat intelligence unit at Pearl Harbor.

11. At a Pearl Harbor hearing, Admiral Kimmel said that he knew the Japanese carriers lacked the necessary range; he assumed that submarines were the main threat. This sort of insight would have been gained by interpreting exercises. Gordon Prange, Donald M. Goldstein, and Katherine V. Dillon, *Pearl Harbor: The Verdict of History* (New York: Penguin Books, 1991), 522.

12. Deception traffic is mentioned in Gordon Prange, Donald M. Goldstein, and Katherine V. Dillon, *At Dawn We Slept* (New York: Penguin Edition, 1991), 424–25. As of 2 December, there had been no radio intercepts of two Japanese carrier divisions for fifteen or even for twenty-five days. This silence could be interpreted to mean that the carriers were close inshore, relying on shore stations to relay their traffic. The previous day the Japanese navy changed all its call signs for the second time in a month. Prange, et al., *Pearl Harbor*, 452.

Timothy Wilford, *Pearl Harbor Redefined: USN Radio Intelligence in 1941* (Lanham, MD: University Press of America, 2001) suggests that TINA (short for SERPENTINA, after its wavy serpent-like trace) or radio fingerprinting (RFP) might have demonstrated that this traffic was deception, but records in RG 457 suggest that these methods were used mainly against U-boats. TINA was given to the U.S. Navy by the British; NRL began an RFP project in 1938 (turned over to the National Defense Research Committee [NDRC] in 1940), but as late as 1942, it was still quite experimental. A U.S. Navy report on TINA and RFP, dated 11 May 1942, stated that a station at Cavite compiled RFP records of U.S. and Japanese HF transmitters between September 1939 and February 1940. A station at Heeia, Hawaii, operated between September 1939 and April 1941, took records of the U.S. fleet. A station at Bellevue, Washington, had operated continuously since January 1939, and in January 1940 it began to record German transmissions.

The British Technical Mission to the United States (presumably 1941) reported the effective use of RFP in England, Australia, Egypt, Canada, and Singapore, achieving high identification rates against French and Italian but not German ships (but they did succeed with *Bismarck*). The British mission also disclosed TINA, and the first U.S. operational results were recorded on 17 April 1941—but apparently work concentrated on the German fleet, given the high priority of the Atlantic theater at this time. "A number of tapes of Japanese transmissions were also received from Cheltenham. These were also plotted in the form of graphs, but it was realised after about a dozen of these tapes had been completed that the method of correlation simply by inspection would not answer the purpose"—TINA had no relevance to Pearl Harbor. NARA RG 457 Entry 9032, Box 192.

13. The Z-Plan (dated 8 March 1944) for future Japanese defensive operations fell into U.S. hands after a plane carrying Japanese admiral Shigeru Fukodome, Combined Fleet chief of staff, crashed off Cebu in the Philippines on 31 March 1944. It was translated at Brisbane. Third Fleet received its copy at Ulithi on 6 October. Halsey and other air-oriented officers were impressed mainly with Japanese interest in shuttle bombing by land-based aircraft, a tactic attempted at Saipan. One of Halsey's intelligence officers, Lt. Harris Cox, was oriented more toward surface warfare and emphasized references to the use of surface striking forces against invasion shipping while Japanese carriers struck from the flanks. As the Japanese surface force converged on Leyte Gulf, he realized that the carriers were exposing themselves to draw the U.S. fleet away. The document naturally said nothing about using the carriers as decoys because it was written well before the destruction of the Japanese carrier aviators at Saipan (a later document, not yet passed to Third Fleet, described the Sho Plan to defend the Philippines with, among other things, a decoy carrier force). The junior intelligence officers convinced their chief, but the chief lost a furious argument with Adm. Robert Carney, Halsey's

deputy. Carl Solberg, *Decision and Dissent: With Halsey at Leyte Gulf* (Annapolis: Naval Institute Press, 1995), 120–25.

14. According to Solberg, *Decision and Dissent*, 125–26, night search aircraft from the carrier *Independence*, which was part of Halsey's fleet, watched the Japanese Center Force turn back toward the invasion beaches, threading the San Bernardino Strait at night. (The pilot remembered seeing the ships' searchlights playing on the steep slopes of the sides of the strait.) This report was rejected after furious argument between the chief intelligence officer and the air officer. Halsey may never have seen it. He forwarded his information that Vice Admiral Kurita Takeo *might* be passing through the San Bernardino Strait to Adm. Thomas C. Kinkaid, the Seventh Fleet (amphibious) commander. Halsey seems to have assumed that, based on his pilots' reports, Kurita was so badly damaged that he was no longer a serious threat. Kinkaid initially assumed that Halsey was covering the strait, but during the night, as the battle in Surigao Strait was ending, he called a staff meeting to see whether everything had been covered. His operations officer pointed out that no one had asked whether Halsey had detached his battleships to cover the strait. Kinkaid's message to Halsey arrived too late because it had to go via the two higher-level fleets rather than directly. Kinkaid's staff ordered reconnaissance by Seventh Fleet flying boats, but the coordinates were accidentally transposed and the wrong area searched. Thomas J. Cutler, *The Battle of Leyte Gulf, 23–26 October 1944* (New York: HarperCollins, 1994), 214–16.

15. Nimitz sent his message after receiving a radio report that the escort carriers were being shelled by Japanese battleships. He had never intervened at this level before. Solberg, *Decision and Dissent*, 153. Halsey could cite Nimitz' explicit disappointment that Spruance had failed to engage the main Japanese fleet at Saipan. In the after-action report, Nimitz wrote that "it may be argued that the Japanese never had any intention of evading [the Fifth Fleet] with part or all of their forces, and making their major attack against our shipping at Saipan. From this premise it can be proved that our main body of carriers and gunnery ships could have pushed to the northward without concern for the expeditionary forces, and that had it done so, a decisive fleet air action could have been fought, the Japanese fleet destroyed, and the end of the war hastened." Cutler, *Battle of Leyte Gulf*, 20. Nimitz' orders to Halsey therefore included the caveat "in case opportunity for destruction of major portion of the enemy fleet offers or can be created, such destruction becomes the primary task." Cutler, *Battle of Leyte Gulf*, 214. Halsey later pointed out that, once he decided that the Northern Force was his main target, it would have been foolhardy to detach his fast battleships because in 1944 it was still quite possible that enemy capital ships, closing at night, could sink his carriers.

16. Writers describe the Operational Intelligence Centre (OIC) as the reaction to stovepiping of intelligence in World War I, but it is not entirely clear that this was the case after 1917, when the code breakers were allowed access to the main plot. The main OIC was ordered set up in June 1937. The Singapore outstation was set up in 1938 and Malta in 1939. Ford and Rosenberg, *The Admirals' Advantage*, 6–7.

17. The 1930 Adm. confidential fleet orders (CAFOs), which announced new developments, included an account of higher frequency radio already in service, ranging from 4 to 300 MHz (for the U.S. Navy, HF generally meant 3 to 30 MHz). Frequencies have

been translated from thousands of kilocycles/sec (kc/s) to the modern usage of MHz (millions of cycles per second). The lower end (4–6 MHz) was used to communicate at up to a thousand nautical miles while comparatively immune from DF; 6–12 MHz for long range in darkness; 12–17 MHz for long range in twilight (and in winter daylight; described as particularly good for communication between England and Australia); 17–21 MHz for daylight long range (more for shore stations than for ships, which would suffer from screening and interference problems); 21–30 MHz for aircraft spotting and submarines; 30–50 MHz for tactical communication (being tested to replace the existing Type 41 tactical set); 50–100 MHz for heavy ship fire control (coordination between ships at short ranges; showing promise in trials); and 100–300 MHz was still experimental. The low end did not show the skipping that gives HF its global range. HF was more immune to DF than lower frequencies.

Like the U.S. Navy, the Royal Navy was aware that higher frequencies did not seem to propagate beyond the horizon. A 1932 CAFO (on DF practice) shows that the Royal Navy still used many lower ones. General fleet communications other than at HF were conducted at 110 kHz; the admiral's wave was at 270 kHz, and the flotilla waves (communication with destroyers) were at 375 kHz. Scouts reported at 170 kHz. A March 1935 CAFO, referring to a 1934 document, enumerated the "Advantages and Risks" of HF communication (CAFO 565/35 in ADM 182/94). The 1937 edition of this document seems to have introduced the designation very high frequency (VHF) (30 to 300 MHz) to British practice. "Although communication on VHF may not, and in fact will not, at the present time be reliable much beyond the optical range [i.e., the horizon], no guarantee can be given that such signals will not be audible at much greater ranges." Thus, VHF did not quite solve the tactical radio problem. The contemporary U.S. Navy was far more optimistic.

18. CAFO 809/36 of 2 April 1936 gave a new system of antenna nomenclature that indicated frequency for the first time (as the second letter: *H* was HF, *A* was alternative MF or HF, *C* was a common antenna for MF and HF to receive both but DF only one). *F* indicated a fixed-frame device, *A* an Adcock (fixed antenna), and *R* a rotating-frame antenna. The HF/DF sets were FH 1 (the cruiser *Berwick*), FH 2 (*Repulse* and other ships), FC 1 (the tender *Maidstone* and other ships), RC1 (the cruiser *Southampton* and other ships), and AH 1 (formerly SLH) for shore stations. ADM 182/95. An 8 August 1936 CAFO announced that outfits would be modernized, heavy cruisers and the minelayer *Adventure* receiving FH-series sets, typically on their funnels and foremast heads. Light cruisers, often used for trade protection, received FA-series sets (RA for the three RAN *Amphion* class). Later some ships were assigned FA and FC sets (the two RAN heavy cruisers were assigned FC). The standard wartime escort HF/DF was FH4. An Adcock used a pair of dipoles to form a directional receiver. Either the antenna could rotate, or two channels could be set at right angles and their outputs compared to find direction, or a receiver could sample the output of the two channels.

19. CAFO 2240/37, "W/T Direction Finder—Capabilities and Limitations" in ADM 182/96 cautioned that these were not to be considered absolute limits. The frequency range for FH sets was 0.7 to 20 MHz, and for the A- and C-series sets, 60 kHz to 20 MHz. A table showed FH in new and modernized battleships and in the battle cruisers (FA in the *Nelsons*; *Hood* had not yet been fitted), FH in new carriers, and FC, FH, and

RC in various modern cruisers. Many had not yet been fitted. Long-range submarines were provided with HF/DF, but not destroyers. A November 1939 CAFO announced the decision to fit HF/DF to J and K class destroyers. (ADM 182/126).

20. TINA used a trace of the pattern of dots and dashes to recognize the "fist" of the operator. RFP and another technique, R/E (range estimation), used photographs of oscilloscope traces of the signals. R/E exploited the way in which phase and other signal characteristics could be expected to change over range. It was apparently accurate to about 10 percent at ranges between 500 and 3,500 nautical miles. Timothy Wilford, "Watching the North Pacific: British and Commonwealth Intelligence before Pearl Harbor," in *Intelligence and National Security* 17, no. 4 (Winter 2002): 131–64, based on British documents in the HW18 series at PRO. TINA and RFP were revealed to the U.S. Navy in 1941. RFP seems to have been invented shortly after World War I. According to Wilford, these methods could identify about a quarter of received transmissions. According to his *Pearl Harbor Redefined: USN Radio Intelligence in 1941* (Lanham, MD: University Press of America, 2001), wartime U.S. and British sources doubted the value of RFP. A 1944 U.S. Navy report claimed only 12 percent successes with it. A British report described the technique as experimental, to be abandoned or improved. In 1944 the British valued RFP/TINA as a means of tracking U-boats if they again lost their ability to read German codes.

21. Several times Naval Group Command West cautioned Luetjens to confine himself to short (three-digit) signals because intercepted messages made it clear he was no longer being shadowed. David J. Bercusson and Holger H. Herwig, *The Destruction of the Bismarck* (Woodstock, NY: Overlook Press, 2001), 236–38.

Chapter 3. Net versus Net: The Battle of the Atlantic

1. German success against high-level British systems peaked in 1940, declined in 1941, peaked again in 1942, fell off through early 1943, and collapsed in June 1943. In 1935 (the first year for which German records were captured), the Germans used the annual British naval exercises to collect traffic; they succeeded against three low-grade British systems, the Government Telegraph Code (used by merchant ships), the Ship Reporting Code, and the Auxiliary Code. The Ship Reporting Code was used extensively to report Italian fleet activities during the 1935 Mediterranean crisis. The more difficult four-digit cipher was not broken until 1939, partly because of a negative attitude toward high-grade ciphers. German records first mentioned the five-digit main Naval Code (used throughout the war) in September 1937. Increased British naval activity during the Spanish Civil War provided more traffic to analyze. They could read 15 to 20 percent at the outbreak of war. British changes in their most important systems (Code 2 and Cipher 4) on 26 August 1939 caused little trouble, the Germans reaching a peak in reading both in the spring of 1940 because of the enormous volume involved.

Ralph Erskine, "The Admiralty and Cipher Machines During the Second World War: Not So Stupid After All," *J. Intelligence History* 2 (Winter 2002), points out that although the British adopted the practice of super-enciphering using long subtractor tables in the 1920s, they apparently did not assess how long a table had to be to last for a given time during wartime. The crucial measure is depth; the average depth is given by dividing the number of groups in messages by the number of groups in the additive tables. The greater the depth, the better the chance that the system can be broken. The situation at the beginning of the war was particularly serious because a generation of British naval officers brought up to believe in radio silence expected that the next war would be almost "silent": few messages would be sent. In December 1936, for example, Vice Admiral Sir William James (deputy chief of the naval staff [DCNS], former head of the Room 40 decryption group of World War I) wrote that "we will [not] again enjoy all the advantages of the 1914–18 war, because people today will be wiser about wireless." The failure of such predictions was disastrous. In June 1942 the depth achieved with Table M for Naval Cypher No. 3 was about twenty (for British, Canadian, and American users), whereas the safe figure was about two. The Admiralty set up a new section, NID 10, specifically to safeguard its ciphers. NID 10 rejected a September 1941 U.S. warning that the codes were insecure. However, a new subtractor system devised in the spring of 1941 was approved in March 1942 and entered service on 1 July 1943. American codebreakers observing German behavior claimed credit for forcing this step.

The British code breakers apparently knew that the Germans were reading Naval Cypher No. 3 as early as August 1942. (The Germans failed to disguise the source of their information.) In mid-1943 the new subtractor system reduced depth sufficiently that the Germans broke this system only for the month of December 1943. When a further new system was introduced, the Germans failed even though they employed 250 people on the task and had captured a copy of the Fleet Order describing the new technique. By October 1939 the Germans were reading 35 percent of Code 2, which dealt mainly with patrol vessels. By November Cipher 4, dealing with major units, was being read with some success. The Germans were reading the daily Admiralty submarine summaries and following British cooperation with the French. Cipher 4 provided warning of the 1940 Allied operation in Norway, the sole major German strategic codebreaking success. When Norway fell, the Germans obtained Code 2 books, but not Cipher 4. The British recast both Code 2 and Cipher 4 on 20 August 1940, among other things making them indistinguishable. The Germans enjoyed only limited success, and matters worsened dramatically on 20 January 1941 with another major revision.

Through 1941 German success was limited, although they were able to read the daily U-boat summaries. Even these successes stopped on 1 January 1942, when new code books were issued, plus numerous one-time ciphers for special areas. However, in October 1941 Combined Cipher No. 3 was introduced for Atlantic convoys. During February and March the Germans read 100 percent of this traffic; 80 percent from June through mid-December; and some from February through June 1943. The gap in April and May 1942 resulted from a change making it impossible to distinguish Combined Cipher traffic, and thus required much more manpower to handle a much larger number of messages (most of them in unreadable systems). The Germans introduced IBM machines to assist them, which led to later success in 1942. A further change by the British (15 December 1942) dramatically reduced German successes (at this time the convoy code and Code 2 and Cipher 4 were being read concurrently). The Germans enjoyed some success in the spring of 1943 because the convoy code book remained in force longer than usual. (It did not change when Code 2 changed on 1 March.) The

Combined Code was replaced by Naval Cipher No. 5 on 10 June 1943, and the Germans never read British convoy codes again. Naval Code No. 2 was read with considerable success until December 1943, but with frequent gaps. Naval Cipher No. 4 was read with increasing difficulty after January 1942.

After cryptanalysis failed, the Germans shifted to D/F and to traffic analysis (and to low-level ciphers that could still be read); particular efforts began in January 1944. At its peak in April 1944, the German D/F system included eighteen primary and twenty-five secondary D/F stations plus four separate D/F detachments, but the Germans considered it a poor source of intelligence. Unfortunately, German traffic analysis records were not recovered at the end of the war, but some German summaries (1944–45) indicate what was achieved, for example, continuing efforts to trace the rhythm of the convoys and their designations. The Germans also intercepted (or thought they intercepted) some diversion orders. Postwar analysis showed that results had been poor, possibly reflecting inexperience in using these sources. U.S. Navy history of German wartime naval communications intelligence, NARA RG 457 Entry 9032, Box 625.

2. As a U-boat officer in World War I, Doenitz saw convoys as arrays of merchant ships, so numerous that he could not possibly fire and reload his torpedo tubes quickly enough to sink many of them.

3. Comment in SRH-368. Doenitz chose sinkings over contacts. That made postwar analysis more difficult, as the usual measure of effectiveness was contacts versus the number of convoys that could have been contacted.

4. The Germans assumed that, as in the past, DF would entail swinging a beam back and forth to determine the direction of maximum strength. That would take a minimum time, and they hoped their messages would be too short to be DFed. Because radio data rate depends on frequency, the Germans associated HF with short signals. To make DF even more difficult, routine messages from U-boats were compressed into three-letter signals.

5. The British system developed by Sir Robert Watson-Watt, who was also credited with inventing radar, used two receiving beams at right angles, driving the plates of a CRT: the screen showed a strobe in the direction of the signal. The shorter the burst, the less chance an operator would notice it. The U.S. Navy adopted the British system and an alternative ITT type using a spinning goniometer (directional element). Shore HF/DF used fingerprinting (TINA and RFP) to track submarines and surface ships. Williams, Kathleen Broome, *Secret Weapon: U.S. High-Frequency Direction Finding in the Battle of the Atlantic* (Annapolis: Naval Institute Press, 1996) and P. G. Redgment, "High-Frequency Direction-Finding in the Royal Navy: Development of Anti-U-Boat Equipment, 1941–45" in F. A. Kingsley, *Radar and Other Electronic Systems* (London: Macmillan, 1995).

6. Introduced in November 1944, Kurier (the "squash" transmitter) sent a maximum of seven letters of text. Signals were tape-recorded at normal speed, then transmitted at higher speed. Kurier defeated wartime shipboard HF/DF, but by 1945 land sites had been modified to deal with it. Its signal began with twenty-five pulses (250/second), which triggered a receiver via a filter. The receiver displayed the signal on an

oscilloscope, and the photograph of that waveform was read off. Total message length was about a third of a second. ADM 220/281, PRO, ASRE Technical Note CX4/48/5 of 20 August 1948, "Appreciation of the German 'Kurier' System of Telegraphy and the Intercept Problem."

7. According to the OIC history, the British first read German U-boat codes in February 1941, but success was intermittent through 1941 (e.g., nothing could be read in March). Between June 1941 and January 1942, all messages could be read; June and July 1941 messages were current thanks to captured documents. August 1941 messages were available with a delay of twenty-four to forty-eight hours. However, nothing at all could be read between February and November 1942. The U-boat plot was maintained by measures such as DF, TINA, and RFP. All messages between December 1942 and October 1944 were read, although at times the delay, for particularly secret messages specially enciphered, was as much as a week. U-boats operating independently, particularly in UK inshore waters, were provided with one-time pads beginning in November 1944, and their messages could not usually be broken. Basic U-boat traffic continued to be read without delay.

8. Some 1940 convoys were escorted by a single trawler. British analysts later commented that this would have been the best time for the Germans to concentrate on killing escorts. Moreover, the Germans were able to prevent air attacks at source (i.e., on U-boats in port) by building massive concrete shelters in France. Through June 1942, only eighty-seven U-boats, a fifth of those built to date, were sunk, but the U-boats sank 8 million tons of shipping. As a measure of improving ASW measures (or of more frequent convoy battles), in the second half of 1942, a total of sixty-four U-boats were sunk; the more numerous U-boats operating at this time sank 8.3 million tons. "The Battle of the Atlantic" (account prepared postwar by the Royal Navy Operational Intelligence Centre [OIC]), PRO HW 11/38.

Like the U.S. Navy, the British became interested in machine ciphers in the 1920s. They set up a committee in 1926. It rejected a proposal to adapt the commercial Enigma, but in 1935 the RAF bought such a machine (Typex) on a private-venture basis. In June 1938 the Admiralty asked for five of the first 350 mass-production machines, and by October 1939 it had 630 on order, of which about 350 were intended for ships. Production proved slow because of limited British industrial capacity, so the machine was never adopted in anything like the numbers of the U.S. Navy's Electric Cypher Machine (ECM) Mk II, which was broadly comparable. In naval service it seems to have been used mainly in combined operations and (modified to feed into an adapted ECM Mk II) in joint operations at high level.

The British had to rely on printed ciphers because of the huge numbers required (Erskine also suggests that Typex would not have lasted very long on board small wet ships). Compared to Enigma, Typex was far bulkier (as a result, in part, to its printers). Compared to Enigma, Typex had five rather than two rotors and enjoyed a more irregular motion; it was also issued with more alternative rotors, and after 1941 it had a plugboard far more complex than that used by the Germans. The British used about 180 to 250 different Typex rotors, compared to only five for the entire German army and air force. U.S. Navy attempts to break Typex toward the end of the war failed because of its irregular internal motion. These notes are from Erskine.

9. Numbers and other statistics are given in C. M. Sternhell and A. M. Thorndike, eds., *A Summary of Antisubmarine Warfare Operations in World War II*, the Summary Technical Report of Division 6 of NDRC (Washington, 1946), also published as OEG 53, divides the antisubmarine war into seven periods: (1) submerged daylight attacks on independents, September 1939–June 1940; (2) night surfaced attacks on convoys, July 1940–March 1941; (3) start of wolf packs, end to end escort of convoy, April 1941–December 1941 (and dispersion of Allied convoys); (4) heavy sinkings on East Coast of United States, January 1942–September 1942; (5) large wolf packs battle North Atlantic convoys, October 1942–June 1943 (and lack of air cover in the mid-Atlantic "gap"); (6) Aircraft defeat U-boats' attempted comeback and force adoption of maximum submergence, July 1943–May 1944; and (7) Schnorchel U-boats operate in British home waters, June 1944–end of war. Average numbers of U-boats at sea in each period were, respectively, 6, 10, 30, 57, 104, 61, 39, compared to 40 during the offensive of 1917–18. Against such figures, in May 1941 (period 3), the Germans had 40 operational U-boats. Their peak (May 1943, period 5) was 250, falling to 170 by fall 1943.

Submarine productivity (merchant ships sunk per U-boat month at sea) was never higher than during the first two periods (4 each); it declined to 1 in the third period, then rose to 1.6 during the "Happy Time," falling to 0.5 during the period of greatest overall success, then to 0.1, rising to 0.2 at the end. The comparable World War I figure was 1.5. Average life of a U-boat at sea was greatest during periods 3 and 4, eleven and twelve months. During the first two periods it was three and five months, and for the rest of the war it declined to seven, four, and then two months (in World War I it was six months).

The tally of U-boats sunk per month began with 2.4 in the first period, then fell to 1.9, rising to 2.8 during the period of convoy dispersion and then to 4.9 during the "Happy Time." Even when the allies were being hammered (October 1942–June 1943), it rose to 14.3, then to 17.1, and then to 18.9 per month. Other postwar analysis examined the importance of particularly aggressive U-boat aces, who would keep attacking even as escorts approached. The summary table in OEG 53 notes that three leading aces were all lost in March 1941 (no similar notes are provided for other periods). They were sunk even though the British did not yet have efficient surface-search radar. Because the U-boats gained French bases during period 2, during period 3, the British had to extend escort coverage all the way across the Atlantic. The table credits the drop in effectiveness to the rapid expansion of the U-boat force and the dilution of expertise. During the "Happy Time," losses peaked with 140 ships sunk in June 1942. Extensive convoying began in July, driving the U-boats away from the U.S. East Coast.

10. According to the U.S. postwar OEG report on communications intelligence, the Germans could estimate position within 500–600 miles north-south and within a day's run (150 to 200 miles) along a great circle route. A pack of ten U-boats (spaced about ten miles apart) could sweep this area in about two days in good weather, with a fair chance of sighting the convoy.

11. OEG Report 68, "Evaluation of the Role of Decryption Intelligence in the Operational Phase of the Battle of the Atlantic," released to the National Archives as SRH-368

(declassified 7 May 1987), dated 1952. This report is almost completely limited to the period between U.S. entry into World War II and February 1944.

12. The first mass-production escorts, the "Flower"-class corvettes, were conceived in 1939 in the context of a submarine war limited by geography to the waters around Britain. U-boats could not operate much farther afield because they would to use up so much of their endurance going to and from patrol areas. Similarly, Coastal Command considered short-range aircraft such as Ansons adequate. Longer-range escorts could not be extemporized when the situation changed dramatically in mid-1940. The "River" class conceived for the new conditions was designed early in 1941 and the first entered service in August 1942, but they did not appear in numbers until 1943.

13. OIC considered special intelligence (code breaking) particularly important between May 1941 and May 1943 as a guide to evasion, when escorts were not strong enough. "After the middle of 1943, although we still diverted convoys where possible, the failure . . . to give timely warning was no longer a cause of grave anxiety, and often afforded the opportunity so eagerly seized by our anti-U-boat forces."

14. Some U.S.-UK convoys were taken off their standard routes for the first time. U-boats were reduced to only one contact in January. BdU apparently had no idea why convoy routes had been stable for the past six months (he wrote of British stubbornness in his war diary) or, therefore, why it was suddenly possible or necessary to change them. The change to active evasion proved permanent.

15. SRH-368 tabulates convoys in the North Atlantic between June 1942 and February 1944. Of 266 convoys in the area of interest, German code breaking compromised the positions of ninety-eight, of which forty-eight were contacted. However, 43 (of 168) convoys *not* compromised by German code breaking were also contacted. A compromised convoy had a 49 percent chance of being contacted, an uncompromised convoy a 26 percent chance. Another measure was the probability per day it was at sea that a single U-boat would contact a convoy: 0.095 percent for compromised convoys, 0.058 for uncompromised. BdU could not always vector U-boats against the convoys that had been compromised. The sinking rate was highest for compromised convoys that BdU designated for attack, that is, against which attacks were feasible: 62 percent of all sinkings were in compromised convoys, whereas only 53 percent of all contacts were against such convoys. The average number of sinkings per convoy was highest for compromised convoys (against which wolf packs were concentrated).

16. The BdU war diary mentions twenty-four cases between 1 July 1942 and 31 May 1943 in which U-boat groups were positioned based on decrypts. According to SRH-368, the most dramatic example was the March 1943 pursuit of convoys SC-122 and HX-229. When he received a decrypt indicating a diversion of HX-229, BdU "reacted so promptly (by canceling an order only a few hours old and directing a radical course change) that the Atlantic section of Op-20-G [U.S. code breakers] (who promptly read BdU's message) were convinced that the Allied cipher had been compromised." This operation sank twenty-two merchant ships, but it induced a code change that ruined later operations. BdU's attempts to use code-breaking intelligence after June 1943 failed. Attempts to vector U-boats against fifteen convoys between September 1943 and March 1944 led to only three contacts, which led to only four sinkings in two attacks.

17. The OIC historian dates the main U-boat effort to the spring of 1943. He argues that, had it been made in November and December 1942, it might have been effective. The North African diversion gave the respite needed to build the ASW forces, particularly aircraft, which won the May 1943 battles.

18. The U.S. postwar report on German communications intelligence describes three Enigma security crises. Shortly after the beginning of the war, the German navy communications department suggested that Enigma M was insecure. Its communications intelligence department suggested enciphering from a codebook rather than from plain text. Units exposed to capture (U-boats) should use lower-level codes. These ideas were rejected. Codebooks would slow communications, and no codebook could suffice for an offensive navy like the German one. Since the Germans were reading British codes; the U-boat code could presumably similarly be read. "It is significant . . . that the leaders of the German communications intelligence service [were] so wholly unaware of the principles according to which German communications procedures were constructed that they could seriously propose measures at variance with these principles" (258). Soon afterward, at Wicher, Poland, the Germans discovered three deciphered messages sent by a German cruiser during the Spanish Civil War. Although repeated interrogations (as late as 1944) elicited nothing, by 1944 some Germans realized that this had been a cryptanalytic success rather than a failure of physical security. It seems that the German navy covered up this episode; its naval communications organization apparently never heard of it.

When the U-boat war began to fail in 1943–44, as U-boats were repeatedly caught on the surface, U-boat personnel and even Doenitz concluded that their communications were insecure. Doenitz ordered an inquiry (others in German communications also made enquiries). Technicians concluded that Enigma could be broken "on the assumption of extraordinary mechanical outlay on the part of the enemy" (262). Based on its long-standing analysis of the degree of security Enigma offered, the naval cipher security department dismissed the suspicions as unsubstantiated. The communications security department preferred to attribute Allied success to aircraft radar, DF, and "a remarkable collaboration between the whole surface location system . . . and the A/S groups using underwater location methods." They concentrated on Kurier (to defeat DF) and on deception devices such as the radio buoy.

19. U.S. intelligence assumed (wrongly) that, given how badly the war had gone against the Germans, the group was heading to the United States could not be intended simply to attack shipping. This final U-boat offensive was therefore associated with strategic attack, perhaps using V-2 rockets towed in canisters. Counterattack was therefore urgent.

20. M. J. Whitley, *German Coastal Forces of World War II* (London; Arms and Armour, 1992), describes actions but not command and control; he confirms that the boats never had effective surface-search radar. The U.S. history of German signals intelligence notes the very detailed reports on coastal operations, clearly intended to support S-boat operations, produced in 1944–45.

21. U.S. methods are described by W. J. Holmes, *Double-Edged Secrets: U.S. Naval Intelligence Operations in the Pacific During World War II* (Annapolis: Naval Institute

Press, 1979). U.S. submarine officers later complained that they missed valuable targets, particularly warships, because of errors in *Japanese* navigation: ships were not where they said they would be (the U.S. Navy did not form German-style scouting and attack lines).

Chapter 4. Commanding the Fleet: Plotting

1. According to Capt. B. C. Decker, USN, a 1914 student at the U.S. NWC, "we are told that [before Tsushima] Admiral Heihachiro Togo [plotted] regular reports of the Russian Fleet as it advanced . . . and was thus able to plan his attack . . . as readily as if the forces had been on the tactical board and a chalk mark indicated the scores." Togo contended with only a single force: "it is possible that [he] could grasp the entire situation without plotting." Decker's speculation that Togo also used a tactical plot seems to have been incorrect. NWC RG 8, answers to queries connected with the 1913–14 Long Course (Box 107, Folder 3, XTAG 1915). No one seems to have followed Togo's lead. In the aftermath of Jutland it seems to have been accepted that Jellicoe was the first to use a plot for control during a battle, rather than only to make the appropriate deployment order at the outset.

2. PRO ADM 1/8662/109, "Action Plotting Arrangements: Standardization of Battleships and Cruisers" (1923–24). The associated file on plotting techniques is ADM 116/2090. A July 1923 CAFO required all capital ships, light cruisers, and aircraft carriers to forward drawings of their plotting arrangements. (ADM 182/82).

3. These instructions appear in CAFOs. The plotting manual was CB 3039 (NARA RG 38 foreign publications series, Box 446).

4. From CB 4357(GB) (December 1945), the Royal Navy *Handbook of Action Information Organization and Plotting*, NHB.

5. A November 1928 CAFO in ADM 182/87 describes the first to be adopted, the Brewerton Mk I*, which recorded ship's track and indicated ship's position as a spot of light on a glass plotting surface. The bug crawling across its chart was driven by a pair of splined shafts driven by a mechanism in the middle of one side of the table, the shafts swinging back and forth. Brewerton Mk II and an Admiralty Research Lab (ARL) table could show two selected enemy tracks in addition to own track. These tables were under armor, but "it is considered that the advantages of plotting the gunnery and torpedo targets below and transmitting the result to outlying stations do not balance the extra cost and personnel involved."

By 1931 two new tables were being built, Brewerton Mk IV and ARL Type B, later designated Mk V to distinguish it from Brewerton tables. The ARL bug was carried on a cross-bar driven back and forth by worm gears. It must have been far more rigid than the Brewerton, hence much more reliable. Its adoption for all future installations was announced in August 1934. Mks VI through IX were in service as of 1948; the latest had its spot of light surrounded by a range/bearing web on which reported contacts could be plotted. The next stage was to project a twenty-four-inch-diameter Skiatron radar display onto an opalescent screen under the translucent plotting surface. CAFO 2462

(ADM 182/90) of 16 October 1931 gives the allocation of plotting tables, including the new types.

6. NWC Archives RG 8, Box 107, folder 3, January 1914 Long Course answers to Query A, the appropriate position of the fleet commander. Capt. B. C. Decker, USN, answered that to make reports (e.g., from scouts) useful and to understand the tactical situation "the CinC must resort to plotting. . . . Distances . . . are now so great that it is impossible to gain a correct idea of the movements of forces except by . . . plotting the observations made by forces in the whole battle area." Lt. Cdr. W. S. Pye (later a leading battleship and force commander) argued that "all plans should be made from this plotting board where the tactical situation can be shown much clearer than from a view from the ship." Cdr. E. S. Kellogg preferred personal observation (by the CinC) to plotting (which depended on multiple observers and plotters) but wanted the CinC to have access to a plot. Other officers who considered plotting vital did not explain why. Others considered the CinC's personal view of the battle sufficient. In a 25 June 1917 "Study in Fleet Naval Tactics," Capt. A. P. Niblack stated that "all flagships should be provided with a plotting room and observing instruments to enable the flag officers to plot and follow the movements of forces" (42), NWC RG 8 Box 109, Folder 7: XTAG 1919–20.

7. The 1924 report of the Ship Control Board in NARA RG 38, "U.S. Navy Technical Publications 1901–1960," Box 33, describes the Flag Bridge Plotting Station (Staff Bridge), containing a battle tracer on a large plotting board with universal drafting instrument (to place plots correctly with respect to the battle tracer), a gyro repeater, a main battery target bearing transmitter, an enemy-bearing solver, plus radio keys and telephones. A separate admiral's conning station contains a plotting board but not a battle tracer. The 1929 edition in Box 38 adds, for the new carriers *Lexington* and *Saratoga*, an Aviation Intelligence Office or Air Plot, a station "in which wing and squadron commanders may be instructed, and necessary last-minute navigational and meteorological information imparted." Features included a dead-reckoning tracking table (replacing the battle tracer) and a plotting table with universal drafting instruments. There was also a wall map board.

8. Wolters, "Managing a Sea," 113–17.

9. This seems to mean time from arrival of a message in a radio room to end of transmission, not including coding and decoding. In May 1923 it was over half an hour. Competition cut the average to four minutes by April 1925, and the fleet flagship average was under three. Wolters, "Managing a Sea," 120.

10. The new formations were proposed to fleet commander Adm. S. S. Robison by his aide, Cdr. Chester W. Nimitz. One day at the Naval War College Commander Roscoe MacFall set the destroyers and cruisers in concentric circles around the battleships on the game board. Compared to the usual rectangular formation, the new circular one concentrated antiaircraft fire and was easier to reorient and also to convert from cruising to approach formation. Many students were impressed, but Nimitz happened to be in a position to introduce the new formations to the fleet. E. B. Potter, *Nimitz* (Annapolis: Naval Institute Press, 1976), 138.

11. Wolters, "Managing a Sea," 128, cites a July 1924 complaint by Admiral Robison, who understood what sort of plot he wanted in a redesigned ship. His requirements may have been met when the fleet flagship USS *California* was fitted with a protected flag plot in 1929.

12. Wolters, "Managing a Sea," 144. Asked about this idea, in 1934 the General Board wanted two specially arranged cruisers made available to CinC U.S. Fleet. It envisaged situations where either a battleship or a cruiser would be best. During World War II cruisers were sometimes used as fleet flagships even when fast modern battleships were available.

13. Wolters, "Managing a Sea," 142–43, notes that for the first time the report of this exercise included Information as a separate topic. A seaborne decryption unit first used in Problem Eight (1928) intercepted only one message, but its potential was understood, hence the more successful operation the following year (Wolters, "Managing a Sea," 161). Such units multiplied in later exercises; in Problem Fourteen (1933), Black ordered at least one for each of his task groups. That raised the question of how the information they gathered could securely be transmitted back to the fleet commander (Wolters, "Managing a Sea," 165).

14. According to the NARA *Naval Security Group History*, 16, by June 1917, Navy Cipher Boxes (NCB) Mks I and II were used to encipher existing codes. A contract for a thousand Mk II was awarded in June 1918. There were no naval codes as such, and the U.S. Navy in Europe used British codes. According to a 1935 memo reproduced in SRH-355, in 1923 training in cryptanalysis began so that effective U.S. codes could be constructed.

In 1925 the graduating class used three months' worth of coded messages from CinC Asiatic Fleet to reconstruct the "E" code then in force. This shock led the U.S. Navy to serious code making. On 2 January 1923 a Navy board had examined the Heburn multirotor machine (work on which began in 1921). Rather than suggest improvements, the Navy decided to buy the machine and then improve it. The success of a service test model in Fleet Problem XIII (1932) sold the fleet the idea of an electric cipher machine. Modernized in 1936, these machines remained in service through 1942, handling all important messages between the Navy Department and the attaché in London between May 1938 and March 1942. However, the Navy cut its ties with Heburn (who went bankrupt) in February 1932. At that time the Washington Navy Yard built a prototype ECM Mk I based partly on the Heburn, but greatly improved. The Teletype Corp put it into production.

Mk I was accepted for service in May 1936, and at least 187 were made. It proved clumsy and unreliable (the prototype had never been service tested). Its problems were solved in Mk II, the prototype of which was delivered in January 1939. As of October 1943, the Navy had had 3,370 Mk II on hand and another 3,380 on order, and the Army had adopted the machine as its SIGABA. Mk II was so successful that it remained in service until 1959 and was not declassified until 2001. Mk II became standard in the Atlantic on 1 July 1941 and worldwide on 10 January 1942. This history is based mainly on a 1 October 1943 memorandum in NARA RG 457 Entry 9032 Box 1340.

15. The standard World War II U.S. VHF radio was TBS. Although the letters were chosen to fit a standard naval nomenclature system (T for transmitter, B and S indicating the place in the sequence of transmitters), they corresponded neatly to "Talk Between Ships." According to Wolters, "Managing a Sea," 188–89, VHF was adopted after an unsuccessful attempt to use underwater sound.

16. Battle Fleet Instructions introduced in 1930 were widely praised. Wolters, "Managing a Sea," 168. "Tentative Fleet Dispositions and Battle Plans" survives in NARA RG 38. The corresponding Fleet Tactical Publication was issued in 1934.

17. Wolters, "Managing a Sea," 167, dates the tactical use of the broadcast to April 1930.

18. In the 1927 Fleet Problem (Seven) a battleship division tracked an enemy force, presumably beyond the horizon, by DF. Shipboard DF was apparently similarly useful in Problem Nine (1929), but the language used may refer to code breaking. Wolters, "Managing a Sea," 175. The use of DF to locate the fleet's own ships is from a private conversation with Dr. Wolters.

19. The Arma Corp., which produced fire-control devices, delivered the first DRTs in 1929; by 1930 they were being installed on board battleships and cruisers and approved for destroyers. Relevant papers are in NARA RG 24 (Bureau of Navigation) under the code S24-7(KA); unfortunately this series does not describe the origins of the DRT, nor does it include a description.

20. Personal conversations with Charles Haberlein, curator of photographs at the U.S. Naval Historical Center. Mr. Haberlein was a member of the Ballard expedition to find ships sunk at Guadalcanal. Observation of where ships were sunk led him to question the validity of ships' track charts, hence the DRT on which they were based. Mr. Haberlein examined the TBS (short-range) radio log of USS *Helena*, which Admiral Callaghan used as his main source of surface information, as she had his best surface-search radar (an SG) on board. Mr. Haberlein recounted a comment by Capt. Russell Crenshaw, USN: the "bug" of his DRT once came off in his hand when he tried to reset it. That suggests something like the Brewerton table the Royal Navy dropped in 1934, whose "bug" was mounted on a moving arm (it could not have happened in a table like the later British ARL).

21. Cap. de Corvette (i.e., Lieutenant Commander) de Bronac de Vezelhas to the French naval intelligence service (EMG 2), 10 February 1921, on the Central Station (Poste Central de maneuvre) and its use by the commanders of naval forces, SHM.

22. Just how complex is clear from David C. Evans and Mark R. Peattie, *Kaigun: Strategy, Tactics, and Technology in the Imperial Japanese Navy, 1887–1941* (Annapolis: Naval Institute Press, 1997), particularly 273–86.

23. Kurita's retreat, with victory nearly in his hands, is an enduring World War II mystery, sometimes blamed on his exhaustion after three sleepless nights. Some of the explanations suggest plotting disasters. One explanation is that that Kurita did not realize how well he was doing; after the war he said that he thought he was facing cruisers and fleet carriers. He also seems not to have realized that he was gaining on the escort carriers he was shelling. For example, he thought the carriers were making thirty knots (in fact they were hard-pressed to make twenty). Such misperceptions may be traceable to a thor-

oughly erroneous flag plot. Kurita had probably lost his strategic plot with his flagship, so he had only a limited idea of where U.S. forces were. That too would have fed into his suspicion that he was facing the U.S. main body, rather than a small vulnerable force. At times after the war Kurita said that he broke off to engage a U.S. main body to his north. He also said that once he failed to find that force, he wanted the chance to run back through the San Bernardino Strait (through which he had come) at night, that is, reasonably immune from air attack. That limited the time he thought he had at Leyte Gulf. Cutler, *Battle of Leyte Gulf*, 262–63 and 286–87. Cutler also suggests that Kurita considered his mission pointless because U.S. forces were already established ashore. When he saw aircraft from the carriers flying toward a field ashore to refuel, he thought they were massing for a strike against him. If Leyte was already lost, better to preserve the surface strike force for another day. Evan Thomas, *Sea of Thunder: Four Commanders and the Great Naval Campaign 1941–1945* (New York: Simon and Schuster, 2006), goes further, arguing that Kurita's announcement of a signal indicating the U.S. main body within striking distance to the north was a ploy to allow the fleet to survive yet save face (308–11, 352–53).

Chapter 5. Picture-Centric Air Defense

1. David Zimmerman, *Britain's Shield: Radar and the Defeat of the Luftwaffe* (Stroud, UK: Sutton, 2001), 4.

2. Zimmerman, *Britain's Shield*, 15–16.

3. Alfred Price, *Instruments of Darkness* (London: Greenhill, 2005 [first edition 1967]), 56–58.

4. Price, *Instruments of Darkness*, 146, describes a May 1943 raid. At this point saturation meant compressing the time of the raid so that each box had too little time (three and a half minutes) to complete most engagements. However, there were rarely multiple bombers inside each box.

5. Price, *Instruments of Darkness*, 147–50, describes the origins of Wild Boar. On 171 he describes a Wild Boar disaster. Without a good overall picture of the battle space over Germany, the Germans were vulnerable to deception. A raid on Peenemunde, the missile development center, was covered by a feint raid against Berlin. The feint succeeded; German fighters concentrated over Berlin. Artillery on the ground fired at them because, despite their recognition flares, the gunners associated engine noise with bombers. The fighter pilots assumed the gunners had valid targets. Those with remaining fuel headed north to Peenemunde only when they saw the first Pathfinder target-marking flares there, a hundred miles away. They caught the last wave of bombers, inflicting considerable casualties. Price points out that the success of Wild Boar led the Germans to abandon their fighter-control system and also to abandon attempts to counter Window (174). However, the Germans began to track the bombers passively, based on their ground-mapping radars and on their "identification of friend or foe" (IFF). Such tracking often made it possible for them to distinguish spoof raids, whose aircraft did not use ground-mapping radar.

6. The RAF jammed the radio uplink used to broadcast the information. Because the Germans used HF radio, it was possible both to jam and to broadcast misleading voice signals from England. Price, *Instruments of Darkness*, 174–75, 182–84, 192–93. At the end of the war, the Germans were beginning to set up a directional data link system, which printed out its messages on paper tape in the cockpit. Its discrete (in effect, digital) signals were inherently difficult to jam.

Chapter 6. The Experience with Radar

1. Henry E. Guerlach, *Radar in World War II*, Vol. 8 of *The History of Modern Physics, 1800–1950* (Tomash/American Institute of Physics, 1987 revision of 1946 book produced for the MIT Radiation Laboratory), 929, based on a report by a U.S. observer, about 1940, after the Tizard Mission to the United States. Guerlach states that the visual plot was invented "as early as 1936." Later British descriptions of plotting practice do not mention it as such.

2. A. E. Fanning, "The Action Information Organization," in Kingsley, *Radar Equipment*, 150–51.

3. R. S. Woolrych, "Fighter Direction," in Kingsley, *Radar Equipment*. Fighter direction in *Ark Royal* was invented by her air signal officer, Lieutenant Commander Charles Coke, who used an aircraft-type plotting board. Initially he used what would later be called broadcast control, passing enemy position, course, and speed to the fighters. They could exploit this information because they carried experienced navigators. Coke found that he could also keep track of friendly fighters, mainly using dead reckoning, so he vectored them to intercept raiders. This method imposed a delay of about four minutes, so sometimes it failed.

4. Woolrych, "Fighter Direction," 176. In the British 1938 summer exercise, the battleship *Rodney* (using her radar receiver) detected radar emissions from the cruiser *Sheffield* at 100 nautical mile range, with a bearing accuracy of 2 degrees. When she first went to the Mediterranean, the carrier *Illustrious* was allowed one radar sweep per hour until she made contact, and she was not permitted to break radio silence to her fighters until the raid was twenty nautical miles from the ship. *Bismarck* detected the emissions of the British cruiser shadowing her.

5. Fanning, "Action Information Organization," 153.

6. Fanning, "Action Information Organization," 155. The policy was promulgated in July 1943. *Valiant* was the example used in CB 4357(GB) (December 1945), cited above.

7. In 1942 a British carrier followed the chosen target with her air warning radar, relying on ships in company to find new targets. Fighter controllers used horizontal plots, so the air summary plot they watched had to be more or less vertical. The 1942 version was a four-foot-diameter plot sloped forty-five degrees to the vertical, the two plotters (one for ship's radars, one for radio inputs) working in front of it. A filter officer stood between them. About two reports per minute were telephoned from the radar scope. The controllers relied on unplotted radar data when they could not see the plot through the mass of personnel. As flagship during Operation Pedestal (August 1942), the Royal

Navy's most intense air action before Okinawa, HMS *Victorious* used this arrangement. Refitting at Belfast, the carrier *Indomitable* was fitted with more radars (Types 277 and 281 in addition to 279), which would require more plotters. A shipyard electrician suggested a way to clear the fighter directors' lines of sight: a vertical transparent edge-lit plot (two sheets of Plexiglas) like the status board at his Home Guard headquarters. Plotters could work behind it, no longer blocking the view, writing backward. The filter officer standing in front of the plot drew target tracks, creating the tactical picture. In April 1943 the Royal Navy began trials with the now-universal plan position indicator (PPI) or map-like display. A good PPI operator could telephone twelve plots per minute. The next step, for both navies, was a twenty-five-inch horizontal plot giving an enlarged PPI picture with black and white reversed, so that grease pencil marks could easily be seen. It was used by fighter controllers in place of their small plotting boards. This device was called Skiatron by the Royal Navy and VG by the U.S. Navy. Woolrych, "Fighter Direction," 182.

8. As in ground air defense, at the outbreak of war German naval radar was technically superior. However, the German navy never saw radar as a situational-awareness device, but only as an all-weather range finder. They apparently never hit on the idea of plotting radar data for situational awareness, possibly because they had never learned to rely on tactical plots. *CIC* (magazine), March 1946, "Radar on *Prinz Eugen*," OA.

9. This account is based on M. J. Whitley, *German Cruisers of World War Two* (Annapolis: Naval Institute Press, 1985), 144–52. Whitley used both British and German sources.

10. The 1951 edition of the British MHQ handbook is in NARA 2, RG 38 (foreign publications), Box 341.

11. The first U.S. ship with an operational air search radar was the battleship *California*. Her CO, Capt. H. M. Bemis, ordered his communications officer, Lt. Cdr. Henry E. Bernstein to create the first U.S. radar plot as a way of integrating the ship's CXAM radar with other command and control elements. This "Geep plot" one deck below Flag Plot contained the radar receiver, two voice radios, intraship phones, a radio direction finder, and a horizontal plot. Bernstein then developed the first U.S. IFF device (which keyed the radar echo) as a necessary complement to the radar. Wolters, "Managing a Sea," 222–23.

12. As reported in David L. Boslaugh, *When Computers Went to Sea: The Digitization of the U.S. Navy* (Los Alamitos: IEEE Computer Society and ASNE, 1999), 20.

13. Guerlach, *Radar in World War II*, 930.

14. Guerlach, *Radar in World War II*, 925, citing USF 74, "Cruising Instructions for Carrier Task Forces," editions dated June 1938 and March 1941.

15. According to Wolters, "Managing a Sea," 220–21, immediately after Fleet Problem Twenty (1939), officers requested radar repeaters. Early the next year NRL said that would be no problem, but nothing concrete was done. NRL also said that it had several methods of sending the radar image to other ships by radio. In August 1940, the CO of *Chester* asked for permission to install repeaters, meaning indicators of antenna bearing/elevation as aids to plotting. Wolters, "Managing a Sea," 224.

16. Guerlach, *Radar in World War II*, 943.

17. In the "X-Ray Formation" adopted after Midway most of the CAP was stationed at a set altitude, with four aircraft five thousand feet above and two five thousand feet below.

18. Guerlach, *Radar in World War II*, 933.

19. Guerlach, *Radar in World War II*, 929 and 934.

20. In spring 1942 CNO Adm. Ernest J. King asked Dr. Vannevar Bush, head of the National Defense Research Council, for a means of relaying patrol aircraft radar data to surface ships (to see "over the hill"). In June 1942 the Joint Committee on New Weapons and Equipment asked the Massachusetts Institute of Technology (MIT) Radiation Laboratory to develop King's device as a means of relaying the radar picture itself. Initial progress, using a lightweight television transmitter, was encouraging, and by the end of 1942, a prototype was ready for flight tests. That summer it seemed that the reliable range was fifty nautical miles. King wanted that doubled. By October King's office (COMINCH) was increasingly worried about the complexity of the system. However, Bureau of Aeronautics (BuAer) was enthusiastic enough to state a definite tactical need for airborne early warning (memo 11 March 1944), and to request forty systems. Admiral King complied.

    The shift from surface search to airborne early warning is probably traceable to Japanese low-altitude night attack tactics practiced from the fall of 1943 onward. Cadillac gained high priority when the Japanese began to use kamikazes in October 1944. The program was granted highest priority at a 5 December 1944 Navy Department meeting; by January 1945 it was a crash program to produce 40 relays (of 140 planned) and 34 aircraft (of 97 required according to a 30 December 1944 program status memo). The Radiation Laboratory began flight tests in August 1944 (Navy tests began in January 1945). The first production set was delivered in March 1945; the others followed by early summer. By the summer of 1945, about a fifth of all Radiation Lab personnel were involved in Cadillac. Just after the war, the carriers *Enterprise* and *Bunker Hill* operated Cadillac aircraft. Others had the necessary antennas and receivers. In early tests single aircraft were detected at twice the usual range, and formations at up to four times the usual range. The horizon to detect surface ships was extended sixfold. Collected copies of the basic Cadillac papers, NAVAIR History (Armstrong series, headed "Acceptances and Reinstatements" beginning 1969–79). These notes include a draft initial chapter of a history of naval airborne early warning begun by Dr. William Armstrong when he was NAVAIR historian.

21. The Navy also considered several other aircraft. A December 1944 BuAer memo reported studies of airborne early warning equipment on board the PBM-5 Mariner, the PB2Y-3 Coronado, and the B-17F, of which the two last seemed best. In January 1945 the Neptune, not yet flown, was added. Work was suspended on 18 January 1945 because of the greater urgency of carrier aircraft installation and "related matters concerning availability of B-17 models." Apparently the B-17 was recommended because it alone of these aircraft could accommodate a larger APS-20 antenna (according to a February note to CNO, the Neptune could not). A December 1975 memo in the Armstrong file on "The Wartime Origins of AEW" refers to 1944 engineering tests on the B-17G. The official request for B-17Gs from the Army is dated 5 July 1945 (NAVAIR History AEW file).

22. In a network-centric attack, the Super Etendard flew below the radar horizon and was cued by the bomber. When USS *Vincennes* was working up for deployment to the Gulf in 1988, this attack technique was described as standard. In the Gulf, aware of Iranian boasts, her commander assumed that an Iranian P-3 circling apparently aimlessly was targeting his ship. He also guessed that Iranian Boghammer boats were part of a planned coordinated attack. Intelligence had not impressed upon him the deep disunity between the regular Iranian armed forces (P-3 and fighters) and the Revolutionary Guards (Boghammers). Sometimes something that may be network-centric is not.

Chapter 7. The Birth of Tactical Automation: The Fleet Air Defense Crisis

1. With ten targets on the PPI, eight were plotted satisfactorily, and the median time to detect a new target was two minutes. With sixteen on the PPI, only twelve were plotted satisfactorily. With fourteen targets, median detection time was three minutes; with twenty targets, it was more than five minutes. The CIC evaluator chose the most threatening raids. In the experiment the criterion was how soon they would arrive within twenty-five nautical miles of the ship. With thirteen raids, the evaluator was 70 percent correct. That fell to 55 percent with eighteen raids and to 35 percent with twenty-two. NRL concluded that a CIC tracker/plotter team could handle four or five targets per PPI/plotter, so a 2-PPI system should be able to handle eight to ten targets; a 3-PPI system tested at NRL handled nearly fifteen. Cdr. J. I. Nichols and Cdr. J. D. Shea, NRL, "CIC Track-Handling Capacity" in *Combat Readiness* 5, no. 1 (January–March 1957), 30–31, OA.

2. OpNav, "Fleet Air Defense," Cdr. Paul van Lounen (Op-41306), "Search, Detection, Countermeasures, and Communications Equipment." Work began on an analog Intercept Tracking and Control Console (INTACC) in 1947. Given coordinates of two interceptors and two targets, it computed interception vectors for the air intercept controller. The production version developed in 1953–55 by Cornell Aeronautical Laboratory entered service in small numbers.

3. The Royal Air Force revived Broadcast Control about the beginning of 1949 on the theory that fighter directors could not cope with fast bombers. At the 1949 American-British CIC conference, British speakers estimated that, whereas a close controller could handle only two simultaneous interceptions, a broadcaster could handle twelve, perhaps sixteen. OEG's 1949 report on fleet air defense was apparently the first to advocate broadcast control for the U.S. Navy. This technique was officially adopted after a series of 1952–53 exercises demonstrated how poor existing methods were. OEG summary report on Fleet Air Defense, 12 July 1956. Successful trials were conducted in 1956 using British GEE navigational equipment because tactical air navigation (TACAN) was not yet operational. For the situation in 1950, see "Fleet Air Defense Capabilities," by J. L. Everett of OEG, 2 August 1950, introductory talk at OpNav presentation to Weapon Systems Evaluation Group, a JCS panel on "Fleet Air Defense as Applied to the Carrier Task Force," NHC Aviation History Office OpDevFor broadcast controls trials were analyzed in OEG Study 555, "A Preliminary Evaluation of Broadcast Control in Fleet Air Defense," issued 23 August 1955 (in OA).

4. "Condition RED in Air Defense," in the March–April 1953 issue of *Combat Readiness* (the first published). Sixth Fleet exercises were considered elementary compared to those carried out of Korea by Task Force 77.

5. OEG Study 540, "Fleet Air Defense Capabilities in 1952 and 1953," 9 July 1954, OA.

6. OEG Summary Report 3, "Fleet Air Defense Improvements," 31 October 1956, reporting a broad study begun in June 1955 to analyze deficiencies and to propose possible corrections that could be made before 1958. This work extended 1952 and 1953 studies and OEG 526 (defensive capability against low fliers).

7. It helped that Sixth Fleet had several carriers, hence numerous fighters. Typically it assigned a Low-Altitude Combat Air Patrol (LOCAP) to orbit over the main body as a backstop, plus an average of seven CAP sections (availability 65 percent) in rings, twenty, thirty, and eighty nautical miles from the main body.

8. A writer in Sixth Fleet pointed out that "the installation of corner reflectors and/or transponders on all ships . . . would make the problem of identification even more difficult." *Combat Readiness*, "Decentralized Air Defense" (1956). U.S. destroyers were fitted with blip enhancers for this purpose.

9. CDS is described in detail in its inventor's autobiography: Prof. Ralph Benjamin, *Five Lives in One: An Insider's View of the Defence and Intelligence World* (Tunbridge Wells: Parapress, 1996). R. V. Alred (Admiralty Signal and Radar Establishment), "Future Techniques for Displaying and Recording of Information in CIC," in "American-British CIC." C. A. Laws of Elliott Brothers, which made the equipment, gave a supplementary talk on the electro-electronic techniques used. See also Eric Grove, "Naval Command and Control Equipment: The Birth of the Late Twentieth Century 'Revolution in Military Affairs,'" in Robert Bud and Philip Gummett, eds., *Cold War, Hot Science: Applied Research in Britain's Defence Laboratories 1945–1990* (Amsterdam: Harwood Academic Publishers, 1999).

10. CDS (and, for that matter, NTDS) design assumed that targets would fly in straight lines, so that the system could dead reckon their positions. Detectors at radar displays entered plots into the system by "hooking" them and moving cursors on their screens using joysticks. Trackers entered target course and speed by associating two positions of the same target. The system fed back a marker (a "tab") at the calculated current position of each target to keep detectors from reentering targets. In tests, operators entered a plot in two seconds (three targets in the projected radar data rate of six seconds). In 1949 it appeared that one tracker could handle up to eight targets. Analysis (filtering) operators hooked markers to gate the radar to display information on the corresponding target. They had expanded A- and B-scopes and precision height displays to enable them to examine target echo characteristics in detail. Using the button on the joystick, the operator could query the corresponding track memory. Apart from analysis, this was much like the U.S. digital NTDS system of a decade later.

11. ADM 1/26038, a 2 August 1955 paper by director, Gunnery Division (of Admiralty) on data link requirements of the new missile destroyers.

12. The annual report on "Progress in Underwater Warfare" for 1947 (ADM 239/421) reported formation of a new Torpedo and Anti-Submarine (TAS) Weapons Control

Committee. Its 1948 request for a specialized TAS plot, as automated as possible, probably inspired CAMBRIA. A short description of ASP, given to the Canadians for comparison with DATAR, is in the report of the 1951 UK electronic mission to Canada, ADM 220/1328. R. V. Alred, "Electronic Operations Plot for Surface and Anti-Submarine Warfare," ASRE report NX/50/28 (second edition, dated 15 March 1951), is PRO ADM220/416. The Staff Requirement dated 9 December 1950 was approved 12 February 1951. EMI received a study contract on 10 March 1951, and a development contract for two ASP for sea trials on 16 August 1951.

13. T. C. Plowman and R. P. Budgen, "Project CAMBRIA, Operation of X3 Model at ASRE," 20 May 1954, ADM220/1067. It was installed on board HMS *Relentless* in August–September 1953 and went to sea that October.

14. The ultimate version seems to have been the British JYA, with two plotting tables, one for antisubmarine action (automatically showing contacts), and one for the local operations plot (ship's radar picture). A control panel on the ASW table selected which of three data sources (visual, ECM, sonar) would be presented automatically in addition to the ship's own surface search radar. For example, a light would indicate that the ship's medium-range sonar was in contact. Pressing a button would cause the sonar contact position to appear as a cross on the plot. The contact position would appear as long as the sonar indicator was on. An electronic cursor could be placed as desired, for example, to indicate a reported consort's sonar contact (displaced as desired from a given position, such as the consort's). On the radar plot table, standard practice was to place plastic plotting symbols atop pips representing ships, one side painted blue and one red (in fluorescent paint). The colors indicated whether a ship was or was not in contact. Plotting was done on Plexiglas "pavements" that could be moved around as the action approached the edge of a table. Lt. Cdr. C. L. McDaniel, USN, "The Automatic Radar Plot in ASW," *Combat Readiness* 9, no. 3 (October–December 1963). McDaniel was U.S. Navy exchange instructor officer at the Joint Anti-Submarine School, Londonderry, HMS *Sea Eagle*.

15. Work began in 1951, using data collected for the BuShips Bell Laboratories—RCA Project COSMOS (1951–56) study of the intercept problem. As in CDS, operators entered data directly from radar repeaters into separate electrical dead-reckoning memories. Paint pens driven by solenoids entered target data onto the usual vertical plot. Like the small version of CDS, EDS could handle up to twenty-four targets. Tests showed that it could handle data much faster than manual CICs (whose net saturated at eight to eleven targets). Associated with EDS was the SSN-21 data link, which could accommodate a twenty-five-ship net. Initial tests on board USS *Willis A. Lee* (14 March 1956–10 May 1957) failed, but an improved version was installed on board the four radar picket destroyers of DesDiv 262 at Norfolk between September 1958 and February 1959. OpDevFor recommended that it be used only as an interim system because the much better NTDS was coming. Operational Test and Evaluation Force report on EDS, Project Op/S480/S67 of 1 February 1960, OA.

16. John Vardeles, "From DATAR to the FP-6000 Computer: Technological Change in a Canadian Industrial Context," *Annals of Computing* 16, no. 2 (1994), credits Belyea with the idea for DATAR. See also Captain (N) D. N. Macgillivray and Lieutenant (N)

G. Switzer, "Canadian Naval Contribution to Tactical Data Systems and Data Link Development" in Commemorative Edition (1985) of (Canadian) *Maritime Warfare Bulletin.*

17. A British report of the 1949 joint CIC conference (ADM220/604) describes the projected U.S. Navy Combat Data Exchange Relay (CODAER) digital data link operating at television bandwidth and frame rate (thirty frames/second) to handle 525 targets. According to a U.S. 1950 presentation, "By 1956 rapid communication for air defense of a Task Group will [use a new digital] surface to surface Data Transmission System. . . . It will be possible for the Command ship in a task group to keep all ships informed of the . . . position, type, number, speed of enemy raids, the number and position of friendly planes or ships in the area, and action being taken to combat the raids. The Data Transmission equipment should also be able to transmit orders and control data. . . . [It] will provide essentially private line communication with up to 100 aircraft." OpNav, "Fleet Air Defense, " Cdr. Paul van Lounen.

18. Macgillivray and Switzer, "Canadian Naval Contribution," 81.

19. Air Force History Office: USAF Historical Division Liaison Office, *Command and Control for North American Air Defense 1959–63*, January 1965.

20. Each contained a pair of IBM's 32-bit FSQ-7 computers with main memory capacity of 8,000 words (in two memories) using magnetic cores and vacuum tubes. By the time the last center in the system was decommissioned in 1984, memory had expanded to 64,000 words—still ludicrously small by later standards. Each machine weighed 175 tons, and the pair consumed three magwatts of power. For a detailed account of SAGE and its impact on the U.S. computer industry, see Robert Buderi, *The Invention That Changed the World: How a Small Group of Radar Pioneers Won the Second World War and Launched a Technological Revolution* (New York: Simon and Schuster, 1996). This is mainly a history of air defense radar, but it explains how SAGE emerged.

21. Major recommendations were concentrate U.S. air defense on the principal centers of population and industry, mainly in the Northeast; disperse SAC and reduce the time to launch its bombers; establish a polar AEW barrier by 1960; build a second DEW line; set up electronic listening facilities as far forward as possible; add forward barriers to the Sound Surveillance System (SOSUS); extend SOSUS north; extend SOSUS to seaward to detect missile submarines; examine the jamming threat to SOSUS; and set up a means of identifying and tracking merchant ships on a global scale. DEFE 7/2084 (British report).

22. Boslaugh, *When Computers Went to Sea*, ascribes McNally's estimates to his knowledge of the kamikaze problem, but more likely they were figures thrown out during LAMPLIGHT discussions. The British LAMPLIGHT report describes the two-step EDS/DATAR plan. McNally probably submitted his NTDS concept to ONR after the conference.

23. Boslaugh, *When Computers Went to Sea*, 118–20.

294 ■ NOTES TO PAGES 75-79

Chapter 8. The Naval Tactical Data System

1. Boslaugh, *When Computers Went to Sea*, 121, based on a 1993 interview with McNally.

2. Graf Associates, "Case Study of the Development of the Naval Tactical Data System," III-4. Report prepared for the National Academy of Sciences Committee on the Utilization of Scientific and Engineering Manpower," 29 January 1964, Post–1 January 1946 Command File: Individual Persons, Box 1787, OA. The project was never completed, but it helps show the extent to which the basic ideas underlying NTDS already existed in the early 1950s. The Navy computer was intended for code breaking.

3. The first of three articles on the subject was Captain Paul Van Leunen, USN, head of the OpNav Combat Direction Systems Branch, "The Naval Tactical Data System— NTDS," *Combat Readiness* 5, no. 4 (October–December 1957). The second was Capt. L. Folsom, head, Advanced Direction Systems Branch, OpNav, "1958—A Year of Decision in Naval Tactical Data Systems," *Combat Readiness* 4, no. 1 (January–March 1958): 5–6. OpNav policy was that NTDS would become "a principal tool of command in the 'new Navy'" offering, beside the usual CIC services, "*maximum aid*" (Folsom's italics) to commanders in decision makings in all types of operation. It would fit within 115 percent of weight, space, and manning currently devoted to CIC functions, and it would be developed largely within the Navy. The third was Advanced Direction Systems Branch, OpNav, "More About NTDS," *Combat Readiness* 7, no. 2 (April–June 1959): 9–10. Its high cost would limit NTDS to ships with considerable remaining service life, for which NTDS would offer a significant gain, and which already had advanced weapons and sensors that NTDS could enhance: carriers, cruisers (new and converted), frigates (DLG), and new destroyers. Installation on smaller and older destroyers and destroyer escorts was under study (soon resulting in the SSCDS project). Probably no more than nineteen ships could be fitted with NTDS by 1963, with about thirty available by 1964.

4. Phase 0 was the Modular CIC split into functional areas. A television monitor in each showed an image of the main plot in the central decision and analysis section (in effect, system track memory). Although what was done in the functional areas could not feed back automatically into the main plot, this was far better than existing CICs. In NTDS computer displays replaced the television monitors, providing two-way communication between functional areas and track memory. Proposed in 1955, the Integrated Modular CIC was approved by OpNav in October 1956, and the first was installed on board the carrier *Oriskany* (completed April 1959). By late 1960, fifty-five such installations were under way. Robert D. Donovan, CIC, Command and Combat Director, Stations Section, BuShips, "Modular CIC," *Combat Readiness* 7, no. 1 (January–March 1959): 2–4 and Instructors of CIC "O" Course, U.S. Naval CIC School, NAS Glynco, Brunswick, Georgia, "A Survey of CIC," *Combat Readiness* 9, no. 3 (July–September 1961): 2–6.

5. The beacon video processing (BVP) computer automatically decided that a beacon signal above a threshold was a real signal (i.e., detected it). The corresponding coordinates were automatically entered. In RVP (radar video processing) the same technique was applied to radar signals. It was more difficult because they were noisier.

6. VCNO Ser 9456P34 of 23 January 1959, as described in the 1962 policy statement described below.

7. List from Op-353/sjt Ser 060P35 of 8 May 1962 in Double Zero files, 9000 series, 1962, Box 10, OA. According to Boslaugh, the new construction installation decisions listed here were made only in March 1962, when it was clear that NTDS was successful: three carriers (*Kitty Hawk*, *Constellation*, and *America*, all of which had Terrier missile batteries); the three *Albany*-class missile cruisers; the ten *Belknap/Truxtun*-class missile frigates (DLG, later CG); and the nuclear frigate (DLGN) *Bainbridge*, which received NTDS in a post-completion refit. *Enterprise* and *Long Beach* received NTDS because they were already receiving computers for their phased-array radars.

8. "USS *Albany* Recommissioned," *Naval Ordnance Bulletin*, 1–69.

9. Double Zero files, 9000 series for 1964, OA; memorandum for VCNO re NTDS, Op-353/mar, Ser 0636P35 of 2 July 1964, signed by L. P. Ramage, deputy chief of naval operations (Fleet Operations and Readiness).

10. Boslaugh, *When Computers Went to Sea*, 244–45. The first two Mk 11 ships were the missile frigate (cruiser) *Jouett* (DLG 29) and the carrier *John F. Kennedy* (which had a Tartar missile battery).

11. Problem J3.4, listed in the Graf report.

12. Macgillivray, and Switzer, "Canadian Naval Contribution," 84–85.

13. Dr. Will O'Neill, who was working at Naval Electronics Laboratory (NEL) on SSDS about 1962, made this point privately to the author.

14. Double Zero files, 9000–9000/5 SEAHAWK for 1964, OA, contains a file of Seahawk memoranda. The earliest was a note from the Long Range Objectives Group (Rear Adm. T. H. Moorer) to the VCNO, Op-93G/ejs of 22 June 1961.

15. See for example Op-951/bj1 Ser 091P95 of 17 December 1964, from OpNav to BuShips, in Double Zero File 1966 Box 59, OA, "Support to Development of ASW Ship C2 System and ASW Ship Integrated Combat System (ICS)." The SOR for Engineering Development of the ASW Ship C2 System was in draft, to be ready for 28 December 1964.

16. Naval Sea Systems Command (NAVSEA) issued Technical Development Plan (TDP-S31-18), "Jr. Participating Tactical Data System (JEEP TDS), in June 1967. The "Jeep" system was included in the FY69–74 five-year R&D plan (OA post-1946 Command Files). Papers were written on installations for both *Adams*-class missile destroyers and *Knox*-class frigates. See also "Junior Participating Tactical Data Systems" in *Naval Ordnance Bulletin*, December 1972.

17. The planned SCS system (eight ships planned through FY81) comprised a single-bay UYK-7, five UYA-4 displays, and one Operational Summary Console. There was no provision for Link 4A. The PF (later FFG: fifty ships planned) system comprised a single-bay UYK-7, three UYA-4 displays, and one Operational Summary Console, with space and weight for Link 11 and for a fourth UYA-4 for the LAMPS III helicopter system. The PHM (thirty ships planned) had a radar repeater (SPA-25) as display. Memory space in its UYK-7 fire control computer was reserved for Link 11.

18. The Composite Combat System proposed by Op-954C was intended to use standard hardware and software: UYK-20 computers, NTDS UYA-4 displays, and options for Link 11 and various fire control systems. This system was advertised as requiring fewer personnel and less space and weight than JPTDS. No track capacity was given. Cost depended on which options were selected: $700k to $1.05 million plus about $750k for installation. Alternatives based on UYK-20 were a radar graphics system (with optional Link 11) and a stand-alone version of the SYS-1 automatic radar detector and tracker (and track fusion device): $1 or $1.5 million. Failed alternatives: DATACORTS, developed under the antiship missile defense (ASMD) program (see chapter 12) could handle fifty tracks. It could not support Link 11, but it could accept Link 14 data. It would cost $1 million, but interfaces to various weapons would add considerably more. The simpler alternative was to upgrade a display by adding a memory and a simple computer. The two candidates were MOSC (Modified Operations Summary Console [OSC], fifty-one tracks, designation to all three frigate weapon systems) and the SPA-25 radar display (Applied Physics Lab: thirty-two rate-aided tracks, control of three weapons). MOSC was rejected because of its inherent limitations (calculator used for processing, poor interfaces, limited growth capacity, and high cost when additional systems such as Harpoon and LAMPS were included). It would cost $400,000. APL's SPA-25 derivative would have cost $225,000. It was rejected as a false economy. In December 1973 JPTDS in a DDG was expected to cost $2.1 million (up to $3 million for a more elaborate system). Because so much of the system already existed, $1.5 million of that was for installation. Link 11 equipment cost $900,000 ($400,000 installation), compared to $450,000 for a postulated low-cost link ($200,000 installation).

19. Plans to modernize the rest of the DDGs were revived in the late 1970s. With few new destroyers in prospect, it made sense to add new features: digital radar (SPS-48) and digital gun fire control (the Mk 86 system), plus missile system improvements. Costs rose, so the program shrank: from nineteen ships to ten (FY80–83 programs: DDG-3, 10, 16–22, 24), then to six (DDG-17, 19, 20, 22–24), and ultimately to only three (DDG-19, 20, and 22). Presumably the resumption of missile destroyer building in the 1980s (the *Arleigh Burke* class) made the program far less worthwhile. Remarkably, public accounts of this program never included the four JPTDS ships.

20. Possibly to avoid admitting that the *Perry* class had high-end combat direction, they were credited with a weapons support processor (WSP) and a Weapon Control System (WCS) serving the Mk 92 fire control system, a U.S. version of the Dutch Signaal "egg." Mk 92 in effect replaced the WDS-fire control combination in a DDG. WSP and WCS were interchangeable UYK-7 computers. Early units had no data link, but UYK-7 could be upgraded to provide it. WSP capacity was only sixty-four tracks plus own-ship position (when Link 11 was added, the system could handle another sixty-four remote tracks). If only one computer was operating, capacity fell to ten tracks, and the system could not evaluate threats. Foreign navies that bought *Perry*-class frigates (Australia, Spain, and Taiwan) received versions of this system.

21. Macgillivray, and Switzer, "Canadian Naval Contribution," 82. Mr. Knights "confessed that they agreed on the name of a well known laundry soap as an acronym in order to capitalize on its universal acceptance."

22. Op-55C/jvc, Ser 08P555 of 13 February 1955, in Double Zero Files, Box 1 of 1959 gives a short history of this link in a letter urging the Federal Aviation Administration to adopt it so that FAA centers could control military aircraft. In November 1955 the Joint Services established Military Characteristics (MC) for a two-way air/ground link that could also be used for automatic landing control. Details were agreed to in 1959 and presented to NATO. The Air Force and Navy let contracts for the necessary USC-2 equipment. Link 4 was first installed on board Phantoms when it was tested on board an F-4G squadron in 1965.

23. Link 4A was a time-division multiplexed access (TDMA) system that paired control and reply messages for easy correlation. Control was allotted fourteen microseconds, after which eighteen microseconds was available for a reply before the system switched to another airplane. Unlike the later Link 16, Link 4A did not rely on the timing of these intervals to identify the airplane; each airplane had its own link address (as in Link 11 in NTDS). From its inception in 1962, it was used mainly for all-weather carrier landing, hence was aboard most naval aircraft. However, fighters could accept vectoring information. By 1970 the Link 4A vocabulary included a DROP command for precision bombing. Fleet Computer Programming Center Pacific, "Link 4A Concept of Operations," 4 September 1970 (declassified 1982), intended to encourage the use of Link 4A for antiair and strike warfare, applications inhibited by "the lack of a definitive statement of operational requirements."

24. One-way Link 4A sent commands to an airplane, such as an F-4J, but the airplane reported its status by voice, and voice was sometimes needed to coordinate action. Using two-way Link 4A the F-14A could provide a ship's combat direction system with its twenty-four targets, and it could receive eight from the ship (or an E-2). The airplane reported its position, course, speed, altitude, weapon inventory, and fuel status. The link could assign the F-14A to either the NTDS tracks or the F-14's own tracks. The ship combat direction system correlated NTDS and F-14A tracks. The airplane display included a pointer operated from the ship, to designate a particular target in a voice discussion.

25. Appendix on NTDS problems to draft U.S. Navy Command and Control Master Plan, 5 December 1979 (declassified 6 December 1985). These problems no longer matter: Link 4A survives only for automatic carrier landing.

26. Notes on the U.S. Navy position on Data Links, 1 October 1963, in Double Zero Files 1963 Box 8 (subjects 1000–3128), referring to 24–26 September 1963 meetings of the U.S. Navy Technical Standards Group, and forthcoming NATO meetings: 7–11 October 1963, NATO AC 181 (Long Range Ship ASW Weapons); 3–4 February 1964, NATO AC 182 (Data Systems for Coastal Escorts and Patrol Ships); and 5–7 February 1964, NATO Electronic Data Transmission Party Subgroup 1. Expected Link 11 cost was cut by 80 percent by eliminating excess channels in its four-channel HICAPCOM communications system.

27. The British rejected Link 11 as too costly and because it used "track quality" to decide which ship's data to broadcast. The British initially thought that Link X would be a fifth the cost of Link 11, but as early as 1969 Moore's Law provided aircraft terminals only

twice as expensive as those of Link X. Link 11 set one of eight quality levels based on target range and quality of tracking sensor. A Link 11 unit became responsible for a track if its track quality was two better than that of the previous reporting ship. In Link X the first ship to spot the target retained responsibility. Unlike Link 11, Link X used just two tones, to indicate zeroes and ones. The word was twenty-four bits plus six error-correcting bits. Words were paired to make the system compatible with Link 11. Link X assigned twelve time slots, 0.8 second each, for a 9.6 second cycle (a ship could have multiple slots). Data rate was 1,200 bits/second, so a time slot was thirty-two words, of which six were for synchronization. Nine targets could be transmitted per slot, so the system could handle up to 108 targets (the requirement was 60). Transmitting amplifying information cut capacity to forty-eight targets. By 1970, the British were considering allocating more time slots (at a higher data rate) for the ultrahigh frequency (UHF) version; ultimately, the limit was thirty-one. Nominal range was sixty nautical miles. For longer range, the data rate was halved or quartered or a relay ship used.

Link X was required to operate on all available bands (MF, HF, UHF) using standard communications equipment rather than special radios, but in about 1970 it was used mainly at HF (an Australian commented that its frequency-shift keying and power level were better suited to UHF). Link X tried to limit multipath by using the highest possible frequency within its band, but Link 11 was considered thirty times better in resisting multipath. Initially, Link X carried eight of the original twelve Link 11 messages, omitting M.7, basic characteristics and track number of underwater emissions; M.9, track management (e.g., drop track or cease reporting or change track number); M.10, coordination and control of forces and weapons; and M.11, engagement status of own ship against specific target or status of interceptor under own-ship control. Using Link X, CAAIS used symbols showing the sensor rather than the type of target (as in U.S. NTDS practice). It emphasized track history, which was important in ASW, for example, in distinguishing a submarine from wake echoes. Ten four-minute track histories (points every thirty seconds) or four longer-term histories (up to eight minutes) could be displayed. CAAIS offered symbols for an ASW datum, nonsubs, bombardment data, and so forth. Ferranti won the Link X contract. Details from Royal Australian Navy (RAN) papers on combat direction systems, 1970 (NCDS/14 and /23), compiled when the Australians were investigating alternatives for their light destroyer. They chose the U.S. *Perry* class and NTDS/Link 11. Papers from RANHB.

28. Probably the earliest effort was Teletype Optical Projection System (TOPS) evaluated in 1962–64 on board the carrier *Oriskany* and the missile frigate (DLGN) *Bainbridge*. Information was projected onto a transparent plotting board manned by human plotters. Both ships reported significant improvements in the quantity, timeliness, and accuracy of Link 14 data. A breadboard version of Teletype Integrated Display System (TIDY) was tested by the missile cruiser *Galveston* off Vietnam between 31 October 1968 and 8 January 1969. (It may also have been on board the battleship *New Jersey*.) The NTDS ship providing Link 14 data tracked the TIDY ship; the TIDY ship recognized its own track number and plotted other contacts relative to it. Each Link 14 message generated a pulsing light projected onto the usual vertical plot, where it could be marked with grease pencil. A separate unit showed track number (TN), category/identity, and last cycle time of the Link 14 report of this particular track. The status

board recorder worked from a unit showing this data plus height, course, speed, raid size, engaging track number, and engaging weapon type for the status board recorder. TIDY plotting errors averaged 1 percent, compared to 7 percent for conventional plotting. Manual CIC capacity was eight tracks (updated once per minute). TIDY handled the Link 14 message rate, about twenty-two tracks/minutes. A maximum of thirty-two individual tracks were plotted at this rate without saturating the plot, although display legibility became marginal.

Given such success, a Specific Operational Requirement (SOR 31-45) was issued on 28 November 1969. Presumably in line with abortive plans to install TIDY on non-NTDS ships, a further UYA-15 version was tested in 1972 on board the destroyer *Hoel*, built around a high-capacity data link 5100R minicomputer (8K memory), which accepted, stored, and displayed tracks. Production versions were expected to cost $96,000, about a tenth or a twentieth as much as a full NTDS installation. OpTEVFOR rejected TIDY as an insufficient improvement over manual plotting. OpTEVFOR evaluation of TIDY, 10 May 1973, declassified 31 December 1985. Calculator Link Information System (CLIPS) was tested was tested on board the frigate *Aylwin* (FF 1081) during a March 1978 NATO operation. Its computer fed a CRT; no manual plotting was involved. It could simplify the tactical picture by suppressing some messages (e.g., those reporting aircraft). It offered sufficient accuracy for Harpoon targeting. OpTEVFOR recommended installation on all non-NTDS ships. ECLIPSE seems to have been an improved version.

29. G. A. Welchman, *The Hut Six Story: Breaking the Enigma Codes* (New York: McGraw-Hill, 1982).

30. All versions divided time into slots in a twelve-second cycle ("epoch"). The proposed naval system could accommodate 1,028 users (twelve microsecond slots); the Air Force, up to 1,536 (7.8 microsec slots). However, the Navy could stack 250 users simultaneously, whereas the Air Force allowed only one at a time.

31. The decision to make the program joint badly delayed it. The Joint Operational Requirement (JOR) drafted in 1976 was not approved until 1981. Phase I was the simpler Air Force TDMA version. Phase II, for the mid-1980s or beyond, was the Navy's preferred DTMA (distributed time multiple access, using a signal hopping in frequency and in time, rather than only in frequency). It was ultimately abandoned as too expensive. Initially, technology precluded the production of terminals small enough for fighter aircraft, so although AWACS was fitted with terminals, the fighters it controlled were not.

Chapter 9. Another Path to Automation: Weapons Control

1. TDS Mk 2 (embodying Designation Equipment Mk 1) accepted input from any two search radars, but its main target indication sensors were the long-range SPS-2 and the fast-spinning three-dimensional short-range SPS-3. One radar was selected at a time. Four optical target designators, used to designate low-flying aircraft at short range, had precedence over the radar channels. Because the input radars had narrow beams, the

system did not establish target tracks. It relied on a large vertical plot, using data phoned from CIC, to give target speed, bearing, elevation, and estimated character, on the basis of which targets were prioritized (predesignated). Close-in radar video also appeared on a fifteen-inch summary CRT. Within the system, radar video was converted into color television video. That made it possible to show the six elevation sectors covered by SPS-3 and also to mix images. Each operator waited for his predesignated target to appear on the short-range CRT, then entered target range and bearing into the system by joystick; the position was confirmed by the appearance of his own electronic marker (circle, square, etc.) over its blip (matching target color entered elevation into the system). As an aid to director assignment, an overlay on the summary CRT showed an outline of the ship, with sectors marked to show which directors were preferred for which sectors. A servo rotated the overlay so that it was always properly lined up. (the CRT, like other radar scopes, was lined up with due North.) The operator selected the preferred director as indicated by the overlay. When an operator assigned a director to his target (by joystick), the director's number appeared, flashing when the director was assigned, and flashing faster when it acquired the target; until then the operator kept his symbol on the moving blip.

The designation officer monitored this operation. The supervisor could move his own symbol across the screens by joystick, and he had a video plotter with a ten-inch screen and a plastic overlay over a video camera. Whatever he wrote on the overlay appeared on the ten-inch screen—and on all the other screens in the system. This kind of video mixing was then being considered for other CIC automation projects. Analog devices converted voltages from the operator panels into coordinates for the directors and added stabilization data. Weapon assignment was manual. OP 2003 (Preliminary) for TDS Mk 2-0, NARA RG 74. In effect, this system further mechanized what was done in simpler versions like TDS Mk 1 on a destroyer: operators with joysticks designated targets directly from a PPI on a special console. Each operator was assigned to one director. TDS Mk 3 sought to automate both target evaluation and weapon assignment. Target priority was based on threat level (time to close the ship, suggesting that this version took account of target speed, presumably maintaining dead-reckoning target channels). Director assignment was based on threat level, availability of director, and director arc. A second-stage evaluator chose the particular guns assigned to the directors and decided when guns should shift to other targets. By 1950 the main development problem was a tendency to oscillate between two targets without opening fire on either. Cdr. N. E. Thomas (Op-344), "A.A. Guns and Their F.C. Systems," OpNav "Fleet Air Defense." According to Thomas, Mk 1 could handle two to four directors (fire channels), Mk 2 could handle more than four, and Mk 3 more than twelve. He rated Mk 3 more than five times as effective as Mk 1, with a sixth the target handling delay, but only twice as complex (which seems far too optimistic).

2. Mk 3 tests began on 15 March 1954. Once a target had been selected, it took the system less than two seconds to assign a gun to it. The system was hampered by the short range of the SPS-3 radar (about 22,000 yards). Preliminary results included a 300 percent improvement in the number of targets effectively covered by the ship's guns. *Combat Readiness* 3, no. 1 (January–March 1955): 6–8.

3. WDE Mk 4, the core of the *Leahy*-class Weapon Direction System Mk 7, was typical. It had one console (for target selection) in the CIC display and decision area. Another seven consoles were located in the adjacent CIC weapon control area: three target tracking consoles (one with target allocation and channel selection panels) with a height console alongside opposite a director assignment console flanked by two weapon assignment consoles. The target selection operator detected and selected targets for tracking and assigned channels to the most threatening targets. His screen showed search radar video. When he decided that a blip represented a potential target, he assigned one of eight channels (and one of three tracking consoles) to it. Each of three trackers entered successive sets of target coordinates into the channel so that the system could measure rates and begin to dead reckon. The operator continued to monitor the channel to make sure that the system was properly tracking. The target selection panels (at the target assignment console and at one of the target tracking consoles) showed missile-in-flight lamps, altitude, and had missile self-destruct buttons. The director console assignment operator evaluated targets and assigned directors; he could also accept target data from one of the four missile directors. Assigning a director released a channel. Its symbols were removed from the display, and its busy lamp went out, so that the channel was freed for a new target. Targets being tracked by directors were indicated by their number symbols (as in TDS Mk 2). The target selection and target tracking consoles could control an arrow to indicate a particular target to other operators, for example, for height data. OP 2717 (15 February 1963), NARA RG 74.

4. Capt. L. J. Stecher, Jr. (CO of the cruiser *Columbus*), "Poor Man's Tactical Data System," *Combat Readiness* 15, no. 2 (April–June 1967): 18–21.

5. Terrier was initially command guided by beam riding. Tartar was semiactive from the beginning. Both missiles had to be guided from the moment of launch; the number of directors on the ship set the number of air defense channels.

6. The first was Bell Labs' 1953–55 Naval Interceptor Program Study to determine the optimum fire-control system for an interceptor. It commented that a subsonic aircraft carrying high-performance missiles might have advantages worthy of further study. It also recommended using a pulse-Doppler radar to overcome low-altitude clutter. On this basis, BuAer bought the APQ-81 pulse-Doppler radar. Follow-ons included "Piloted Fighter Weapons System Providing Outer Perimeter Fleet Air Defense" (OPFAD), completed in September 1956 by the Air Warfare Department of the Naval Air Development Center (NADC). It compared a subsonic fighter equipped with an APQ-81 and with long-range air-breathing semiactive missiles (i.e., capable of engaging one target at a time) to a supersonic fighter (faster than the Phantom then about to fly) armed with missiles better than its Sparrow III. The subsonic fighter was rated two to four times as effective against a Mach 2 threat flying at high altitudes and against medium-altitude Mach 0.9 and low-altitude Mach 1.0 raids. It would be easier for a carrier to operate because its cycle time would be longer, it would burn less fuel, and it would be easier to control. Cornell Aeronautical Laboratory's "Study of Fighter System Requirements for Task Force Air Defense" compared the subsonic fighter with two versions of the Phantom, with a vertical takeoff or landing (VTOL) fighter (which could be widely dispersed within the fleet), and with CAL's "Bogey Buster," an airborne early warning airplane carrying twelve thirty-nautical-mile missiles. CAL liked Bogey Buster

best, but Grumman showed that its radar could not yet be built and that it was so heavy that carrier operation would be marginal. That left the subsonic fighter. A further BuAer Research Division Research Analysis of Fleet Air Defense (RAFAD), completed in July 1958, examined a spectrum of fourteen aircraft, ranging from subsonic to Mach 2.2, from 39,000 to 85,000 pounds gross, all using APQ-81. It showed that a subsonic fighter with long-range high-performance missiles was best. Eagle-Missileer development plan in the Double Zero file, OA, folder 3010/2 for Developments (Weapon Systems) 1-1-60/6-30-60. The studies of subsonic fighters are listed in "Project Report for Advanced Air to Air Missile Aircraft," dated 1 November 1958, referring to project approved 7 December 1957, in NAVAIR History F6D (Missileer) file. There were also North American's "The Effect of Supersonic Fighters on the Problem of Fleet Defense" (27 December 1956), and Sperry Gyroscope's "Fleet Air Defense Systems" (8 January 1957). Bids for the fighter were requested 11 December 1959, Douglas being selected on 24 May 1960.

7. Once Aegis was mature enough for installation, it faced a cost barrier: by law, absent a waiver, any U.S. warship displacing over eight thousand tons had to be nuclear powered. Unable to afford numerous nuclear ships, CNO Elmo Zumwalt Jr. ordered Aegis squeezed into a five thousand to seven thousand-ton DG/Aegis. It failed. Aegis went to sea because, probably at the suggestion of Rear Adm. Wayne E. Meyer, the head of the program, it turned out that the system could be shoehorned into a modified *Spruance*, to produce the current *Ticonderoga* class.

8. The "New Threat" was the much faster Backfire bombers carrying standoff missiles. In 1974 the assistant secretary of defense for research and engineering requested a study to see whether the Tartar/Terrier system could be further improved, probably as an alternative to Aegis, which was then in trouble because no affordable yet effective platform was in prospect. Simply upgrading the existing command system bought a great deal. New Threat Upgrade (NTU) was briefed to the Navy in 1976. MarionOliver, "Terrier/ Tartar: Pacing the Threat," *Johns Hopkins APL Technical Digest* 2, no. 4 (October–December 1981): 259.

9. In a 2001 All Services Combat Identification Evaluation Team (ASCIET) test, a CEC net created 1.06 tracks per object, compared to 1.35 for Link 16 and 1.5 for Link 11.

10. When a unit loses track, instead of dead reckoning or coasting it, CEC continues the track using data from other units. To limit false alarms, radars normally do not declare a target valid unless its strength exceeds some threshold. However, a radar can declare a signal below its own threshold a valid target if it appears to be on a track already known to the net. It can try to confirm that by turning up power and sensitivity only around the area indicated by the track.

11. New engagement modes were cued (sensors on the firing ship are cued by remote data against longer-range targets); Aegis Engage on Remote (EOR, another SPY-1 or NTU FCS radar provides target tracking data to an Aegis C&D/WCS); NTU Engage on Composite (EOC, another SPS-48, SPG-51, or SPY-1 is tracking source); remote vertical launching system (VLS) launch (the Aegis control ship controls a missile fired by another ship from prelaunch to in-flight control); and Forward Pass (another ship takes over missile control either during midcourse or during transition to terminal

guidance). CEC made non-Aegis ships spare magazines for Aegis ships. It also extended the effective horizon of a ship such as an LHD or a carrier firing short-range defensive weapons.

12. CEC was Phase III of the Battle Group Antiair Warfare (AAW) Coordination (BGAAWC) program. Phase I sought to solve the long-standing common grid (gridlock) problem; without good gridlock, ships cannot use one another's data. A surface-gridlock system was installed on board the *Ticonderoga* class. Air gridlock was demonstrated in the *Vinson* battle group, and Aegis autogridlock technology was transferred to non-Aegis ships. BGAAWC Phase II concerned force-control items to place weapons on target, for example, improved gridlock using Global Position System (GPS) satellites and improved Aegis displays.

13. Initially each ship sweeps its array antenna to link with the two closest CEC ships. Once linked, all simultaneously switch to identical (individually generated) schedules, indicating which unit communicates with which in any multimicrosecond time frame (cesium clocks maintain the schedule on a microsecond scale). Each "dumb" CEC node passes on whatever data it receives. The resulting duplication limits how many units can participate in a net to about twenty. Those who had developed CEC proposed Solipsys' Tactical Component Network (TCN) about fifteen years later. Its "smart" nodes edit data flow, based partly on seeking changes from what dead reckoning would predict. At government behest, Solipsys set up a TCN-based air tracking system to support domestic air defense immediately after the 11 September 2001 attacks. It was valued for its ability to spot unexpected events, such as diversion of airliners from their projected flight plans. Three mobile sites were in service within a day. The Navy tested TCN as a possible low-bandwidth tactical data link but did not abandon CEC because integrating and validating a new system would have taken too much time and effort.

14. The typical prenuclear submarine form of Target Motion Analysis (TMA) was a strip (navigational) plot, in which a series of bearings was plotted at regular intervals. If both own submarine and target were moving at constant speed along constant courses, the bearing lines would cut the target's course at regular intervals. A plastic strip could be maneuvered until regular marks matched, indicating target course. However, the target could be faster or slower, corresponding to shorter or longer range. This ambiguity was typically resolved by turning the submarine to take a new series of bearings. If the strip still worked, the solution was correct. Otherwise the solution would break up. The slower the submarine, the more laborious the process, as target bearing would change slowly.

15. "Fire Control System Mk 113 Mods 1 and 2" in *Naval Weapons Bulletin*, 1–63. The version on board *Thresher* was changed from Mod 1 to Mod 0 when odd numbers were reserved for ballistic missile submarines. The main TMA mode was CHURN, a matrix solution using four target bearings (the submarine maneuvered between taking two of them). It could also solve using one or more range inputs (one range and three bearings or two ranges and two bearings). The computer could also calculate target course and speed based on bearings plus an operator's target speed estimate. As in NTDS, an operator at a Mk 51 analyzer entered sonar data into the computer by placing a cursor on a sonar blip. He could also assign an analog tracker to a target. Each operator handled

a single target. Operators also evaluated generated solutions on their analyzer screens. Mk 130 had only 4,000 words of memory, operating at 25 KOPS for addition or logical operations or 2.5 KOPS for multiplication or division. Such speeds may have been acceptable because the maximum speed of a ship or submarine was less than a tenth the speed of an airplane. The Mk 113 Mod 0 prototype in *Thresher* had four Mk 51s, but the Mod 2 in *Permit-* and *Sturgeon*-class submarines had only two. Target solutions were passed to the two analog Mk 75 attack directors, which set torpedoes or passed data to the SUBROC computer. Like the old Torpedo Data Computer, a Mk 75 could dead reckon (position keep) a target, so in theory a Mod 2 could handle three targets simultaneously. Mod 0 also had a Mk 50 summary display CRT showing all four targets, that is, providing situational awareness. Little-used, it was deleted as a space-waster in later versions. Given two Mk 75s, a Mk 113 fire-control system could engage two targets simultaneously. Mk 113 Mod 3 was an abortive version (using the Mk 130 computer) for later ballistic missile submarines of the SSBN616/640 class. Mod 4 was an abortive two-target attack submarine version. Ballistic missile submarines time-shared their Mk 84 ballistic computers with their fire-control systems in the Mod 5 version, but attack submarines continued to use the Mk 130 computer in the Mod 6 version (Mod 2 adapted, like the strategic submarines' Mod 7, to the Mk 48 digital torpedo). Mod 8, the final Mk 130 version in later *Sturgeon*-class submarines, reverted to four analyzers. It had a more powerful Mod 1 computer that corrected sonar data by estimating the acoustic path.

16. Feasibility studies of a long-range acoustic link were ordered in June 1953, and an Operational Requirement was issued in October 1955. They were intended to support cooperative antisubmarine submarines (SSK) operations. Thus "Use of Underwater Telephone," *Combat Readiness* (March–April 1953) described coordination between the submarines *Ronquil* and *Volador* at ranges of up to 38,000 yards, about 20 nautical miles. The sophistication of the devices brought to the test stage indicates the perceived importance of netting in ASW. In 1962 the main competitors were SESCO (Secure Submarine Communications) and SPUME (Short Pulse Message). SPUME sent eight short high-powered broadband (100 kHz) pulses with six-tone modulation omnidirectionally. Like many Russian systems of this era, it could measure distances between transmitter and receiver. Messages received at twenty-nautical mile range were too distorted to recognize. The lower frequency SESCO (1.5–2.5 versus 2–5 kHz) sent its pulses slowly (as in HF radio) to overcome multipath distortion, using a three-level code. Detection used the LOFAR technique used to detect submarines. The system achieved its advertised hundred-nautical mile range, but it suffered badly from multipath and was too easy for enemy submarines to detect. Reportedly, both systems relied heavily on synchronized timing, beyond the capacity of existing clocks. The programs died after *Thresher* was lost with the prototypes on board. Their collapse was evident in how quickly documents involved were declassified. The U.S. Navy again tried to develop an acoustic data link in the late 1970s (using UYK-20 computers). Development finally succeeded in the late 1990s, when there was finally enough computer power to overcome the complicated changing multipath distortions because of the sea. It inspired the Manta unmanned underwater vehicle (UUV) proposed by the U.S. Naval Underwater Center (NUWC).

17. According to the in-house history of the main Russian sonar developer, Morphizpribor, all integrated Soviet submarine sonar systems incorporated acoustic links. The Russians first became intensely interested in underwater communications when they tried to set up coastal sonar systems, for example, for harbor defense, in the 1940s. Soviet submarine communication was audible throughout the world's oceans by the 1970s. Different systems were given NATO nicknames.

18. Submarine Integrated Control (SUBIC), begun in 1958, was the basic computerization effort. Its reports covered such topics as the Digital Multibeam System (DIMUS) sonars, digital fire control, and displays providing better situational awareness so that a ballistic missile submarine could better evade detection. SUBIC sponsored the CONALOG (CONtact AnaLOG) and the Submarine Quickened Response (SQUIRE) maneuvering aids (CONALOG was the "road in the sea" display, which notoriously put helmsmen to sleep). Fast-Reaction Submarine Control (FRISCO) was also concerned with submarine control. It was redirected about 1964 to emphasize near-term improvements and was cut back during 1965. The Combined System Electronic Design (CSED) electronic "work study" program was intended to improve ships' command and control performance through changes in system configuration.

19. The situation late in 1965 is described in Planning Research Corporation (PRC), "Submarine Data Processing Applications and Current State-of-the-Art Capabilities," PRC-R-658 prepared for BuShips, dated 1 December 1965, in NARA, RG 344, Box 1. This report was part of the FRISCO project. The writers considered their objectives similar to those of the A-NEW aircraft project that produced the P-3C. A single central computer (or computer complex) could deal with navigation (including automatic calculation of SINS updates), steering (including automatic stabilization), communications/message handling (including automatic radio frequency control), fire-control/situational awareness, sonar processing, and submarine safety monitoring. The computer could perform sonar processing not normally carried out at all, or else handled only by special-purpose equipment, such as target classification, measurement of sonar performance, measurement of sonar data quality, sonar range prediction, propagation error correction, and sound velocity calculation; it might also automatically calculate target range and bearing using the PUFFS system of multiple arrays. Unlike RCA, PRC envisaged merging TMA and other fire-control calculations with overall situational awareness, much as later happened in the Mk 117 system. A single computer system was far better than a mass of separate specialized units because responsibilities for different functions would overlap so extensively that the separate computers would have to communicate masses of data. Their data standards might well be incompatible, errors would be introduced, and the sheer mass of electronic equipment might be unacceptable.

20. NARA, RG 344; one was marked "the attached CO displays look about as good as any I've seen" (19 August 1966). Arma's work was based on the submarine monitoring system it developed for the experimental deep-diving *Dolphin*. Thus it envisaged two own-ship monitoring displays plus a third showing the geographic situation plus essential own-ship data, such as speed and keel depth.

21. Delays in adopting computer control are often blamed on Adm. Hyman G. Rickover and on the general conservatism of submarine officers. Rickover rejected automation of nuclear power plants, on the grounds that flexible humans would more likely avert disaster. Similarly, the U.S. Navy rejected one-man control (as other navies did) and X-sterns (which reduce stern plane area, hence drag, but require a computer). Admiral Rickover is probably best seen as standard-bearer for submarine officers, acutely aware that a computer problem could easily kill them. The *Los Angeles* class adopted a computer complex for all noncontrol and nonpropulsion functions.

22. The digital system in *Thresher* had been conceived to some extent for this purpose, but the idea lapsed in the U.S. Navy. It was pressed aggressively by the Royal Navy, with which the U.S. Navy had close relations. Thus an RCA paper (1966) referred to British escort trials using HMS *Dreadnought*. The direct support mission was explicit in 1966 AGSSN command and control documents. At least some of the contractor reports on the electronic requirements of the escort mission are in NARA, RG 344, Entry S11.

23. Admiral Rickover first proposed shifting to a destroyer reactor in November 1963 (for FY67 and later submarines). The following April he ordered preliminary studies from Electric Boat, and in July he presented the idea to Rear Adm. Eugene Wilkinson, director of the OpNav submarine branch, and thus in charge of future submarine design. In September OpNav ordered BuShips to produce preliminary designs. That took about a year. Attention then moved to sonar and command and control. Meanwhile, Secretary of Defense Robert S. McNamara announced that all new projects should be preceded by trade-off studies called concept formulations (CONFORM). Although his motive seems to have been to delay or kill expensive projects, CONFORM seemed to participants to be a more rational way of developing new designs. The AGSSN (i.e., experimental prototype) designation was adopted in 1966 (as in an FY68 design study completed that March) as protective coloration (experimental designs were exempt from CONFORM). Formal CONFORM studies began in August 1966, and at one point Rickover had to agree in writing that his AGSSN would be followed (probably in FY71) by whatever submarine CONFORM recommended.

24. RCA Service Company, "AGSSN Escort Operations Command Control Electronic Systems Design Requirements Study Report," dated 21 February 1966, based on three 1971 scenarios: direct support of a carrier battle group, operation with a hunter-killer (CVS-centered) task group, and convoy support. Direct support required quick (hence computer-assisted) decisions: a twenty-eight-knot battle group might close a twenty-five-knot enemy SSN at fifty-three knots. To cope with high speeds of advance, RCA envisaged sprint-and-drift tactics, the AGSSN using her active sonar at maximum speed (given as thirty-three knots; the best any U.S. submarine had yet done was four thousand yards at thirty knots by USS *Scorpion*). The twelve-target capacity in the report was derived from that of the projected new sonar. A March 1966 review by Sanders (now BAE Sanders), which had more experience in submarine warfare, showed that RCA's estimate of sonar performance was overoptimistic. For example, that the system was expected to classify targets within two minutes and complete a fire-control solution within three. At maximum direct-path range (fifteen nautical miles), a ping would take thirty-seven seconds to go back and forth: two minutes meant four pings. At maximum bottom-bounce range, given as fifty nautical miles (which seems excessive), only two

pings (two bits of data) would be available. Classification was typically based either on target Doppler or on the use of multiple short pings to establish target angle (a concept called the acoustic short-pulse echo classification technique [ASPECT]). The single long pings needed for long range seemed to offer neither possibility. Hence the more complex pings of modern sonars.

25. RCA envisaged using a modified NTDS console, which could be supplemented by totes giving numerical data. In addition to the usual NTDS data on the overall situation, RCA wanted the single display to provide the CO with own-ship data like heading, speed, and depth, which would otherwise appear on dials in the ship's attack center. Thus, the CO could concentrate on the tactical situation, instead of scanning the attack center. Much the same argument justifies heads-up and other integrated displays in tactical aircraft. Other additional functions included rapid means of evaluating the target and determining kill and survival probabilities. RCA proposed using television to provide the CO with the periscope picture and also with a view of the (sonar) bearing-time recorder. The Mk 113 fire-control system in the existing *Sturgeon* class could solve the TMA problem, as long as the target did not zigzag, but the manual plot (the CO's only means of maintaining situational awareness) was slow and ill-adapted to multiple targets. "Commanding Officer's Tactical Display Study AGSSN," dated 30 June 1966, in RG 344.

26. Solution time depended on how fast bearing rates were changing, which often meant how close the target was. The only way to obtain instant passive solutions was triangulation, using arrays spaced down the side of the submarine. In the 1980s the U.S. Navy introduced a new Wide Aperture Array (WAA) for this purpose. At long ranges (e.g., bottom-bounce or convergence zone) its main virtue was that it could give much more precise bearings for TMA.

27. MATE was devised at Naval Underwater Ordnance Station Newport by a group headed by Earl Messere, beginning in 1965. John Merrill and Lionel D. Wyld, *Meeting the Submarine Challenge: A Short History of the Naval Underwater Systems Center* (Washington, D.C.: GPO, 1997), 105–6. The prototype was developed by Joseph DiRuzzo (who went to sea as test operator) and his supervisor, Herbert W. Headle. It went to sea to support SUBASWEX 2-68. When the sea test was analyzed (1969–71), it became clear that MATE solutions were consistently closer to true target position than solutions using other TMA techniques. Additional TMA modes were then added: Endpoint (using only two parameters instead of the usual three [range, course, speed]) and Set Speed (using a speed taken from a turn count, then adjusting only one parameter). MATE was expanded to include FLIT (frequency line integration tracking) data in 1974–75 and towed array data in 1978–81, and multiple sensor inputs (including bearings, conical angles, depression/elevation, inverse ranges, and frequency) in 1981–85. A later development was a Parameter Evaluation Plot (PEP), which could generate and evaluate alternative solutions. In the ballistic missile submarines, MATE required about two thousand lines of computer code. Information courtesy of Pat Clayton of NUWC, via Ernest Correia of NUWC. MATE was associated with the effort to develop the new (digital) Submarine Sonar/Fire Control System (TDP S 23-26). As of 1966 it was expected to track twelve targets simultaneously (four times existing capacity). Digitized submarines did much better because connecting a digital sonar to what amounted to

NTDS would move the track-while-scan burden to the system memory, or else set up categories of more- and less-precisely tracked targets (tracked inside the sonar or in the larger command system). The 1966 development plan called for a prototype in FY74–75 and a production version in FY77–78.

28. The first Polaris submarines had no missile fire-control computers, instead carrying punched cards giving corrections corresponding to the submarine's planned patrol area. For Polaris A3, which operated over a much wider patrol area, submarines were fitted with a Mk 84 digital geoballistic computer intended to produce such cards en route to the patrol area. It also replaced the Mk 130 computer in these submarines' Mk 113 Mod 5, the first U.S. submarine fire-control system to use a programmable general-purpose digital computer. Computer memory and precision were valued for bearings-only TMA conducted over a protracted period. Mod 5 had only one Mk 51 analyzer, so it was a track one, fire one system. "Fire Control System Mk 113 Mod 5" in *Naval Weapons Bulletin*, 1–65, and "Rearrangement of Fire Control System Mk 113 Mod 5 Equipment (ORDALT 6538)" in *Naval Ordnance Bulletin*, 4–67. Mod 7 was Mod 5 adapted to fire the Mk 48 torpedo. Once Mod 9 succeeded, NUSC modified Mod 7 to conduct MATE on a single target. A 1971 Mod 7 manual in the Navy Department Library (1971) describes single-target MATE.

29. This potential seems not to have been realized. Ballistic missile submarines typically tracked and engaged one target at a time. Alternative display modes of the single sixteen-inch circular CRT of the Mk 78 analyzer (in effect, the sole computer display) were MATE, CHURN, time-bearing plot (TBP), and situation display (SIT). TBP was a smoothed plot of bearing versus time (waterfall) for single target, and SIT was a geographical (PPI-like) plot of two contacts. Thus, Mod 9 did not exploit the situational awareness potential inherent in MATE. It was not considered reliable enough to provide a TMA solution on a second target (its stacks of dots often tipped over, for example). The first Poseidon conversion was USS *James Madison*, completed 28 June 1970. Mod 9 was first installed on board USS *Stonewall Jackson* (SSBN 634), modernization completed 29 October 1971. Mod 9 was accepted for service in 1972.

30. Mk 81 modes included MATE, multitarget tracking, multimode tracking, data storage and evaluation, weapon attack evaluation, generation of computer-recommended presets, and a PPI-like geographical display of all the system tracks. The traditional dials, indicating the progress of a fire-control solution, could be represented in video form.

31. The three analog trackers of BQQ-2 gave way to eight trackers (five digital plus three analog) in the initial BQQ-5. A tracker produced a steady stream of bearings, typically once every fifteen seconds. A Mk 117 operator applied MATE to such a string, then shifted its tracker to a new contact while the computer dead-reckoned the first (which would later be cycled back to a tracker). In this way Mk 117 could handle up to two dozen contacts. The analog trackers were dropped in BQQ-5A or -5B, and the total number of trackers doubled. BQQ-5C had enough memory to handle 200 to 250 contacts.

Chapter 10. Spreading CIC Automation

1. DCA used two consoles and CAAIS rather than ADA software, but it was always described as ADA for submarines. It is not clear whether it had a summary display.

2. Plans initially called for a single class of simplified destroyers that could be armed with either Sea Dart (Type 42) or Ikara (Type 17); later the Ikara destroyer was abandoned in favor of modifying existing *Leander*-class frigates. Both ships, as well as the later Harrier carriers (*Invincible* class), were given versions of ADAWS.

3. Development of further versions of ADAWS was simplified because the software was modular. Mk 7 (1988) added a data link processor (full Link 4 and Link 11 capacity) and a captain's console. Mk 8 added an interface to a new digital Type 2016 sonar. Mk 12 was a major ADAWS improvement program. Mks 9 and 11 were probably reserved for new Type 43 and Type 44 AAW destroyers conceived in the late 1970s. Mk 10 was a modernized carrier version.

4. Compared to NTDS, as envisaged in 1967, CAAIS handled fewer tracks (sixty, including twenty autotracks) over a smaller area (48 x 48 rather than 512 x 512 nautical miles).

5. The British tried but failed to sell CAAIS to NATO, presenting it at Brussels in November 1967, and demonstrating a prototype off Zeebrugge on board HMS *Wakeful*. On a cruise ending 27 November 1967, the crew of *Wakeful* showed the system to the Belgian, Danish, French, Norwegian, and Swedish navies. As of October 1968 other navies that had either requested or received demonstrations were the Argentine, Royal Australian (twice, in connection with the abortive RN/RAN frigate that became Type 21), Canadian, German, Indian, Italian, Royal New Zealand, Pakistani, Portuguese, South African, Turkish, and U.S.

    Roughly in parallel, Ferranti, Elliott, and Decca began a private-venture system for the new Vosper Thornycroft export frigates. It used much the same hardware but some proprietary software. Confusingly, it was also called CAAIS. The first went to sea on board the Argentine carrier *25 de Mayo* (the Argentines wanted compatibility with the ADAWS/Link Y on board their Type 42 destroyers).

6. The digital weapon control system of the Type 21 frigate was called Weapon System Automation (WSA) 4. Marconi's Sapphire digital fire-control system was an export version. The company developed it further into a "mini Action Information Organization (AIO)" for Egyptian October-class missile boats. The operator could track and allocate four targets. A second (identical) display alongside the surface display controlled the Otomat missile. Further systems were sold under the Ferranti name because that company provided the FM 1600 series computer (as in British naval systems) and the necessary software. Marconi provided the radars.

    The first export versions were WSA 401, 402, and 403 in the Brazilian *Niteroi* class (with commercial CAAIS), which could be considered export derivatives of the Type 21 frigate. There was apparently no WSA 410 series. The simple WSA 421 is in the Brazilian *Inhauma* class, with a CAAIS. WSA 422 equipped the Egyptian *Ramadan* class; with a CAAIS, it equipped the Kenyan *Nyayo* and the Omani *Al Sharquiyah* (her sisters have

9LV300-series systems). WSA 422 could handle as many as sixty tracks (the weapon director typically handled ten to twelve; CAAIS capacity was 120 tracks, 100 of them automatic). South Korea bought CAAIS and WSA 423 for later *Ulsan*-class frigates and for later KCX-class frigates, and the systems were license-made in South Korea. Chile apparently bought at least the WSA element of the system to upgrade *Almirante Williams*–class destroyers. Separating weapon control from the tactical data system made it relatively simple to add Seawolf self-defense missile to some *Leander*-class frigates. Using a separate computer, the Seawolf element was fed by the Type 967 radar. It could pass up to forty tracks back to the ship's CAAIS.

7. The logic of the advanced radar and the associated computer system is put in a 6 November 1959 report to the Conseil Superieure de la Marine, the advisory council for the minister, in 3BB8/CSH12, SHM. The existing combination of 2-D and 3-D radar (DRBV22C, DRBI 10) was considered sufficient to guide Masurca I against Mach 1.5 targets, and a carrier interceptor (Etendard) against a Mach 1 target under simple conditions, with two or three targets, at limited range (seventy nautical miles) and limited angles of approach (0 to 15 degrees). Data rate was slow (2.5 revolutions per minute [rpm] for DRBI 10), and the combination would have limited resistance to ECM. The French considered such limits inadequate for a ship entering service after 1966. The proposed DRBI 23 could reach out to 150 nautical miles and 70,000 feet in altitude, it could resist jamming by varying its frequency, and it offered a much better data rate (6 to 10 rpm). The combination of the new radar and a computer would make it possible to engage the high- and medium-altitude Mach 2 to Mach 3 targets to be expected in 1965–70.

8. Alain Denis, "L'Aventure des Systemes Informatieses de Commandement Dans La Marine Nationale," 14, in *Les Systemes d'Information et de Commandement 1955–1975: Actes du colloque organise le 29 Mars 2001 a l'Ecole militaire* (Paris: Lavauzelle, 2002).

9. SENIT 4, begun early in 1969 for the carrier *Clemenceau*, switched to a French IRIS 55M computer. This system was modular; a down-rated version equipped *Georges Leygues* (F70) –class frigates.

10. Vega I and II were both offered in two-computer versions, the second computer maintaining a tactical picture and displaying it on a digital table. Vega I used the hybrid BCH (*Bloc Calcul Hybride*: analog ballistics but digital track-keeping). The single-computer version was effectively an export version of the standard French navy CTH fire-control system. It could carry six air or surface tracks, one sonar track, and one electronic support measures (ESM) strobe. It could handle two gunnery targets simultaneously. The two-computer version (sixteen tracks in the tactical table) may have equipped Portuguese *Baptiste de Andrade*–class frigates.

Vega II used CDI (the designation simply advanced by one letter over BCH), with hardwired digital ballistics. The single-computer Vega II could handle sixteen tracks. The two-computer version could handle another sixteen to sixty-four (typically thirty-two). Versions equipped Exocet-firing missile boats sold to Greece, Iran, Libya, Nigeria, Peru, Qatar, and Tunisia. At least some had the two-computer version. Vega II/83 (German-built *Almirante Padilla*–class frigates for Colombia) used Vega II computers. It seems unlikely that any of these versions incorporated a data link.

Vega was scaled up to become a full frigate combat direction system, Tavitac (Traitement Automatique et Visualization Tactique) or Vega III. It used the fully programmable IRIS 15M, in the same series as that in SENIT 4. It could handle up to 128 tracks and could automatically evaluate air threats and engage air targets. Vega IIIC, sold to Saudi Arabia (*Al Madinah* class), incorporated Link W (named for the SaWari program under which the Saudi ships were built), an unlicensed French adaptation of Link 11. It was intended mainly to support Otomat antiship missile targeting. Vega III was probably also sold to China. In 1976 the French navy announced that it would adopt Tavitac for its new A69-class corvettes as SENIT 5, but that never happened.

11. The agreement to buy the destroyers was concluded 11 May 1964, and the contract was signed 1 April 1965. The Germans withdrew from the SENIT program in 1967.

12. The first Chinese SADOC 2, designated ZKJ-1, was installed on board the Luda-class destroyer *Hefei* in January 1984, an imported Italian equivalent going aboard the destroyer *Dalien*. A frigate version went aboard the first Jiangwei III-class frigate, *Huangshi*, in April 1986. This and related systems equip other Chinese destroyers and frigates and also the four Thai *Chao Praya*–class frigates built in China. The Indian equivalent, known by its Italian IPN-10 export designation, was widely installed on board Indian warships, including the now-defunct carrier *Vikrant*, *Godavari*-class frigates, and missile corvettes. Link 11 was not exportable outside NATO, and Italy produced no equivalent of the Anglo-Dutch Link X/Y, so the export version never incorporated a data link. That seems not to have been a sales liability.

13. Macgillivray and Switzer, "Canadian Naval Contribution," 83.

14. Boslaugh, *When Computers Went to Sea*, 334.

15. Eight ships, somewhat smaller than contemporary U.S. DEGs (398 x 46 vs 415 x 43 ft, 3,300 tons), were included in the projected 1963 program. Into this smaller hull would have been squeezed much more than in a DEG: one twin five-inch/thirty-eight-mount (Signaal M26 fire-control system), one Mk 22 missile launcher (sixteen Tartars with two Mk 74 directors), two Sea Mauler short-range launchers (seventy-two missiles), two triple Mk 32 torpedo tubes, and a single Limbo mortar (sixty projectiles). There would also be a U.S.-type light helicopter (the primary ASW standoff weapon). Complement was given as 236, compared to 246 for the nonautomated U.S. DEG with a comparable missile battery. Estimated cost was $34.25 million. The Canadians adopted the Tartar missile in hopes that the U.S. Navy would develop the projected ASW version of the missile (then unfunded), to carry either a homing torpedo or a depth bomb. Where the U.S. Navy relied on a massive bow-mounted low frequency sonar (SQS-26), the Canadians held to medium-frequency sets but included a variable-depth sonar aft, which would have made processing at least as complex. An unusual feature was a requirement to support two hundred troops for up to fifteen days. The design emphasized human engineering, automation (she could steam with her machinery spaces unmanned), and centralized command/control. Much of the equipment had not yet been developed. Memo for the (U.S.) CNO, Op-42/1m, Ser 0558P42, in Double Zero Files, 9000 series, Box 10 of 1962, OA.

16. The Action Information System was called AIS-240. In April 1963 the Canadian navy let a design contract to Canadian Westinghouse. Much of the work was done by Westinghouse in Baltimore. Given its very small complement and its ASW mission, the hydrofoil was much like a patrol aircraft. During the winter and spring of 1964, Canadian programmers working at NEL on the A-NEW automated ASW airplane became increasingly involved in the program. AIS-240 could handle sixty-four tracks plus consort tracks, using Links 11 and 14. It could remotely control the craft's sensors and weapons. The system used three NTDS displays but a new Westinghouse twenty-four-bit computer (16,000 word memory, about half as many as in the standard NTDS computer, each word slightly more than half as long as an NTDS word). The computer arrived late and had nothing like enough capacity (65,000 words operational program), so software had to be read off the system disk as the system ran. The novelty of this programming added more delays.

By the time the command system was ready, the hydrofoil escort program was dying However, the Canadian navy was already deeply involved in two more command system programs, one for a new escort (which became the DDE 280 "Tribal" class) and an abortive one for the midlife update of the existing *Restigouche* class. In November 1967 AIS-240 was chosen as the tactical direction system training aid that would clearly be needed. On 4 July 1968 it was formally accepted as the Marine Tactical Data System (MARTADS) trainer.

17. Sensor, Weapon, Control (SEWACO) II (ordered 1975), for the Dutch version of the "standard frigate," is probably much the version in the Argentine *Almirante Brown* and Nigerian *Aradu* classes (both MEKO 360s). No SEWACO III was announced. SEWACO IV was ordered in 1974 for the Belgian *Weilingen*-class frigates. (SEWACO MA in the Malaysian FS 1500 class may have been similar.) SEWACO V was ordered in 1976 for the midlife modernization of the Dutch *Van Spejk* class (later sold to Indonesia). SEWACO VI was ordered in 1985 for Dutch "Standard"-class frigates (AAW version). SEWACO VIII was ordered in 1979 for Dutch *Walrus*-class submarines.

18. Users were: Argentina (*Espora* class), Egypt (*El Suez* class, 1978), Korea (*An Yang Ho* or KCX class with WM-28 FCS), Morocco (*Errhamani* class, 1979), Norway (*Storm*-class fast attack boats [probable]),Singapore (110-ft Type B fast attack boats [probable]), Spain (*Descubierta* class, 1974), Thailand (*Ratanakosin*, with WM-25). Reportedly, the two Mini-Combat Systems on board Greek *Gearing*-class destroyers lacked the "egg" usually associated with this system.

19. The system maintains a tactical picture, carries out navigational calculations, displays weapon danger zones, carries out threat evaluation and weapon assignment (TEWA), manages the ship's ECM system, and controls her torpedoes and missiles. Track capacity depends on the required refresh rate: twenty-four tracks if they must be updated every two minutes, six if they must be updated every thirty seconds.

20. Other designations: DEPLO (Danish [C]EPLO) and MARIL (Swedish: MARInen Eldlegnings) with various suffixes. The MARIL 880 version, which may be CEPLO, can accept over-the-horizon (OTH) targeting data from helicopters and from a shore command center via a digital data link.

21. Systems were sold to Denmark for frigates and for missile boats, to Norway for fast attack craft, and to Cold War neutrals or semineutrals (9LV200 Mk 1 to Malaysia and to Yugoslavia; Mk 2 to Bahrain, Finland, Iraq, Kuwait, Norway, Oman, the UAE, and Yugoslavia). It is not clear whether any buyers of 9LV200Mk 1 and Mk 2 did *not* receive the associated CEPLO system. That no sales of STRIKA were announced proves nothing because coastal command and control systems generally are not reported. Many countries bought Swedish coast defense weapons.

Chapter 11. Fleet Netting in Action: Vietnam and After

1. The reference to the airliner (generally described as the Pan Am flight from Tokyo to Manila) as the motivation for Positive Identification Radar Advisory Zone (PIRAZ) comes from a conversation with Cdr. (later Capt.) Hal Cauthen about 1975; he had served with Seventh Fleet off Vietnam.

2. J. L. Lockett, "Naval Operations in Southeast Asia, 1964–1973: History of PIRAZ," Center for Naval Analysis (CNA)76-0720 of 21 July 1974.

3. On 1 July 1966 the missile frigate (DLG) *Coontz* and the gun destroyer *Rogers*, on search and rescue (SAR) station fifty-five nautical miles southeast of Hanoi, were attacked by a North Vietnamese P-6 class torpedo boat. A five-inch gun destroyer was therefore assigned to all PIRAZ missile cruisers and *Leahy*-class "frigates." Although the cruisers had five-inch guns, they were considered ineffective. Lockett, "Naval Operations in Southeast Asia," 3.

4. By keeping track of friendly traffic using non-NTDS means (such as prefiled flight plans and IFF beaconry), PIRAZ stayed within NTDS capacity. Given its excellent picture, the PIRAZ ship was naturally assigned control of the Combat Air Patrol (CAP) (two to five sections) between targets in North Vietnam and the fleet. PIRAZ missions included the earlier Tomcat mission (delousing returning strikes), control of search and rescue, and arrangements for tanking for returning strikes. CO USS *Chicago*, "PIRAZ: New Concept in Strike Warfare," *Combat Readiness* 14, no. 2 (April–June 1968): 1–4: "It is generally accepted that the concept of PIRAZ is one of the most promising developments in the area of tactical AAW." Commander Collins (Op-353F) commented that "for the first time the Cruiser-Destroyer force is actively contributing to Air Warfare as well as performing their classical Anti-Air Warfare role. The PIRAZ flight-following concept and services that can be provided to aircraft of all Services over the Tonkin Gulf and the target area, in effect enable the PIRAZ ship to provide the interface between sea strike forces and land targets."

5. Malcolm Muir Jr., *Black Shoes and Blue Water: Surface Warfare in the United States Navy, 1945 to 1975* (Washington, D.C.: GPO,1996), 174–75, cites depressing exercises. Hot Stove, in the summer of 1965, included the new missile cruiser *Chicago*. Thirty-seven raids generated 150 bogey reports. Numerous friendly and nonexercise aircraft—but only eight attackers—were (notionally) shot down. The after-action report cited poor intraship and intership communications. In Exercise Rag Weed a few months later, 38 percent of enemy aircraft were shot down, but 57 of 104 missiles were fired at friendlies. In other exercises at about this time (Base Line, Range Bush) fewer friendlies would

have been shot down, but only one raider in four would have been hit. Eager Angler (November 1966) was a first test of the new PIRAZ procedures as a way of reducing Blue on Blue attacks. It simulated the situation on Yankee Station off Vietnam, with two carriers, two AEW aircraft on station (one in the area of Point Yankee, the other over the PIRAZ ship), and five pickets. Three Orange raid periods (seventy-six raids) lasted a total of sixty-two hours. They included conventional aircraft, simulated missiles (surface and air launched), and ECM/reconnaissance flights. The maximum density in any one fifteen-minute period was ten raids (aircraft). Another eleven raids that should have proceeded to the vital area were prematurely terminated.

These figures presumably reflect contemporary U.S. estimates of the threat carriers off Vietnam might encounter. Because pickets were placed too close to land (and did not use MTI radar), they often detected raiders too late. Anomalous propagation ("severe trapping"), which would also be met in Vietnam, did not help. Raiders also took too long to evaluate; the lag between first detection and display (after evaluation) averaged thirty-nine nautical miles. Destruction improved from 50 percent on the first day to 72 percent on the last. If only the first five raids of each period are counted, the success rate was 67 percent, indicating slow reaction to suspected or known threats. The missile pickets did not destroy anything. PIRAZ did protect friendlies (only two were splashed during each raid period) but not unknowns (non-exercise aircraft)—like airliners over the Gulf. They did not respond to IFF, and there was no other way to identify most of them. PIRAZ used a new Single Net Information and Position (SNIP) reporting. It did not realize its full potential because many of those involved were not sufficiently familiar with proper authentification procedures and because the required "heads-up" and "hold" reports often were not issued. However, the net was never saturated, and this was a considerable advance. Ships, particularly those without NTDS, poorly organized the flow of information from radars to evaluation. They were unable to apply all possible means of identification to each contact or to correlate and disseminate identification data. Identification was often too late. There were too few trained and qualified CIC personnel, partly because the U.S. Navy was at full stretch. CIC personnel did not get the opportunity to train in depth. For example, most air intercept controllers never got to control aircraft. Final Report of Exercise Eager Angler, 2 December 1966, in the Post-1946 Reports File, Box 237, OA.

6. During 1966 the Joint Chiefs of Staff rejected numerous requests to fire Talos "for fear an errant missile might destroy a U.S. plane or fall into a North Vietnamese city." Command/control capability might not match weapon performance. *Long Beach* received permission to fire (May 1968) after she had tracked 500 MiGs. She hit one at a range of sixty-eight nautical miles, and the debris from it brought down a second. These were the first aircraft ever shot down by naval surface-to-air missile fire. She shot down another MiG in September 1968 at a range of sixty-one nautical miles. Five later attempts missed. After a MiG escaped a missile fired by the missile "frigate" (DLG) *Jouett* by radical evasion, the Joint Chiefs prohibited overland shots. Muir, *Black Shoes*, 158.

7. Because they were heavily laden and had to fly at low altitude, the mining aircraft were considered particularly vulnerable to MiG attack. The missile CAP was provided by the Talos cruisers *Chicago* and *Long Beach* and the SM-1 "frigate" (DLG) *Sterett*, with nom-

inal missile ranges of 100 and 60 nautical miles, respectively. Aircraft from the carrier *Coral Sea* provided backup CAPs, *under positive control of the cruisers*, orbiting to seaward of the cruisers. An EC-121M ELINT airplane (Big Look) provided ESM and tactical warning in support. Aircraft from the carrier *Kitty Hawk* made a diversionary strike. Four destroyers shelled antiaircraft and coast defense sites at the entrance to Haiphong harbor. MiGs approached as the mining aircraft neared their objective. *Chicago* shot one down with a Talos missile at an estimated range of forty-eight nautical miles. A second may also have been shot down. R. A. Ross, (CNA) 00449-73, 16 November 1973, "Air Defense During the Mining of Haiphong Harbor on 9 May 1972," OA.

8. According to Ford and Rosenberg, *The Admirals' Advantage*, 38–39, the practice of sending junior intelligence officers to sea on board surface ships, dropped after World War II, was revived in the early 1960s, presumably as the U.S. Navy became involved in combating Communist insurgencies. The 1964 Tonkin Gulf incident began with a typical electronic intelligence-gathering mission, U.S. ships stimulating North Vietnamese coast defenses so that they could collect operationally useful information. Unfortunately, Ford and Rosenberg do not distinguish between then-Lt. Cdr. William Manthorpe's experience as deputy to an intelligence admiral (and, they say, the first junior intelligence specialist to go to sea on board a surface ship) and junior officers serving as cryptanalysts and operational intelligence collectors.

9. This is presumably the Rota Opintel effort recounted by Ford and Rosenberg, *The Admirals' Advantage*, 56–59; they place special emphasis on SIGINT reporting during the October 1973 Middle East War, when Soviet naval forces built up in the Mediterranean into what some imagined was war status.

Chapter 12. Intraship Netting: ASMD

1. Op-72C3/ns Ser 00213P72 for DCNO (Fleet Operations and Readiness), 26 June 1967, established the executive committee. This paper referred to the report of the ad hoc committee, 25 April 1967 (DCNO(D) Op-72C3 Ser 06206P72). Double Zero files, Box 31, 3900 series, 1967, OA.

2. "The Ships Anti-Missile Integrated Defense (SAMID) Program," *Naval Ordnance Bulletin* 2–68 and "SAMID—Immediate Program," *Naval Ordnance Bulletin* 1-70. The ships were DLG (CG)-30, -31, and -33; DLGN (CGN)-35; DDG-9, -13, and -14; and DD-717, -718, -784, -806, -808, -832, -836, -851, -852, -869, -875, -886, and -887. Computer modifications are described in "NTD's [*sic*] Three-Computer OP-Program for DLG's," *Naval Ordnance Bulletin* 4-71.

3. June through August 1967, according to a footnote in Muir, *Black Shoes*. Presumably First Fleet's tentative tactical manual was the fruit of these experiments.

4. Ships' WLR-1 ESM sets scanned frequencies mechanically, hence too slowly to detect pop-up threats. Plans called for emergency upgrades (QRC 68/9) for FRAMS and new threat receivers for missile ships. The chaff launcher was developed under an urgent August 1966 CNO requirement, as described in "Chaffroc: A Ship-Launched Chaff Decoy System," *Naval Ordnance Bulletin* 1-69.

5. The QR sector was 1–360 degrees wide. The operator designated a maximum CPA (closest point of approach: either preset as one nautical mile or variable between one and twenty nautical miles) as a criterion for considering quick reaction (QR) response to a target. Maximum range at which an incomer could be identified as a QR threat was preset at 120 nautical miles, but could be varied between 60 and 250 nautical miles. Response range (maximum for reacting to a QR target) was preset at sixty nautical miles but could be varied between 20 and 120 nautical miles. Preset ASMD zones were Late Detect (twenty nautical miles) and Low Flier (forty nautical miles preset, variable between twenty and sixty nautical miles).

6. Major program innovations included a QR mode (with a table of appropriate responses to each of up to twenty-seven threats), automatic track correlation, automatic emission control (EMCON) monitoring, and a threat emitter library to assist in identifying signals detected by the ship's WLR-1 ECM receiver. The system could operate in automatic, semiautomatic, or manual mode. The computer contained a threat-weapon table giving guidelines for weapon assignment. In semiautomatic mode, the system recommended weapon assignment. In manual mode, it presented only target data. Operator-assist functions included correlation between all NTDS and electronic warfare (EW) tracks and chaff placement (the launcher was controlled by NTDS). The operator was assisted, not replaced. Thus, correlated tracks had to be confirmed by the ECM or track supervisor before they were entered into the computer track database. New NTDS symbols were added to indicate in-flight missiles and hostile missile platforms. There were also new display formats adapted to short-range missile defense.

7. Missile-control radar (SPG-55B) was given two quick-detection modes, HS (horizon search) and SS (sector search), both within selectable elevation sectors. In a new sector scan engage (SSE) mode, a missile was fired along a narrow sector around the center of a line of bearing without any lock-on by the fire-control system. In continuous boat tracking (CBT), the system could fire at an incoming missile while tracking its launch platform. Continuous wave acquisition tracking (CWAT) provided the a second tracker operating on a different band. A new track module improved target detectability and range resolution. Long-range air search radar was given a minimum-range (reduction) kit.

8. Ships received a new multibeamed (i.e., wide-open rather than scanning) antenna for their passive intercept receivers and a new Threat Recognizer/Programmer (SLQ-21) for the H-J bands (i.e., for missile seeker bands).

9. By 1986 the preset threat list had grown to fifteen, with three numbers left blank for reassignment: Styx (QR 01), Samlet, Shaddock (SS-N-3), Scrubber (SS N 1), SS N 7, SS-N-9, Kennel (AS-1), Kipper (AS-2), Kangaroo (AS-3), Kitchen (AS-4), Kelt (AS-5), AS-6, Goa (SA-N-1), Goblet (SA-N-3), and SAN-4. Note the absence of the French Exocet, which a year later would be fired at USS *Stark*.

10. According to "SAMID—Immediate Program," *Naval Ordnance Bulletin* 1-70, automated DLG reaction times before and after SAMID modifications were: 107/33 seconds for search radar, 51/17 seconds for fire-control radar, and 107/23 seconds for EW. For a DDG the corresponding figures were 97/43 seconds, 23/14 seconds, and 119/24 seconds, respectively. The DLG would not have had time to fire her guns before SAMID.

Destroyer (DD) time to open gunfire: 69/57 seconds relying on search radar, 51/16 relying on fire-control radar, and 73/48 seconds relying on ESM. Fire control radar seems to have given the quickest reactions. These figures were based on 635 test runs in 1968–69. Because time was short, the tests used only the basic mode of operation; they did not test the reflexive mode.

11. "SAMID Evaluated in Baseline Integrated Ship Antiair Warfare System, NAVORD SYSCOM," *Naval Ordnance Bulletin* 3-69.

12. According to the *Naval Ordnance Bulletin* 1-70 article, the 1970 ships were the carriers *Bon Homme Richard* and *Shangri-La*; the cruisers *Chicago*, *Little Rock*, and *Long Beach*; and four missile "frigates" (later cruisers): DLG-11, 29, 30, and 31. Neither carrier nor *Little Rock* had NTDS. Ten ships were listed for 1971: the carrier *Forrestal*, the cruiser *Springfield*, the fast replenishment ship *Sacramento*, three missile "frigates" (DLG-16, 17, and 26), and four missile destroyers (DDG-4, 13, 22, and 35; DDG-9, 12, 15, and 21 were substituted). Only the carrier and the "frigates" had NTDS. According to a December 1972 account of the ASMD-financed JPTDS program, ASMD improvements had already been made in some ships of the following classes: CVA, CG, CLG, DLG, LPH, LPD, and DD. It is not clear what was done in the amphibious classes listed.

Chapter 13. Crisis and Transformation

1. The ship's master tape, used to reload the entire NTDS program, could not be modified.

2. Appendix on NTDS problems in draft U.S. Navy Command and Control Master Plan, 5 December 1979, declassified 6 December 1985. The germanium-based components used in the CP-642A computer (in seven carriers and eleven missile cruisers) were no longer being made. These computers could not be supported after 1985. All CP-642 computers were at or near saturation, and all available program memory in the follow-on UYK-7s had been used. Because of limited computer power, NTDS displays were confusing, requiring the operator to work too hard to assemble something meaningful. In the *Virginia* (CGN-38) class, data sometimes had to be hand-copied from one program to another. NTDS index numbers for EW did not correspond with standard signal notation. NATO nicknames for suspected threats could not be displayed.

3. As of November 1969 only one ship had Dynamic Modular Replacement (DMR). It could be expensive in terms of memory because it entailed duplicating instructions. In 1969 it took two CP-642s to make DMR possible, but it was expected that the future single-UYK-7 configuration would make do with one computer.

4. The command and control processing (C2P) operational requirement was issued in December 1985, and the first UYK-43 computers intended for operational evaluation of the Version 0 system were acquired under the FY88 program. Version 0 was released to the fleet in FY92. It completed technical evaluation in April 1994. (V)1 was first tested in 1994.

5. Mod 2 (November 1980: four computers) was Mod 1 adapted to a Taiwanese fifty-meter patrol boat. Mod 3 (delivered beginning in March 1980: two UYK-19, eleven microprocessors) was for even smaller missile boats.

6. Egypt bought MCS to create an over-the-horizon targeting picture for Harpoon missiles on board *Descubierta*-class frigates on the basis of data links (Links YE and Z) and ESM data. Taiwan bought MCS to control antiship missiles and forty-millimeter guns on board its modified *Perry*-class frigates, whose JPTDS-derived combat systems had not been designed for those roles. MCS marketing ceased after Honeywell sold its combat direction business to Hughes Ground Systems in 1988.

7. The federated SEWACO VII (designed beginning in 1985 for Dutch M-class frigates) was sold to Korea for *Donghae*- and *Po Hang*–class frigates (hulls 756–65) and to Turkey as Signaal Tactical Command and Control System (STACOS) Mod 3 (capacity 512 tracks). The Turks switched to the fully distributed Tactical Information and Command System (TACTICOS). Mod 1 equipped Portuguese and Turkish (Track I) MEKO frigates, and Mod 2 equipped Greek MEKO frigates. SEWACO IX, for Tripartite minesweepers (except French), was derived from SEWACO VII. SEWACO X was designed for the abortive Dutch-Belgian-Portuguese mine hunter. SEWACO XI was a modified SEWACO VII for the Dutch *De Zeven Provincien*–class missile frigate. The fully distributed STACOS Mod 4 or STACOS FD (fully distributed) became TACTICOS. It is fully scalable, so users range from fast attack craft to the most sophisticated AAW frigates. About when it appeared, Signaal was sold to Thomson-CSF, which made the French TAVITAC systems. It became Thales (ex-Thomson) Nederland Naval Systems. TAVITAC and TACTICOS are now probably effectively identical. The French followed roughly the same path as the Dutch. Systeme d'Exploitation Navale des Informations Tactiques (SENIT) 6 in their *Cassard*-class destroyers is federated (SENIT 8 is the equivalent for the carrier *Charles de Gaulle*). Because it is modular, SENIT 8 is scalable down to platforms such as Norwegian fast attack boats. SENIT 7 (Tavitac 2000) for the *La Fayette*–class frigates, is a federated version of the earlier TAVITAC, entirely distinct from SENIT 6/8. By spring 1996 Thomson-CSF (now Thales) was calling its system TAVITAC-FD, in analogy to SEWACO-FD, and it was advertising TAVITAC-NT (new technology).

8. Private remarks to the author by a Ferranti engineer, about 1990.

9. Frigate versions were sold to Brunei, Malaysia, and New Zealand. Egypt and Thailand bought smaller-ship versions. The mine countermeasures version was adopted by Australia, Saudi Arabia, Spain, the United Kingdom, and the United States (for the *Avenger* class).

Chapter 14. Extending Combat System Automation: Aircraft

1. The OpNav requirement for the Airborne Tactical Data System (ATDS) was issued 2 November 1955, and the BuAer Type Specification (OS-139) on 23 November. The interim airplane was originally designated WF-2, Grumman having received a 1952 contract (canceled in 1954) for a WF-1 based on its S2F Tracker carrier ASW airplane.

In early summer 1955 Grumman began work on an unsolicited proposal for an early warning version of its TF-1 carrier onboard delivery airplane. Wind tunnel tests (July 1955) showed that it could carry a radome large enough for a stabilized 17 1/2 x 4 foot antenna, much larger than the usual carrier APS-20 (using similar electronics). Stabilization made it possible to use the radar for height finding by lobe comparison, something impossible in earlier aircraft. Work on the formal proposal began in September. Several other such proposals had already been turned down as unsuited to carrier operation. Grumman and Hazeltine (electronics) jointly submitted their proposal in January 1956. A 27 February 1956 BuAer memo recommended buying the Grumman airplane immediately as an interim step "considering the urgent operational need for an improved carrier-based AEW capability." There were two CIC operators, each with an analog intercept computer. (Memo in NAVAIR History file on E-1B, folder "A Summary of the WF-2 Program through January 1959.")

2. The three-phase get-well program ensured a successful first E-2A deployment in November 1965. In August the Office of the Secretary of Defense (OSD) approved FY66 procurement and authorized a follow-on version. The new tactical situation, close to land, required urgent changes ("MOD Ax"), the original hard wired computer being replaced by a programmable unit. In August 1966 the Navy verbally suggested to OSD that the FY66 purchase be deferred, all E-2As backfit, and an E-2B developed. This was approved in November, including the APS-111 "overland" radar replacing the earlier APS-96. The E-2A/APS-111 program was formally approved on 18 April 1968, and money was released in mid-May 1969. APS-111 offered much better overland performance and somewhat better overwater performance (180 versus 160 nautical miles), and it could control strike aircraft 1.5 nautical miles circular error probable [CEP]). Integration of the carrier air inertial navigation system greatly improved its positional accuracy (a drift of 1.25 versus 2.50 nautical miles per hour). Reliability rose from 9.6 to 50 hours between failure. The new version offered automatic jamming alert. APS-111 was later described as the breadboard version of the APS-125 in the initial E-2C, whose rated range was 125 nautical miles. The Program Change Recommendation (PCR) refers to this new program as the E-2B, but it shows characteristic E-2C features. Data largely from the draft PCR for what became the E-2C, in the "E-2 Background File" folder in NAVAIR History Aircraft Collection Box 69.

3. C. E. Hutchinson and Edward J. Thaubeld, "E-2C/F-14A—A Formidable Team," *Selected Readings for Naval Operations 1977* in NWC Archives, RG 4. An E-2C could exchange data with NTDS on board a carrier at a rate equivalent to twenty-eight targets/second.

4. Versions of the P-3C were designated updates. Update III increased channel capacity from thirty-one to ninety-nine, partly to make up for shorter individual buoy detection ranges and also to use more sophisticated buoys (Directional LOFAR Sonobuoy System [DIFAR] and the Directional Command (Controlled) Active Sonobuoy System [DICASS] and then buoys with depressed beams), which required more than one radio channel per buoy. Buoys were processed separately; the U.S. Navy experimented with coherent processing, in which all the buoys in a field were handled as a single entity. The mission computer would have been changed to match. For such a technique to work, the computer must have precise sonobuoy positions, which means Global Position

System (GPS) receivers on all buoys. The main current development is bistatics, to detect quiet diesel submarines. An array of sonobuoys detects echoes from a small controlled explosion or a pinger. Each receiving buoy carries a GPS receiver.

5. The A-6A system was built around the ASQ-61 ballistic computer, which navigated it to the target and assisted in bomb release. Navigational inputs were an inertial system (ASN-31), a Doppler radar (speed over the ground), and the CP-528A air data computer. The inertial system sensed aircraft pitch and roll. Near the target the pilot used the APQ-92 search radar. He switched to the APQ-88/112 tracking radar to lock onto a target (it was also used for terrain avoidance).

6. The Intruder entered combat in Vietnam in June 1965. It was the first U.S. all-weather bomber. (The Air Force F-111 later offered somewhat similar capabilities.) Based on combat through 31 March 1968, the CEP with an undegraded system against a complex target was 450 feet, compared to 152 feet (160 feet on the first pass) in tests. In degraded mode (generally meaning without target-tracking radar), estimated CEP was 630 feet. About 20 percent of the time the target was not identified at all. CNA proposed expanding collection of radar scope photography for use in mission planning, so that bombardier-navigators would have a better idea of what targets looked like when they arrived. It also recommended a program to provide more accurate range and bearing data for use in offset bombing, that is, in attacks based on more distinct radar objects. CNA Operations Evaluation Group Study 721, "Effectiveness of the A-6A in Combat in Southeast Asia," 24 January 1969, OA.

7. On average 51 percent of aircraft were ready at the beginning of each flying day. According to the CNA report, on only about 20 percent of missions the airplane had all systems running. About 16 percent of the time performance was badly degraded, the crew using "manual range time" to drop bombs (i.e., their target-tracking radar was not working). The least reliable element of the system was the ASQ-61 ballistic computer (the bomb-aiming computer).

8. The A-7A was much larger than its A-4E Skyhawk predecessor: maximum takeoff weight was 38,500 versus 24,500 pounds. It could carry more bombs (up to 15,000 pounds versus 8,000)and it had a longer combat radius (with a low-level run-in and standard fuel reserves, 620 versus 215 nautical miles). Because they flew in daylight, A-7s over North Vietnam faced light antiaircraft guns and so could not use A-6 style low-altitude tactics. They normally flew above 3,500 feet. The test CEP was based on predeployment training runs using standard speed (450 knots), release altitude (5,000 feet), and dive angle (45 degrees). W. Nunn, CNA Operations Analysis Group Study 731, "Combat Introduction of the A-7A Aircraft," released June 1969, OA.

9. Accuracies in mils (thousandths of a radian) were standard for dive-bombing, as they were for gunnery. CEPs were given in feet for level delivery: 181 feet for radar bombing, 328.8 feet for normal attack, 374.2 feet for navigational bomb flyover, 430.9 feet for navigational bombing with heads-up display HUD update, 548.2 feet for navigational bombing with offset, 920.6 feet for radar bombing with offset, and 1,011.7 feet for navigational bombing with radar update. Navigational meant that the airplane was guided to the target by its inertial system. In normal mode the pilot designated the target visually or from the radar display. The HUD showed mainly own-airplane data, including

navigational cues from the main computer and the command to pull up for weapon release. Once the pilot entered the target into the computer, it began tracking, holding it even if he lost sight of the target, continually computing appropriate release points. CNA Operations Evaluation Group Study 767, "Evaluation of the A-7E Weapons System" released 26 December 1972, OA.

10. This application of Link 4 is mentioned in a book of major accomplishments published by the Naval Ordnance Test Station (NOTS), China Lake in November 1982. NOTS worked on Operational Flight Programs (OFPs) for both aircraft. According to the book, NOTS produced all the A-6E OFPs, including E-110 (released 1980), which provided strike attack vectoring, presumably by E-2C. The NWC-2D OFP of the A-7E offered strike attack vectoring from an E-2C; NWC-3 was compatible with the forward-looking infrared (FLIR) on board some A-7Es.

11. Analytics, Inc., "Design of Air Strike Planning Aids: Lessons Learned from the ONR Operational Decision Aids Program," 15 May 1982 report for ONR: NTIS ADA 121939. ONR had been developing planning aids for about eight years, but there was no indication that air strike planning had been automated.

12. Analytics, Inc., "Design of Air Strike Planning Aids."

13. The delay was ascribed to two factors, the need to pass strike plans all the way up the chain of command, and a requirement to warn the State Department to give its employees enough time to take cover from the expected poststrike rioting. Similar requirements seem to have ruined the 1998 Tomahawk attack against terrorist training camps in Afghanistan.

14. In 1986 Secretary of the Navy John Lehman ordered a strike planner developed. It was the first attempt to unify a service's systems. The Navy selected the McDonnell Douglas Tactical Aircraft Planning System (TAPS). It entered service in 1986 aboard the carrier *Vinson*. The Navy took over management (as TAMPS) in October 1987, and the system was first operationally evaluated in 1991. TAMPS supported both wing- and squadron-level planning. The system uses a general-purpose core plus modules for different aircraft and systems. That made it possible to extend TAMPS far beyond the A-6E for which it was originally designed. The initial version 4.x defined the strike route; calculated time, speed, distance, fuel consumption, and aircraft weight; and analyzed known en route threats. Operators could test alternative routes (what-if questions). Inputs included automated intelligence information and weather applications. The output was hard copy, such as kneeboard strip maps for pilots. Version 5.0 added a data transfer device, which plugs into F/A-18s at flight time. In addition to route data, it sets Link 16 and IFF and programs some weapons. Version 6.1 (1996) was designed for distributed collaborative planning, and thus supported a shared map, e-mail, voice conferencing, and white boards. Institute for Defense Analysis, "Assessment of Aviation Mission Planning Systems" (Project leader J. Walsh), May 1995, for ASD (C3I) Further versions followed; the successor is the Joint Mission Planning System (JMPS).

Chapter 15. U.S. Ocean Surveillance after 1945

1. This account of the origin of SOSUS is based on Cross Associates, *Sea-Based Airborne Antisubmarine Warfare 1940–1977*, published in 1977 at the Secret level and declassified on 31 December 1990. A copy of this three-volume study is in OA ("Other Organizations, post 1974 series, C"). SOSUS origins are in volume II, 122ff. SOSUS was tested operationally in the Atlantic between 26 April and 7 June 1954 (Antisubmarine Development Exercise [ASDEVEX] 1-54); work had begun in 1950 with a research contract to Western Electric (the parent company of Bell Labs). The concept was theoretically proved late in 1950, and a working model was produced by 2 May 1951, for tests in shallow water off Sandy Hook. It achieved ranges of forty to fifty miles. ONR then authorized a deep-water installation (a forty-hydrophone array in two hundred fathoms off Eleuthera in the Caribbean). After successful tests in April 1952, in June CNO authorized BuShips to procure and install six stations in the Atlantic (the 1954 test used Eleuthera and Bermuda stations plus the submarine K-1 with long-range listening equipment, presumably simulating a third station). Aircraft with passive sonobuoys were sent to the point at which the system detected a submarine, succeeding 50 percent of the time. The Atlantic network was declared operational in December 1956, and a Pacific network followed beginning in March 1958.

   By 1956 twelve Atlantic stations were planned or being built, plus seven in the Pacific. Arrays were set at 1,060 fathom depth, giving them access to the deep sound channel. By this time average range was 300 to 400 miles, and ranges as great as 600 miles were being reported. By January 1956 the eight operational Atlantic stations had reported 3,400 contacts, of which 64 were classified as possible non-U.S. submarines, but air resources limited investigation to five of them. By 1959 eighteen of the original nineteen stations were complete, and two more were under construction, and another (deep-water) station was planned northwest of Bermuda, plus a shallow-water system at Argentia. These twenty-three stations formed the original SOSUS system. By 1956 a shallow-water system (to preclude end runs around the system) was under development, and a deeper-water version was being investigated. During 1960–64, positive annual submarine contacts in the Atlantic varied between eight (FY62) and forty-five (FY65), except for FY63 (169, mainly in the Norwegian Sea). The first Soviet submarines positively identified in the western Atlantic were the four "Foxtrots" deployed during the Cuban Missile Crisis (Vol. III, 13). By 1968 the Atlantic SOSUS system included four arrays in Iceland for Norwegian Sea surveillance, plus four deep-water arrays at Argentia, and two arrays at Shelburne, Nova Scotia, manned by the Canadian navy. During 1968, SOSUS detected 467,677 contacts, of which 4,755 were submarines (1,716 U.S. nuclear, 2,451 U.S. diesel, 303 Soviet nuclear, and 285 Soviet diesel).

   In 1965 proposed additions to SOSUS off the U.S. coast were canceled in favor of the "forward concept": arrays would be installed abroad, particularly around the Norwegian Sea and the Northwest Pacific, to detect submarines in transit to operating areas or even in home waters. This alternative to detecting submarines in their operating areas was chosen because submarines were becoming quieter, hence more difficult to track at greater ranges. Later it was argued that the mid-Atlantic ridge was the ultimate barrier to detection by arrays off the U.S. coast, and in the 1970s stations were built in the

Eastern Atlantic under Project Backscratch. Initially the forward policy was inspired by the success of the OBOE array installed in 1962 at Adak, which gave excellent coverage of the area near the Petropavlovsk submarine base. Unfortunately, there was no good coverage of the mid-Pacific area through which Soviet ballistic missile submarines transited. Pacific Fleet developed new tactics: OBOE would develop an initial track, and P-3s would then pick up the submarine using high-altitude large-area (HILAST) tactics, creating a square pattern of nine sonobuoys spaced seventy-five miles apart, monitored from 20,000 feet. A P-3 monitoring this 50,000-square mile field had a 95 percent probability of picking up a nonnuclear transitter at least once. These HILAST tactics spread to the Atlantic.

2. Until about 1960 sonobuoys were simple broadband microphones. Then narrower-band microphones capable of providing LOFAR detections were installed in the buoys to exploit newly miniaturized spectrum analyzers suited to aircraft installation.

3. Relays were the ASW equivalent of a radar link distributing raw video. LOFAR (narrowband analysis) was the central technique of U.S. ASW. Submarine signatures were embodied in Lofargrams ("grams")—which the relays transmitted. They made it possible to compare a new gram with those in a distant library, or to know that two SOSUS arrays were detecting the same submarine (for a cross-fix) or to know that two trackers were detecting (or had detected) the same submarine, so that a track could be drawn. They were needed between NAVFACs (Naval Facilities, the SOSUS centers), between NAVFACs and Evaluation Centers (patrol plane command centers); between NAVFACs and hunter-killer groups (prosecuting SOSUS contacts); between patrol aircraft and Evaluation Centers; and between carrier-based ASW aircraft and their carriers. They turned U.S. ASW into a netted operation. By 1962 the single-channel HEIFER HF modem had transmitted grams over a thousand miles from patrol aircraft, and grams had been received successfully on board the carriers, at the NAVFACs, and at the Evaluation Centers. In April 1962 the National Security Industrial Association (NSIA) ASW Advisory Committee recommended LOFAR relays as a way of reducing ASW reaction time, reduce classification time, making for better evaluation and correlation of data, improving flexibility, and making it easier to decentralize ASW command and control. Double Zero files, 1962 Box 14, 5000 series, OA. A relay for carrier ASW aircraft transmitted sixteen grams simultaneously over eighty-eight nautical miles, in trials on board USS *Kearsage* (30 October–18 November 1962). ComOpTevFor, Weapons/Weapon Systems Summary, 1 April 1963 in Double Zero Files, 1963 (Stack Files), OA.

4. ASCAC began as a Pacific Fleet program to improve ASW classification, largely by setting up a submarine signature library on board an ASW carrier, against which sonobuoy records could be compared. It was approved by CNO for installation using repair funds aboard the carriers *Yorktown* and *Kearsage* in 1961, *Hornet* following in 1962. The Atlantic Fleet began its own evaluation of a somewhat similar concept in September 1961 on the different basis of coordinating SOSUS and land-based patrol aircraft. As of 1962, efforts to set up a single program were being frustrated by the deep differences between Pacific and Atlantic concepts of operation. RDT&E file in Double Zero 1962 Box 15 (5000 series).

5. According to a report quoted in the Cross Report.

6. This idea may have originated with the 1957 Gaither Committee on the threat of surprise attack. SOSUS information became an important WWMCCS indicator.

7. A 1976 NWC paper treated detection of ballistic missile submarines as the primary SOSUS role. Even after the Soviets had long-range missiles that could be fired from "bastions" off their coasts, they continued to operate "Yankee"-class submarines in patrol boxes off the U.S. coast—knowledge of which must have come from SOSUS. In the 1970s SOSUS was extended to forward areas such as the Norwegian Sea, where it could detect sorties by the submarines with shorter-range missiles (and also movements of attack submarines into the North Atlantic). "Navy's Undersea Surveillance Program," Appendix A to "Ocean Surveillance" referenced below, a compilation of data prepared in July 1976, based on a paper by CDR H. N. Walther USN; NWC RG 4.

8. Array positions were determined by bottom topography and by the requirement to connect each forty-hydrophone array to a shore processing station. Initially cable length was limited to three hundred nautical miles.

9. First-generation submarines shared a common power plant, with common acoustic characteristics: November-class attack submarines, Hotel-class ballistic missile craft, and Echo-class guided-missile submarines. Second-generation submarines shared a different common power plant: Victor-class attack submarines, Yankee-class strategic submarines, and Charlie-class guided missile submarines (one rather than two reactors). The 1976 claim of improved silencing predated the emergence of the Victor III, with its rafted power plant. It may have referred to the Alfa class, which also had a rafted power plant (so quiet that it was credited with turboelectric propulsion), but was rarely seen.

10. The 1976 paper describes a SOSUS improvement program. Goals were better sensitivity so that a second-generation submarine at patrol speed (or the postulated third-generation at transit speed) could be detected, greater holding time for each contact, improved target localization and tracking accuracy (for faster interception by forces vectored by the system), increased target-handling capacity, and significant reductions in delays in target reporting to tactical forces. To this end signal processing was being automated and a digital multibeam (multiple beams simultaneously) configuration adopted. A longer-term improvement program called for the creation of a Main Evaluation Center and Regional Evaluation Centers for each ocean. There were also new sensors. The Suspended Array Surveillance System (SASS) was a large-aperture array suspended in the deep sound channel (typically six thousand feet down in the Atlantic) in mid-ocean, that is, not limited by bottom topography near the shore. The Fixed Distributed Subsystem (FDS) was a string of upward-looking hydrophones or arrays winding back and forth on the bottom in or near a choke point. A submarine passing overhead would be detected repeatedly, its course and speed measured. The Moored Surveillance System (MSS), which could be deployed rapidly, used one or more buoys from which were suspended near-bottom acoustic arrays; data were transmitted by satellite for shore processing or stored to be read out by an airplane. MSS could be deployed in depths down to 21,000 feet, by aircraft, ships, and submarines—that is, rapidly and/or covertly. Lifetime would be at least 180 days.

11. The first three experimental towed array ships, using existing oil exploration arrays (and no special processing) appeared in the Mediterranean in June 1970. According to the 1976 NWC paper, they proved the idea was feasible. All were retired during the fall of 1973, replaced by six towed surface ship surveillance arrays (TASS) ships (three Atlantic, three Pacific) with SQR-15 arrays that (at less than five knots) could detect Soviet diesel submarines at fifty nautical miles, and transiting second-generation nuclear submarines at over a hundred nautical miles (presumably at three convergence zones), but not patrolling second-generation submarines. Nor could they communicate effectively with the SOSUS net ashore. They inspired the T-AGOS surveillance towed array ship, with its satellite link to the system ashore, conceived as a mobile SOSUS array, capable of detecting the 50 Hz line of a Soviet second-generation submarine (the line SOSUS and LOFAR detected) at a range of 900 to 1,200 nautical miles. It offered coverage where fixed arrays might be politically or economically prohibited, it could respond to changing Soviet operating patterns, and it could make up for SOSUS outages.

12. Several navies have shifted toward active systems using low frequency broadband signals, their processors handling many narrow frequency bands separately and simultaneously to limit reverberation. (This kind of processing may be compared to hyperspectral processing of images). Such systems offer good shallow-water performance. Foreign examples are the French Combined Active-Passive Towed Array System (CAPTAS) and the British Type 2087; the towed sonar planned for the U.S. DDG-1000 *Zumwalt* class is probably in this category.

13. Lt. Col. Robert R. Dailey, USAF, "The Worldwide Military Command and Control System," in College of Naval Command and Staff, *1976–1977 Selected Readings in Naval Operations: Systems, Sensors, and Platforms Study,* Vol. II-5, NWC RG 4. This 23 June 1976 paper submitted to the NWC and then used as a text was declassified on 31 December 2003.

14. By about 1970 the Soviets had learned to curtail submarine HF signals, so HF/DF and SOSUS seemed to deal with entirely different targets. SOSUS coverage did not include the main areas of Soviet surface activity, such as the Mediterranean, the Baltic, and the Norwegian Sea. In the mid- and late 1970s SOSUS extensions and the advent of long surveillance towed arrays in the Mediterranean changed the situation, and long-range acoustics came to be seen more as a surface sensor. The U.S. HF/DF net had been conceived for Atlantic and Pacific ASW and thus did not cover much of the world. HF/DF was also subject to considerable uncertainties. Other (intermittent) sources, such as regular patrol plane overflights in the Mediterranean, offered better accuracy. In that sea the aircraft saw about half the ships of interest. Because of its connection with wide-area ASW, the Cross Report describes shore HF/DF development in detail. Other data in what follows came from declassified naval communications handbooks and from Internet descriptions (particularly from the Federation of American Scientists) of the Bullseye system. In 1960 the most active U.S. DF net (WestPac) was handling about 200 to 250 "flashes" each day, of which it fixed about 60 percent of targets within about 100 nautical miles. Under optimum conditions, the time delay from initial interception at the control station to measurement of bearing at outstations was a minimum of twenty seconds; no shorter signal could be localized, hence the system was helpless

against highly time-compressed signals. The standard HF/DF set then in service was ITT's GRD-6, using a U-Adcock array like that of the wartime ITT set (DAJ) using five masts and a spinning goniometer (and a cage array for higher frequencies). Range was 2 to 32 MHz in four bands (like DAJ). It could be operated remotely by teletype or radio signals by a GSW-1 control station (using pushbuttons to set frequency) to form part of an automatic DF net. The GRD-6 designation was assigned in 1951, so presumably it was a direct successor to DAJ.

The goal in 1960 was to detect and fix transmissions as short as one microsecond (one thousandth of a second). The solution seems to have been a combination of electronic beam steering (to detect short signals) using a Wullenweber array receiver, and retrospective DF developed by NRL under Project Boresight. All stations recorded their signals, so that they could correlate them (for DF) even after the short signal had vanished. The associated equipment was the FLR-7 receiver and the FRA-44 recorder. Bullseye used a new type of circularly disposed wide-aperture array with significantly better accuracy and signal collection, FRD-10. It was the first operational U.S. Wullenweber; because its beam swept around electronically, it could intercept even very short signals. NRL produced its first report on the German Wullenweber in 1947 and built an electrically steered four hundred-foot prototype in the 1950s. Bullseye was a scaled-up version. A third innovation was the use of computers (GYK-3) in DF nets. According to a 1997 NRL booklet, Bullseye innovations made HF/DF "a principal means of global ocean surveillance, with special capabilities against critical targets." Classic Bullseye was later renamed Classic Flaghoist. Classic Bulldog was a further upgrade. The Air Force system of FLR-9s, installed from 1964 on, was called Iron Horse, using an intercept building at the center of the array. Under a program to unify the services' HF/DF resources (Unitary DF or Crosshair), Iron Horse data were provided to the Navy under the Classic Centerboard program. The first new-generation (Bullseye) station entered service on Okinawa in 1961, followed by thirteen more through 1964: Adak; Edzell, Scotland; Galeta Island, Panama; Guam; Hanza, Okinawa; Homestead, Florida; Imperial Beach, California (the last built); Marietta, Washington (dismantled 1972 when the Canadian Masset array entered service); Northwest, Virginia; Rota, Spain; Sebana Seca, Puerto Rico; Skaggs Island, California; and Winter Harbor, Maine; plus two at Sugar Grove for communications intercepts. Further stations opened to make up for the loss of British stations resulting from the retreat from east of Suez: Udorn, Thailand (December 1972); Masirah, Oman (October 1974); and Diego Garcia (August 1974). They worked with an existing Australian station at Pearce. There were also Canadian stations at Gander and Masset, British Columbia. The antennas are large Wullenwebers called circularly disposed array antennas (or "elephant cages"), using inner and outer rings of antennas. The inner ring (230-meter diameter, forty folded dipoles) covers the 2–8 MHz range; the outer ring (260-meter, 120 sleeve monopoles) covers 8–30 MHz. Inside each ring is a wire mesh reflector. Nominal range is 3,200 nautical miles. The Wullenweber measures the elevation angle at which signals arrive. The FRD-10s were supplemented by smaller arrays called Pushers (FRD-13), including Canadian units at Bermuda, Leitrim, and Alert.

Compared to the earlier GRD-6, FRD-10 could record intercepts; offered four times the accuracy and four times the gain; and it was better able to select wanted signals and reject interfering signals and noise. At least some of the earlier GRD-6 arrays, such as those in Iceland and in Bermuda, were retained after FRD-10 entered service. The U.S. FRD-10 system was closed down during the 1990s, leaving only the two Canadian units at Leitrim and Alert.

15. Ford and Rosenberg, *The Admirals' Advantage*, 56, suggest that Rota was created in response to an August 1968 request by Vice Adm. David Richardson for a Mediterranean Surveillance Net. Rota was considered a Sixth Fleet, rather than an ONI, asset. According to Ford and Rosenberg, it concentrated on indications and warning for Sixth Fleet, producing both a daily morning message (in time for the morning briefing on board carriers) and flash messages. They credit Rota with particular success in exploiting Soviet communications for operational warning. That may be a reference to practices like the successful Tonkin Gulf operation (not mentioned by Ford and Rosenberg). According to Ford and Rosenberg, 59, Vice Adm. Dan Murphy, Sixth Fleet commander, described the Rota report on Soviet C3 activity during the 1973 Middle East War as the most important single piece of intelligence he received at that time.

16. ONI intelligence computerization projects are listed in Double Zero 1963 Box 10 (3800-5050), OA.

17. Op-92P/lhk Ser 03520P92 of 5 September 1967 in Double Zero file 1967 (3800 series), OA.

18. SOR 31-10 for SODS, Subordinate Operations Control Center Data Systems, was established on 5 June 1964. BuShips was designated principal development activity. SODS was part of the abortive super-NTDS plan. Thus papers mentioned in the SOR included the 1961 summer study on ocean surveillance (published 17 November 1961), the CNA (Institute of Naval Studies) Ocean Surveillance Study dated 25 April 1963, and also the latest SOSUS evaluation study (TRIDENT, by Arthur D. Little) and even the 1955 LAMPLIGHT report. SODS would manage and display the wide-area pictures subordinate commanders needed for tasks such as ocean surveillance, shipping control, and ASW. Desired performance gives an idea of what early ocean surveillance automation was intended to achieve. Required tracking accuracy was ten nautical miles for ships and ten nautical miles or six minutes' flight time (whichever was larger) for aircraft. SODS would display all known vehicle positions (which might be updated up to four times a day) and dead reckon them; time to update all vehicle positions was not to exceed thirty minutes. Time to locate all units within a given area and to update a hundred of them was not to exceed five minutes. Display was to be selective by category (e.g., all submarines), by area, by category within an area, and by particular vehicle. Display area should be selective (e.g., 180, 360, 720, 1,500, and 3,000 miles square). The center of the display area should be variable and selectable. Two versions were envisaged. The smaller would store information on 10,000 vehicles, of which 2,000 would be moving at any one time (1,900 ships, 75 aircraft, 25 objects in space). The larger version, for CNO CinCUSNAVEUR, and COMNAVEASTPAC, that is, for the shore European and Far Eastern command centers, should have three times the capacity of the smaller. A few SODS would be air-transportable on two-hour notice. SODS and other planned command systems may have been intended to use the CP-667 high-capacity computer, under development by Univac to a 1962 Navy specification for a thirty-six-bit machine.

(It never entered naval service.) The 9 July 1964 SOR is in NARA RG 19 Entry 1044M1 (72A6481, Box 8: NTDS materials). I am grateful to Chris Wright for this document.

19. In 1970 principal sources were the National Security Agency (including HF/DF), the Coast Guard (merchant vessel reports), Lloyds of London, the Naval Environmental Data Network (weather reports, which identified the ship sending them and her position), the Movement Report Control Center (reports of planned movements of U.S. naval vessel lasting more than twenty-four hours), and SOSUS. SOSUS and other acoustic systems were to be used against both submarines and surface ships. The Naval Intelligence Processing Support Center (NIPSSA) was modernized with new computers and displays to become the Naval Operational Intelligence Center (NOIC), the main station of the OSIS system. Extracts from the report of the 1970 Defense Science Board panel on Ocean Surveillance, in NWC Tactics Department, "The Role of Ocean Surveillance in Naval Warfare," in *Selected Readings in Naval Operations: Sea Control Study* 4, no. 3, NWC Archives RG 4.

20. Letter reporting the lease, 16 August 1966, in Folder 2, Double Zero files 1968 Box 12 (3800 series), OA.

21. The surveillance system is described in CNA Operations Evaluation Group Study 683, "Contribution of ASW Patrol Flights in the Western Atlantic to Surface Surveillance," released 3 December 1964, in OA. The study showed that systematic surveillance flights could not make up for the limits of the intelligence-based surveillance system. ONI estimated that an average of 1,890 ships were in the area covered, including 80 U.S. naval units (versus 64 in the ocean surveillance database). The surveillance system typically detected 499 distinct ships (discounting double counts), of which 12.8 percent were U.S. naval units, 10.7 percent were Soviet bloc merchant ships, and 76.5 percent were other ships. Although average patrol plane navigational error at this time was twenty-five nautical miles, over 75 percent of the time the positions found by patrol aircraft for ships in the database were more than one degree of latitude or longitude (sixty-five miles) from predicted positions. Typical errors in course and speed were fifteen degrees and three knots. Most patrol plane contacts were not in the areas covered by the surveillance system and hence could not be compared with its predictions. About a third of patrol plane contacts could not be identified because of bad weather and darkness.

22. CTG 81.2, Quonset ASW Group; CTG 81.3, Norfolk Air ASW Group; CTG 81.4, Jacksonville ASW Group; CTG 81.5, Bermuda ASW Group; CTG 81.8, Argentia ASW Group; CTG 81.9, Azores ASW Group; and CTG 302, Canadian Atlantic ASW Force.

23. CNA Operations Evaluation Group Study 685, "Effectiveness of Surface Sea Surveillance During the Cuban Crisis," distributed 30 April 1965, in OA.

24. A line at least five hundred miles from Cuba was more than three times the length of a four hundred-mile line from Florida to the Bahamas to Hispaniola, which would have sufficed if the acceptable distance had been shorter. The greater distance was presumably required so that ships of interest could be shadowed and turned back.

25. New programs included the remote-control carrier ELINT package ultimately installed on board the ES-3A (at that time called the Tactical Airborne Signal Exploitation System [TASES] and later Carrier Horizon Extension Surveillance System [CHESS]), the high-

flying EP-X aircraft (see chapter 16), TASS, and unmanned aircraft. Op-095 Issue Paper (September 1973) in 1973 Double Zero files, Box 59 (3800), OA, and a list of sensor programs, in the same box, in a 20 July 1973 memo to the chairman of the JCS.

26. Op-76/scm Serial 0047P76 of 12 February 1971, "Operational Exploitation of Soviet Surveillance System," in 1971 Double Zero file, OA (3800/1: Ocean Surveillance, folder for January–March 1971). Defense Intelligence Agency (DIA) reports on Soviet reconnaissance satellites in NWC, RG 4, make the nature of Cluster Buster obvious.

27. According to Ford and Rosenberg, *The Admirals' Advantage*, 63, in November 1975 OSIS began to receive electronic reports of the positions, port arrivals, and departures (and course changes) of all U.S. merchant ships, using a system developed the previous year in cooperation with the Maritime Administration. Presumably it was a replacement for the previous American Vessel Report (AMVER) messages, adapted to the emerging OSIS. Ford and Rosenberg, in *The Admirals' Advantage*, 75, claim that the merchant ship reports (for U.S. ships in Middle Eastern waters) were urgently demanded during the 1973 Middle East War.

28. In box 34, 1977 Double Zero files, OA: Naval Audit Service report S 30506 of 2 September 1976, enclosed in an 18 October 1976 report on OSIS management.

29. SEAWATCH was the Ocean Surveillance Information Handling System. According to Ford and Rosenberg, *The Admirals' Advantage*, 66–67, the first SEAWATCH summary was sent to Atlantic Fleet in September 1972, but the first-phase batch processing system became operational only in March 1973. (Software problems were not resolved until at least October.) Initially, SEAWATCH was limited to merchant ships. Running on new CDC 6400 computers it replaced the earlier FYK-1s system. It expanded to become the core of the OSIS system. In March 1975 Soviet open-ocean naval aircraft flights were added. Installation of the essential dead-reckoning function began in December 1976. Ford and Rosenberg give the impression that, at least initially, the flood of new ELINT ship-tracking information (presumably from satellites) was handled separately.

30. "Ocean Surveillance" in College of Naval Command and Staff, *1976–1977 Selected Readings in Naval Operations: Systems, Sensors, and Platforms Study* 2, no. 5, NWC RG 4.

31. Descriptions of HF/DF systems mainly from the NWC paper, ibid.

32. Curtis Peebles, *Guardians: Strategic Reconnaissance Satellites* (Novato, Calif.: Presidio Press, 1987), 294, based on an 18 October 1965 report in *Aviation Week & Space Technology*. According to a 2008 account by Dwayne Day, based on declassified material, the Manned Orbiting Laboratory (MOL) was mainly an Air Force optical reconnaissance project, carrying a massive telescope (four-inch resolution). According to Day, the National Reconnaissance Office killed MOL in 1969; its resolution was not needed, and the astronauts themselves would cause problems.

33. Peebles, *Guardians*, 301–2, based in part on an article, "Navy Will Develop All-Weather Ocean Monitor Satellite," in the 28 August 1978 *Aviation Week & Space Technology*. The other radar satellites then under development were a Central Intelligence Agency (CIA) reconnaissance radar and an Air Force air vehicle tracker.

34. Peebles, *Guardians*, 302. The Army satellite presumably became Lacrosse, which reportedly uses synthetic aperture radar. Integrated Tactical Surveillance System (ITSS) seems not to have figured in the ocean surveillance or targeting studies of the 1980s.

35. White Cloud apparently became operational in 1976. Ford and Rosenberg, *The Admirals' Advantage*, 61–62, coyly refer to an ELINT revolution because of the arrival of a secret new system that year, producing a flood of data that "soon allowed analysts to track virtually all ships and other ELINT emitters at sea on a near real-time basis. . . . ELINT of surface combatants [soon] constituted as much as 80 or 90 percent of the information incorporated into the operational intelligence (OPINTEL) analyses." They may also be referring to Tactical Exploitation of National Capabilities (TENCAP), which began about 1973 as an army program to exploit National Security Agency (NSA) information. The Navy joined about 1976.

36. Hull-to-emitter correlation (HULTEC) is defined in Naval Electronic Systems Command, "U.S. HULTEC Vulnerability Program: Plan of Action and Milestones," 25 April 1975, declassified 31 December 1982. The object was to determine how easily U.S. ships could be fingerprinted and thus tracked by the Soviet Ocean Surveillance System (SOSS). This project began with a 25 July 1974 vice chief of naval operations (VCNO) directive. It embraced all emissions from ships: radar, communications, navigational aids, IFF, acoustic, or IR, but concentrated on radar and radio rather than acoustics and IR. The document also described "handprinting," which correlated electronic emitters on a class of ships. It notes that communication fingerprinting might involve stereotyped operating procedures for particular ships rather than physical peculiarities of their systems. Ford and Rosenberg, *The Admirals' Advantage*, 62, concentrate on acoustics (completion of a library of acoustic signatures for specific ships and submarine was completed in 1974 as a prerequisite for OSIS) to the exclusion of radar and radio signatures.

Chapter 16. Netting Tactical Intelligence: IOIC and Its Successors

1. Informal meetings to define a future reconnaissance system, attended by the CNO, were held in February through September 1957. A single airplane, to enter service in 1963–67, would replace both photographic and electronic intelligence aircraft. It would have cameras, ECM collection sensors, IR, television, side-looking radar (SLAR), nuclear sniffers, and weather recorders. BuAer received CNO development characteristics in January 1958. In February the A3J (later A-5) Vigilante was chosen as the interim solution. A competition for the roughly parallel Air Force SR-195 system was held in October and November 1958. The Navy, but not the Air Force, saw tactical ELINT and COMINT as essential complements to other sensor outputs. The Air Force was more interested in IR sensing. Each service had its own side-looking radar. OSD tried to force both to adopt a common airplane, preferably the A3J. Air Force refusal was one of the few instances in which Secretary of Defense Robert S. McNamara was thwarted. Box 29, 1963 Double Zero files, OA (12000–13000 series).

2. The distinguishing external feature of the RA-5C was the "canoe" under its belly, which accommodated cameras, an infrared camera (AAS-21), a side-looking radar (APD-7),

and an ELINT system (ALQ-61 "passive ECM," or PECM). ELINT data were recorded on magnetic tape (112-minute capacity). Photo capability amounted to six inches forward oblique, eighteen inches panoramic, three inches panoramic, six inches side oblique, and six inches vertical. The RA-5C also had an ASQ-56 communications/navigation/identification system (a term usually associated with the Joint Tactical Information Distribution System [JTIDS]). Left over from the bombing mission was an inertial navigation system. There was also defensive ECM.

3. The problem was set forth in detail in an Op-92 memo, Ser M-001-59 of 6 May 1959. CNO Adm. Arleigh Burke ruled that the problem justified resort to OpNav and bureau resources; Op-923/mvg Ser 005115P92 of 8 June 1959, "Mechanization of Naval Intelligence Processing," in Double Zero files, 1959 Box 9 (5550–5710/2), OA.

4. Double Zero files for 1967, 3800 (Intelligence) series, including the 10 November 1967 OpNav memorandum, signed by J. H. King, executive assistant to the CNO.

5. Reference to Fleet Intelligence Centers and Facilities Study, 25 July 1967 in Double Zero files 3900 series, Box 31 for 1967, OA.

6. A March 1979 thesis produced at the Naval Postgraduate School, "Operational EA-6B Mission Planning Programs" (NTIS ADA 067581), mentioned a first EW mission planning effort completed by Beaudet and Watts in June 1977. Watts developed a way of choosing an optimum jamming route.

Chapter 17. A New Kind of Fleet Command: FCC and TFCC

1. MAT-03 status report on Mediterranean and Pacific Extended Surface Plot, 10 February 1971, in 1971 Double Zero file, OA (3800/1 folder for January–March 1971). This report refers to 30 September 1970 and 10 December 1970 reports detailing establishment of the system in the Mediterranean. It includes the 30 September memorandum, "Mediterranean Surface Surveillance Plan," by T. D. Davies. The reference to surfaced submarines reflects a Soviet practice of operating on the surface at night to evade sonar detection.

2. A U-2 would be available between 15 August and 15 October 1972 (i.e., beginning in FY72) for tests. The Defense Directorate for Research and Engineering (DDR&E) actively supported the program, but early in 1972 the U.S. House Committee on Appropriations rejected proposed FY72 emergency funding as, it turned out, a protest against the use of such funds for the space-based Program 749. FY73 was no problem. Op-986B1 letter of 28 March 1972 by Lt. Cdr. C. D. Kimble in 1972 Double Zero (3800) file, OA. To some extent a carrier-borne aircraft with Tactical Airborne Signal Exploitation System (TASES) was considered a passive complement to EP-X.

3. "Selected Readings in Tactics 1973–74: Sea Control Study, Vol. 4–6: A Study of Fleet Performance and Factors Inhibiting Performance," 20, in NWC RG8. The reference is to recent First Fleet exercises.

4. Fleet Command Centers (FCCs) achieved full operational capability late FY77 (Atlantic), early FY78 (European), and mid-FY78 (Pacific), according to a September 1977 report on Tomahawk targeting.

5. Memorandum to Adm. D. H. Bagley, CinCUSNAVEUR from OpNav (Admiral Boyes, then chief of naval communications), laying out the test program, 8 July 1975, in 1975 Double Zero file Box 21 (2000 series—C2), OA.

6. The CNO authorized the Tactical Flag Command Center (TFCC) on 17 December 1974. The term Naval Command and Control System (NCCS) was in use by 1975 (e.g., in connection with the FCC-TFCC combination), but the 3 December 1979 draft Navy Command and Control Plan (declassified 5 December 1985) stated that existing systems were not properly integrated, hence that a single unified NCCS plan was needed. A briefing prepared at about this time (declassified 31 December 1983) categorized ongoing efforts as concept development, system development, and management. Concept development included efforts to support Harpoon over-the-horizon targeting using a ship's own sensors, including Outboard/Outrigger (HF/DF), and attack submarine direct support (renamed Coordination in Direct Support, CIDS). The major new system development was to use OSIS to support Tomahawk antiship targeting, demanding much timelier information. CIDS required management development, because submarine, air, and surface forces all had to be coordinated. A new requirement for flexible tactical nuclear targeting was associated with the new Schlesinger Doctrine of flexible response to possible Soviet attacks. It and CIDS made submarine communication more important than ever. Submarines could receive HF messages at periscope depth, and the projected extremely low frequency (ELF) system could reach a submarine at four hundred-foot depth, albeit at a very low data rate. A slide on future submarine communications showed an ARIENNE acoustic transmitter off the U.S. coast that could reach a submarine at seven hundred-foot depth. A future Integrated Acoustic Communications System (IACS) with hundred-nautical mile range and a low probability of interception would allow a surface ship to contact a submarine at any depth, and it would support submarine-to-submarine communication. IACS did not materialize. (Uniquely among communications systems listed in the draft 1979 Command and Control Master Plan, it had no expected in-service date.)

7. Memorandum from OpNav to VCNO concerning OSIS management, Serial 942/107816 of 21 November 1977, in 1977 Double Zero Files, 3800 series (folder 1 July–31 December), OA. The command level involved indicates the seriousness with which OSIS problems were taken.

8. J. Tuttle, "A Brief History of JOTS," in V. DiGirolamo, ed., Naval Command and Control: Policy, Programs, People, and Issues (Fairfax, Va.: AFCEA International Press, 1991). Apparently the acronym originally meant simply the "Jerry O. Tuttle System," but it was always officially the Joint Operational Tactical System.

9. The Officer in Tactical Command Information Exchange System (OTCIXS) led to a new concept, the Battle Group Information Exchange System (BGIXS), in which a battle group flagship could send messages in the format used for Submarine Data Exchange System (SSIXS) traffic. A submarine equipped to receive the SSIXS satellite

broadcast could participate in the BGIXS net. It could routinely transmit periscope pictures, graphics, and even video back to the flagship.

10. JOTS systems were renumbered when they were deployed fleet wide. JOTS I (USQ-112) was the version running on a DTC I (Hewlett-Packard HP 9020) computer. JOTS II(1991) was USQ-112A, running version 1.15 software. The baseline NTCS-A implemented on DTC II computers was USQ-119. The initial upgrade version (with TAC-3 computers) is USQ-119A. The JMCIS baseline version was USQ-119B. The integrated C4I version was USQ-119C. The TAC-4 version was USQ-119D.

Chapter 18. Using Ocean Surveillance: OTH-T

1. Desired range was 300 nautical miles, which the missile would reach more than half an hour after it received the last updated target position just before launch. Initial calculations showed that, given multiple passes to find the moving target, a Mach 0.8 missile would need to fly about 550 nautical miles to hit a target 300 nautical miles away. Even with an aerodynamic range of 600 nautical miles, a Mach 0.65 missile would not hit a target more than 250 nautical miles away.

2. Quoted in Appendix C (OTH Targeting) of the draft Navy Command and Control Master Plan, 5 December 1979 (declassified 6 December 1985).

3. The terminals showed no graphics. The track-keeping computer was a 64,000 word (sixteen-bit words) Rolm 1666 with 4 million words of RAM disk storage in the surface ship and 2 million in the submarine. *Daniels* tested the idea of systematically sanitizing more highly classified information for insertion into the GENSER (non-codeword) net. A separate terminal sanitized information from her Classic Outboard HF/DF system for input into the Rolm computer. ComOpTevFor Test Plan for CNO Project 310-1-OT-1A, "Over the Horizon Missile Targeting Definition Demonstration," 28 February 1978, declassified 31 December 1983.

4. Beside specifying the search area for the target, the missile had to be set in one of five basic radar search modes, its passive identification/direction equipment (PI/DE) receiver set to a specific kind of target radar, and one of three combinations of radar and PI/DE function chosen.

5. On board the destroyer, the single Tactical Data Display System (TDDS) computer supported three display stations, two in Combat Information Center (CIC) (one for the commanding officer, one for the CIC analyst), and one in the Ship Signals Exploitation Space (SSES) collocated with Outboard equipment. It was fed with sanitized Classic Outboard information, which could be correlated with whatever the ship received via satellite. The Shore Targeting Terminal Display System (STTDS) was similar, but had only a single operator station. The Airborne Information Correlation System (AIC) was an airborne equivalent to Submarine Tactical Data Display System (STDDS), but with a scratch display for the tactical evaluator. In addition to data from the airplane sensors, it could accept data manually from the senior evaluator. Track files could go from AIC, STDDS, and TDDS to the tactical net, for display and (in STDDS and TDDS) to missile

fire-control systems. Initial Pacific Fleet experiments used the submarine USS *Guitarro* (SSN-665) and the destroyer USS *Merrill* (DD 976).

6. DEFE 24/1022, "Northwood: Modernisation and Centralisation," dated 1976. In 1967 the Royal Navy and the Royal Air Force agreed that naval and maritime air commands would be centralized at Northwood by 1972. In 1969 Northwood was the main naval headquarters that exercised operational control over forces in the Eastern Atlantic and in the Channel via headquarters at Pitraevie in Scotland and at Plymouth in England. Both needed urgent modernization. The hope was that a single computer-assisted plot at Northwood (replacing a number of separate manual plots) could support command without the intermediate layers at Pitraevie and Plymouth. (Pitraevie was to be retained as an alternative naval headquarters in the event that Northwood was destroyed.) The automated plot was part of a projected Computer Command Information System (CCIS), which was sometimes described as primarily a message-handling system. The British approached NATO to agree to a parallel reorganization of command structures in the Eastern Atlantic and the Channel, and thus to help finance Northwood. CCIS would be connected to with the new computerized NATO Integrated Communications System (NICS). Apparently the British decided in about 1970 that Northwood had to be computerized. The application to NATO was temporarily withdrawn as the cost and scope of computerization became clear. (The British decided to prefinance the project and apply to NATO for later payment.) According to a paper in this file, "the basic layout of the Northwood Headquarters dates from Second World War. The manual operating plots and display systems, the internal communications and working conditions generally are primitive by modern standards and were badly outdated in the 1950s. The volume and flow of signal traffic and information is progressively outstripping the capacity of the present organization. Despite the best efforts of those who man the present Headquarters, signals can take over an hour to reach Desk Offices; there have even been instances where they may have been misplaced. Information tends to become distorted in the plethora of verbal messages passed from individual plots situated remote from the [Command]." The CCIS would use the same information base to form all the different plots command required.

Chapter 19. The Other Side of the Hill

1. By 1963 the Soviets were conducting long-range reconnaissance flights against Pacific Fleet carriers; they added Atlantic Fleet carriers in spring 1964. Op-932C21/wgb Ser 001093P093 of 24 October 1972 (in 1972 Double Zero files, OA), referring to an EMCON program. This memorandum calls for an attempt to measure the Soviet ability to fingerprint U.S. radars by placing three identical units close together, rotating their radar transmissions in an irregular way such that certain transmissions occur. All-source analysis, including Cluster Buster (apparently interception of Soviet satellite downlinks), would be used to see whether the Soviets could determine how many ships there were.

2. Navy Field Operational Intelligence Office, "SOSS Trends," 17 May 1976 (ONI-CR-82-2-76), copy in NWC RG 4, used as a reading in the Naval Operations course, 1977, now declassi-

fied. The 1951 date is from a section describing SOSS development in 1951–61, implying that the system was created in 1951. During this period, each fleet controlled its own surveillance assets, from Krug down to Soviet intelligence-gatherers (AGIs). Surveillance was simplified by the use of choke points between the Soviet coast and the open sea; any enemy unit not emitting (hence not detectable by SIGINT) could be picked up by AGIs and minor combatants in the choke points. Krug used multiple receivers to cover the 2–28 MHz range. Accuracy at 5,000 nautical miles using a 400-foot diameter array was 1.5 degrees (equivalent to about 90 miles). Accuracy at less than 2,000 miles was half a degree (circular error probable [CEP] 25 nautical miles); maximum range was 8,000 nautical miles. There were twenty-six Krug sites in 1973, nine of them capable of tracking the Pacific Fleet. It was not always clear how much this national sensor was devoted to naval surveillance. Apparently the first Soviet HF/DF was the Adcock Thick Eight (0.5–5 and 1.5–15 MHz, accuracy one degree at 4,000 nautical miles), which was also used by the KGB, and was exported to China. By 1970 it was being replaced at Soviet naval SIGINT sites by Fix-24 (2–20 MHz, accuracy 2–5 degrees), which was simpler hence cheaper than Krug. Development of HF/DF sites seems to have ended by 1970.

NWC Tactics Department's 1973–74 pamphlet, "Planning Considerations for Cover and Deception," NWC, RG 4 (now declassified), 1974 readings on electronic warfare (NWC, RG 4), "Soviet Electronic and Electro-Acoustic Intelligence Collection Sensors," STIC-CW-05-1-70 of 31 July 1970), and 1974 Third Fleet report on Soviet surveillance (declassified in 1982). None of the reports includes the mobile DF system described in post–Cold War Russian books, which was probably associated with mobile coastal missiles.

3. V. P. Kuzin and V. I. Nikolskiy, *The Soviet Navy 1945–1991* (Historical Naval Society: St. Petersburg, 1996), distinguish Whiskey (Project 613) and its successor Romeo (Project 633) from Zulu-class cruiser submarine (Project 611) built to operate off distant enemy bases and on the broad oceans. According to them, plans called for 350 Whiskeys (of which 215 were built) and then for 560 Romeos (perhaps including replacements for unbuilt Whiskeys). Plans called for 40 Zulus (26 built) and then for 160 Foxtrots (58 built). That Foxtrot construction continued after Romeos were no longer being built suggests a shift away from the coastal submarine screen.

4. According to a 1973 U.S. analysis, in 1953 the Soviets first assigned intelligence officers to the crews of Soviet merchant ships. In 1955 permission was granted to develop the AGI program. The first Lentra (Project 391)–class fishing trawler carrying Brick series ESM equipment and a small electronics van began operating in the Sea of Japan in 1956. At least seven were converted. Next came six Mirny (Project 393R)–class whale hunters, twice the Lentras' size, converted from 1965 on (four may have been non-naval). These small intelligence ships (MZRK) carried radio, electronic, and hydro acoustic intelligence equipment. Other small intelligence gatherers were up to twenty Mayak-class trawlers (Project 502, built 1965–70; some were used as training ships for reservists and as small transports; six in AGI service 1984–85), up to twenty East German–built Okean-class trawlers (built in Stralsund 1965–69; fifteen in service in 1984–85), and three Hungarian-built Telnovsk class (Project 650RP, built 1949–57). Two of the three Swedish-built Pamir-class rescue tugs and two Dnepr-class (Project

734) repair ships were also converted. To accelerate intelligence gathering, hydrographic survey ships were converted: three medium intelligence-gathering ships (SZRK) of Project 850 (*Nikolai Zubov* class, 1965–66; there was no NATO nickname; conversions were indicated by assignment of SSV auxiliary ship numbers) and nine small Project 861M (Moma class: 1968–70; Pavlov lists ten ships).

Six *Primor'ye*-class (Project 394B, later Project 994) Large Data-Collecting Ships (BRZK were built in 1960–71 based on the design of the *Mayakovskiy*-class large ocean fishing trawler. U.S. analysts were impressed by the great enclosed volume of the *Primor'ye*, which they assumed provided more intercept operator positions, associated with its larger number of intercept antennas. These ships had much greater communications capability than previous AGIs, including specialized antennas previously seen only on board major combatants such as *Moskva*-class carriers and Kresta-class cruisers. To U.S. analysts their presence implied the existence of a high-capability onboard processing system that could pass processed intelligence to task group commanders and to naval headquarters in real time. They suspected that the ship could analyze data collected by less-capable AGIs. The six provided two each for the oceanic fleets (Pacific, Black Sea/Mediterranean, and Northern). Among other advantages, these ships had great endurance (100 days' stores, 13,000-nautical mile range). The four follow-ons were the somewhat smaller Project 1826 (Balzam) built in 1978–87. At about the same time seven medium Vishnaya-class (Project 864 and 864B, completed 1985–87) were built in Poland to operate in sea and near-ocean zones. These three classes all had the Prokhlada radio and electronic intelligence system (lesser types seem to have had only separate receivers).

Follow-on small AGI conversions were four Al'pinist-class (Project 503M) trawlers and two Polish-built Yug-class hydrographic ships (Project 0862.1 and 0862.2, completed 1989–90). Early in 2008 fifteen AGIs were still in service: six Vishnaya, three Alpinist, two Bal'zam, two Yug, and three Moma, though they rarely deploy far from home. A new AGI, *Vitse Admiral Yuriy Ivanov* (Project 18280), was under construction. According to a 1976 paper on SOSS trends (referenced below), after about 1973 the number of deployed AGIs declined, and after 1973 no new AGIs were seen. (The later ones appear to have been a replacement program for existing high-capacity units.) Data on AGIs is from Kuzin and Nikolskiy, from A. S. Pavlov, *Warships of the USSR and Russia 1945–1991* (Annapolis: Naval Institute Press, 1997), and from A. D. Baker III, editor emeritus of *Combat Fleets*. Kuzin and Nikolskiy list few of the smaller-ship conversions (they are taken mainly from Pavlov). The Smith paper on the SOSS gives the 1974 AGI order of battle (all AGIs deployed since 1970) as: Northern Fleet, sixteen; Baltic Fleet, seven; Black Sea Fleet, thirteen; and Pacific Fleet, fifteen, for a total of fifty-one ships.

5. We now know that AGIs were split between those gathering operational intelligence, for example, registering the departure of a carrier group from its base, and those gathering technical or national intelligence, for example, missile or radar characteristics revealed in tests. This distinction is familiar from U.S. practice.

6. See, for example, primary U.S. naval objectives offered by senior retired flag officers, in Special Flag Dope for 20 October 1966; Double Zero Files 1967, Box 32, 3900–3900/2,

OA. Seven broad objectives included developing and maintaining ocean-wide surface and subsurface surveillance; and developing worldwide C2 for afloat compatibility with the unified commands and the national military command center (NMCC).

7. The best-known case in point was submarine tracking: during the 1960s and 1970s, Soviet units appeared near U.S. submarines far too frequently. When John Walker was caught, it became clear that for years he (and possibly others) had sold the Soviets the key cards the U.S. Navy used. These sales became a serious threat when the Soviets obtained the code machines the North Koreans captured in 1968 on board the intelligence-gathering ship *Pueblo* in 1969. It is not clear why the cryptology significance of the *Pueblo* incident was not appreciated at once. Submarine interceptions inspired a massive U.S. SSBN security program, which concentrated on exotic sensors—and concluded that they were unlikely to succeed. A U.S. naval intelligence officer later wrote (in *Proceedings*) that he deeply regretted not having pressed his suspicion that Soviet success reflected a leak or, more likely, code breaking. Accounts of World War II code breaking suggest that victims generally refuse to blame what happened (such as the interception of U-boats) on code breaking. The code makers refuse to acknowledge that anything could have gone wrong. The best-known exception was the World War II decision to change the British-supplied convoy code. Note that the postwar U.S. analysis of SIGINT in the Battle of the Atlantic concluded that it was U.S. code breakers who forced the British to acknowledge that their code was insecure, hence to change it, after observing German exploitation of orders to a convoy to change course.

8. As described in the Cross Report (Vol. III, 70–72). Contact XRAY-5 was tracked between 4 December 1967 and 19 January 1968. She emerged from Petropavlovsk, ran down the Aleutians, tested the West Coast SOSUS system in close coordination with the AGI *Gavril Sarychev*, and then intercepted the carrier. The nuclear cruiser *Truxtun*, escorting the carrier, gained sonar contact on the submarine and vectored a P-3, which surprised it on the surface at dusk. Intelligence implications of the operation included the likelihood that the Soviets were aware of at least the approximate locations of West Coast SOSUS stations, possibly deduced from the positions of the shore Naval Facility (NAVFAC) sites supporting them; and also that the Soviets were probably aware that the carrier was about to depart the West Coast, prompting them to test their ability to intercept her. There may have been two other attempted interceptions, by N285 on 5 January 1968 and by N4/5 about 12 January 1968. The AGI may have contributed intelligence while in the Hawaiian area.

9. Deployment began the last week in March 1970 with thirty-five AGIs and seventy-two submarines. Major surface combatants began to deploy the second week in April. The ASW phase lasted from 14 through 18 April, followed by an anticarrier phase (14–18 April), an amphibious phase (25–28 April), and a coast defense phase (24–28 April); the exercise officially ended on 5 May 1970. Participants included at least 177 surface ships (88 combatants) and 72 submarines; aircraft flew about 700 sorties, including two consecutive 125-sortie days. There were concurrent attacks against multiple simulated carrier battle groups in the Atlantic and Pacific at ranges of up to 1,500 miles from Soviet bases. Concurrent ASW operations were conducted in the eastern and western Mediterranean basins by task forces based on the two *Moskva*-class helicopter carriers; another ASW operation was conducted in the Norwegian Sea by a task group

built around three Kresta-class cruisers. The amphibious operation, conducted over a distance of 1,500 nautical miles, culminated in a three-battalion assault landing. U.S. observers were struck by the fact that deploying seventy-two submarines for Okean-70 (including twenty-six covertly to the Pacific) did not interfere with normal Soviet submarine deployments. Also striking was the apparent use of Navy Bear D maritime patrol aircraft as pathfinders for missile strikes (using the AS-3 Kangaroo) by long-range aviation Bear B and C aircraft in the Iceland/Faroes area, indicating a degree of interservice coordination that might seem unusual in the West. The canned character of the exercise showed in a comment that only the first wave of Badgers (in a morning attack in the Norwegian Sea) seemed to have properly tracked a specific ship target so as to attack it. All other waves either did not track the target or simulated release from beyond the range of the AS-2 missile the aircraft would have carried in combat. Okean-70 demonstrated what Admiral Sergei Gorshkov had achieved during Khrushchev's Seven-Year Plan (1959–65) and the subsequent Five-Year Plan (1966–70). The only previous announced Soviet exercise, and the largest prior to Okean, was Sever (Warsaw Pact, 1968), involving 79 surface ships, 26 submarines, and about 160 aircraft sorties. The follow-on was Okean-75; apparently there was no Okean-80. "Sea Control: Multiple Threat Environment," a 1975 Selected Reading in Tactics (NWC RG 4).

10. The system was formally approved on 16 March 1961. In January 1964 the Defense Ministry included it in the next five-year space reconnaissance plan (1966–70) as Morya-I (Seas-I); this name was later changed to Legenda (Legend). Initially one satellite would have carried active and passive radars. After Krushchev fell, the launch vehicle was changed from his UR-200K to the smaller Tskiklon-2 (modified SS-9), and weight had to be reduced. Separate active (US-A) and passive (US-P) satellites were planned, using the same bus; US meant Controlled Satellite in Russian. US-A was nuclear powered because it had to fly at low altitude (250 to 265 kilometers) to gain sufficient resolution. At such an altitude large solar panels would have generated excessive drag. The reactor section was to be fired into a permanent storage orbit (900 to 1,000 kilometers) at the end of a forty-five-day operational lifetime. In two cases the boost system failed, and the satellites fell to earth, creating a scandal. Satellites were intended to operate in pairs, providing two looks twenty to thirty minutes apart at any ship. Ten test vehicles were launched between 28 December 1965 and January 1969, followed by two full-scale dummies (April and December 1971), and then by the first radar satellite in August 1972. The system was declared operational in October 1975 (two were launched to support the Okean-75 exercise), but it was still experimental in 1978. Series production began at Arsenal KB in Leningrad in 1978. Twenty-four production US-A were launched, not all successfully. US-P used interferometric direction finding (it had an X-shaped antenna). The first operational test satellite was launched in October 1975. Improved versions were US-AM, US-PM, and US-PU (there was no US-AU, because the US-A program died).

11. As observed by U.S. Naval Intelligence, according to the paper on SOSS trends.

12. The level of detail of U.S. information on the satellites' capabilities suggests that the downlinks were intercepted. Satellite operation was programmed from the ground as the satellite passed over its control station in Moscow, and data was all downlinked to Moscow. There was slight evidence of data dumping elsewhere. Later it became clear

that satellites could be commanded to dump data to places where ships could be commanded to receive it. U.S. documents described a Generation I package aboard Type A photo/ELINT and photo/ELINT/scientific satellites; a Generation II package on board satellites using SL-8 launchers; and a Generation III package launched by SL-3s. Generation I was pretuned to selected frequency bands, primarily to intercept the UHF radars (such as SPS-43), which then equipped major U.S. warships. (A later document noted that it had collected data on radars with frequencies of 200–225, 400–450, and 1250–1350 MHz.) On a single pass, the satellite could locate the emitter within 50 to 100 nautical miles by noting when a radar vanished over the horizon. It also measured antenna rotation rate, possibly to correlate the emitter with a specific hull. The data rate (340 samples/second) was too low for the sort of detailed pulse measurements that might be used for HULTEC, but it sufficed for radar lobe width and scan rate. By 1973 Type A was being retired. Generation II was intended for strategic warning, using ten scanning receivers to cover the 100 to 3600 MHz radar band. It could not locate an emitter on a single pass. Nor could any of the receivers stop scanning when it encountered a signal of interest. Generation III covered the same band, but its receivers could stop scanning when they located a signal of interest. It was stabilized so that it could locate an emitter within perhaps twenty-five nautical miles. When programmed for ocean surveillance, it was limited to the UHF radar band. At this time only the Royal Navy and the French navy were also using UHF air search sets, whereas radars operating at higher frequencies were common. None of these was the US-P EORSAT. The 1973–74 document speculated that this choice might indicate limitations in the database the Soviets used to identify U.S. naval radars. "Selected Readings in Tactics" for 1975: "Excerpts from Reconnaissance Space Systems " (ST-CS-12-23-74 of 14 January 1974), NWC RG 4.

13. As described in the 1976 U.S. naval intelligence paper on SOSS trends.

14. U.S. Navy Net Assessment Organization, "Soviet Ocean Surveillance System" (Extracts) in NWC, *Selected Readings for Naval Operations 1977: Sea Control Study* (NWC Archives, RG 4). Information cutoff date was 30 September 1974. This paper emphasized the likely role of Soviet submarines as surveillance assets, observing that during the 1973 Middle East War Soviet submarine HF traffic tripled. It described Soviet underwater communications, as then understood, in some detail.

15. A 1974 Third Fleet tactical memo on countersurveillance tactics (declassified in 1982) described Soviet ESM systems as then understood. Bear D (Tu-95Ts) could DF sources above 400 MHz (i.e., many radars) with an accuracy of 2 degrees. Reconnaissance Badger Ds could DF 1–16 GHz sources with an accuracy of 3 degrees. "The task group commander can anticipate the presence of either Bear D or Badger D prior to an open ocean attack by Soviet missiles." The Air Force Bear C was credited with 2 degrees DF at 1 to 10.3 GHz, which it probably needed to target its huge AS-3 (Kangaroo) missile. The reconnaissance aircraft could intercept signals over much wider ranges. There was also a SIGINT version of the An-12 Cub transport. It appeared that submarine ESM was suitable only for situational awareness and not for precision location, as it was credited with an accuracy of only 5 or 10 degrees. Some surface ships were credited with HF/DF (3–24 MHz, using an antenna called High Ring to attain 10 degrees accuracy).

16. According to the paper on SOSS trends, the first anti-Polaris AGI patrols were set up at Charleston and Rota in 1962, followed by Guam in 1964, and Holy Loch in 1965. Other AGI patrol areas were Tonkin Gulf (1965), East Pacific (1966), Mediterranean (1967), East China Sea (1968), English Channel (1970), and Arabian Sea (1974). This U.S. list does not indicate whether AGIs were assigned to British and French strategic submarine bases.

17. Eventually arrays in the Soviet Far East were identified and given code names, the best-known being Cluster Lance (Dnestr). For the story of the long-range systems, see Norman Friedman, *The Naval Institute Guide to World Naval Weapon Systems*, fifth edition (Annapolis: Naval Institute Press, 2006), 21–24. This account in turn is based largely on the history published by Morphizpribor, the Russian sonar developers. Dnestr is the bistatic system called Cluster Lance by the U.S. Navy. Claimed range is 150 kilometer, but the arrays can be deployed up to 400 kilometers offshore. After several false starts, Dnestr was certified for service on 2 December 1993, then modernized with better electronics. It is currently offered for export as Searchlight, but no buyers are known. Some U.S. observers expected the Soviets to develop coastal arrays like those in SOSUS. Lt. Edward A. Smith, Jr., USN, "The Soviet Ocean Surveillance System," 15 November 1974, ONI-CS-52-22-74, in the NWC readings on ocean surveillance referenced above.

18. The Soviet Navy called this Bambuk-class (Project 10221, based on the Project 1288 refrigerator trawler) underwater situation illumination ships (OPO). *Kamchatka* was completed for the Soviet fleet (her sister became the Ukrainian fleet flagship). Her tall tower superstructure housed the hoist for the massive pinger of the Dnestr bistatic system (the Soviets also tried fixed offshore pingers). The U.S. Navy tried something similar in the late 1950s, when it seemed that Soviet silencing might render the passive SOSUS useless. A massive pinger was placed aboard the tanker *Mission Capistrano*, the SOSUS arrays acting as receivers (better signal processing made this effort unnecessary).

19. U.S. Navy Net Assessment Organization, "Soviet Ocean Surveillance System," 15 November 1974, ONI-CS-52-22-74.

20. "Identification and Exploitation of Soviet Maritime Weaknesses," a January 1981 report by the British Maritime Tactical School (PRO DEFE 69/707). "The SOSS appears to be optimized for a pre-emptive strike. Its degree of effectiveness in war, when elements of it will be quickly destroyed or degraded, is open to question. Many intelligence analyses point to preemptive or massive strikes being planned to occur in a 'valley of death' close to the point at which allied forces could launch strikes on the Soviet Union. There is a feel of entrenched defence, more in keeping with land based military thinking than that of flexible maritime operations. . . . In time of tension the Allies must threaten but not venture into the 'valley of death' until at least some of the high ground, held by the SOSS in peacetime, has been denied to the enemy." The paper went on to comment that much had to be done to educate Western naval personnel to deny the SOSS information by closing down emitters. Few in Western fleets understood that OSIS was, in effect, the West's SOSS.

21. Particular modes were associated with the video data link used for targeting. Despite long nominal ranges, the Soviets preferred to fire their antiship torpedoes at short range (1,000–5,000 yards for conventional, 6,000–8,000 yards for nuclear) so as not to waste weapons in short supply. That would bring submarines well into reliable detection ranges, and they would spend more time maneuvering into position once vectored by the SOSS. DEFE 69/707.

22. As indicated by a commemorative photograph in the first 2001 issue of *Morskoi Sbornik*. No article accompanied it.

23. The November 1999 issue of *Morskoi Sbornik* carried a commemorative article. The Observation and Communications Service was created on 23 November 1909. It received radar and fixed sonar after World War II. When the Soviets adopted the bastion concept (operating strategic submarines in offshore areas) the coastal system expanded to protect them using "permanently operating fields" of air, surface, and underwater surveillance. Presumably the underwater component was the long-range sensors under development from the 1960s on. In the 1970s automated data processing systems were developed to support the surveillance system. Apparently, this was the first approach to an integrated system. After a 1971–72 study, the Naval Institute (NII) for electronics created a new Department of the Navy Shore Surveillance System, which conducted feasibility studies to formulate an operational requirement for a system to be ready by the end of the Ten-Year Plan (1980). It sought means of "illuminating the situation," that is, creating a tactical picture; this phrase was associated with ships carrying pingers to work with shore acoustic arrays. The new program produced automated information systems (ASI-1, 4, and 5) to replace the earlier manual plotting systems (Styag and Sten'ga), a new shore radar system (MRSTs-1 Uspekh), and automated coastal surveillance sonars (Amur, Liman, etc.). Fleet efforts (1973–74) resulted in a new doctrine embodied in a 1975 manual on naval radar units and combat information posts. Development of new surveillance systems continued through the 1980s, producing the Podsolnikh OTH (HF) radar, the Sopka mobile radar, the Gites-B electro-optical device, new fixed sonars (Sever, Vektor, Dnestr), and the Komor fixed electromagnetic submarine detector (presumably a standard harbor-floor device). Note the absence of the satellite systems, associated with a separate *oceanic* surveillance system.

24. Unfortunately, the Russians do not specify what they mean by computer speed, so these comparisons are not precise.

25. The follow-on Almaz (MVU-133) SSBN system for Project 667BD (Delta II) and Project 667BDR (Delta III) uses two side-by-side workstations and a central computer (500 KOPS, 320,000 words), which can track ten targets and attack two of them. It automatically evaluates the threats represented by various targets and distributes fire among them. Antiship missile submarines had a separate line of command systems, beginning with Brest, for the Charlie (Project 670A and 670M) class. Completed in 1967, it was separate from the integrated navigation system and from missile and torpedo fire controls. The city name suggests that it was an analog position keeper (Leningrad was a torpedo position keeper). The digital follow-on for the Oscar I class was Antey.

26. Traditional stations (radio, radar, sonar, navigation) were abandoned. One-man consoles were arranged around a horseshoe in the control room: commanding officer,

propulsion control, weapon control, steam-generator control, electric-power control, shipboard-system control, navigation, information, and communications and ESM (single console). The captain's combat management station had a television screen (rather than a circular CRT) showing submarine position, under-ice situation, compartment status, and periscope picture, plus panels showing radiation status and submarine condition (list, trim, speed, etc). Note the absence of a separate sonar position. Five men operated the submarine under normal conditions (ten when she was at general quarters).

27. The computers and the system were devised by two Americans who defected to the Soviets in 1950. Their story is told in Steven T. Usdin, *Engineering Communism: How Two Americans Spied for Stalin and Founded the Soviet Silicon Valley* (New Haven, CT: Yale University, 2005). Their system was not upgraded during the Soviet period because they fell into disgrace after the 1973 party celebrating the Tango system: they always brought a bottle of "cognac" to Soviet parties, drinking it instead of the vodka plentifully supplied. At this party someone found out that the "cognac" was tea—the two would not get drunk and thus were not to be trusted. Their computer development institute was closed.

28. The associated Rubikon sonar is analog. The display is a circular presentation of sound level versus bearing, so notches indicate sound sources. TMA uses simple relative-rate calculations, for example, the submarine runs at speed toward the target to measure speed across. There are three comparators (analog beam-formers), one for search and two for tracking. Beam width is about a degree. The sonar operator (separated by a partition from the fire-control display) searches for targets. He can juggle two or three, but only with some difficulty. There is no plotter and no summary plot. The computer solves the target triangle and indicates whether an attack is possible. The main display shows the computer estimate of target position, based on a relative motion calculation. Wire-guided torpedoes follow a pure pursuit path, controlled by the sonar man. Since the torpedo is running down the sonar beam, it has to be slowed periodically so that the target becomes visible. The system is designed primarily to attack surface ships, which are fast enough to provide the desired high bearing rates. The submarine is intended to ping to verify range. (The Russians disliked using periscopes.) In support of the anti-ship mission, the submarine is designed for fast reloads, and torpedo controls *except for depth* are centralized. The upgraded version, probably on board modernized Indian Kilo-class submarines, has a digital sonar. Computer capacity is increased by 50 percent and speed by 40 percent. This system can accept data on fifty targets and can generate tracks on fourteen of them, but it is still limited to simultaneous attacks on two targets. The follow-on Amur class is intended to use a more sophisticated Litei system capable of maintaining eighty tracks and conducting TMA on fifty-four of them.

29. The Tron system for the frigate *Neustrashimyy*, completed at the end of the 1980s, is presumably of a later vintage. Because the frigate was scaled up from a much smaller ship working with a coastal control station, it may be intended for a different kind of operation.

Chapter 20. Net versus Net: U.S. Ocean Surveillance versus the SOSS

1. "EMCON Effectiveness Study," produced as part of Selected Readings in Tactics for the 1975 Sea Control Study of the NWC (NWC, RG 4); it is portions of a Naval Weapons Center study of EMCON conducted during FY72 for the chief of naval development. The release notice was dated 4 October 1972.

2. At least in the 1970s, surface tattletales were the rule in the Mediterranean and the Norwegian Sea. By 1973 submarines were the main tattletales in the Pacific. Early in 1973 Commander Attack Carrier Air Wing Fourteen convened a board to study the Soviet Pacific threat; its April 1974 conclusions reflect existing tactical conditions. The board assumed that a carrier would be trailed by a November-class nuclear attack submarine, which would pass targeting data to Echo II–class antiship missile submarines and to Soviet naval headquarters as soon as the carrier's course and speed were determined. Then a pair of Bear Ds would be sent to find the force, locate targets, and relay a radar picture to the Echo IIs and to provide targeting data to Charlie-class missile submarines by HF or VHF voice radio (presumably such relays had been seen in exercises). Exercises suggested that the Echo-IIs would try to position themselves ahead of the carrier, widely dispersed so that they could not be destroyed at the same time, but with their fields of fire overlapping. The Bear D would try to position itself ahead of the carrier, along its course. (NWC, RG 4 , "Multi-Threat Environment," cited above).

3. Declassified message from COMFEWSG (naval EW training group), 13 June 1973, to Second Fleet.

4. The ships involved were USS *Columbus, Belknap, R. E. Byrd, E. Montgomery,* HMS *Devonshire,* and FGRN *Rommel.* Neither a threat alert net nor special ASMD procedures were used. A phase in which the carriers defended themselves using their Combat Air Patrols and their short-range defensive missiles (BPDMS) seems to have been more successful.

5. The Integrated Cover and Deception System (ICAD) comprised a shipboard electromagnetic element and a towed acoustic element. The Phase I electromagnetic element consisted of four HF transmitters to deceive HF/DF systems plus a simulator for the SPS-43 radar that then equipped U.S. carriers and other high-value ships. It produced radar signals and also simulated the scanning pattern of the radar. There were also simulators for other carrier emitters, such as TACAN and VHF and UHF radios. Phase II included a false target generator to deceive both airborne radars and radar satellites. The acoustic element simulated the sound of a carrier. Further decoy development was urgent because of the advent of the Soviet SS-NX-13 (KY-9) antiship ballistic missile, which was designed to home on particular radars. NWC readings (for 1973–74) on "Naval Deception: Past, Present, and Future" in NWC, RG 4. This document quotes a 31 January 1973 demand for a countermeasure beyond the developmental ICAD. It explicitly rejects what was later clear, that the Soviets would depend on visual targeting (tattletales) for their long-range standoff missiles.

6. An early example was Commander Third Fleet, "Tactical Memorandum 510-1-74: Passive/Active Project" (dated 5 June 1974, declassified 31 December 1982), a study conducted by Cruiser-Destroyer Group Five and then by Group Three; an interim report was

submitted in December 1973. Its tables showed detection vulnerabilities of various U.S. radars and sonars. It was assumed that the Soviets used radio fingerprinting. The report suggested countermeasures, such as rotating which transmitters a ship used, detuning the antenna load, switching power supplies between units, and reducing the loading of the power amplifier. Alternatives to HF were LF/MF radio (probably not detectable on Soviet territory), middleman transmission (an HF unit linked to the carrier by line-of-sight radio), Autocat (line-of-sight radio relay using an airplane, sometimes called a "poor man's satellite"), bean bag (delivery of a physical message by helicopter or high wire), pigeon post (radio from a helicopter), visual communication, blind terminations (message received but not answered), ship/shore simplex circuit, command by exception (to reduce communication volume), the use of two-letter call signs on uncovered circuits (to make it more difficult to identify the source), and the use of covered (encrypted) circuits. Communication channels could be simulated. Radar signatures could be changed, and different radars (such as the SPS-10 surface search set) used to simulate others (e.g., missile control radars). Another characteristic carrier emitter, the TACAN aircraft homing beacon, could confuse the enemy by changing channels and identifier codes. Other ships could take over the carrier's channel. Soviet satellite radar DF could be countered by using other emitters to match major radars. The characteristic pings of the long-range SQS-26 sonar, ordinarily a give-away, might be used for cover and deception. Noise generated by high-powered sonars could cover attempts to break away from submerged tattletales.

7. According to the 29 October 1974 OpNav Decision Coordinating Paper advocating its construction, the point of the Tomahawk-armed strike cruiser (CSGN) was to offset increased Soviet offensive power by fielding a non-air ship armed with Harpoon and Tomahawk.

8. The U.S. government may have been aware of, and have abetted, this misunderstanding. The Reagan administration tried to induce the Soviets to waste scarce defense resources by revealing programs that, had they been real, would have been altogether impractical. Making a program "black" was almost certain to convince the Soviets it was worth penetrating. Apparently Soviet political leaders imagined that the Americans could accomplish anything they tried to do—whereas their own scientists were incompetent. For example, they ordered the U.S. Star Wars program copied (at huge cost) even though their own scientists said that it would not work.

Index

About the Author

Norman Friedman is a strategist known for his ability to meld historical, technical, and strategic factors in analyses of current problems. Author of thirty-three books, he often appears on television, writes a monthly column on world and naval affairs for the *Proceedings* of the U.S. Naval Institute, and is a frequent contributor to many other periodicals. His Cold War history, *The Fifty Year War: Conflict and Strategy in the Cold War*, won the 2001 Westminster Prize for the best military history book of the previous year, from the British Royal United Services Institute. His *Seapower as Strategy* won the Samuel Eliot Morison prize awarded by the Naval Order of the United States in November 2002.

Dr. Friedman has testified before the U.S. House and Senate on U.S. Navy programs, has lectured widely in forums such as the U.S. Naval War College, the Naval Postgraduate School, the Industrial College of the Armed Forces, the Air War College, the Australian and Canadian junior and senior national staff colleges, the Royal United Services Institute, the British Ministry of Defence, and at a series of seminars for the Naval Air Systems Command managed by the University of Virginia. In the fall of 2002 Dr. Friedman served as the Royal Australian Navy's Synott Professor, lecturing on seapower in several Australian cities. For some years he was Visiting Professor of Operations Research (for the naval architecture course) at University College, London, concerned mainly with the formulation and consequences of ship operational requirements.

Among Dr. Friedman's many books are *Naval Firepower*, which describes gunnery in the battleship era; *Terrorism, Afghanistan, and America's New Way of War*; *The Cold War Experience*, a short history of the Cold War with accompanying reproduced documents; *Seapower as Strategy*; *The Fifty-Year War: Conflict and Strategy in the Cold War*; *Seapower and Space*, an account of the role that space and information assets now play in naval warfare; five editions of *The Naval Institute*

Guide to World Naval Weapon Systems; and his renowned illustrated design histories of U.S. warships (volumes on cruisers, destroyers, battleships, carriers, small combatants, amphibious ships and craft, and submarines).

Dr. Friedman's articles have appeared in *Joint Forces Quarterly, Jane's International Defence Review, Asian Pacific Defence Reporter, Defense Electronics,* the *Journal of Electronic Defense, Armada, ORBIS, Military Technology, Naval Forces, Signal,* the *Wall Street Journal,* the *Journal of Cold War Studies, Proceedings* of the U.S. Naval Institute, and many others.

A longtime consultant to the media, he frequently appears on national television, including specials on various forms of weaponry, on warships, and on the Gulf War, for the Discovery and History networks and the "Warplanes," "Warship," and "Seapower, " series as well as NOVA on the U.S. Public Broadcasting System.